The Dominican People:
A Documentary History

THE DOMINICAN PEOPLE

A Documentary History

Edited by
Ernesto Sagás
and
Orlando Inoa

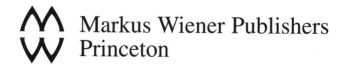 Markus Wiener Publishers
Princeton

Cover design by Maria Madonna Davidoff

For information write to: Markus Wiener Publishers
231 Nassau Street, Princeton, NJ 08542
www.markuswiener.com

Library of Congress Cataloging-in-Publication Data
The Dominican people: a documentary history/edited by Ernesto Sagás and Orlando Inoa.
    Includes bibliographical references.
    ISBN-13: 978-1-55876-296-1 (hardcover)
    ISBN-10: 1-55876-296-5 (hardcover)
    ISBN-13: 978-1-55876-297-8 (paperback)
    ISBN-10: 1-55876-297-3 (paperback)
    1. Dominican Republic—History.   I. Sagás, Ernesto.   II. Inoa, Orlando.
F1938.D645 2002
972.93—dc21
2002071318

Markus Wiener Publishers books are printed
in the United States of America on acid-free paper,
and meet the guidelines for permanence and durability
of the Committee on Production Guidelines for
Book Longevity of the Council on Library Resources.

Contents

*To our students of Dominican history,
past, present, and future*

*Man is a history-making creature who can
neither repeat his past nor leave it behind.*
—W.H. Auden

Introduction

The written history of the Dominican people now spans more than five centuries. On a fateful December 6, 1492, Christopher Columbus and his men landed in the western part of an island the natives called *Bohío* or *Haití* (nowadays officially named Hispaniola). Since then, the history of the inhabitants of this island has been indelibly marked by the trends set in motion by that casual encounter between two dissimilar worlds. The history of the Dominican people has been written in fire, whether it was by the extermination of the island's original native inhabitants, the enslavement of thousands of Africans brought there against their will, the numerous foreign interventions the country has been subjected to, or the cruel and bloody domestic dictatorships that characterized most of the nineteenth and twentieth centuries. It is a history of heroes and villains, of martyrs and despots, of patriots and traitors. Of a Juan Pablo Duarte, but also of a Pedro Santana; of a Francisco Caamaño as well as of a Rafael Trujillo.

Fortunately, all that struggling has not been in vain. Today the Dominican Republic is an electoral democracy, where ample respect is paid to most basic human rights. Though much remains to be done to improve the quality of its democratic system, a quick glance at the historical record will immediately show how much has been accomplished. Since the country's independence in 1844, the majority of Dominican governments have been authoritarian. Only with the collapse of the Trujillo dictatorship in 1961, and particularly since the 1978 elections, have free, competitive, regularly-scheduled elections become the norm, giving the people the opportunity to have some political input and to exercise some accountability over their leaders. For the first one hundred and thirty-four years of independence, democratic or democratically inclined administrations were a rare exception in a deeply authoritarian political system. For the last twenty-four years, however, electoral democracy has reigned and it is now widely accepted as the main means of governmental legitimacy. We remain optimistic that Dominican democracy will succeed in shedding its authoritarian legacy and will survive the test of time.

The present annotated compilation of documents serves as a testimony to the centuries-long struggles. Without any doubt, the history of the Dominican people is the most complex in the region. The island's territory has been occupied by Spain, France, Haiti, and the United States–often on more than one occasion. The country was a Spanish colony three times, was invaded by Haitian armies at least six times, by U.S. military forces twice, and achieved its independence on three separate occasions. Moreover, it is one of only a handful of divided islands in the world, as it is shared by the Dominican Republic and Haiti, two culturally distinct sovereign nations. Such a complex and rich history deserves a detailed, accurate documentary record.

Over the course of several years spent researching and teaching Dominican history, both in the United States and in the Dominican Republic, we realized that in spite of a plethora of available textbooks, we still lacked a good, comprehensive, and manageable compilation of Dominican historical documents. Most existing documentary collections were outdated, incomplete, out of print, or simply too "dry," being just simple listings of treaties and other documents of "high politics." In the particular case of the United States, we were faced with the additional problem that most documents were available only in Spanish, and thus were out of reach for our English-dominant students. This work will finally fill this major gap in Dominican historiography.

A few comments about the "documents" selected for this work should be made. While recognizing that treaties, constitutions, and other documents of "high politics" are necessary to the understanding of the history of any nation, we strove to achieve some balance between these often dry, lifeless documents written by the elites, and depictions of the daily life of the Dominican people—a people often without history. Thus, we combined the essential documents of Dominican history with "snapshots" that tell us how ordinary Dominicans, including women, slaves, and other often-ignored historical subjects lived. To achieve this objective, some unavoidable choices had to be made. Some official documents had to be left out, while others which may not qualify as real documents under the strictest definition of the term were included in order to fill gaps left by the former. As a result, and as is the case with all documentary compilations, this is an ongoing process. For example, early on we had intended to include documents about Dominican culture. However, we soon realized that just that topic alone would amount to an entire new book, and that, at least in our case, it would have required us to add several extra chapters and several hundred pages to this book. And it would have still been an incomplete job given the Herculean task of adequately covering so many different cultural manifestations. Nevertheless, the reader may rest assured that, in spite of its logical imperfections, this work is the most comprehensive compilation of documents related to the history of the Dominican people available in any language.

Also, we decided early on to stick to the original usage of the authors of these documents, while at the same time striving to offer the public a readable manuscript. Particularly whenever we translated documents into English, we tried to be as faithful as possible to the original words of the authors. For example, Latin American and Spanish authors—and Dominicans are no exception—refer to the Western Hemisphere as "America"—a single land mass—and not as "the Americas" as is common usage in the United States. Thus, readers should be aware of the document's context, including its author, when reading it. When a Dominican or Spanish author uses the term "America" the reference is obviously to the continent, and not to the country known as the United States *of* America. Moreover, we tried to respect the authors' original capitalization and punctuation. So, terms such as "the Government," "the State," and others that are not usually capitalized in English, are capitalized in this book to reflect the authors' original usage. We also tried to maintain the authors' original, often-flamboyant writing styles by strictly adhering to it at the time of translating the documents into English. Of course, at some points it was obviously impossible to offer a literal translation of the documents, so some rewriting was needed. Also, there were some terms for which no literal or reliable translation was available. Those are explained in footnotes on first mention in the book. As in the case of choosing which documents to use and which to leave out, translating also involves certain inherent choices that are sometimes unavoidable. Still, we believe that we have achieved a coherent and readable product.

This book was originally the idea of Orlando Inoa when we were both graduate students at the University of Florida in the early 1990s. He had patiently collected many of the documents and images now in this book, hoping to publish them upon his return to the Dominican Republic. Professional obligations eventually precluded him from publishing that book, but the dream remained. A few years ago, I was introduced to Markus Wiener, who was visiting my department chair, Luis Martínez-Fernández, to discuss with him the idea of publishing a documentary history of the Cuban people. Given the fact that Markus Wiener already publishes a documentary history of the Puerto Ricans, both of them suggested that I write the third installment in this trilogy of the peoples of the Hispanic Caribbean. A quick call to Orlando and the answer was yes. Thus, this book's first debt of gratitude is to Markus Wiener and Luis Martínez-Fernández for their vision and for their help in making this idea a reality. In addition, Professor Martínez-Fernández has been a close friend, colleague, reader, and advisor for years at the Department of Puerto Rican and Hispanic Caribbean Studies of Rutgers University. I just have no way of repaying him.

Rutgers has been a very stimulating environment in which to prepare this book. I must thank my colleagues/friends (listed in alphabetical order) Yanet Baldares, Pedro Cabán, Frank Freyre, Humberto García Muñiz, Larry La Fountain-Stokes, Ana Y. Ramos-Zayas, Asela Rodríguez de Laguna-Díaz, and Carmen Whalen for making it such a great place to work in. Frank in particular shared with me countless hours of stimulating dialogue, and often just mundane, funny, stress-relieving, plain talk. Our chats during the hot summer months and the freezing winter break made the drudgery of translating the documents more bearable. Special thanks go to Monica Licourt, our administrative assistant, for her incredible knack for solving big and small problems, and for her enlightening hallway conversations. My "History of the Dominican Republic" students at Rutgers during the 2001 spring and fall semesters also contributed to this book by providing rough translations of some of the documents and commentaries as part of their class research projects. They are just too many to list individually, but my thanks go to all of them. Finally, I would like to thank Lorgia García Peña, a brilliant graduate student in Spanish literature, who did some editorial work on the translations.

More personal thanks are also in order. First, to my parents, who have always supported my professional endeavors and have transmitted their unconditional love to me in so many ways. To my children, Antonio Ernesto and Anaís, who are my window into the future and who inspire me to excel on a daily basis. And finally, to Alba Mota, for being my companion, friend, advisor, confidante, and so many things at once. Her love and support have kept me going during the toughest of times. Thanks for always being there for me.

Ernesto Sagás
North Brunswick, New Jersey
September 2002

CHAPTER ONE

Hispaniola: Conquered, Colonized, and then Forgotten

On October 12, 1492, two worlds collided: Europe, which was just emerging from the Middle Ages; and America, which had remained isolated from the new technological developments taking place in the Eurasian land mass. The encounter was far from equal; the Amerindians' Stone Age culture was no match for European military technology. The initial encounter took place on the Caribbean island of Hispaniola, part of which is now the Dominican Republic.

This first chapter examines the saga of "discovery" and the Spanish conquest and colonization of the island of Hispaniola, which for a few decades became the center of the Spanish colonial enterprise in the New World. It was in Hispaniola where the first major contacts between Europeans and Amerindians took place, where the first exploitative economic activities in the New World were developed, where Europeans first established permanent settlements and colonial institutions, and where the stage was set for the colonization of the rest of the New World.

The history of the Spanish colony of Hispaniola during the century that followed was erratic at best. The island economy quickly boomed and busted as it moved from being the center of the colonizing enterprise to a depopulated backwater of the Spanish empire by the late sixteenth century. Early on, the island had witnessed an impressive number of "firsts," including the first permanent settlement of Europeans in the New World, the establishment of the first city (Santo Domingo de Guzmán), the first church, and the first university. On the darker side of colonization, it also witnessed the first massacre of Amerindians, the first exploitative industries (gold mining and sugar), the first importation of black slaves, and the first rebellions against the Spanish authorities. However, the eventual exhaustion of gold deposits, the extermination of the Taínos, the colonization of new lands elsewhere, and the legendary wealth of the Aztec and Inca empires, drove scores of Spanish colonizers to turn elsewhere. By the early seventeenth century, the island was so depopulated that the Spanish authorities decided, for security reasons, to reconcentrate the remaining population in the eastern part of the island, closer to the city of Santo Domingo, the center of Spanish authority.

On the Brink of Discovery

The European "discovery" of the New World was more than a fortuitous event. If Christopher Columbus[1] had not done it, certainly it would have been just a matter of time before other European explorers would have landed in the Western Hemisphere. However, in 1492 a combination of historical currents, junctural events, and Columbus's own perseverance and determination came together and led to the bewildering saga of his journey into the unknown. For seven centuries, the peoples of the Iberian Peninsula had been fighting the Moors, Muslim invaders from northern Africa who conquered almost the entire peninsula. The war against the Moors forged a nation based on Catholicism and on the political marriage of two monarchs, King Fernando de Aragón (Ferdinand of Aragon) and Queen Isabel de Castilla (Isabella of Castile). This new nation, Spain, finally defeated the last Moorish stronghold in 1492, while at the same time expelling its Jewish population. Spain was now a heterogeneous,

---

1. Originally Cristoforo Colombo, he later changed his name to the Spanish Cristóbal Colón.

powerful nation bent on expanding its empire, increasing its foreign trade, and joining the ranks of European powers. After some initial reluctance, the Crown finally decided to support the proposal of Christopher Columbus to open a new trade route to the Indies by sailing west. Since open-ocean navigation was far from an exact science in the late fifteenth century, Columbus's venture carried great risks. Still, the potential rewards, if the expedition was successful, were enormous. Both the Crown and Columbus envisioned this exploratory trip primarily as a commercial enterprise, so a contract was in order. The end result was the Stipulations of Santa Fe, the agreement by which Columbus was guaranteed the three things that many fifteenth-century Spanish men dreamed of: a nobility title, political power, and wealth. Neither Columbus nor the Crown ever imagined the global repercussions this fateful voyage would bring. This surviving copy is an amended document signed in Granada a few days later.

THE STIPULATIONS OF SANTA FE[2]

For as much of you, *Christopher Columbus*, are going by our command, with some of our vessels and men, to discover and subdue some Islands and Continent in the ocean, and it is hoped that by God's assistance, some of the said Islands and Continent in the ocean will be discovered and conquered by your means and conduct, therefore it is but just and reasonable, that since you expose yourself to such danger to serve us, you should be rewarded for it. And we being willing to honor and favor you for the reasons aforesaid; Our will is, That you, *Christopher Columbus*, after discovering and conquering the said Islands and Continent in the said ocean, or any of them, shall be our Admiral of the said Islands and Continent you shall so discover and conquer; and that you be our Admiral, Vice-Roy, and Governor in them, and that for the future, you may call and stile yourself, D. *Christopher Columbus*, and that your sons and successors in the said employment, may call themselves Dons,[3] Admirals, Vice-Roys, and Governors of them; and that you may exercise the office of Admiral, with the charge of Vice-Roy and Governor of the said Islands and Continent, which you and your Lieutenants shall conquer, and freely decide all causes, civil and criminal, appertaining to the said employment of Admiral, Vice-Roy, and Governor, as you shall think fit in justice, and as the Admirals of our kingdoms use to do; and that you have power to punish offenders; and you and your Lieutenants exercise the employments of Admiral, Vice-Roy, and Governor, in all things belong-

2. From Francis N. Thorpe, *The Federal and State Constitutions, Colonial Charters, and Other Organic Laws of the State, Territories, and Colonies Now or Heretofore Forming the United States of America* (Washington, D.C.: Government Printing Office, 1909), vol.1, 39–40.
3. *Don* is a formal Spanish form of address equivalent to Mister or Sir.

ing to the said offices, or any of them; and that you enjoy the perquisites and salaries belonging to the said employments, and to each of them, in the same manner as the High Admiral of our kingdoms does. And by this our letter, or a copy of it signed by a *Public Notary*: We command Prince *John*, our most dearly beloved Son, the Infants, Dukes, Prelates, Marquesses, Great Masters and Military Orders, Priors, Commendaries, our Counselors, judges, and other Officers of Justice whatsoever, belonging to our Household, Courts, and Chancery, and Constables of Castles, Strong Houses, and others, and all Corporations, Bailiffs, Governors, Judges, Commanders, Sea Officers; and the Aldermen, Common Council, Officers, and Good People of all Cities, Lands, and Places in our Kingdoms and Dominions, and in those you shall conquer and subdue, and the captains, masters, mates, and other officers and sailors, our natural subjects now being, or that shall be for the time to come, and any of them, that when you shall have discovered the said Islands and Continent in the ocean; and you, or any that shall have your commission, shall have taken the usual oath in such cases that they for the future look upon you as long as you live, and after you, your son and heir, and so from one heir to another forever, as our Admiral on our said Ocean, and as Vice-Roy and Governor of the said Islands and Continent, by you, *Christopher Columbus*, discovered and conquered; and that they treat you and your Lieutenants, by you appointed, for executing the employments of Admiral, Vice-Roy, and Governor, as such in all respects, and give you all the perquisites and other things belonging and appertaining to the said offices; and allow, and cause to be allowed you, all the honors, graces, concessions, prehaminences, prerogatives, immunities, and other things, or any of them which are due to you, by virtue of your commands of Admiral, Vice-Roy, and Governor, and to be observed completely, so that nothing be diminished; and that they make no objection to this, or any part of it, nor suffer it to be made; forasmuch as we from this time forward, by this our letter, bestow on you the employments of Admiral, Vice-Roy, and perpetual Governor forever; and we put you into possession of the said offices, and of every of them, and full power to use and exercise them, and to receive the perquisites and salaries belonging to them, or any of them, as was said above. Concerning all which things, if it be requisite, and you shall desire it, We command our Chancellor, Notaries, and other Officers, to pass, seal, and deliver to you, our Letter of Privilege, in such form and legal manner, as you shall require or stand in need of. And that none of them presume to do any thing to the contrary, upon pain of our displeasure, and forfeiture of 30 ducats[4] for each offence. And we command him, who shall show them this, our Letter, that he summon them to appear before us at our Court, where we shall then be, within fifteen days after such summons, under the said penalty. Under which same, we also command any Public Notary whatsoever, that he give to him that shows it him, a certificate under his seal, that we may know how our command is obeyed.

GIVEN at *Granada*, on the thirtieth of April, in the year of Our Lord 1492
I, THE KING, I, THE QUEEN

---

4. gold coin

Columbus in a New World

On August 3, 1492, Columbus's expedition left Spain. It sailed the breadth of the Ocean Sea, as the unexplored Atlantic was known then, in three small ships, the *Niña*, the *Pinta*, and the *Santa María*. On October 12, 1492, they reached the island of San Salvador in what today are the Bahamas. A New World had been "discovered," or more correctly "encountered," as the Spanish found the land inhabited by several indigenous people, including a well-organized agrarian people: the *Taínos*. Columbus, bent on proving that he had reached the Indies, incorrectly labeled them Indians. After some weeks of exploration, particularly in search of wealth, Columbus arrived on December 6, 1492, at a mountainous island the Taínos called *Bohío* (and also *Aytí*). Presumably because it resembled Spain (Columbus had a penchant for exaggeration), Columbus named it *La Española* (the Spanish island; now Hispaniola). It was near La Española that the expedition suffered its first major disaster: the *Santa María* ran aground and had to be scrapped. Thus, by pure chance, the island of La Española came to harbor the first Spanish settlement in the New World, as Columbus was unable to take back all his men on the two remaining ships. The settlement, called *La Navidad* (because the Santa María foundered on Christmas Day), began a long series of first events as La Española fortuitously became the center of the Spanish colonial enterprise in the New World. The description of these events, taken from Columbus's letter to his friend Luis de Santangel, is one of the few documents in Columbus's hand that survive to this day. Copies were made in several languages and distributed throughout Europe. The letter provides a brief description of the people Columbus encountered. As seen below, Columbus portrayed the Taíno people in rather rosy terms and exaggerated the potential wealth of the territories he had explored. His description excited the imagination of the European public, for whom the seemingly peaceful and benign Indians would become an object of much curiosity.

LETTER OF COLUMBUS TO LUIS DE SANTANGEL[5]

I understood sufficiently from other Indians, whom I had already taken, that this land was nothing but an island, and I therefore followed its coast eastward for one hundred and seven leagues to the point where it ended. From that point, I saw another island, distant about eighteen leagues from the first, to the east, and to it I at once gave the name "Española." I went there and followed its northern coast, as I had followed that of Juana,[6] to the eastward for one hundred and eighty-eight great leagues in a straight line. This island and all the others are very fertile to a limitless degree, and this island is extremely so. In it there are many harbors on the coast of the sea, beyond comparison with others that I know in Christendom, and many rivers, good and large, which is marvelous. Its lands are high; there are in it many sierras and very lofty mountains, beyond comparison with that of Tenerife. All are most beautiful, of a thousand shapes; all are accessible and are filled with trees of a thousand kinds and tall, so that they seem to touch the sky. I am told that they never lose their foliage, and this I can believe, for I saw them as green and lovely as they are in Spain in May, and some of them were flowering, some bearing fruit, and some at another stage, according to their nature. The nightingale was singing and other birds of a thousand kinds, in the month of November, there where I went. There are six or eight kinds of palms, which are a wonder to behold on account of their beautiful variety, but so are the other trees and fruits and plants. In it are marvelous pine groves; there are very wide and fertile plains, and there is honey; and there are birds of many kinds and fruits in great diversity. In the interior, there are mines of metals, and the population is without number.

Española is a marvel. The sierras and the mountains, the plains, the champaigns are so lovely and so rich for planting and sowing, for breeding cattle of every kind, for building towns and villages. The harbors of the sea here are such as cannot be believed to exist unless they have been seen, and so with the rivers, many and great, and of good water, the majority of which contain gold. In the trees, fruits and plants, there is a great difference from those of Juana. In this island, there are many spices and great mines of gold and of other metals.

The people of this island and of all the other islands which I have found and of which I have information, all go naked, men and women, as their mothers bore them, although some of the women cover a single place with the leaf of a plant or with a net of cotton which they make for the purpose. They have no iron or steel or weapons, nor are they fitted to use them. This is not because they are not well built and of handsome stature, but because they are very marvelously timorous. They have no other arms than spears made of canes, cut in seeding time, to the ends of which they fix a small, sharpened stick. Of these they do not dare to make use, for many times it has happened that I have sent ashore two or three men to some town to have speech with them, and countless people have come out to them, and as soon as they have seen my

---

5. From Cecil Jane, ed. and trans., *The Voyages of Christopher Columbus: Being the Journals of His First and Third, and the Letters Concerning His First and Last Voyages, To Which He Added the Account of His Second Voyage Written by Andrés Bernáldez* (London: The Argonaut Press, 1930), 259–263.

6. Name Columbus gave to the island of Cuba.

men approaching, they have fled, a father not even waiting for his son. This is not because ill has been done to any one of them; on the contrary, at every place where I have been and have been able to have speech with them, I have given to them of that which I had, such as cloth and many other things, receiving nothing in exchange. But so they are, incurably timid. It is true that, after they have been reassured and have lost this fear, they are so guileless and so generous with all that they possess, that no one who has not seen it would believe it. They refuse nothing that they possess, if it be asked of them; on the contrary, they invite any one to share it and display as much love as if they would give their hearts. They are content with whatever trifle of whatever kind that may be given to them, whether it be of value or valueless. I forbade that they should be given things so worthless as fragments of broken crockery, scraps of broken glass, and lace tips, although when they were able to get them, they fancied that they possessed the best jewel in the world. So it was found that for a thong a sailor received gold to the weight of two and a half castellanos,[7] and others received much more for other things which were worth less. As for new blancas,[8] for them they would give everything which they had, although it might be two or three castellanos' weight of gold or an arroba or two of spun cotton. They took even the pieces of the broken hoops of the wine barrels and, like savages, gave what they had, so that it seemed to me to be wrong and I forbade it. I gave them a thousand handsome good things, which I had brought, in order that they might conceive affection for us and, more than that, might become Christians and be inclined to the love and service of Your Highnesses and of the whole Castilian nation, and strive to collect and give us of the things which they have in abundance and which are necessary to us.

They do not hold any creed nor are they idolaters; but they all believe that power and good are in the heavens and were very firmly convinced that I, with these ships and men, came from the heavens, and in this belief they everywhere received me after they had mastered their fear. This belief is not the result of ignorance, for they are, on the contrary, of a very acute intelligence and they are men who navigate all those seas, so that it is amazing how good an account they give of everything. It is because they have never seen people clothed or ships of such a kind.

As soon as I arrived in the Indies, in the first island I found, I took some of the natives by force, in order that they might learn and might give me information of whatever there is in these parts. And so it was that they soon understood us, and we them, either by speech or signs, and they have been very serviceable. At present, those I bring with me are still of the opinion that I come from Heaven, for all the intercourse which they have had with me. They were the first to announce this wherever I went, and the others went running from house to house, and to the neighboring towns, with loud cries of, "Come! Come! See the men from Heaven!" So all came, men and women alike, when their minds were set at rest concerning us, not one, small or great, remaining behind, and they all brought something to eat and drink, which they gave with extraordinary affection.

In all the islands, they have very many canoes, which are like rowing fustas,[9] some

7. Spanish coin
8. coins
9. small sailing ship

larger and some smaller; some are greater than a fusta of eighteen benches. They are not so broad, because they are made of a single log of wood, but a fusta would not keep up with them in rowing, since their speed is an incredible thing. In these they navigate among all those islands, which are innumerable, and carry their goods. I have seen one of these canoes with seventy or eighty men in it, each one with his paddle.

In all these islands, I saw no great diversity in the appearance of the people or in their manners and language. On the contrary, they all understand one another, which is a very curious thing, on account of which I hope that Their Highnesses will determine upon their conversion to Our Holy Faith, towards which they are very inclined.

I have already said how I went one hundred and seven leagues in a straight line from west to east along the seashore of the island of Juana, and as a result of this voyage I can say that this island is larger than England and Scotland together, for, beyond these one hundred and seven leagues, there remain to the westward two provinces to which I have not gone. One of these provinces they call "Avan," and their people are born with tails. These provinces cannot have a length of less than fifty or sixty leagues, as I could understand from those Indians whom I have and who know all the islands.

The other island, Española, has a circumference greater than all Spain from Collioure on the seacoast to Fuenterabia in Vizcaya, for I voyaged along one side for one hundred and eighty-eight great leagues in a straight line from west to east. It is a land to be desired and, when seen, never to be left. I have taken possession of all for Their Highnesses, and all are more richly endowed than I know how or am able to say, and I hold all for Their Highnesses, so that they may dispose of them as they do of the kingdoms of Castile and as absolutely. But especially, in this Española, in the situation most convenient and in the best position for the mines of gold and for all trade as well with the mainland here as with that there, belonging to the Grand Khan, where will be great trade and profit, I have taken possession of a large town, to which I gave the name Villa de Navidad, and in it I have made fortifications and a fort, which will now by this time be entirely completed. In it I have left enough men for such a purpose with arms and artillery and provisions for more than a year, and a fusta, and one, a master of all seacraft, to build others, and I have established great friendship with the king of that land, so much so, that he was proud to call me brother and to treat me as such. And even were he to change his attitude to one of hostility towards these men, he and his do not know what arms are. They go naked, as I have already said, and they are the most timorous people in the world, so that the men whom I have left there alone would suffice to destroy all that land, and the island is without danger for their persons, if they know how to govern themselves.

The Island of *La Española*

Gonzalo Fernández de Oviedo is known as the "Chronicler of the Indies." His 1526 account gave Europeans one of the first descriptions of this new, intriguing, and strange world. By this time the Spaniards had reached the continental mainland, where they had met new Indian groups and encountered unknown animal species. Fernández de Oviedo was commissioned by the Crown to describe these new lands; a monumental task in itself. He describes the natural features of the territories Columbus explored, noting their potential wealth if properly exploited. The work also included some drawings, which pictured some of the tools used by the Indians, as well as tropical plants. A small section of the book is devoted to Hispaniola, in which he gives meticulous descriptions of the flora and fauna of the island, not an easy task considering how alien they were to Europeans, and delineates Hispaniola's main features. Oviedo also briefly describes Hispaniola's indigenous inhabitants, the Taíno people, and the town of Santo Domingo, which by then had become the capital of the colony and the center of Spanish activity in the Caribbean region.

FROM OVIEDO'S CHRONICLE
The Island of Hispaniola [10]

Hispaniola, from Higuey Point to Cape Tiburón is more than one hundred and fifty leagues in length. From the coast of Navidad in the north to Cape Lobos in the south, the island is fifty leagues wide. The city of Santo Domingo is in the southern part of the island at about nineteen degrees north latitude. There are many beautiful rivers and streams on the island and some are quite large, such as the Ozama River, which empties into the ocean at Santo Domingo. Other rivers are the Neyba, which flows close by the town of San Juan de la Maguana, the Artibonito, the Haina, the Nizao, and many smaller ones which I do not care to mention. On the island there is a lake [Lake Enriquillo] about two leagues inland, near the town of Yaguana, which extends fifteen leagues or more to the east. In some places it reaches a width of one to three leagues, but for the most part it is considerably narrower. Most of the lake is salty, but where rivers and springs flow into it the water is fresh. The truth is that this lake is really a "sea eye," which is very near the sea and contains many different kinds of fish, especially large sharks, that enter the lake from the sea by coming under the land or through a place or places through which the sea flows and forms the lake. This is the opinion of most of those who have seen this lake.

At the time of the discovery, Hispaniola was populated by Indians and was ruled by two great kings, Caonabo and Guarionex, and afterwards it passed to the rule of

10. From *Natural History of the West Indies* by Gonzalo Fernández de Oviedo, translated and edited by Sterling A. Stoudmire. North Carolina Studies in the Romance Languages and Literatures, No. 32. Copyright (c) 1959 by the University of North Carolina Press, renewed 1987 by Sterling A. Stoudmire. Used by permission of the publisher. Pages 8–13.

Anacoana. I do not wish to dwell on the conquest or the cause of the reduction in numbers of the Indians, and thus go about describing things I have described in detail elsewhere. This is not the subject I am to treat here, but other details that Your Majesty may not know so well or may have forgotten. Concerning this island, however, I wish to say that there are very few Indians there now, and not so many Christians as there should be, since many of those who once were on the island have gone to other islands or to Tierra Firme.[11] Being men fond of adventure, those who go to the Indies for the most part are unmarried and therefore do not feel obligated to reside in any one place. Since new lands have been discovered and are being discovered every day, those men believe that they will swell their purses more quickly in new territory. Even though some may have been successful in this, most have been disillusioned, especially those who already have established homes and residences in Hispaniola.

I believe beyond any doubt, and this opinion is held by many, that if a prince had no realm except this island, in a short time it would not be inferior to Sicily or England, nor at present is there any reason why either of those islands should be envied. Hispaniola is so rich in natural resources that she could enrich many provinces and kingdoms. In addition to having more rich mines and better gold than have yet been discovered in such quantity anywhere in the world, so much cotton grows wild that if it were cultivated and cared for it would become the best and the most productive in the whole world. There are so many excellent drumstick trees that large quantities of the pods are already being brought to Spain and from Spain they are carried and distributed to many parts of the world. This is increasing so rapidly that it is really a marvel. On that island there are many rich sugar plantations. The sugar is of very good quality and ships loaded with it come to Spain every year.

Plants native to Spain that have been transplanted and cultivated there grow better and in larger quantity than in any part of Europe. They grow and multiply in spite of the fact that they are neglected and not well cared for. The men want the time they would employ in agriculture for other gains and enterprises that more rapidly swell the wealth of covetous souls who have no desire to work. For this reason the settlers do not occupy themselves with growing grain or setting out vineyards, for in the time necessary for these to produce fruit, these products can be had at good prices, for ships carry them there from Spain. In mining, trading, pearl fishing, or in other pursuits, the colonists become wealthy more quickly than they would by sowing wheat or planting vines, as I have said. Some, however, especially those who expect to remain in that land, are engaged in agriculture. There are also many fruits native to Hispaniola, and those that have been carried there from Spain and planted have grown remarkably well.

Farther on I shall describe in detail those things that had their origins on that island and in other parts of the Indies, which have been found there by the Christians. Of the things which have been carried from Spain there can be found on that island, throughout the year, many good vegetables, many fine cattle, sweet orange and bitter orange trees, and very beautiful lemon and citron trees, and these fruits are to be

11. the mainland or continental landmass

10

found in abundance. There are many figs throughout the year, many date palms and other plants and trees that have been carried there from Spain.

In Hispaniola there was no quadruped except two species of very small animals that are called *hutía* and *corí*, which are very much like rabbits. All other quadrupeds that are there now have been carried from Spain. Consequently it seems to me unnecessary to speak of them, nor is it necessary to say more than that the cattle as well as other animals have multiplied greatly. Cows have multiplied at such a rate that many cattle kings have more than a thousand or two thousand head, and there are quite a number who have up to three or four thousand head. An occasional herd may have more than eight thousand head. Herds of five hundred or more are quite common. The truth is that the land furnishes some of the best pasturage, clear water, and one of the most temperate climates in the world for such cattle. Consequently the animals are larger and more handsome than those in Spain; and since the weather is mild, and not cold, the cattle are never lean and of bad flavor. Likewise, there are many sheep and swine, and many of the swine and cattle have become wild. Large numbers of dogs and cats that were carried there from Spain for the use of the settlers have escaped to the forests and have become quite vicious, especially the dogs, and they eat the cattle because of the carelessness of the shepherds, who guard the flocks poorly. There are many mares and horses and all the other domestic animals that have been bred from original stock carried from Spain.

There are a number of small towns on this island, concerning which I desire to say only that they are so located that in time they will grow and become famous, because of the fertility and the abundance of the land. Concerning Santo Domingo, the principal city, I wish to point out that with regard to the buildings, no town in Spain, unless it is Barcelona, which I have seen many times, is superior in general. The houses in Santo Domingo are for the most part of stone like those in Barcelona, and the walls are strong and beautiful, constructed of wonderful masonry. The general layout of the city is much better than that of Barcelona, because the many streets are more level and wide and incomparably straighter. Since the city was founded in our own time, there was opportunity to plan the whole thing from the beginning. It was laid out with ruler and compass, with all the streets being carefully measured. Because of this, Santo Domingo is better planned than any town I have seen.

The city is so near the sea that on one side there is only space for the street, which is about fifty paces at the widest point. On one side the waves beat upon live rock and a rugged coast, while on the other side, near the houses, flows the Ozama River, which forms a marvelous port. The ships anchor there near the shore, under the very windows of the houses and no farther from the mouth of the river than the distance from the foot of Monjuich Mountain to the monastery of Saint Francis or to the Exchange of Barcelona. In this area, the fortress and castle are located, beneath which, and about twenty paces away, the ships pass in order to anchor somewhat further up the river. From the time the ships enter the river until they drop anchor, they are never more than thirty or forty paces away from the houses of the city, for on that side the city extends to the edge of the water. One could not find such a beautiful port or river mouth anywhere in the world.

There must be some seven hundred citizens in this city, living in such houses as I have already described. Some of the private homes are so luxurious that any grandee in Spain would find himself most comfortable there. Admiral Diego Columbus, Your Majesty's Viceroy, has such a magnificent house that I cannot remember one in Spain a quarter as good. It is well constructed of stone and located on the port. It has many fine rooms and commands a beautiful view of both land and sea. The rooms to be added later will harmonize with the part already constructed. Here your Majesty would be as comfortably lodged as in one of the finest houses in Castile.

A cathedral is now being constructed, and the Bishop and other dignitaries and canons are well provided for. Since there is an abundance of materials and labor, it should be completed soon. From what I have already seen, I believe it will be a magnificent building of good proportions.

There are also three monasteries (Dominican, Franciscan, and Saint Mary of Mercy) which have handsome but modest buildings which are not so grotesque as some of those in Spain. But speaking without prejudice toward any religious order, Your Majesty may rest assured that in these three communities God is worshiped most devoutly, because they are inhabited by holy and exemplary monks. There is also a fine hospital to which poor people may be carried and where they are well cared for. It was founded by Miguel de Pasamonte, Your Majesty's treasurer.

Day by day the city is growing larger and becoming more noble, and this is certain to continue since the Viceroy and Your Majesty's high court of justice and Royal Chancellery are located there. Likewise, most of the rich people of the island live in or near the city of Santo Domingo.

The Natives of Hispaniola

The natives of Hispaniola are somewhat smaller than Spaniards, and are of light brown color. Each Indian has his own wife and no man marries his daughter or his sister nor does he couple with his mother. They may couple with and marry women of any other degree of kinship. Those Indians have wide foreheads and very straight black hair. Neither the men nor women have beards or any hair on any part of their bodies. It is a very rare thing for either a man or a woman to have any hair on the body. They go naked as they were born, except that over their privates they wear a loincloth, of linen or some other kind of cloth, about the size of a man's hand. But this piece of cloth is not worn in such a way as to fulfill the purpose for which it is intended.

The Taínos

Fray Ramón Pané was the first "anthropologist" of the New World. A missionary priest, he was entrusted with learning the customs and language of the Taínos and describing them to the authorities. Even though Pané's biases are obvious (for example, he considered the beliefs of the Indians pure superstitions), his descriptions are among the most-detailed accounts of the Taíno way of life. It must be kept in mind too that Pané wrote this account in 1498, just before the Spaniards began their merciless exploitation of the Indians, ending in their eventual extermination. As such, Pané describes a people about to experience culture shock, domination, and soon genocide. This fragment describes one of the most important members of Taíno society: the *behique*. Healer, shaman, counselor, and oral historian, the behique exercised different roles that gave coherence to the world of the Taínos. He was the intermediary between the living and the Taínos deities, and his skills in interpreting the gods' wishes guaranteed his people's future well being. Because the Taíno way of life was so quickly and radically altered within a few years, Pané's account remains as a valuable snapshot of a people now extinct.

FROM PANÉ'S ACCOUNT[12]
Concerning the observances of these Indian behiques, *and how they practice medicine and teach the people, and in their medicinal cures they are often deceived*

All or the majority of the people of the Island of Hispaniola have many zemis[13] of various sorts. Some contain the bones of their father and mother and relatives and ancestors; they are made of stone or of wood. And they have many of both kinds, some that speak, and others that cause the things they eat to grow, and others that make it rain, and others that make the winds blow. Those simple, ignorant people believe that those idols or, more properly speaking, demons make such things happen because they have no knowledge of Our Holy Faith. When one of them is sick, they take him to the *behique*, who is the aforesaid physician. The physician is obliged to keep the same diet as the patient and to put on a sick face. This is done in the manner you will now see. He must also purge himself as the sick one does; and in order to purge themselves, they take a certain powder called *cohoba*, inhaling it through the nose, which inebriates them in such fashion that they do not know what they are doing; and thus they say many senseless things, affirming therein that they are speaking with the zemis, and that the latter tell them that the sickness has come from them.

A Colony of Exploitation

The Spanish conquest and colonization of the New World was a commercial enterprise. Indians, though legally vassals of the Spanish Crown,

---

12. From Fray Ramón Pané, *An Account of the Antiquities of the Indians*, edited by José Juan Arrom, translated by Susan C. Griswold (Durham, N.C.: Duke University Press, 1999), 21.
13. idol

were to provide the necessary labor and pay taxes as required by the authorities. For this purpose, the Crown established the system of *encomiendas*, grants of lands and Indians to individual Spanish colonists. The Indians would work for the Spaniards, who would be entrusted with their care and Christian education. In reality, the *encomienda* system worked the Indians to death. Together with warfare and diseases previously unknown among the Indians, this exploitative work regime virtually exterminated the Taínos within a few decades. Bartolomé de las Casas knew this reality firsthand. A former *encomendero*, he later became a priest and an ardent defender of the Indians. His work describes, and sometimes exaggerates, the atrocities committed by the Spanish in the New World. Decrying the Spaniards as merciless, bloody profiteers, Las Casas tries to make his case for the preservation of the Indians. At one point, he even suggested importing slaves from Africa to replace the declining Indian labor force, not an abomination from his point of view, since the Indians were vassals of the Spanish Crown, while Africans were deemed slaves with no rights or human condition. He later regretted this standpoint as an error. One of his most famous works was his *Brief Account of the Devastation of the Indies*, which was translated into several languages and eventually gave rise to the *Spanish Black Legend* by which the northern European nations accused Spain of the genocide of millions of Amerindians.

FROM BARTOLOMÉ DE LAS CASAS'S ACCOUNT[14]

On the Island Hispaniola was where the Spaniards first landed, as I have said. Here those Christians perpetrated their first ravages and oppressions against the native peoples. This was the first land in the New World to be destroyed and depopulated by the Christians, and here they began their subjection of the women and children, taking them away from the Indians to use them and ill use them, eating the food they provided with their sweat and toil. The Spaniards did not content themselves with what the Indians gave them of their own free will, according to their ability, which was always too little to satisfy enormous appetites, for a Christian eats and consumes in one day an amount of food that would suffice to feed three houses inhabited by ten Indians for one month. And they committed other acts of force and violence and oppression which made the Indians realize that these men had not come from Heaven. And some of the Indians concealed their foods while others concealed

---

14. From Bartolomé de las Casas, *The Devastation of the Indies: A Brief Account*, trans. Herma Briffault (New York: Seabury Press, 1974), 42–45, 51–53.

14

their wives and children and still others fled to the mountains to avoid the terrible transactions of the Christians.

And the Christians attacked them with buffets and beatings, until finally they laid hands on the nobles of the villages. Then they behaved with such temerity and shamelessness that the most powerful ruler of the islands had to see his own wife raped by a Christian officer.

From that time onward the Indians began to seek ways to throw the Christians out of their lands. They took up arms, but their weapons were very weak and of little service in offense and still less in defense. (Because, of this, the wars of the Indians against each other are little more than games played by children.) And the Christians, with their horses and swords and pikes began to carry out massacres and strange cruelties against them. They attacked the towns and spared neither the children nor the aged nor pregnant women nor women in childbed, not only stabbing them and dismembering them but cutting them to pieces as if dealing with sheep in the slaughterhouse. They laid bets as to who, with one stroke of the sword, could split a man in two or could cut off his head or spill out his entrails with a single stroke of the pike. They took infants from their mothers' breasts, snatching them by the legs and pitching them headfirst against the crags or snatched them by the arms and threw them into the rivers, roaring with laughter and saying as the babies fell into the water, "Boil there, you offspring of the devil!" Other infants they put to the sword along with their mothers and anyone else who happened to be nearby. They made some low wide gallows on which the hanged victim's feet almost touched the ground, stringing up their victims in lots of thirteen, in memory of Our Redeemer and His twelve Apostles, then set burning wood at their feet and thus burned them alive. To others they attached straw or wrapped their whole bodies in straw and set them afire. With still others, all those they wanted to capture alive, they cut off their hands and hung them round the victim's neck, saying, "Go now, carry the message," meaning, Take the news to the Indians who have fled to the mountains. They usually dealt with the chieftains and nobles in the following way: they made a grid of rods which they placed on forked sticks, then lashed the victims to the grid and lighted a smoldering fire underneath, so that little by little, as those captives screamed in despair and torment, their souls would leave them.

I once saw this, when there were four or five nobles lashed on grids and burning; I seem even to recall that there were two or three pairs of grids where others were burning, and because they uttered such loud screams that they disturbed the captain's sleep, he ordered them to be strangled. And the constable, who was worse than an executioner, did not want to obey that order (and I know the name of that constable and know his relatives in Seville), but instead put a stick over the victims' tongues, so they could not make a sound, and he stirred up the fire, but not too much, so that they roasted slowly, as he liked. I saw all these things I have described, and countless others.

And because all the people who could do so fled to the mountains to escape these inhuman, ruthless, and ferocious acts, the Spanish captains, enemies of the human race, pursued them with the fierce dogs they kept which attacked the Indians, tearing them to pieces and devouring them. And because on few and far between occasions, the Indians justifiably killed some Christians, the Spaniards made a rule among themselves that for every Christian slain by the Indians, they would slay a hundred Indians.

After the wars and the killings had ended, when usually there survived only a few boys, women, and children, these survivors were distributed among the Christians as slaves. The *repartimiento* or distribution was made according to the rank and importance of the Christian to whom the Indians were allocated, one of them being given thirty, another forty, still another, one or two hundred, and besides the rank of the Christian there was also to be considered in what favor he stood with the tyrant they called Governor. The pretext was that these allocated Indians were to be instructed in the articles of the Christian Faith. As if those Christians who were as a rule foolish and cruel and greedy and vicious could be caretakers of souls! And the care they took was to send the men to the mines to dig for gold, which is intolerable labor, and to send the women into the fields of the big ranches to hoe and till the land, work suitable for strong men. Nor to either the men or the women did they give any food except herbs and legumes, things of little substance. The milk in the breasts of the women with infants dried up and thus in a short while the infants perished.

And since men and women were separated, there could be no marital relations. And the men died in the mines and the women died on the ranches from the same causes, exhaustion and hunger. And thus was depopulated that island which had been densely populated.

I will speak only briefly of the heavy loads the Indians were made to carry, loads weighing three to four arrobas, Christian tyrants and captains had themselves carried in hammocks borne by two Indians. This shows that they treated the Indians as beasts of burden. But were I to describe all this and the buffetings and beatings and birchings endured by the Indians at their labors, no amount of time and paper could encompass this task.

And be it noted that the worst depredations on these islands in the New World began when tidings came of the death of Her Most Serene Highness, Queen Isabel, which occurred in the year one thousand five hundred and four. Because, up to that time, only a few provinces on the island of Hispaniola had been destroyed in unjust wars, but not the entire island, since, for the most part, the island was under the royal protection of the Queen and she, may God rest her, took admirable and zealous care of these people, their salvation and prosperity, as we saw with our own eyes and touched with our hands.

Another rule should be noted: in all parts of the Indies, wherever they have landed or passed through, the Christians have always committed atrocities against the Indians, have perpetrated slaughters and tyrannies and abominable oppressions against innocent people that we have described, and have added worse and more cruel acts, ever since God allowed them most suddenly to fall into dishonor and opprobrium.

The Decline of the Taínos

With the establishment of the Laws of Burgos in 1512, the Spanish Crown realized the precarious situation of the Taíno population of Hispaniola. Church missionaries had warned of the impending demise of the Indians unless drastic measures were taken to protect them. However, these humanitarian concerns clashed with the demands of the Spanish colonizers, who required a steady supply of labor to extract gold, and the needs of the Spanish Crown for revenues. In 1513, the Crown ordered Rodrigo de Alburquerque to carry out a *repartimiento*, that is, the apportionment of the remaining Indians among the Spanish *encomenderos*. His instructions are reproduced below. The apportionment was far from equal; powerful Spanish officials received the largest share of Indians. The *repartimiento* also serves as an informal census of the remaining Indians. According to it, some twenty-six thousand Taínos still lived on the island. While the figure most likely underestimates their actual number, it still reflects the precipitous decline of the Taíno population within just two decades of a Spanish presence on the island. Alburquerque's *repartimiento* portrays a people on the verge of extinction and a colony in crisis. The lack of Indians to work the gold fields would accelerate the flight of Spaniards to other islands (e.g., Cuba and Puerto Rico) and eventually to the mainland (Mexico and Peru).

INSTRUCTIONS GIVEN BY THE MONARCHS TO RODRIGO DE ALBURQUERQUE AND TO LICENTIATE IBARRA TO BE CARRIED OUT DURING THE GENERAL DISTRIBUTION OF THE INDIANS IN THE ISLAND OF HISPANIOLA. VALLADOLID, OCTOBER 4, 1513.[15]

This copy was faithfully transcribed from a decree given by the King.
The King: What you, Licentiate Ibarra and Rodrigo de Alburquerque, must do, in your position of *encomendador* of the Indians, so that, according to the lettered men's resolution, they would be treated and indoctrinated in Our Holy Catholic Faith is to abide by the following:

1. First, once you have, with good fortune, arrived there, and before doing anything else, you must present the decrees you carry with you to our Admiral,[16] judges

---

15. Translated from Luis Arranz Márquez, *Repartimientos y encomiendas en la Isla Española: El Repartimiento de Alburquerque de 1514* (Santo Domingo: Fundación García Arévalo, 1991), 263–273.
16. Diego, Christopher Columbus's son

and officials, and once presented, they should be announced to the public.

2. Second, by the virtue of the decree you carry, you shall revoke and annul, through a public announcement, the current Allocations of the Indians, this is, as determined by our erudite men, in order to cleanse our conscience. And you should order that everyone, including our officials, anyone under our name, the Admiral and his wife, the appellate judges, as well as our officers and all the people, of every class and condition, report each of the Indians they possess, and the name of the caciques under whose command they are, and the name of each Indian, be it men or women, boys or girls, to the Indian Visitor and a delegate, who will be elected in every town for such, and other, purposes. The procedure by which the delegate must be elected, which will be discussed in the next chapter, will take place in front of the town's council secretary.

3. And then, to elect the previously mentioned delegate, the people of each town should name three or four men from among themselves as candidates so that one should become the delegate. The names of the candidates should be placed in a bowl and one person should pick one of the names. The person whose name is picked shall become the delegate of that town. This elected person will become the witness in front of whom the Declaration of Indians will take place, as ordered, taking into account that a punishment of twenty pesos in gold per head, be it large or small, will be applied to those who decide to hide them, and if he has Indians, two will be taken away from him, and if he hides ten or more, he will not be given any Indians.

4. And then, you should order each of the town mayors to visit, within a twenty-day period, the Indians in the neighboring farms and ask their caciques for a list of names and allocation of each of their Indians. The lists should be sent to you by the mayors within a reasonable period of time.

5. And then, you should order that a record of all the people that live in each town should be created under the supervision of the mayor and the secretary of each town. And these records should be signed by the mayor and the secretary and brought to you by the delegate, as well as the list of the declared Indians, and a report of the visit that the mayors paid to each of the caciques.

6. Having completed all the instructions, and after receiving all the reports from each of the towns, including the list of Indians and the report on the population of each town, you shall compare the numbers in the reports provided by each of the mayors.

7. Completed this first part of the task, what you shall do next is to see that the general distribution of the Indians is just, according to its population, so that no town is affected by having fewer Indians. At the same time, you should consider if a town has been allocated too many Indians in respect to its population. This is so that no one feels the need to present a protest as in the village of Puerto Real where people were affected. They say they have very few, and extremely necessary Indians, who are very useful in the trade with Cuba. Make sure that no other town, but the one already mentioned, is affected. And, to my opinion, this matter should be mended there, without causing any changes in the other towns. The Indians should stay in their original places to avoid the inconveniences of moving them around. But if a general redistribution of Indians is necessary, make sure you privilege those communities that have mines in them, because they will be more useful to us.

8. If a new Distribution should be done within the various towns, you may request the mayor and council of each town, along with the delegate, to come for this duty. Once the Distribution is completed, the mayors and councils could return to their towns while the delegates shall stay to perform the various allocations.

9. Completed the general Allocation, and if changes must be made in order to meet the needs of each town, and if nothing else needs to be done, then you should proceed to make the individual distributions.

10. In this matter, the first thing to be considered, as determined by the Lettered Men for the relief of our conscience, is that no Indian shall be allocated in two places at the same time. This is because by their [the Indians] being in several places, the control as to their instruction and doctrine in our sacred Catholic faith and in the communication with Christians as to their good treatment, in the hands of the people who have them, cannot be clearly maintained. And it is for these reasons that you shall carry my ordinances. If they are not followed, as ascertained by the Lettered Men, I cannot, with good conscience, allocate them nor can they accept it. And in that case, neither I nor they, with good conscience, can reap the profits of gold nor the other goods their work provide, and we, indeed, will be deprived of the gratification of those earnings.

11. Afterwards, it should be manifested to everyone that they shall follow these ordinances, which were decided upon in Valladolid according to the resolution of the erudite so that I, in good conscience, can allocate them [the Indians], as you shall do in my name. Therefore, expressively order them to obey the ordinances as they are, during their entire lifetime and during the lifetime of one of their inheritors, a son or a daughter, if they have one. So that, in my name, you may take away their allocations of Indians, if the ordinances are disobeyed. And in this case, the burden should fall on their conscience, and not ours, as well as other punishments that may be applied to them.

12. And because it has been called to our attention that the number of Indians in the island has been declining, and at the same time, some people have too many of them and cannot, therefore, indoctrinate them and teach them the tenets of Our Holy Faith nor can they all be well treated, as reasonable, and because more can now communicate in Christian, and in order to expedite their individual allocations, we mandate that you adhere to the instructions, following the number of Indians allocated without exceeding them.

13. In our Haciendas you may leave the number of Indians that are now there, as long as that number does not exceed one thousand. The Admiral shall keep three hundred and his wife, María de Toledo, two hundred Indians. To the people who serve me but are not in the island, who are: the First Chaplain of my Council, the Reverend in Christ Father Don Juan Fonseca, Bishop of Palencia, shall receive two hundred Indians; Fernando Vega, Comendador Mayor of Castile, two hundred; Chamberlain Juan Cabrero, two hundred; Secretary Lope Conchillos, two hundred; to the judges, officers, mayors, I order each shall receive two hundred; and to the descendants of the Admiral and their uncles two hundred Indians each.

14. The rest of the people who live in the island to whom you shall allocate Indians, should be divided within four groups as follows: The most honorable and respectful people, among which you will surely find my servants Villoria and Porros

amongst others, should receive the largest possible number of Indians which will be of one hundred and fifty.

15. The second group will be of one hundred Indians and those would be allocated to the next following honorable people you hear of.

16. The third group shall receive seventy-five Indians.

17. The last group shall receive forty Indians, and the rest of the people shall receive none because I understand that less than forty are of no use, and of no profit because those who have them would not bring the one-third profit that was established in the ordinance.

18. And also, because we have been informed that many people have ten or fewer Indians and for this small number we receive no profit. So we order that you collect those Indians from the people that only have three, four, or six and up to ten, so that they may be relocated, especially the Indian men. But the Indian women can stay because many of them are used as house servants and maids, and they shall be indoctrinated and taught in the house. This is so long as they are not married, because according to the Lettered Men, the married women and the children under thirteen years of age must do as the Indian man orders, for they are subjected to his will. If any of these Indians hold vital positions in the mines such as blacksmith or similar occupations, they should be left there.

19. In addition, if an Indian is learning a skill from one of our officers, let him be; those who are truly learning, who are being taught by the officer and not used merely for his service shall be let to learn, for the Erudite have determined that the Indians should be free to learn a skill.

20. And also, make sure that the Indians are not overworked as they have been until now, a matter that has caused a lot of harm and a decrease in the number of Indians. Those who have Indians, as it has been determined, shall have them use oxen to plough their land, to the extent that this could be possible, so that the Indians can preserve energy. You shall order anyone who has more than fifty Indians to obtain a pair of oxen as well to help work the land; and those people who have more than a hundred Indians shall have two pairs of oxen, and those with over two hundred should have three pairs. That is so that the more oxen they have the less overworked the Indians shall be, therefore they could serve us better, and they could have more time to be indoctrinated and to celebrate their festivities and holidays.

21. And also, since that island needs to be populated, we order that the widowed women or those who during the near future lose their husbands, that is, if their husbands had Indians at the time of their deaths, keep the Indians for a year, this is so that the man's will could be carried out. But if she marries within a year, they shall both keep their Indians, as long as the number does not exceed the regulations stated above.

22. And, we order that no foreigner that lives or stayed in the mentioned island shall be allocated any Indians, unless it has been specifically mandated by us, or unless he, with our consent, marries one of our own. In that case, if he is married with our consent or we have given him our permission to obtain Indians, he can receive them.

23. Because we have had complaints from the residents that the Admiral has taken away Indians from them and given them to his servants without due process or any

cause, and because they may not take the case to court here without great expense, we order that you, along with our appellate judges there, or at least two of them, grant them justice.

24. For we have been told that the Admiral, after being notified of these Orders and exceeding his authority, has been giving away the Indians that were not declared, without following the correct procedure, we order that these Indians are collected and then, reallocated to other people, according to the rules, as you see it fit.

25. Because there ought to be two general visitors, who visit all the Indians of the island, and these ought to be very good people, and they must do it in a good and faithful manner, we order that they get forty more Indians with their commission, besides the ones already allocated to them. And we also order that thereafter those forty Indians go with them because it is beneficial to all Indians in general.

26. Because in each place there ought to be a visitor who visits the Indians of each location, we order that he should be given twelve Indians for this commission, besides the ones already allocated to him.

27. And so that the aforementioned ordinances are kept according to the determination of the lettered men, a number of them, which will be determined by our main chaplain, the bishop of Palencia, and our secretary, Lope Conchillos, shall be printed. This will be determined according to the following:

28. So that the bishops and all their representatives shall have a copy; that every monastery must receive a copy; that the Admiral and his mayors, and all of our appellate judges and our officers will each have a copy; and that in each town council one copy must be posted; that each council secretary shall have one in his house; that each officer, as well as the generals of each town must have one; that the miners who bring the Indians to the mines, shall, according to your considerations, also have a copy; and that in the same manner, the prosecutors of those places shall have a copy. This is so they may not argue ignorance. The copies must be signed by the aforementioned bishop of Palencia and the secretary Lope Conchillos.

29. And also, since we have granted the friars, guardians, and monasteries in the cities of Santo Domingo and La Concepción, a number of Indians to be taken care of, among whom they have some of the caciques' sons, nothing shall be changed in this. So that this arrangement may continue to be carried out in the same manner, so that the mentioned sons of the caciques are well provided for, and so they do not because of lack of care, fail to learn the teachings of our faith.

30. You shall mandate that those people who receive Indians as a result of the distribution in our name, must maintain the same number of Indians that was allocated to them originally.

31. After arriving in the island, you shall proclaim the decree that you carry in which all former allocations of Indians are revoked, either by our power or by special decrees that we have issued up to the day in which we granted you the power to carry out this new allocation.

32. Furthermore, because as you already know, there are very few Indians in the island and there are many settlers without them, we have ordered to lower their distribution as mentioned above. I order you that no person shall receive more that two hundred Indians in the distribution even if they are council members. Make sure that those functionaries that have less than one hundred Indians receive another twenty

for holding the position, but not those who have over a hundred Indians.

33. In the same manner, since the Indians from Mona Island fall under the allocation of the island of Hispaniola, and there is a great lack of Indians in the island of San Juan, and since they are so close to the island of San Juan, we believe that they could be moved without endangering their health, we order that you leave the Indians from Mona Island out of the distribution of the island of Hispaniola and that you apply them to the island of San Juan, and that you order that, if possible, they be moved to the island of San Juan, if it can be done without endangering their health as we believe. If not, you shall order haciendas to be built in Mona Island for the sustenance of the Indians in the haciendas of San Juan in spite of the fact that we had ordered that the Adelantado Don Bartolomé Colón use them with our permission, because that complies with our service and the well being of our possessions.

34. Once you establish your mandate, you shall remove the Indians from the possession of the functionaries and the Admiral. The ones in the hands of Marcos de Aguilar, you shall give to the incumbent judge; those that the licentiate Carrillo has shall be given to the lieutenant that replaces him, so that the incumbent judge and his lieutenants have the Indians for as long as they are in office, or for as long as I determine.

35. And, from what I understand, the clinics in the island have been given some Indians. You shall respect this and do as you see fit so that they shall continue to receive their share from the tithe of the island, as well as other contributions that we have ordered for them to receive.

36. Also, we order that the Indians will be distributed among people who are over twenty years old and who reside in the town where such distribution is taking place, or its environs. And those who do not live, at least eight months of the year, in the town where the distribution took place, shall be fined one hundred castellanos for the first offense; one third of which will go to our chamber; another third to whoever accuses him; and another third to whoever sentences him. And if there is a second infraction, he is to lose his Indians, except for those obtained through inheritance.

37. In the same manner, so that the given orders are maintained and obeyed, it is necessary to have two visitors.[17] It is not possible for us, from a distance, to assign which visitors would be best suited for the happiness of the Indians and for them to learn Our Holy Catholic Faith. Since you already know the people over there, you would perform this duty better. Trusting that you shall carry out the orders accordingly, with the well being of the Indians in mind, we give you special authority to appoint those visitors. Make sure that you assign the best-suited people to carry out this duty of visitors; and that you appoint those you see necessary for the good treatment of the Indians. Also, make sure to give them instructions on how to carry out their duties for the good treatment of the Indians, as we have done so far. Also, make sure to add instructions as you see fit for the implementation of these orders for the good treatment, conservation and development of the Indians, and so that they are taught our Holy Catholic Faith, and for this we trust your consciences. I understand that for the aforementioned to be carried out, it is necessary that the disputes of these visitors be heard only by the appellate judges of the island, and you carry a letter in

17. inspectors

which I order that. After appointing the visitors, you must announce this letter so that our orders are known by all. So that the visitors carry out their duties they shall be appointed to two-year terms. For that, you carry our letter and shall announce it.

38. Since from here we cannot provide for all of the things that are necessary for the distribution as particularly as it is convenient, and if by chance when you arrive some of the ordered things are already in place, and if by chance you must change the orders that you now carry, and trusting that you work at the service of the serene Queen, my very dear and loved daughter, and at mine, for the benefit and development of the island, by the present one I grant you the rights and power, so that you three together do whatever needs to be done otherwise, or in addition to these orders in the carrying out of this service.

I command you and everyone else to read the mentioned orders and to obey and follow, and to have them obeyed and followed in their entirety, and in everything contained therein. And against their spirit and form, you shall not let time pass nor consent it to pass by for any reason or you should fine ten thousand maravedís[18] for my chamber to each one who fails to comply with them.

Given in Valladolid, on the fourth day of October 1513.
I, the King. The Bishop of Palencia, Earl.

Enriquillo, the Last Cacique

Enrique (or Enriquillo as he was called by the Spanish) was a Christianized Taíno Indian who rebelled against the Spanish colonial authorities between 1519–1533. By this time, the Taínos were almost gone, after decades of military raids, enslavement, epidemics, and hard labor in the gold fields. By the same token, the colony, which had been once the center of the Spanish colonial enterprise in the New World, was no longer an attractive destination. With gold becoming scarce and the Taínos quickly disappearing, the economic future of Hispaniola did not look promising, so the Spaniards started to leave. The European exodus to other islands and to the mainland endangered Spanish rule in Hispaniola and the authorities tried to contain it. Thus, both factors seemed to have overlapped in sparking the rebellion. Moreover, by this time the remaining Taínos understood Spanish military technology and were well aware of the Spaniards' weaknesses. Enriquillo carried out a successful insurrection centered on the highlands of southwestern Hispaniola. The Taínos's

---

18. Spanish coin

knowledge of the region and the dry, rocky, mountainous terrain made it extremely difficult for the Spanish to crush the rebellion. Moreover, maroon African slaves also joined the rebellious Taínos and together launched attacks against Spanish plantations and unwary travelers. Eventually, the Spanish colonial authorities negotiated a truce with Enriquillo, by which his people would be granted lands on which to live unmolested by the Spanish. In exchange, they had to acknowledge the King's authority and to turn over the escaped slaves. The following is a letter from Enriquillo to King Carlos (Charles) V.

LETTER FROM ENRIQUILLO TO KING CHARLES V[19]
Your Catholic Majesty,
I received, through Francisco de Barrionuevo, governor of the mainland, a Royal decree that Your Majesty granted me and grateful for the favor and mercy Your Majesty serves me, I kiss your hands and feet. After reading your Royal orders I, with the required obedience and as your lower servant, obeyed and carried out your commands and moved along with all the other Indians of my land to the towns of the Spanish. After capturing some maroons who were in other parts of the island, I came to this city to speak to the president and other officials, about some things that are convenient to Your Majesty for the peace and tranquility of the land. In them and in the rest of the Spaniards, I have found much good will and I depart to uproot some of the Indians that are not in the service of Your Majesty, in which I shall occupy myself for the rest of my life to the utmost. To Your Majesty I beg that you allow me to be counted as one of your servants and vassals. I have communicated this to the vicar friar of Our Lady of Mercy Francisco de Bobadilla, who with very good intentions and deeds will express this to your majesty. I beg your majesty about this matter and hope for the growth and development of your kingdoms and possessions, as your imperial heart desires for Santo Domingo.
Sixth of June, 1533 . . . your humble servant and a lower vassal of Your Majesties . . . who kisses your hands.

A Fleeting Sugar Boom

By the early decades of the sixteenth century, with the gold reserves practically exhausted and the native population virtually extinct, Hispaniola faced a crisis of major proportions that threatened the very existence of the colony. The colonial authorities sought a solution in plantation

19. Translated from César A. Herrera, *Divulgaciones históricas* (Santo Domingo: Editora Taller, 1989), 51–52.

agriculture, particularly the production of sugarcane, using African slave labor. Sugar was in high demand in Europe, but producing it required of considerable capital investment. Land, machinery, such as *trapiches* or sugar presses, as well as animals, buildings, skilled technicians and a considerable number of slaves were needed to

A rudimentary sugar mill or *trapiche*.

run a mid-sized plantation. Not many Spaniards were willing to risk so much capital in a distant, decaying colony. Moreover, attacks from maroon slaves made inland travel dangerous, while pirates and Spain's enemies threatened sea lanes. As a result, the sugar boom in Hispaniola was short-lived and it was over by the 1570s. Still, it represents the first colonial plantation system experiment in the New World. The model developed in Hispaniola would be copied in other islands and it sparked a large-scale African slave trading system across the Atlantic. Gonzalo Fernández Oviedo describes the state of the sugar industry in sixteenth-century Hispaniola.

FROM GONZALO FERNÁNDEZ DE OVIEDO'S HISTORY[20]

Regarding the sugar mills and trapiches that exist in the island of Hispaniola, to whom do they belong, and how this wealthy agricultural production began in this island.

Since sugar is one of the richest crops that any province or kingdom in the world could have, and in that island there is so much and of such good quality, and it has been so recently developed and acquired, it is true that (though the land and its fertility, and the use of the waters and the utilization of the great forests of firewood for such great and continuous fires, are in such purpose as they are for such haciendas), even more should be the graces and the prize given to the one who taught it [sugar

---

20. Translated from Gonzalo Fernández de Oviedo, *Historia general y natural de las Indias* (Madrid: Gráficas Orbe, 1959), chap. VIII, book IV, 106–107.

production] and first installed it. So everybody had their eyes closed until bachelor Gonzalo de Velosa, at the cost of his great and excessive expenditures, based on what he had, and with a lot of personal work, brought the first sugar masters to this island, and built a horse-driven trapiche, and was the first one to manufacture sugar on this island; to him alone we owe thanks, as the main inventor of this rich crop. Not because he was the first one to bring sugar canes to the Indies, since some time before his arrival, many had brought them and grew them and made molasses out of them; but he was, as I have said, the first one to produce sugar on this island, because based on his example, later, others did the same. The aforementioned, as he had a lot of cane, built a horse-driven trapiche on the banks of the Nigua River, and brought the employees for it from the Canary Islands, and milled and produced sugar before anyone else.

But, in fairness, after inquiring, I have found that some credible old men, who now live in this city, say something else and affirm that the first one who brought sugar canes to this island was a Pedro de Atienza, in the town of Concepción de la Vega, and that the mayor of La Vega, Miguel Ballester, a native of Catalonia, was the first one to manufacture sugar. And they affirm that he did it more than two years before Velosa did; but, together with this, they say that what the mayor did was very little, and that all, one and the other, found their origin in the canes of Pedro de Atienza. In such a manner that, one way or the other, it is the sugar of this island and the Indies; because since Pedro de Atienza started it, it multiplied so that this crop reached the state where it currently is, and every day it increases and becomes greater, since from fifteen years ago until nowadays, some mills have gone bankrupt and deteriorated due to causes that I will mention; but others have been improved.

Just as, thanks to him, this crop has become better understood, the overseer Cristóbal de Tapia and his brother and warden of this fortress, Francisco de Tapia, joined him, and the three of them built a mill in the Yaguate, a league and a half from the banks of the Nizao River. Some time ago they broke up, and the bachelor sold his part to the Tapias. Later, the overseer sold his to Joan de Villoria, who later sold it to warden Francisco de Tapia, and he was left by himself with the first mill that existed on the island.

Since at that time, or at the beginning, it was not well understood how convenient it was for such crops to have a lot of land and water and firewood and other things that are foreign to such crops (of which there was not as much as needed there), the warden Francisco de Tapia depopulated that mill, and he moved the copper cauldrons and supplies, and all that he could, to a better place, on the same banks of the Nigua, five leagues from this city, where until said warden died, he had a very good mill and one of the powerful ones in this island.

So that what I am going to say now is not repeated many times, the reader should notice about this mill, as for all the others, through this warning, that each mill, of the powerful and well-stocked ones, besides and beyond the heavy cost and value of the building and factory of the house in which sugar is made, and of another house in which it is purged and stored, there are some that exceed ten or twelve thousand gold ducats or more, until it is up running and milling. And even though fifteen thousand ducats are mentioned, I do not extend myself, because it is necessary to have, at least, eighty or a hundred Negroes continuously, and even a hundred and twenty and some more, so that they are well-stocked; and nearby one or two good cattle ranches, of one or two or three thousand heads for feeding the mill; besides the heavy cost of the technicians and masters who manufacture sugar, and of the carts to haul in the cane to the mill and to carry firewood, and full-time people to make bread and prepare and irrigate the canes, and do other necessary things requiring of continuous expenditures. But in reality, the master of a free and well-stocked mill is very well and richly endowed; and those mills are of very great usefulness and wealth for the masters.

So this was the first mill that existed on this island; and it should be noticed that until sugar was made there, the naos returned empty to Spain, and now they go back loaded with it [sugar] and with larger loads than those they bring back here, and with more profits. And thus this crop was begun on the banks of the Nigua, I mean to say the other mills that are near the same river.

Hispaniola by the Mid-Sixteenth Century

What was Hispaniola really like back in the early days of the Spanish colony? As the Taínos were replaced by African slaves during the first half of the sixteenth century, the racial makeup of the colony changed. Mestizos and mulattos were born from sexual encounters of Spanish colonists with their Indians or African slaves. Moreover, as immense wealth was discovered in Mexico and Peru, many Spaniards began abandoning the colony in search of greater fortunes elsewhere. The short-lived sugar boom did not solve the colony's economic problems and Hispaniola was slowly but steadily becoming a backwater of the Spanish empire. Administering such a vast empire was a complex endeavor. Communications were extremely slow and sporadic. With no easy way of knowing what was going on in the colonies, or even what their colonies looked like, Spanish monarchs relied on detailed reports from their officers stationed in or visiting the colonies. The following is a description of the colony of Hispaniola by magistrate Echagoian, prepared in 1568. Notice the author's pains in trying to describe tropical fruits and plants for which there were no equivalents in Europe. The description remains a valuable snapshot of Hispaniola when it was just a remote outpost of the Spanish empire.

Sixteenth-century view of Santo Domingo city.

ECHAGOIAN'S DESCRIPTION OF HISPANIOLA, 1568[21]

First of all, it should be said that the city of Santo Domingo is the head of the island of Hispaniola, which is formed also by many other cities and provinces, of which I will speak to you later on. Santo Domingo is composed of other villages and cities; and it is located on the coast, about a quarter of a league from the ocean. From the ocean and up to the beach of Guiaia the city is bordered by a rock wall, which is constantly battered by the sea. To enter the city, people must navigate a river that has about four leagues of salty water, changing to sweet thereafter, as it borders many beautiful curves, surrounded by beautiful forests, where one can find estancias,[22] which here people call estates; as well as cattle and goats. We can also find a variety of native fruits as well as fruits from Spain, which grow to be good and even better here, and also gardens, some that produce vegetables and others that do not. The cabbage crops last from ten to twelve years, because as you cut one, the next flourishes in its place. And from the sprouts, although they might not have roots, one gets as much cabbage as little branches are planted. This is an eggplant land, just like Toledo, and a land of cucumbers, and of many citrons; there are countless types of oranges, and lemons of all kinds. The potato growth on this land, however, is poor. And it seems that the good roots have been ruined and lost. In terms of the native fruits, there are wild grapes and some grapevines from Spain, and some muscatel grapes that produce good wine. In Nigua were some vineyards that produced many grapes,

---

21. Translated from "Relación de la Isla Española enviada al Rey D. Felipe II por el Licenciado Echagoian, Oidor de la Audiencia de Santo Domingo," *Boletín del Archivo General de la Nación*, vol. 4, no. 19 (1941): 441–461.

22. farms

but because of the lack of care, they have been lost; however, if we bring wine shoots from the Canary Islands, we could have powerful vineyards like the ones on those islands. There is also a lot of pomegranate, because this fruit grows well here. And there are about six quince trees, which produce fruits that are as good as those that grow in Spain. Among other local fruits, there are three main ones that I will mention here. There are plantains: some are very small and are called "dominicos" while others are larger. Those trees are tall and are a beautiful sight which are called platanales. The leaves of these trees are very long, four yardsticks in length, and over half a yardstick wide. Once peeled, they can be eaten using only the hands, with no need for utensils. They are white, like marmalade, with a sweet apple scent. This tree never grows off fruit after the first bunch because later on it rots. The fruit comes out of a beautiful blue and white sleeve, which opens as the plantain grows anywhere from three to four bunches with over a hundred plantains. The fruit is good, when it ripens in the bunch, which does not happen unless they are cut when they are green, and in fifteen days they will ripen. It is noticeable that while the tree is producing some, others grow at its base. It is the main staple of this land. There are more than two hundred thousand of these trees in the aforementioned city, sugar mills, and estancias.

There is another fruit called pineapple: some of white and others, which are the best, of a yellowish color. The external texture of these fruits is similar to the ones of our country. This fruit has a soft scent and it enhances the appetite. It does not have stones, grows cholera, is brought to Spain as preserves and loses some of its good color.

There is another fruit called mamei,[23] which grows in both small and large sizes. Some have four pits while others have two; they have the size and roundness of a ball, big or small. Its scent and flavor is very similar to peach, but the texture is harsher. The trees are as tall as poplars and hold up to two thousand or more of these fruits, depending of how large they are, there is a large number of these trees. This is all regarding the main fruits, except for a fruit called guava, which I will mention later on, when I talk about cattle.

Amongst the rivers of this island, some are called the golden rivers, and rightly so, because anywhere in them one decides to search, gold can be found, and it is believed that even more now than there was before, in those times when about two hundred ducats' worth was extracted every year. The water drags down the gold all the way from the sierras and mountains to the actual rivers where people find them in various forms of thick and thin dust, according to how much the sun's rays have touched it. Some of this gold is dragged by the streams and mixes with the sand, other sticks to the rocks that border the banks of the river. We have news of and familiarity with these panning fields, but not of gold mines, for the reasons that will be mentioned below, when we talk about the state and the conditions of the people of that land.

I sent Your Majesty some grains worth six hundred ducats each and smaller than the ones that the French took, as it was mentioned in one of the aforementioned letters, by the fault of the masters, who later on paid for their cost.

---

23. Sapodilla plum, now spelled mamey.

In this land, particularly in the village of Cotui, located sixteen leagues from Santo Domingo, there is a lot of copper, from which coins were minted during my stay in this city. This copper, which lies on the earth's surface, almost the same way as the gold, something I will later explain, is somewhat rough, but can be malleable. There are in this great village of Cotui many beautiful azure mines, something of great value in Spain, but unlike the metals, the azure mines are found deep in the land, not as we have said about metals.

The countryside of this city and its land, as it has been said, is very fertile in many ways. There are large meadows and there are forests of four and five leagues covered with a tree named guayacán,[24] which is called around here "the healthy tree." It is used against syphilis and other diseases, and when cut off completely it takes four years to grow back. A lot of this wood is taken to Flanders, where it is carved into plates, mortars, and other wares, because in addition to being so healthy, it is as resistant as steel.

There is in the aforementioned city and the island a large number of drumstick trees, which grow well there and can also be found in Yayguana, a village that has one hundred settlers and a seaport within is district. These drumstick trees are very tall; they have a yellow flower of very admirable scent, which can be boiled to make preserves, and is so healthy that we should bring some to Your Majesty's royal house. By the same token, when a drumstick tree is very small, so that it is very tender, very good preserves is made from it, that is almost as good as the one made from the flower. This drumstick product is merchandise that is brought to Spain. Later on we have found an herb called china, so prolific that is has no value.

From this city to the aforementioned village of Yayguana, there are more than thirty sugar plantations and some of them are sugar mills, which move their wheels with horses, not water. Two of these sugar plantations, which belong to Melchor de Torres, a gentleman from the aforementioned city, have over nine hundred Negroes,[25] the rest of them have about two hundred, some three hundred, and some even have one hundred, and one hundred fifty Negroes.

The workers in these sugar plantations and *estancias*, as already mentioned, are Negroes, only the overseer and the master, and some of the sugar technicians are Spaniards. The rest of the skills, like tradesmen, blacksmiths and carpenters, are taught to the Negroes, so that they can handle these duties. There is so much wood for heating the pans where the cane juice and molasses are deposited that there is no land in Christendom or beyond it as suitable for sugar plantations as the aforementioned island of Hispaniola, and also for the amounts of meat consumed by the Negroes, though it is now declining.

The Negroes who serve in *estancias* and sugar plantations, as well as those who work in the city and in the household, who are about twenty thousand in total, sustain themselves by eating casabi,[26] which is made from a tuber that is planted into mounds. Once this tuber is fully grown in the mound, it is scraped and then washed, and with a mold for this purpose they make a somewhat toasted large cake, and if this

24. a hard, tropical wood
25. Obviously referring to black slaves.
26. Cassava bread

tuber is further squeezed, they make another very thin, delicious cassava bread called *sablao*. From the flower of this plant, which is called *anaiboa*, a white porridge is made with milk, which is also very delicious, and it is so strong, and is so nourishing that in spite of how little one consumes, it makes one perspire. This food is widespread, for the neighbors as well as for those who come from overseas, because there is no bread in that land and if there is, it is not enough, and it is usually brought from here [Spain]. There could be a lot of wheat if it were planted, because from one dry measure[27] of wheat that I planted near Manguana, thirty leagues from the aforementioned city, over four grain measures[28] of wheat were harvested, and the bread was very good. They concentrate more on the cassava bread, and also argue that if there is bread and wine very few naos[29] will arrive, and they will not be able to sell the fruits of their haciendas.

There is a lot of cattle on this land, however, it used to be even greater, something with no comparison as the cattle multiplied by three and there were initially about four hundred thousand head of cattle. The number has reduced because the demand for meat by the settlers has grown lately, and in order to satisfy this need, the settlers have been killing not only grown cattle, but also the pregnant cows and the ones that are about two or three years old. And although this has been prohibited and publicly denounced to prevent it, it continues to happen. At the same time, in certain places of the island inland, there are ports where foreign ships come to and since they do not carry licenses from Your Majesty, they barter cheaply hides and sugar, and they take away the gold dust, and the settlers, without having any other considerations, kill all the cattle that they have. For prohibiting this, and punishing the officials who allow foreigners in those parts, since the damage continues and there are others to be mentioned later, I have been hated and despised by many, by my colleagues, the president and the magistrates, as I have proven well. Since the skins of the cows must be registered, people will be punished if [the cows] are killed while they are still too young or pregnant, as for the rest of the cattle, bulls, and wild and maroon cattle, they are allowed to be killed without restrictions. These measures are to prevent the depopulation of the land, because the land is occupied by sugar plantations; and every sugar plantation is a town, and the cattle are the main sustenance for these plantations, and its workers, the Negroes, who do not have any other food, and consume a lot. There is also a lack of meat because dogs have reproduced so much, that their number has reached over one hundred thousand, and these dogs, who are known as maroon dogs, are like wolfs, they kill the cattle, especially the small ones, and they drink the blood, leaving the meat, which is later eaten by the pigs, both domestic as well as wild pigs, of which there are many. The third, and most damaging reason for the shortage of meat, is the existence in the aforementioned city of a very large tree, although some are also small, known as *guayabal*. This tree produces a very rich fruit, which is as big as a quince, red on the inside and yellow on the outside, with many seeds, called guava. Since cattle can reach and eat this fruit, when it defecates, since the land is so fertile, each seed turns into a tree. That is the reason why so many guava trees have

27. a unit of capacity
28. a unit of area, equivalent to 0.66 hectares
29. trading ships

grown in that island: three-quarters of the countryside is shaded by those trees. The shade is so dense that people cannot walk or ride their horses through there, and therefore cannot hunt for cattle, leaving the maroon dogs as the masters of the land. The shade also makes it difficult for the grass and grains to grow on the ground, therefore the cattle has transformed from domestic and tame into wild and maroon. Lots of remedies have been tried short of God's. If the land were as populated as it was before, it would be more trodden and treated, and this remedy as well as the establishment of estates to help settlers, which Your Majesty has already ordered the Audience to do by granting them a six-month stay for each debt claimed by deposit, would have been sufficient. In terms of the minor cattle, there is also a shortage. There are up to fifty thousand sheep, three thousand goats, and a countless number of mares and mules and wild horses. They are lassoed, and their value resides only in domesticating them. Lots of pigeons, hens, and countless Guinea fowl, which look and taste like partridges, except they are larger in size. And so many sweet, sour, dry and tangerine oranges, which have been causing as much harm as the guava tree I have mentioned before.

The city of Santo Domingo has at its entrance, which is at the mouth of the river, a very strong fortress, commanded by the warden Don Rodrigo de Bastidas, son-in-law of Oviedo, Your Majesty's chronicler. This fortress counts with a good amount of new bronze artillery, enough for three fortresses. This fortress defends the mouth and entrance of the river, where not a single or many ships can attempt to enter without risk of being sunk. The defects in this fortress and the great need that it has are: that it has on its river side a big hole carved out by saltwater, that unless it is fixed soon, it [the fortress] may soon collapse by its own weight, and that of the artillery, and it will destroy the rocks at the entrance of the river in such a manner that no naos will be able to go in, and the commerce of that land will cease. I had warned about it, and something was to be done which I do not remember what it was. In this there is a particular need, as I am saying. The hole must be filled by blocking the water with boards, so that it can be done, and with care. I cannot stress it too much because the aforementioned city is the entrance and stopping point to the Indies, and its future conservation is extremely important, mostly for the Royal Treasury, because of duties levied in the cities of Sevilla and Cádiz on the merchandise that arrives in that city, and for other evident effects.

The main external danger to this city is mainly the beach of Guinia, a quarter league from it, because with rowboats and small ships one may land, and since the aforementioned city is so desolated that it has now little defense, it could be easily taken, mainly by calling on and appealing to the Negroes, who many times have tried it. The remedy suggested for this beach is, since it is so close to the aforementioned city, it could be covered up with one hundred or two hundred boatloads of rocks. To cover it up is easy because in this area there is not that much water, and this would become a strong wall.

In this river and port there is such a good pier, so that with one gangplank the naos are loaded, being so close to land. There is a great need to repair this pier because pieces have come off it, and the waters have carried so much sand that it is turning into a beach, in such a way that in its main part, no naos or boats can enter, and Negroes enter into a good portion of the river to wash clothes. This and other things, since I was so envied by my colleagues, have been delayed, and I informed about it and about some other things for which I have presented several memoranda.

Since the city has so much money from the excise tax that is imposed, it is necessary they spend some money on this, little as it may be, and the needs related to the aforementioned fortress.

In this city they started building a very strong and tall wall, and three main gates are already completed. Because when in the beginning the wall was started, the island was very populated, and it was expected that the city would keep on growing. They made the aforementioned wall so long that there are now lots of trees and estancias inside the aforementioned wall. This is no obstacle to continuing and for the city to be finally walled, by spending some of the island's money.

This way, the wall would become a strong and secure defense against external enemies, as well as against inland enemies, of which the Negroes are the most feared. This is very much needed in order to improve the structure of that city, and so that Your Majesty will have that entrance and gateway to the Indies secured, and out of risk, not in the dangerous situation it is now. I will also deal with other remedies for the inland population later on.

This city has many main buildings and it is very beautiful. Each house is a fortress, and there are not in Christendom better materials for buildings, an opinion shared by many who know about this. The city is a beautiful sight.

The city has in its vicinity many places, most of which are almost depopulated, but were formerly well inhabited; and most of them with more residents than Santo Domingo currently has. The aforementioned city has five hundred residents, if that much. Buena Ventura, which is five leagues from Santo Domingo, used to have more and today has no residents. And in the same manner, the city of Santiago, maybe twenty or thirty residents. The village of Cotui has at least one hundred residents and it is a very good seaport. It trades with the Mainland, and its business consists of hides and drumstick trees, and some sugar from a sugar plantation that is over there. The city of La Vega was and still is a bishopric. The church is collegiate; it fell with an earthquake and the only remains left are right where the wooden cross of La Vega is, as it will be mentioned below. Similarly, a port named Monte Christi, which has been described: it had up to twenty residents.

Puerto de Plata, with about thirty or forty residents, is a seaport. Its trade is sugar, because it has four or five sugar plantations and some cattle. This port is far stronger than the one in Santo Domingo, and with very little force, it could defend itself from others. I bought some artillery, which is in a small fortress that I ordered made based on an old decree from Your Majesty. I do not know if it is finished. Its warden is, until Your Majesty desires, Fernando de Savallos, resident of the aforementioned village of Puerto de Plata. In all these ports, and in Puerto Real, which is in the same region and should have a little over twenty residents, there are mayors and council members, and lieutenants of the officers of the Royal Treasury from the aforementioned city of Santo Domingo. All of these places are in the northern region.

The Devastation of the Colony

By the end of the sixteenth century, Hispaniola was a forgotten colony. The wealth created by gold and sugar that had attracted Spanish colonists earlier in the century had run out decades before. Most well-to-do Spaniards, and many poor ones as well, had moved elsewhere. What remained was a mostly poor, racially mixed remnant that clung to the fertile soil for survival. Few ships arrived from Spain, so trade was very limited and sporadic. The few thousand colonists and their slaves had become virtually self-sufficient and survived by planting their own crops and hunting the wild cattle that roamed throughout the island. Cattle ranching, or more precisely, cattle hunting, became the island's most important economic activity when foreigners, particularly the Dutch, began bartering much-needed European products for hides and food crops the locals produced. These activities took place in remote coves and on beaches far removed from Spanish control, though there is plenty of evidence that some Spanish authorities profited from the illegal trade. Contraband thus became a primary livelihood for Hispaniola's remaining settlers. Alarmed by the spread of the contraband trade and the proliferation of Protestant Bibles found in the hands of some local smugglers, the Spanish authorities considered several solutions to the problem until finally settling on the most radical one: the devastation of parts of the colony. By a royal decree issued in 1603, Governor Antonio de Osorio was ordered to move settlers, their possessions, and their cattle, from the western and northern parts of the island to within a few miles of Santo Domingo, where they would not be able to engage in contraband trade. Entire villages were burned and thousands of heads of cattle were lost in the process. Imaginary borders were drawn and anyone caught beyond them was considered an enemy of Spain. What the Spanish authorities did not realize, however, was that now the western flank of the colony was open to foreign penetration, and soon, Spain's enemies started arriving. Osorio's instructions follow below.

OSORIO'S INSTRUCTIONS[30]

The following is Our Majesty's resolutions for providing a Remedy for the issues concerning communications and trade relations between the people of Hispaniola and the enemies; so that certain villages, regularly frequented by the enemies may be moved inland.

The King

Don Antonio Osorio, my governor and captain general of Hispaniola and president of my royal audience, because of your letter and those written by the archbishop and by many others, it is understood that the trade relations have continued, as well as contacts between the villagers of that island, and the French, English, and Flemish, who frequent it. And that, from this great inconveniences have resulted and are still ensuing. And that greater [problems] may occur because of these interactions, and because of the sect books that they [the foreigners] bring, as well as the defrauding of the royal rights, and the condition of scarcity in the island that this whole situation has caused. In all the possible ways, attempts have been made to remedy these damages. We have tried, by all means, to remedy this damage. Censures have been used and judges have been sent to apply the punishment to those who commit these crimes, that is without damaging their souls. But even these rigorous penalties, as they have been implemented, have not been sufficient to stop these interactions and trades, and the robberies [piracy] that take place in the sea and on land, causing harm to our servants. Through these violations, the enemies of Our Holy Catholic Faith, who are also my enemies, have acquired strength. Being that these trading relations are a matter of such magnitude, and considering it greatly offends Our Lord and my Royal Crown, I have ordered it treated with special attention so that it can be remedied. And in order to do so, I have revised reports and documents made by people experienced in the issues that concern the island, people who are compromised with maintaining the public well being, and the comfort of the island. Among proposed remedies for this matter, it seems convenient that the three posts located in the ports of Puerto de Plata, Vayaha, and La Yaguana should be moved inland. These villages are located in the northern region of that island and are very distant and isolated from the city of Santo Domingo, where this audience resides. And being these the most populated areas, the enemies visit them regularly, and are given there shelter and provisions by the local villagers. These villages should be moved inland to inhabited places near the neighboring area of the city of Santo Domingo, five, six and eight leagues away from it, and reduced to two good settlements in comfortable places, with abundant pastures for their cattle and farms, as they had, and also enough timber and materials to make houses. Being so close to the audience and further inland will ensure that these villagers will have difficulties in trading with the enemy. This will be more peaceful for them than being in those places without law and exposed

---

30. Translated from "Real Cédula a Antonio de Osorio, Gobernador, Capitán General y Presidente de la Real Audiencia comunica lo que su Majestad ha resuelto para La Española," in J. Marino Incháustegui, ed., *Reales cédulas y correspondencia de gobernadores de Santo Domingo: De la regencia del Cardenal Cisneros en adelante* (Madrid: n.p., 1958), vol. 3, 791–793.

to the assaults of enemies, where they risk having their properties burned down as they [foreigners] have done so many times. The move would be easy and little damaging because the villagers' present houses are made of straw. Those parts of the island to where they will relocate have many good pastures and watering places for cattle. The abandonment of those ports is not a matter of consideration, since there are another forty-two ports, as good and even better, and uninhabited, where enemies enter and stay for the time that they want with great security, and not having there someone to trade with them and to provide them with the things that they need, they will stop going there as they have done in other places that are not populated. Many benefits would follow from moving these towns because by moving everyone closer together, all the strength of the island would be concentrated in one region, if ever needed, and it will provide security against the maroons. Trade and commerce will increase by sending their crops to Spain, and by importing and exporting everything through the port of Santo Domingo. The mines will benefit from this relocation and the population will increase. Having considered and reviewed very attentively what has been said, and after consulting me, it seemed good and convenient to move the three villages. The cattle in and around these villages shall be taken inland to the new places to be settled. No cattle shall be left near the shore or many leagues near these ports, so that the enemies cannot supply themselves from them nor profit from them in any way for food or for their hides. I have decided to make you and the archbishop of that city, accompanied by the judges of that royal audience and other people who prove to have no other personal interest than a concern with the service of God Our Lord and mine, and on the public well being, responsible for executing these orders. And only after having very carefully looked at these resolutions, and after viewing them under close consideration and attention, will you proceed to move the villagers of these three places (Puerto de Plata, Vayaha, and La Yaguana), having, before that, carefully selected the most comfortable places you can find five to twelve leagues from the city of Santo Domingo, so that these villagers can settle there. I want you to give the order and execute the plan in the most convenient way that will facilitate their move there along with their cattle, so that it will be done with the greatest ease, comfort, speed, and security that can be provided. You must provide them with the necessary means to establish these settlements, facilitating and overcoming the difficulties that might arise. The least amount of discomfort and harm must be assured to the new settlers of these lands and to those interested in the matter, making sure also that the three mentioned villages are condensed into two. And with great justification for the establishment of these places and estancias and farmlands, you are to provide those who move there with the appropriate living areas and comforts, as needed, without injuring third parties. Taking this very seriously and with much fervor in order to help you with this task and entrusting the implementation of what is finally resolved to Licentiate Manso de Contreras, whom I have provided as my judge of that royal audience and who is informed of this matter, or to Licentiate Marcos Nuñez de Toledo, who also is a judge, and to Valtazar López de Castro, chamber secretary of that audience, who as a well-versed person of that land and of good character, his intelligence and diligence will be of benefit, by doing the honors and the favor of facilitating it. Of everything that is done and of the lands that are distributed, you shall inform me in detail and if any major difficulties arise in the implementation of this task, and if any other more useful means come up in order to accomplish what is planned, you will give me an account of all the steps taken as soon as possible and with great punctuality.

And so that, with the greatest ease and comfort, the move can take place, and in order to have mercy for persons accused of trading with the enemy, and so that those who are hiding for those crimes are appeased and pacified can return to their homes, farms, and ranches, I have had and have for good decreed that those who move to these new settlements and establish residence in them or in the city Santo Domingo will receive a general pardon for the crimes committed up to the publication of this amnesty which I am enclosing. Those who thereafter commit these crimes again and are found guilty of illegally trading and interacting with any other kingdoms that are not Spain's will lose their lives and properties. You will proclaim the aforementioned pardon everywhere and whenever you deem it to be convenient so that what I have ordered is implemented. In Valladolid, on the sixth of August 1603.

I, the King.
Countersigned by Juan de Ibarra and supported by the Council

CHAPTER TWO

Shifting Colonial Masters

In the seventeenth and eighteenth centuries, the history of the Spanish colony of Santo Domingo (as it was commonly known by this time) took new and unexpected turns. For more than a century after the 1603 devastations, the colony languished in poverty and oblivion to such an extent that the seventeenth century is known as the "Century of Misery" in Dominican history. While the Spanish colony stagnated, the French established a colony on the western end of the island, which they called Saint-Domingue. Starting in the 1630s, French buccaneers, pirates, and adventurers settled on Tortuga Island and within a few years, the French government took control of the situation and established a permanent colony. Spanish attempts to drive the French out were largely unsuccessful, and by the mid-eighteenth century Saint-Domingue had become France's most profitable colony. The Treaty of Aranjuez (1777) formalized the partition of the island into two separate colonies: French Saint-Domingue, wealthy, capital-intensive, and with hundreds of thousands of slaves; and Spanish Santo Domingo, poor, economically backward, with a Creole population that eked out a meager living on the land and by selling some cattle to the French. An irrevocable split between east and west had been created. The exploitative French colonial rule came to a sudden halt in 1791, however, when the slave population launched a large-scale insurrection. Eventually, political infighting between whites, mulattos, and blacks led to civil war and a social revolution. The result was the birth of the Republic of Haiti, a nation ruled by former slaves and the first black republic in the world. Spanish Santo Domingo was directly affected by these events taking place to the west. In 1795, Spain ceded Santo Domingo to France, and in 1801, Toussaint Louverture, the Haitian revolutionary leader, enforced its cession by occupying the former Spanish colony. In 1802, French troops, sent by Napoleon Bonaparte, occupied Santo Domingo and helped defend it against an attack by Jean-Jacques Dessalines, Haiti's first president and an avowed enemy of the Europeans. In 1809, the Dominicans got rid of the French army only to

return to the Spanish empire. The embrace was of short duration. In 1821, a group of Dominicans declared the nation's independence and its annexation to the newly established Republic of Gran Colombia in South America, while several towns in the interior favored joining Haiti. The 1821 "Ephemeral Independence" was short-lived, though. In January 1821, President Jean-Pierre Boyer of Haiti took over the eastern part of the island again and annexed it to the Republic of Haiti. For the next twenty-two years, the island was a single political entity.

A French buccaneer.

40

Fighting Spain's Enemies

A few decades after the devastations in the early seventeenth century, the Spanish authorities came to realize the magnitude of their mistake. The depopulation of western Hispaniola had opened the door to European competitors who established settlements there. By the 1630s, adventurers from France, England, and other European nations formed a settlement on Tortuga Island, from where they engaged in piracy, hunted cattle in the vast, depopulated regions of western Hispaniola, and eventually began planting tobacco as a cash crop. The French government saw a great potential in this development and quickly sent colonial officers and troops to tame the adventurers, establish permanent colonial institutions, and foster the planting and export of cash crops. The Spanish authorities carried out periodic punitive raids to dislodge the French, but mostly without results. The French settlers would simply scatter into the forests and return weeks later to rebuild their villages. The following document describes an early (1634) attack on Tortuga Island, in which the Spaniards took the French by surprise and caused some casualties among them.

SPANISH OFFICERS DESCRIBE THE ATTACK
ON TORTUGA ISLAND[1]

Sir,

In accordance with the prior communication that we wrote to Your Majesty on the fourth of January of the current year, and of which we include a copy (we are remitting a duplicate of it to you, along with this one) [*sic*], we would like to refer to the four Armada ships that left this port under the command of Captain Francisco Turrillo, as ordered by Your Majesty, to join General Ruy Fernández de Fuenmayor at the Port of Bahaya, where the one hundred and fifty men that he had recruited from inland, as well as the other official captains mentioned in this letter, waited in the aforementioned port for the Armada to sail to the Island of Tortuga, in order to evict and punish the enemy who had settled and fortified there. It is in reference to this incident that we write to Your Majesty, so as to tell you the results and the effects of the aforementioned incident. Having arrived at the Port, the aforementioned General and everyone else, including the fifty infantrymen from this Presidio and people from overseas, reaching a total of about three hundred individuals, and after having determined and resolved the different factors that needed to be considered prior to the

---

1. Translated from "Los oficiales de la Real Hacienda refieren el ataque a la Tortuga," in J. Marino Incháustegui, *Reales cédulas y correspondencia de gobernadores de Santo Domingo: De la regencia del Cardenal Cisneros en adelante* (Madrid: n.p., 1958), vol. 4, 1185–1188.

attack, they arrived on the coast of the Island that is located right across from La Tortuga, and decided to stay there until night, when they would cross the water, this was to avoid being detected by the enemy. But they were not able to take over the port where the three ships and one cargo boat were left unguarded and exposed, so they disembarked at the first landing spot where they could anchor the ships, and put people ashore. In the midst of this confusion, the darkness of the night, and the noise and the voices heard all around there, people started to jump overboard, causing many to drown. Captain Camacho's lieutenant, Pedro de Vargas, who was armed, warned the people and went to the windlass to bring up the artillery that needed to be moved. Having streamlined it and set up, they started to fire it and play the bugles, which stirred up the people of the Island who took up arms. General Ruy Fernández de Fuenmayor, having landed with Captain Turrillo went to seek out the Admiral and Captain Gonzalo de Frias with up to twenty-four people. Feeling exposed with such a small number of people and facing the risk that the others would run for the water, he seized the fortified position, with infinite risk due to the shelling from the ships. When it was clear that he was in control and before sunrise, with the people that he could gather, who had come on land by swimming or in the captain's dingy, he marched inland to the settlement of the Governor of the aforementioned Island, who came to face them with as many people as he could assemble. Having killed him [the governor] with two spears, and fifteen of his men, and captured thirteen or fourteen Englishmen, they took over the Governor's house and others, and they killed everyone they found there. The General set up Camp in the aforementioned house with all the dispositions in maintaining the success that God had granted them. When they returned to the forces on land, they found the enemy prepared with six mounted pieces [cannons]. They detached two of them and, after firing them at the ships, the wooden blocks holding them in place, because they were rotten, collapsed, broke into pieces and came unmounted. One of the shells, a nine pounder, did a great amount of damage to the water port of one of the ships. The next day, the General met at the Camp, joined by more people from his flagship, and the admiral's ship and other ships that, although damaged, had escaped danger. After being warned that the enemy from the other settlement, along with the people that they gathered, some one hundred and ninety French- and Englishmen, was coming toward him, the General fortified the Camp and came out to face the enemy's attack. He fought them with so much determination and courage, that having beheaded the majority of them, the rest turned and fled, which made it easier to catch up to them, so that very few of them escaped. In the scuffle, two of our soldiers were killed and three were injured, among them Don Juan Mor, the young man I referred to you in my prior correspondence, shot in the head. He was a sergeant in the aforementioned Island, and had come to this one [Hispaniola].

With these measures, General Ruy Fernández had the aforementioned Island under control, and he was able to supply it with enough troops to replace the individuals who were missing, as well as with thirty or forty Negroes. Later, it was learned from some prisoners captured during the battles that those people who escaped had embarked in a boat and traveled to this shore. All this to which I refer, took place from the twenty-first of January, which was the night they crossed, until the twenty-fourth, when an enemy cargo boat and a nao arrived in Port. They and three small ships sailed, all of them with flagship's flags, and only one cargo boat remained. The general sent people to the fortress to procure some artillery to expel the ships from the Port, and mounted two pieces (though with difficulty) on top of some thick logs. The remaining enemy ship fired an emery shot, and they [the Spanish] responded from the fortress with one piece that went through the ship's sides, so it tried to sail away, a thing facilitated because another shot broke its anchor line.

On the twenty-seventh and the twenty-eighth, all four of our ships, which had not been able to enter the Port before because of the naos that occupied it, were able to do so. The General gave orders to burn two boats that were astride, and to fix another cargo boat the enemy left dismantled. He sent a man to this Island [Hispaniola] with news of everything and a list of what was required to stop the boldness of these rebels. The number of deaths was one hundred and ninety five, and thirty-nine prisoners were taken, among them three women. He reports that in two or three days, a ship will leave and bring the six pieces of artillery, and even the muskets and the ironwork of the burnt boats, and some Brazil wood that he found cut and stacked in piles. And so that Your Majesty receives the good news as soon as possible, he is dispatching Doctor Don Alonso de Corixidae, who leads a frigate, who will stop on the coast of Puerto Rico, and someone will go to that city, so that the letters will leave in the boats of that Port, and in two other ships which arrived there from New Spain's fleet General Don Lope de Hoes. He also sends the report submitted by the aforementioned Ruy Fernández regarding the details of this event.

The expenses of the four ships and the pay for the sailors and the one hundred fifty infantrymen, in addition to the men from the Presidio, is quite considerable. Given the dire straits of our treasury, we will be forced to use our deposits from the sales of Miguel Fernández de Fonseca's slaves, as well as the possessions of President Don Gabriel de Chaves, in order to meet this payment. As it is done for the San Martín charities and other occasions of Sublimations, in the meantime we sent for the expenses to the treasury of Mexico, for which we beg Your Majesty to issue a decree without impediment, as usually done on occasions like this one. This we beg, as we have done many times before, so that there would be no difficulties, because it would be an obstacle to satisfy the aforementioned deposits when the order from Your Majesty arrives. May God protect your Royal Catholic person, as well as Christianity. Done in Santo Domingo, on the sixteenth of February 1634.

Signed and stamped,
Francisco de Tajagrano   Diego Nuñez de Peralta

Fighting the Maroons

As early as the mid-sixteenth century, blacks (most of them slaves) outnumbered all other racial groups in the Spanish colony of Santo Domingo. Keeping a tight rein on these thousands of slaves became an increasingly difficult problem for their white masters. Slaves escaped into the wild interior of the island, where it was almost impossible to recapture them. Moreover, they began organizing themselves in *manieles*, communities from which they often attacked unsuspecting Spanish travelers, sugar plantations, and occasionally small settlements. Punitive expeditions to dislodge and recapture them were periodically organized by the Spanish military authorities, but to no avail. The territory was too large, the topography too rough, and the raids were often very expensive endeavors for a poor colony. Many of these maroon leaders became household names for their exploits, such as Diego de Ocampo and Lembá.[2]

As the colony's economy declined in the late sixteenth century, and particularly after the devastation of the colony's western lands in 1605, the pervasive economic malaise prompted many white colonists to leave for wealthier, safer lands. As the "century of misery" progressed, slaves found it increasingly easier to escape into the hinterland and to organize independent communities there. The following letter from 1662 reports on the activities of these runaway slaves and discusses the intractable nature of the maroon problem.

FRANCISCO, ARCHBISHOP-ELECT OF SANTO DOMINGO TO THE KING OF SPAIN, FIFTEENTH OF SEPTEMBER 1662[3]

Sir.—

In the uninhabited regions of this island, some fifty leagues from this city [Santo Domingo], there are some sierras (a place called Maniel) which are very tall and fertile. After all the native Indians of this island disappeared, and the Spanish had to resort to black slaves to work the land, all the fugitive slaves escape to these sierras where they live without any doctrine nor priests to teach them. It is a robbers' cove of barbarians, because every year slaves escape from their owners' rural farms, and that is one of the main causes for the miserable state of this island.

There are four towns in this sierra, which "it is said" have six hundred families, and with children and wives should be more than two thousand persons. They have no churches nor do they worship images; some who were baptized before escaping put crosses in their homes, yet they do not get baptized nor do they have laws. They are governed by ladino[4] Negroes; their weapons are arrows, which they use with skill; they use short, broad swords they fashion from the iron and steel that they purchase

---

2. Maroon derives from the Spanish word *cimarrón*, meaning "wild."

3. Translated from Fray Cipriano de Utrera, *Dilucidaciones históricas (I–II)* (Santo Domingo: Secretaría de Estado de Educación, Bellas Artes y Cultos, 1995), 325–327.

4. slaves born in the colony

from other Negroes in this city. They cultivate just enough land for their subsistence, because they have an abundance of meats and native fruits. They collect tomines[5] of gold and of silver in the rivers, and with this they buy clothes, wine, liquor, and whatever they need, from other Negroes. The militias have launched some attacks against them, in which women and children have been captured, because the rest escape to the heights of the sierras, and so far this robbers' cove has not been destroyed. Some of them pray the Holy Father and the Ave Maria, and mistakenly worship idols. They guard and watch their sierras with care. If someone commits a grave crime, they throw him down a cliff; and if he escapes, they search for him so that he may not give their location away. And they remain restless until they kill him. And if they cannot achieve that, they move their villages elsewhere so that escapees cannot serve as spies to entrap them.

Slave owners live in uneasiness, because they cannot safeguard their slaves, and if their [the maroons'] barbaric government were not so rigorous, all the slaves would be in the Maniel to obtain their freedom.

A few days after I arrived in this city, concerned about so many lost souls, and with the colonists—who are the interested party—inclined to offer them [the maroons] liberty at the time, and knowing that God's and Your Majesty's service was to pacify this people, after communicating the matter to President Don Pedro de Carvajal and others, I resorted to writing them a letter, in which I promised to beg Your Majesty their pardon, and that they all would be free if they left the Maniel and moved their towns to places to be indicated. There, Your Majesty would place them under the rule of justice, and my ministers of the church would teach them, so that thereafter they would live like Christians. And they shall not admit any more fugitive slaves, and if any are missing, they would be in charge of locating and delivering him. To deliver this letter I used a slave belonging to treasurer Don Diego Soria Pardo, who is brother of the captain of the largest [maroon] village. And though we know that he delivered it and talked to them, he has been detained and I have received no response from them, although a group of them went to a farm and said that I should be told that they do not trust whites, who in the past have betrayed their word.

And they have told me that if I travel alone with a servant, they would come to talk to me, as long as there are no other people present. If they decide to talk to me, certainly, God will subdue them. I have decided to seek them by early November, and to try to talk to them. This is important, Sir, to Your Majesty's service, because it is a robbers' cove (as I have said) of fugitive slaves, and from other Negroes they have news of whatever happens in town. And we have these barbarians on our backs, and if the enemy again tries to invade this island, we must guard ourselves from them [the maroons] as well as from the enemy, though during the [16]55 events[6] they were quiet. They cause damages like stealing female slaves and admitting those slaves who flee. I will inform Your Majesty of whatever happens, since up to now nothing has been achieved, and the President believes that it is impossible to subdue them, so

---

5. Spanish measure of weight
6. Reference to the 1655 British attack on Santo Domingo. The British invasion force was defeated and from Santo Domingo they proceeded to attack Jamaica, which they were able to take.

nothing will be informed until this matter develops, though nothing would be lost by trying.

Santo Domingo, island of Hispaniola, the fifteenth of September 1662.

Francisco, Archbishop-elect of Santo Domingo (signed).

Class, Color, and Gender in the Colony

The extinction of the Taíno Indians in the sixteenth century, the large influx of African slaves to work in the island's sugar plantations, and the poverty that engulfed the colony of Santo Domingo in the seventeenth century contributed to defining its racial makeup. While the colony still had sharply differentiated racial groups in the sixteenth century, by the end of the seventeenth most of Santo Domingo's population was mulatto—the mixed descendants of blacks and whites. Pervasive poverty helped to soften class distinctions and the colony's declining population restricted the number of available sexual partners. So, in spite of the efforts by the Spanish authorities to uphold European social mores, interracial liaisons were common in the impoverished colony, giving rise to a largely mulatto population within a few generations. This ethnic character has been maintained to this day, as more than three-quarters of Dominicans can be classified as mulatto.

The following document is a 1680 legal dock describing an "incident" between Juana Maldonado—a poor mulatto woman—and an upper class white man. Apparently, Juana's crime was an affair with this man that had become the town's main gossip. Since Juana was poor, mulatto, and a woman living in a race- and status-conscious patriarchal society, she was summoned by the authorities and told to break off the relationship and to move from her neighborhood. The man—out of respect for his status—is not even mentioned by name in the document. This case is illustrative of the double standard the Spanish authorities applied regarding "social" offenses. While men were often left unscathed, different standards applied to women, who also had to bear the brunt of being publicly shunned and humiliated.

46

THE CASE OF JUANA MALDONADO[7]

On the fifth day of the month of May of the current year [1680] Your Honor the President issued a summons indicating that he had true and individual news that Juana Maldonado, a free mulatto woman who lived in the neighborhood of San Miguel for a long time, has had contacts[8] illicitly and basely with a person whose name, out of respect for his status, is omitted. This [situation] caused a great deal of gossiping and scandal in this Republic and proceeding with the investigation and information your Honor acknowledged the inconvenience of this [situation] becoming even more public and the other inconveniences that may stem from it. And attending only to prevent public wrongdoing which is the principal task that concerns your Honor, you ordered to notify her that from hereon she shall not contact that person (naming him in secret) and that within fifteen days she shall move from the house where she lives to another one in a different neighborhood, due to the grave inconvenience caused by her staying there, as Your Honor acknowledged.

On the aforementioned fifth day of May, after eight in the evening, Juan Pinto Galindo, court bailiff of Your Honor, brought to your presence the said Juana Maldonado as ordered. While in the palace houses, your Honor took her aside and scolded her as it seemed convenient, and mentioned to her the person named in this summons, and ordered me, the scrivener, to notify her, as I did.

A Foreign Portrait of a Poor Colony

Pierre-François-Xavier de Charlevoix was a French Jesuit priest who published several accounts about foreign, exotic places for a European public. One of these was his 1730 history of Hispaniola. His description of early eighteenth-century Spanish Santo Domingo highlights the colony's poverty, the frugal, yet carefree, lifestyle of its inhabitants, and the potential wealth of the colony—if properly exploited. At this time, Santo Domingo was still recovering from its "Century of Misery" and slowly engaged in the business of selling cattle to the French colony. This intra-island trade helped the Spanish Creole colonists acquire much-needed European goods that Spain could not provide, due to the small size and inefficiency of its industry and its trading fleet. Thus, the Spanish colony was far behind neighboring Saint-Domingue in economic development, as the French had made heavy capital investments in their colony and had

---

7. Translated from Frank Moya Pons, *La vida escandalosa en Santo Domingo en los siglos XVII y XVIII* (Santiago: UCMM, 1976), 159.

8. euphemism for a sexual liaison

imported thousands of slaves to work the sugar, coffee, and tobacco plantations. Charlevoix's account also underscores the radically different attitudes about life and work of the French colonists versus that of the pre-capitalist, semi-feudal Spanish Creoles, who still lived in an essentially pastoral society.

FROM THE HISTORY OF HISPANIOLA BY PIERRE-FRANÇOIS-XAVIER DE CHARLEVOIX (1630)[9]

Poverty of the Spaniards.

This is what this Spanish colony was like at the beginning of 1717. There were 18,410 souls living there. This count includes the thirty-seven [military] companies, which were conformed by 3,705 armed men, this is without counting the French men, which amounted to about four hundred, scattered in villages or settlements, nor the seamen who navigated along the coast in Spanish ships. Regarding other matters, there is no greater poverty than the one experienced by those settlers. This is, with the exception of the capital, where there still remain some mansions and palaces that reflect some of the former splendor. Everywhere else only cabins and huts can be seen, where they [the colonists] can barely cover themselves. When ancient houses in Santo Domingo are dismantled due to age or accidents, no repairs or constructions are done to amend this. Everywhere around, furniture reflects the primitive condition of the lodgings. For that reason, in most places, there is neither commerce nor manufacturing. Its numerous herds of cattle nourish them [the colonists]; and it is from here that the French colony gets all its meat. In exchange, we give them what satisfies their most basic needs in life; because from Spain almost nothing is sent nowadays, and they will not work to satisfy their necessities by means of their industry and labor.

Their Occupations and their Sobriety.

Truly, we ought to acknowledge that they are tough men who know how to live with little. Their cattle ranches feed them, and their chocolate supplies what is lacking in this rural nourishment. They do nothing during the day; they will not even use their slaves for difficult labor. They spend all of their time gambling or rocking in their hammocks. When they are tired of sleeping, they sing, and they do not leave their beds except when they are hungry. To get water from the river or from fountains, they ride a horse even if they would only have to walk twenty steps; there is always a horse tied to a pole for this purpose. The majority of them despise gold, over which

9. Translated from Pierre-François-Xavier de Charlevoix, *Historia de la Isla Española o de Santo Domingo: Escrita particularmente sobre las memorias manuscritas del Padre Jean-Baptiste Le Pers, jesuíta, misionero en Santo Domingo y sobre los documentos originales que se conservan en el Depósito de la Marina* (Santo Domingo: Sociedad Dominicana de Bibliófilos, 1977), 385–388.

they walk, and they mock the French whom they see getting involved in projects that shorten their lives in order to accumulate wealth, which they will have no time to enjoy in peace. Their tranquil and frugal life allows them to reach a very old age.

Their Pride and Ignorance

The care of cultivating their spirits occupies them as little as that of achieving life's comforts. They do not know anything and hardly recognize the name of Spain, with whom they no longer trade. Moreover, because their blood is extremely mixed, first with the islanders, afterwards with the Negroes, they come in all shades; depending on whether they have more [blood] from the European, the African, or the American. The character of their spirit partakes from all three of them and has contracted overall the majority of their vices. Nevertheless, they still believe that they are the greatest men in the world and express a great contempt for the French. On a certain day I asked a Spaniard what were they so worthy of so as to underrate their neighbors in such a manner: "We are real men," he replied. Certainly, there has been a need to sustain such pride on occasion: these men have been, throughout many years, pawns of all the European nations that have navigated these waters. When their largest ships could hardly defend them against petty thieves, ordinary sloops took a big number of them and their most powerful colonies are surrounded by savage nations that they have never been able to subjugate. They have become courageous with time, and their Santo Domingo militias, no less than those of neighboring islands, do not fear fighting in the seas and on land with the English and the French, and they frequently do it with success.

Their Religion

The inhabitants of the Spanish part of Santo Domingo do not go out into the countryside at night, whose shadows serve some of them as veils to cover their wrongdoings; because most of them are extremely corrupted. Nevertheless, they practice all the external trappings of religion with an accuracy to which it is not possible to add anything. It is unbelievable the extent, in particular, of their respect for sacred things and their blind submission to everything that is preached by their pastors. I have noticed that although, their houses, their furniture, and everything they use, reflects the most extreme poverty, their churches are magnificent and are well decorated. They pray almost daily and they religiously observe all the holidays, of which there are plenty in this diocese. Whenever they can, they will attend Mass. The rosary as well, which is prayed every afternoon in the churches. It does not matter where they find themselves, they will not refrain from praying it [the rosary], whether in public, with their families, or each individual in particular, and they are not seen without a rosary around their necks. With this, if any reproach could be made about them dishonoring religion with their depraved customs, one also has to agree that Christianity owes this nation [Spain] most of the progress that it has achieved in America. No other [nation] was in the condition of establishing it [Christianity] there, when this New World was discovered. All the European provinces, with the exception of Spain, were deeply involved in internal or external wars and they soon became the unfortunate stage in which heresy provoked the bloodiest tragedies. Only these kingdoms [Spain] remained calm in the midst of so much turbulence and conserved faith in all its purity. One must also confess that they have shown a great zeal in the conversion of idolaters, and in securing their spiritual conquests in these vast regions. The magnificent institutions that they have built everywhere will become eternal monuments that no other nation can ever erase.

Their Virtues.

In spite of the upheavals that I have referred to, the Spaniards (at least those in Santo Domingo) also practice virtues that honor Christianity. I said that they were great beholders of hospitality and are given frequent occasions to practice it. We have, within our borders, a large number of drifters, whose pastime it is to crisscross the country; and wherever they find Spaniards, in spite of the reciprocal animosity of both nations, they are received with ample charity. These good people take out from their basics to give something to their guests. Finally, even if the frugality and the simplicity in which they live were not the result of their idleness and indolence, more than of their view of life, they cannot be praised enough for bringing to this island the stories of the first men and of those ancient patriarchs,[10] of whom sacred men and lay historians have given us such pleasant images. They live in the wealthiest country in the universe, they step on the most precious metals with their feet; moderate labor could provide them with plenty of all sorts of goods, yet they have found the secret to do without and despise them. It is not only at home that they behave like that. They come frequently to our districts with large herds of horses and it is rare to see even one enter into a tavern. They camp alongside the paths, they let their horses graze in the countryside, they cover themselves under huts, which they build in a hurry, and they make their meals with a piece of roasted meat that they carry with them, plantains, which are found everywhere, and chocolate. If they enter a bakery to purchase bread, they consider it corruption. It is true, if a Frenchman invites them to eat, they accept the invitation, but they would drink very little, and if someone overdoes it until he is intoxicated, which is very rare, they retire without noise and go to sleep. Such life, no doubt, could be seen as delicious, if considered that comforts, which these colonists lack, are not even known to them; and that they enjoy everything that nature offers them. Ambition and interest do not perturb them, and their ordinary pleasures are pure and without any kind of worries. Concluding what matters to this colony, Father le Pers believes that, besides our fugitive slaves mentioned in the diary of Mr. Butet, there is a considerable number of them who have not surrendered to the Spanish and are barricaded in mountains where they live equally independent of both nations, whose common interest would certainly suggest to prevent them from multiplying too much.

10. Bible stories

A Local Portrait of a Poor Colony

In 1785, just a few decades after the publication of Charlevoix's description of colonial Santo Domingo, another priest, this time a Spaniard, produced a similar work. Like Charlevoix, Antonio Sánchez Valverde sought to describe the colony to a European public, while defending Spain's colonial interests. He replies to Charlevoix's (and other foreigners') "insulting" remarks and defends the work habits and morality of the Spanish Creoles. The difference in wealth between the two colonies, Sánchez Valverde argues, stems solely from the lack of slave labor in Santo Domingo. Had the Spanish Crown fostered importing slaves into the colony as the French did in Saint-Domingue, Santo Domingo would have been a very wealthy colony. The section reproduced here is Sánchez Valverde's appeal to the Spanish Crown to recognize the importance of slave labor in a tropical colony. He argues for the intensive use of the plantation system and slave labor, which has been so successful in Saint-Domingue and elsewhere. Moreover, in a moralizing tone, he lashes out against the "sins" committed by Spanish Creoles, such as sexual liaisons between masters and slaves, slave prostitution, and the practice of allow-

Slaves working in a sugar boiling room.

ing slaves to buy their freedom. These practices, he argued, are not only immoral, but they undermine the use of slave labor and production, thus threatening the colony's future.

ANTONIO SÁNCHEZ VALVERDE'S APPEAL OF 1785[11]

It is with substantial evidence, based on commonsense facts, that we have manifested how the personal activity of the *French* in the *Americas*, rather than making them superior to the *Creoles* [Spaniards], whom they call and see as lazy, is very much inferior to the relentless labor and sobriety of the latter. And this will be confirmed better when we speak about our ranchers; and show that the French are in fact the real sensual drifters of the Island. But this truth will become more perceptible with the testimonies that I shall quote here from Weuves himself, with the objective of uncovering the real causes from which such a noticeable difference in production derives. Weuves states: "Secondly, could it be ignored in France that it is impossible to cultivate the lands of the *Torrid Zone* without Negroes? It is ignored that those burning climates do not allow *Europeans* to resist the fatigue of their labor? All of them put together and assembled would not be enough for this task. Only those who have been born in the Tropics can handle the heat of the sun." Further down: "The Businessmen of *Bordeaux* should not ignore that without the use of the labor of the *Negroes*, our Colonies would not have survived." In conclusion, discussing the necessity of seeking a way to lower the price of *Negroes*, whose labor is the main force in so many products, he says: "Since the production of the soil of our Colonies is the general goal that we set in their Establishment, since the abundance of these products depends as much on a good soil as on the hand that works it, since the *Torrid Zone* is an extremely hot Country for white men to be able to resist continuous exercise there, it is necessary to supply them with men toughened by the heat of the burning sun; only *Negroes* would be able to resist the fatigue."

This is the first and main cause for the vast difference between the wealth of *French Santo Domingo*[12] and the poverty of the *Spanish* side. What is the purpose of having, not two-thirds of the *Island*, but more than three-fourths of it, a territory that is more united, better watered, and more fertile, if all this wealthy fund is a hidden treasure in the entrails of the land, for which the key to opening it and taking advantage of it still needs to be found? Without this key, nothing can be extracted by the Owner, and the *Colonists* or Inhabitants are but Guards who live on the salary of the master and some scraps, which they grow by themselves. The wealthiest Mines do not give their metal unless they are worked, nor does the most fertile land give all the abundance of its crops without labor and plough. Do the *Spanish Colonists* or *Creoles* ignore, by any chance, what the key is? Certainly: they know well that it is the labor, mainly of *Negroes*. Do they have it, or is it within their reach to have it? Neither one, nor the other. Thus there is no reason for either to accuse them of being indolent, or

---

11. Translated from Antonio Sánchez Valverde, *Idea del valor de la Isla Española* (Santo Domingo: Editora Nacional, 1971), 167–173.

12. Saint-Domingue

censoring them as having little genius or talent. Give them this key as it has been given to the *French*; and if they do not do as much or more than those [the French], it could be said that they are left-handed and that they do not know how to use it. How much does the small district of our neighbors produce, which in 1777 had more than three hundred thousand *Negroes* in the Registers of *Guárico*, not including in this number fifty thousand under the age of fourteen, noting that, at least, half of these minors serve the same purpose as the same number of adults; because the former do jobs that would embarrass the latter. There are barely twelve or fourteen thousand slaves in all of the extension of our Possessions.

To this number of *Negroes* we must take into account the few holidays in which they do not work for the benefit of their Owners, which are only Sundays and other unusual Holiday. Our Slaves rest or work for themselves for almost one-third of the year, the days that we call of two or three crosses.[13] The abusive practice of hired-out slaves,[14] way too extended in our *America*, renders unusable a great part of the few we have, because these kinds of *Negroes* live without discipline or subjection; they earn their living, the females, regularly by making the wrong use of their body, and the males, usually by thievery. They hide and protect each other and especially those who escape from haciendas. The few who work, do it without orderliness and, if they earn a week's wages to satisfy the wages of two weeks, they rest the second one. Besides the fact that they frequently cheat their masters out of half of the assigned wages. This abusive practice begs not for reform, but for its extinction and total extermination, by prohibiting these Workers in the Capital and other Cities.

There is no doubt that many Individuals, Widows and Minors, possess Slaves without having any land to use them for, and we also know that the wages for slaves are their only means of support and not receiving these wages would be of great harm to them. This matter could be solved the same way it was combated in the city of *Cuba*,[15] which secured that the Owner would receive the wages while assuring that the Public would have use of the labor that was idle most of the year; and in terms of Religion, achieving a reduction in the increasing number of scandals and sins that this type of Slaves commit, either women, through the use of their bodies to earn their daily wages, or men through robberies and hiding in their huts other Slaves, who steal from their Masters, organize breakouts, or seek asylum for their instincts. This measure consists in that Farmers are absolutely prohibited for years or for months, in the conduction or leasing of their Workers, by the threat of a hefty fine for the first and second convictions, and the loss of the Slave to the Royal Treasury for the third one, to lease them within Cities or Towns, even to known and specific people. Regarding the benefits that would accrue thereafter, a lengthy and solid discourse could be formed, arguing that, besides what we have already written, it will result in the employment of many *Negroes* and free *Mulattos* of both sexes and of poor whites, who nowadays lie inactive and indolent, because there is not anyone who would

---

13. This refers to very sacred Catholic holidays.

14. Slaves who were sent out into the streets by their owners and had to sell their labor in order to return home with a predetermined amount of money (or wages) every day.

15. It refers to Santiago de Cuba.

employ them due to the *Negroes*; that many [women], even of the lower class and who have no money to buy Slaves, would desist from their vanity of destroying their poor husbands with the wages that they must pay to exempt them from the household chores that they could do themselves.

A misunderstood religious principle, which consists of favoring by all means and without any discernment the freedom of Slaves, has brought us and still brings us to another pernicious situation, which the *French* have rationally limited. Among us, it is an act of mercy to give or grant freedom to the Slaves. It is so, in effect, on some occasions, but generally it is an act of lack of religion, merciless and seriously sinful. When freedom is granted to a male or female Slave who is knowingly devoted, hard-working, and free of vices by a master who has no ancestors, descendants, or poor relatives, to whom it would be a greater virtue for these Slaves to go to, then freedom is a religious and meritorious act. But this case, or also that of a Serf who saves the life of his Master, is extremely rare.

These emancipations are regularly granted by infatuated old folk led by inexperienced confessors. Leaving lots of relatives in poverty and some lazy, unkempt freedmen, who will almost necessarily survive from iniquity, an act which, far from being merciful, is a notorious scandal that hampers civil and ecclesiastical legislation, because the frankness of granting those freedoms, infinitively multiplying sins, fills the Towns with robbers, prostitutes, and the authors of vices, taking away the most useful hands for labor, whose disorder we commented on and visibly experienced in our *Island*.

The second source from which this abusive situation derives is far more delinquent and therefore worthier of being eliminated. The emancipations that are graciously given do not begin with the male Slaves but with the female Slaves. Their Owners or Masters, particularly those who are not married and live away from Trade with other people in the countryside, usually use them [sexually] and mix in a sinful familiarity. The female Slave agrees, not because of the power or the violence of the Master, but by the appeal of the freedom he promises her and which the law permits. In trying to stop adultery, it has established the impediment of *crime*, preventing from marrying those who, while married, received the promise of marriage once the spouse died. It should equally order that excesses between Masters and female Slaves would serve as a legal obstacle to their freedom, stopping [the practice of] concubinage which is much too common. The State thus retains the labor of these female slaves and their descendants, and eliminates their prostitution, who after becoming free have no trade to survive on than the one which helped them get rid of slavery.

Those who do not obtain the benefit of their freedom by their wrongdoing with their own Master will obtain it through the same crime with a stranger, either for themselves, or for the resulting progeny. The mother, after giving the Master the amount of two hundred and fifty pesos, is assured of her freedom, without the Master being either able to ask for more, unless he had purchased her by title for a bigger amount, or to ask where that sum comes from, which often is, if not in its entirety, from his own stolen wealth. The son is removed, even before he is born, from the Master's control with just one hundred silver reales, and after he is born, with twenty-five pesos, which the owner is required to accept, if he resists. Who cannot see the inequity and the prejudices of this system that wants to look merciful? If the Royal Treasury would hold an investigation regarding these kinds of liberties with the presence of the Master, in order that it would apply the price offered for such freedoms to Public Funds or to a policy Treasury, the female slaves would neither prostitute themselves with the frequency that it occurs, nor would there be in the Settlements of the *Indies* so many useless and delinquent members. When the amount that the slave offers for his freedom is acquired by his efforts and extraordinary labor, it is very fair that he should be favored and the Republic gains a person who will serve it with usefulness and without prejudice.

The *French* have wisely stopped these abuses and their consequences, with the provision that the Master or person who grants freedom to a Slave has to pay one hundred fifty pesos to the King and guarantee the maintenance of the freedman until his death through means determined as sufficient by Justice. Before this law, emancipations were more frequent in their Colonies than in ours, resulting in the large number of them [freedmen], mainly *Mulattos*, but after this law, one can hardly find any freedmen. On the other hand, they have taxed with a contribution of three pesos per year each domestic Negro, male or female, who lives in the Cities or Towns, whether freed or enslaved. From this very prudent ordinance, it results that Masters do not have the sumptuous luxury of *Spanish* Settlements, where the rich acquire the silly vanity of filling their houses with lazy and useless Slaves and that the free ones should apply themselves to working the land.

The Island Divided

Since their arrival on Tortuga Island in the 1630s, the French had been colonizing the western part of Hispaniola, clashing with the Spanish, who first tried to dislodge them, and later, to contain them. After several decades of conflict between French and Spanish colonials in the seventeenth century, and the achievement of a modus vivendi in the eighteenth, a treaty was finally signed by the two monarchs which settled the partition of the island. By the 1777 Treaty of Aranjuez, Spain finally and formally recognized the French colony of Saint-Domingue (a tacit, implicit recognition had taken place in 1697 with the Treaty of Ryswick). The treaty was a belated, de facto recognition of the control the French had held for more than a century over western Hispaniola where they established a thriving colony. The Treaty of Aranjuez furthermore provisioned the establishment of a fixed border between the two colonies to prevent future conflicts over territory, a task carried out by a bi-national commission. Hispaniola thus became a geographic oddity: a small island divided into two different colonies. This colonial duality, formally established in 1777, would eventually lead to today's division of the island into two separate independent states: Haiti and the Dominican Republic. The details of the treaty follow below.

THE TREATY OF ARANJUEZ, 1777[16]

Treaty Agreed to by the Plenipotentiary Ministers of Their Christian and Catholic Majesties Related to the Boundaries of the French and Spanish Possessions in Santo Domingo, on June 3rd, 1777.

The sovereigns of France and Spain [. . .] wish to reach an agreement, according to the cases and circumstances, to settle the difficulties and obstacles that could have opposed such a healthy end. The frequent disagreements [. . .] between the French and Spanish inhabitants of the island [. . .] have obliged the two sovereigns to take into consideration this important matter and to issue orders and instructions to the governors in the aforementioned island, urging them to apply the utmost care and sincere desire of success, to establish the greatest possible harmony among the respective colonists. Also, that they [the governors] survey themselves the main lands and draft very exact charts and to finally conclude a border agreement, clear and positive enough to put an end forever to the difficulties and assure the closest unity among the inhabitants. In accordance with the orders of the two monarchs, all of the tasks and possible surveys were carried out and in the end, Monsieur De Vallière, commander and governor of the French part of the island, and Don José Solano, commander and Captain General of the Spanish part, signed a provisional agreement, on the twenty-fifth of August 1773. However, the two Courts, judging that this agreement did not completely convey the mutual desires and that it was a matter of vanishing forever any motive or pretext of discord and that it was necessary to clear up much more certain parts, issued new orders in relation to this matter.

The two governors, seriously prompted by the same desires, came to an agreement and signed a new convention or description of the limits, on the twenty-ninth of February 1776, and also appointed commissars and engineers to jointly draft a topographical chart of the whole extension of the border, from one end to the other, from north to south, and to place in a set distance, the necessary markers or milestones. This task was carried out, as it is verified by the document signed by the commissars the following twenty-eighth of August.

The two sovereigns, completely informed about all these antecedents and wishing to place the seal of their approval on a definite arrangement that would establish forever unity among their respective subjects, determined that a treaty related to the limits of the French and Spanish possessions in the island of Santo Domingo be drafted in Europe, based on the agreement of the twenty-fifth of August 1773, the agreement

16. Translated from M. L. E. Moreau de Saint-Méry, *Descripción de la parte española de Santo Domingo* (Ciudad Trujillo: Editora Montalvo, 1944), 26–45.

concluded on the twenty-ninth of February 1776, and above all the document signed by the respective Commissioners on the twenty-eighth of August 1776.

And to this effect, his excellency the Marquis of Ossún, and his Excellency Don José Moñino de Florida Blanca, after conferring among themselves and informing each other about their full powers, agreed to the following articles:

ARTICLE I

That the limits between the two nations will be perpetually and invariably fixed at the mouth of the *Dajabón* or *Masacre* River on the north side of the island and on the mouth of the *Pedernales* or *Anses-á-Pitre* River on the south side, in the terms to be specified in the immediately following article, remarking here only, that if in the future any doubt should surface regarding the identity of the *Pedernales* and *Anses-á-Pitre* Rivers, it is from now on and forever decided, that it is the river popularly called *Pedernales* River by the Spanish the one which the plenipotentiaries have designated to serve as limit.

ARTICLE II

Considering that the last operation the Viscount of Choiseul and Don Joaquín García have accomplished in their role as commissars, together with the respective engineers and with some native inhabitants, has been carried with utmost detail, with knowledge of the arrangement agreed between the French and Spanish commanders, on the twenty-ninth of February 1776, and that having surveyed the various terrains, have been in condition of clearing up all the doubts or mix-ups that might have derived from the literal expression of the aforementioned arrangement; attending also to the circumstance that commonly agreed markers have been placed alongside the border and that more precise charts have been prepared, in which the markers are indicated one by one; upon those considerations, the aforementioned plenipotentiaries stipulate that the said document prepared and signed by the aforementioned commissars, on the twenty-eighth of August 1776, and in which all the points, rivers, valleys, and mountains, where the line of demarcation passes are clearly and distinctly designated, will be included in the present article, of which it will be part, as follows:

Description of the limits of the island of Santo Domingo, agreed and convened in the final Treaty sub sperati signed in Atalaya on the twenty-ninth of February 1776, by the honorable gentlemen Don José Solano and His Excellency Seigneur Víctor Theresa Charpentier.

Who, after having signed the aforementioned original treaty, as adults, they issued according to it their instructions, on the same date, to the undersigned Don Joaquín García, Lieutenant Colonel of His Catholic Majesty's army and Commander of the regular militias of disciplined infantry of the Spanish colony; and Jacinto Luis, Viscount of Choiseul, Brigadier of His Very Christian Majesty's Armies, respectively named commissars with the task of implementing the articles of the treaty, which invariably fix the limits of the respective possessions of the two Crowns; and placing pyramids and markers where they see fit, in order to put an end to the disagreements that could disturb the good harmony between both nations, with the assistance of a sufficient number of Engineers to draft the enclosed Topographic Chart and which the undersigned sent for greater clarity, noting that the aforementioned chart has not been signed, as mentioned in the treaty, by Chief Engineer M. Boisforet, because he is currently at work, by superior orders, in other urgent functions related to his job.

[A detailed description of the border line follows.]

The Island Ceded

In 1795, at the end of another European war, Spain found herself once again on the losing side. Defeated by France, she had no choice but to pay war reparations. The price stipulated by the Treaty of Basel was the eastern part of the island of Hispaniola. The French, who already controlled Saint-Domingue, would now own the entire island. Unfortunately for them, political developments in Saint-Domingue prevented them from immediately carrying out the formal annexation of Santo Domingo. The social revolution that was taking place in Saint-Domingue was a major setback for French colonialism in the Caribbean, particularly as they lost effective control of the colony. For the inhabitants of Santo Domingo, the cession had traumatic repercussions. For more than three hundred years, Santo Domingo had been a Spanish colony. It was the place where Spain's American empire began, and the colony's elites felt the pride of having been "first" in many historical deeds. Moreover, the cession to France brought with it fears of the Haitian revolution spilling over into Santo Domingo. Soon, members of the Spanish Creole elites, afraid of losing their privileges—and their slaves—started to abandon the colony and move to Puerto Rico and Venezuela. But most troubling for the former Spanish colony was the uncertainty over when the French would actually enforce the treaty. For six years (1795–1801), Spanish governors ruled Santo Domingo in the absence of authorities from the French government. The 1795 Treaty of Basel is shown below.

STIPULATIONS OF THE TREATY OF BASEL, 1795[17]
The French Republic and His Majesty the King of Spain, equally animated by the

---

17. Translated from Carlos Calvo, *Colección completa de los tratados, convenciones, capitulaciones, armisticios y otros actos diplomáticos de todos los estados de la América Latina comprendidos entre el Golfo de Méjico y el Cabo de Hornos: Desde el año de 1493 hasta nuestros días* (Liechtenstein: Topos Verlag, 1978), vol. 6, 348–352.

desire of stopping the calamities of the war that divides them, intimately convinced that between their two nations exist respective interests that demand a reciprocal return of friendship and of good intentions, and wanting through a solid and lasting peace, to reestablish the good harmony that during a long time was the basis of the relations between the two countries, have entrusted this important negotiation as follows:

The French Republic, to citizen FRANÇOIS BARTHELEMY, its Ambassador in Switzerland; and his Catholic Majesty, its Plenipotentiary Minister and Extraordinary Envoy before the King and of the Republic of Poland, DON DOMINGO IRIARTE, Knight of the Royal Order of Carlos III, etc.

They, after having informed each other of their full powers, have decreed the following articles:

Article 1—There will be peace, friendship, and good understanding between the French Republic and the King of Spain.

Article 2—In consequence, all of the hostilities between the two signing powers will cease after the exchange of ratifications of the current treaty, and none of them are permitted from that same date, under any circumstances, to use against the other any aid or group of men, horses, supplies, money, war munitions, or warships or other things.

Article 3—Neither one of the signing powers will allow the use of its territory by the enemy troops of the other.

Article 4—The French Republic returns to the King of Spain all of the conquests that have been made during the course of the current war; French troops will evacuate the outposts and countries conquered within fifteen days after the exchange of the ratifications of the current treaty.

Article 5—The strongholds mentioned in the preceding article, will be returned to Spain, with the cannons, war munitions, and things for the use of these strongholds that existed at the moment of the signing of this treaty.

Article 6—Contributions, deliveries, provisions, and war loans will cease entirely fifteen days after the signing of the present act of pacification. All arrears to this day, as well as the promissory notes and promises given or taken in this sense, will be annulled. Those taken or collected after said date will be returned immediately for free or paid in cash.

Article 7—Both parts will appoint next, commissioners to proceed with the preparation of a border treaty between the two powers. They will use, whenever possible, this treaty as their basis, and in relation to the lands that were contested before the current war, the crests of the mountains that form the watersheds between France and Spain.

Article 8—Each signatory power will, a month after the exchange of ratifications of the current treaty, be able to place within its respective borders the same number of troops as deployed before the current war.

Article 9—In exchange for the restitution dealt with in Article 4, the King of Spain, by himself and for his successors, cedes and abandons in all property to the French Republic, all of the Spanish part of the island of Santo Domingo in the Antilles.

A month after the ratification of the current treaty is known in that island, the Spanish troops will be quick to evacuate the forts, ports, and buildings they occupy there, in order to turn them over to the French troops when they show up to take possession of them. The aforementioned forts, ports, and buildings will be given to the French Republic with the cannons, war munitions, and things necessary for their defense that exist in them at the moment that the news of the current treaty reaches Santo Domingo.

The inhabitants of the Spanish part of Santo Domingo, who by their interests or by other motives prefer to be transferred with their goods to the possessions of His Catholic Majesty, will be able to do so within a year from the date of this treaty.

Article 10—The respective individuals of the two nations will receive the wares, rents, and goods of any kind that were detained, seized, or conquered as a result of the war that has existed between the French Republic and His Catholic Majesty: and likewise there will be quick justice in relation to particular debts of any kind, that those individuals could have with the States of the two signatory powers.

Article 11—While a new trade treaty is being drafted by the two signatory parties, all communications and commercial relations will be established between France and Spain in the same position as they were before the current war.

Article 12—All prisoners, respectively captured after the start of the war, without taking into consideration the difference in number or in rank, and understanding that the marines and sailors taken from French and Spanish ships, or of other nations, as well as, in general, all those detained by any of them as a result of the war, will be handed over at the latest in the course of the two months after the exchange of ratifications of the current treaty, without any reclamation from one part or the other, and only paying them the particular debts that they could have contracted during their captivity. It will be done in the same way for the injured once they recover.

Both parties will immediately name commissioners for the implementation of the present article.

Article 13—The Portuguese prisoners, who are part of the Portuguese troops who have served in the army and in the ships of His Catholic Majesty, will be likewise included in the aforementioned exchange.

Article 14—The same peace, friendship, and good relations stipulated in the current treaty between France and the King of Spain, will take place between the King of Spain and the Republic of the United Provinces allied to the French Republic.

Article 15—The French Republic, wanting to give testimony of friendship to His Catholic Majesty, accepts his mediation in favor of the Queen of Portugal, the King of Naples, the King of Sardinia, the Infant Duque of Parma and other States of Italy, for the reestablishment of peace between the French Republic and each one of these princes and States.

Article 16—The French Republic knowing the interest that His Catholic Majesty has in the general pacification of Europe, consents likewise in offering its good offices in favor of the other belligerent powers that would come to enter into negotiations with the French government.

Article 17— The present treaty will not take effect until after it has been ratified by the signatory parties and those ratifications will be exchanged within the time limit of a month or as soon as possible, if it is possible, from this date.

In witness whereof, we the undersigned, plenipotentiaries of the French Republic and of His Majesty the King of Spain, by virtue of our full powers, have signed the present treaty of peace and friendship and we have placed on it our respective seals.

Done in Basel, the fourth Thermidor[18] in the third year of the Republic (July 22, 1795).

Signed: François Barthélémy   Domingo D'Iriarte

The Slaves Rebel

In 1793, the French government, fearful of the potential fall out from the civil war raging in Saint-Domingue, abolished slavery. In Spanish Santo Domingo, on the other hand, slavery remained intact even after the colony was ceded to France in 1795. Although compared to Saint-Domingue, Santo Domingo always had, numerically and proportionally, fewer slaves, its elites nevertheless feared a slave uprising and a social revolution like that in Saint-Domingue. Moreover, light-skinned elites in Santo Domingo also feared that free blacks and mulattos would join their "brothers" and massacre all the whites in the colony in a bloody racial war. These fears seemed to be confirmed when the slaves of the Boca de Nigua sugar plantation—near the city of Santo Domingo—rebelled in 1796. Though Santo Domingo had very few plantations (as compared to Saint-Domingue), slaves working them were exploited as brutally there as in the neighboring colony. Moreover, these slaves were aware of the latest political developments, such as the abolition of slavery in Saint-Domingue and the cession of the colony of Santo Domingo to France. When news of the rebellion reached Santo Domingo, the Spanish authorities lost no time. Well aware of the potential consequences of a slave uprising, they acted swiftly and brutally to suppress it. The following document reports details about the slave insurrection, its outcome, and particularly, how the Spanish authorities doled out harsh, cruel sentences to those involved, so as to serve as an example to other slaves and freedmen.

18. After the French Revolution, the Republic adopted a new calendar and the months of the year were renamed.

LETTER FROM THE GOVERNOR OF SANTO DOMINGO, DON JOAQUÍN GARCÍA, TO THE PRINCE OF PEACE, GIVING HIM AN ACCOUNT OF HAVING DEFEATED THE UPRISING OF THE NEGROES OF THE HACIENDA DE BOCA-NIGUA, AND OF REESTABLISHING ORDER WITH THE PUNISHMENT OF THE CRIMINALS. WITH A MARGINAL RESOLUTION.[19]

Your Excellency, the Honorable Prince of Peace,

On the morning of the thirty-first of October, the most unexpected news of an organized Negro uprising arrived in this Capital. The incident took place in the Hacienda del Cargo owned by Don Juan de Oyarzabal, and along with the news, we learned that the life of this man was in great danger. Two [individuals] who refused to join the disorder, putting their own lives in danger, were able to escape the Hacienda and come to us to announce the incident. This sugarcane Hacienda of two hundred Negroes, named Boca-Nigua, is located five leagues away from this Capital, on the coast, and it is the best established, wealthiest, and better administered of all of the Spanish part and even of the whole Island nowadays.

Its location forced [us] to guard it in this war with arms and munitions, which could defend it from the Piracy which was menacing it, and these were the aids that they [the slaves] took advantage of in this formal and surprise attack against their Master. They then planned to follow up against any whites counting on getting their Haciendas, enslaving those who did not take up arms in their favor or killing them, rapidly increasing their numbers with the groups of Negroes who fled from neighboring Haciendas upon hearing the sound of liberty, exterminating the whites, taking over the Port and Battery of Jayna, following up to the San Gerónimo Castle, and based on these favorable events, they were counting on taking possession of the City, and establishing a government like the one in Guarico, and others in the French part.

These Negroes, who, based on the good conduct and the loyalty they had demonstrated to their masters, were not treated like Negro slaves. They were never subjected to any commiseration or mistreatment until Captain Franco started to antagonize them. His rudeness and indecisiveness drove him to this extremist behavior based on two fantastic events: First, He found a foremen in the same Hacienda to serve the roles of Commander of Artillery, of Dragoons, Infantry, and others he conceived in his whim, and outside he had consultants and a Collaborator who disputed the command when the captain manifested weakness toward the Negro companions who pretended loyalty to the Master. His woman was unalterable and praiseworthy. Not being able to assist them in the preceding days that were occupied with the plotting, she warned the Master with insistence, and with opposition of the conduct of another Negro woman who, though more attended to and distinguished by her Master, volunteered to be the assassin, and was made Queen in the disorder, reciprocating with prizes and rewards.

---

19. Translated from J. Marino Incháustegui, *Documentos para estudio: Marco de la época y problemas del Tratado de Basilea de 1795, en la Parte Española de Santo Domingo* (Buenos Aires: Artes Gráficas Bartolomé U. Chiesino, 1957), 332–335.

Some demonstrations that took place forewarned Oyarzabal and put him on his guard. He took the precautions that the short notice permitted him and which could not be other than the recourse of waiting for them, because he did not have what was needed to undo the plan, as it was proposed for the following day.

On the afternoon of the thirtieth, the alarmed Negroes rose up. They attacked the Master's House once but without success. They attacked a second time more bravely, and every time they were conducting themselves more boldly. The Master, armed in the House for his defense with the aid of some White Domestics and villagers, always resisted the violence and in this defense some Negroes were injured.

The persuasions of the Negro captain for the Master to escape were effective, either because he was judged with the same contempt as his companions, or because the Parties that were to surprise him were ready. The major effort seemed to be to separate him. The greatest hatred was toward Don Pedro Abadia, and the Foreman, who were destined to die; one drowned inside a liquor barrel, the other under the harshness of the Whip.

Oyarzabal escaped through the most remote route, and all the Whites escaped before the number [of slaves] grew and resistance [to them] became impossible.

Then the Negroes took over everything, destroying and smashing to pieces anything under lock and the furniture that they were not fond of. They burned down the Tile-making Ranch so as not to leave an emplacement for any Enemy, the Sugar Fields, some Houses, they speared the beasts, and they tried to annihilate and destroy so that rebuilding would be less likely.

In this situation arrived the troops composed of two officers and fifty-four Grenadiers of the Cantabria Regiment, and the Regulars of Santo Domingo, who worked fruitlessly the night before in the crossing of the Nigua River, which the Negroes contested. By sunrise, they were already able to remove them from two Positions that they had protected with a four-pound cannon each, which they used with grapevine shot, and the troops took up positions in the Main House and other buildings, and then the Commissioned Hearer was able to start working on the details of justifications, acknowledgments, and others ways of conducting the punishment and disciplining [of the slaves], and the escaped Negroes, so that they were documented and well justified.

[. . .]

Because the measures that I, of course, adopted everywhere had the efficiency and desired effect so that everywhere in the region up to Azua and San Juan the villagers were up in Arms, it was not long before the mutinous Negro rebels dispersed in order to escape. They have been hunted down and captured in all distances; there are no more of them dispersed. The countryfolk with spears and machetes, and some with rifles or carbines have been the most useful for the pursuit in the woods, particularly with the incentive of cash gratifications, offered and paid by Oyarzabal.

Seven Negroes died in the Battle and its aftermath. Seven were hanged and dismembered after a month because they were leaders. Among them, the Negro captain, the named Queen Ana Maria, and her husband; the rest of the group of Negroes, males as well as females, were whipped at the pillory the former (one hundred lashes) and inside the Jail the latter (fifty lashes), and then were paraded under the gallows after witnessing the executions, and sentenced to work in the same Hacienda as

I order, with shackles on their feet and grapples around their necks for a ten-year term. Three of the Collaborators with their instructions from the *Briganes* of the Colony were sentenced and sent to the prisons of Cartagena, Vera Cruz, and Havana, and one of the former to Panama because it was deemed suitable to remove him from the company of the others.

In proportion to the fatal appearances of this event from the point that it manifested with so much gravity, it has been my satisfaction, since it did not seem possible in a Country like this, that such a disorder could be suppressed so quickly and so completely. A very exemplary punishment has taken place to the surprise of all residents. All of the neighboring areas of Boca-Nigua replied to Oyarzabal's request. The city and the countryside were, of course, placed on alert and under observation. Judgment day was frightening and had we not taken some measures capable of containing so many Negroes, freedmen as well as slaves, and so many foreigners loyal to Liberty and to Equality, and closing the Doors, establishing Patrols, putting all the Guards in Arms, and one hundred Grenadiers for the execution, all the troops ready in their Barracks with their Officers, and simply put on alert all of the Garrison, we could have experienced a commotion like that which took place in the Island's vicinity,[20] and conceivable in a City that has one year and four months of being ceded to the French Republic.

The role played by Don Juan Bautista Oyarzabal in the suppression of this uprising should not be minimized. His character and genius, his wealth, and compensations have been constant and timely, crediting him with the greatest particular disinterest as proof of his Love to the King's Service, and to the Motherland, for which he is worthy of all public gratitude, and of the praise of those who have seen him serve on this occasion.

Santo Domingo, the thirteenth of December 1796
Joaquín García (signature)

Toussaint Louverture Takes Over

Toussaint Louverture is one of Haiti's founding fathers. A former slave, he became a revolutionary military leader who initially fought against the French, and once they abolished slavery, he became a defender of the French Republic. By 1801, Toussaint Louverture was in full control of the French colony, and though he still pledged loyalty to the French Republic, it was clear that the French had no real power in Saint-Domingue. Confident of his power and authority, he enforced the Treaty of Basel in 1801 by annexing the eastern part of the island. His troops

---

20. This refers to the slave insurrections in French Saint-Domingue.

found no resistance along their way to the city of Santo Domingo, where he abolished slavery upon his arrival. Though some historians categorize this event as the first Haitian "invasion" in Dominican history, Toussaint Louverture instituted many progressive measures during his brief administration. In 1802, Napoleon Bonaparte sent a French expeditionary force to regain control of the island. The first landings took place in the eastern part of the island and Louverture decided to withdraw his troops to the West, where he was in a stronger position. For the rest of the decade, Santo Domingo remained in French hands, ruled by the officers of Napoleon's army. Toussaint Louverture would later be tricked by the French, arrested, and deported to France, where he died in prison in 1803. The following is a description of Louverture's takeover ceremony, where the Spanish authorities surrendered control of the city—and the colony—to him.

ENDOWMENT CEREMONY FOR SURRENDERING THE CITY OF SANTO DOMINGO TO TOUSSAINT LOUVERTURE[21]

Given in the city of Santo Domingo, on the twenty-sixth of January 1801. The Town Council assembled at this Town Hall, accompanied by its Board, Judge, and Regiment; as well as by Doctor Don Adrián Campuzano, Counsel to the Royal Audience, and Don Andrés Angulo, Sublieutenant of the Infantry Volunteers, Ordinary Majors of First and Second Vote, Don Rodrigo de la Rocha, Captain of the Fixed Infantry of this plaza, and Interim Chief Bailiff: Don Francisco de Tapia y Caridi; and Don Pedro Fernández de Castro, Regents of this illustrious Body; also present was the Major Attorney General for the act of granting possession as decreed by the Superior Government of this City to the General in Chief of the Armies of the French Republic Toussaint Louverture, as informed by the Governor and Captain General in the note dated twenty-third, for the enlightenment of this Illustrious Body; in consequence, being about 1:30 in the afternoon, into this City Hall entered together Don Joaquín García y Moreno, Field Marshall of the Royal Armies, Governor and Captain General of this City and Island, and with the Mayors, and Regents standing, the aforementioned Captain General Don Joaquín García, in front of the Illustrious Body, and I, the undersigned Secretary, asked the aforementioned General in Chief to swear before God, and the Holy Trinity, Father, Son, and Holy Spirit, that he was taking possession of this Capital, and of the Spanish part of this Island in the name of the French Republic, one and indivisible. And that his subordinates would observe and carry out the treaty of Basel in all its parts and articles as well as the agreements between both Leaders, ratified on January twenty-second of the current year (Second

---

21. Translated from Gustavo Adolfo Mejía Ricart, *Historia de Santo Domingo: Una interpretación objetiva* (Ciudad Trujillo: Editores Pol Hermanos, 1948).

of Pluviôse). And he said: That he could not take the oath that was demanded because the French Republic has not mandated to receive the Plazas, under this condition: that after having ratified the articles proposed by the Spanish government, the possession Ceremony was completed; that nevertheless he will sign the surrender act with the Spanish Governor in the presence of the Town Council, and other circumstances: promising on this day, that if the Spanish General on his own, or the Town Council on its own, or both together would ask him for something, in favor of the locality, that he would grant it or respond to what corresponds. With this, the aforementioned Field Marshall Don Joaquín García, taking the keys of the three doors to this City, that were already arranged on top of the table, handed them over to the aforementioned General in Chief, Toussaint Louverture, who received them in his hands, and acknowledged their receipt, in the name of the French Republic. With this the act was concluded, that having been read by means of the interpreter of General in Chief, was signed by the Generals and other Individuals of the Illustrious Body, to which I the Secretary attest.—Joaquín García, Adrián Campuzano. Andrés Angulo, Rodrigo de la Rocha, Francisco de Tapia, Luis Franco, Pedro Fernández de Castro. For the City, Francisco de Lavastida.—Secretary.

Jean-Jacques Dessalines Attacks

After Toussaint Louverture made peace with Napoleon's expeditionary force, he was tricked and arrested. The French deported him to France, where he died in prison in the French Alps. His generals continued the fight for freedom. One of them was Jean-Jacques Dessalines, a former field slave, who led the revolutionary struggle until the French armies were defeated and Haiti became an independent nation on January 1, 1804. In a break with their colonial past, the leaders of the new nation decided to adopt the Taíno name for the island: *Aytí* (i.e., Haiti). Since the fighting had been confined to the western part of the island, French troops in Santo Domingo refused to lay down their arms when their comrades-in-arms surrendered to the Haitians in the west. The presence of the hated French in Santo Domingo presented a grave security risk for the fledgling Republic of Haiti, which feared a potential invasion from the east. In 1805, Dessalines launched a two-pronged attacked on the eastern part of the island. The Haitian armies quickly advanced through the southern end and the Cibao region, converging on the city of Santo Domingo, where they were stopped by thick walls, artillery, and the French garrison. Dessalines, who lacked the firepower to breach the walls, decided to lay siege to the city and starve its inhabitants into surrendering. For weeks, the French and the local inhabitants defending Santo Domingo city feared the worst, when suddenly a French fleet appeared on the horizon. Dessalines interpreted this as a signal of an impending invasion of Haiti and retreated to the safety of the western part to prepare for his country's defense. In the course of this retreat, the Haitian army carried out a "scorched earth" campaign, burning towns and villages, and taking groups of people hostage, so as not to leave anything of military value to the French. The feared French invasion never materialized. The following excerpt is from the memoirs of a French military officer who survived the siege.

FROM THE MEMOIRS OF A FRENCH MILITARY OFFICER DESCRIBING THE SIEGE OF SANTO DOMINGO[22]

Once again Ferrand had achieved his objective: to prove to the enemy that we are still very far away from being defeated. But the fleeting advantage that we had achieved did not change our position. However, for twenty-four hours, the topic of our conversations was that sometimes it was forgotten that when the hour neared, in which, like the brave men who had fallen in that attack, we were also going to succumb in turn.

In this skirmish we had lost eleven men, and twenty-five had been injured.

At last, the twentieth-first day of the blockade had started to take its toll. Hunger prevailed everywhere. In some catacombs, which had served in the past as graves for the nuns of Santa Clara or Clarisas, some spoiled flour was found, and initially abandoned, because it was unhealthy. That flour, mixed with the bones of the poor nuns, served to prepare a horrific bread. Everything had been devoured: horses, donkeys, dogs, rats. A piece of bacon, the size of a flintstone, was being sold for five francs; a caged parrot was purchased for 60 francs.

And this bread, which the stomach rejected, was also going to run out. In the presence of so much misery, courage declined. The ladders that the enemy prepared to begin the assault were regarded with a dull gaze; the threats the Negroes yelled from their trenches were heard with indifference: "*Demain, blancs, zantes va mourir*" ("Tomorrow, whites, you are going to die").

Summons by Dessalines

In his last summons, Dessalines had indicated, in writing, the punishment reserved for each one of the Chiefs: Ferrand was to be sawed between two boards; Aussenac, disemboweled like a pig. The other officials were destined to perish in a bonfire, and the soldiers were to be beheaded.

---

22. Translated from Jean Baptiste Lemonnier-Delafosse, *Segunda campaña de Santo Domingo: Guerra domínico-francesa de 1808* (Santiago: Editorial El Diario, 1946), 114–118.

These threats against him did not worry our brave general; but, how much did he suffer for his soldiers!

We did not know until much later to what extent his moral sufferings went.

Lucia, a quadroon in charge of his house, told us that every night, the general [Ferrand], alone, surrendering to his reflections, cried like a child, thinking about the fate of so many valiant soldiers who had followed his destiny.

But, at dawn, he was the general once again, giving encouragement to all and committing them to defend themselves to the death.

Surrender is not an option when you are faced with a man like Dessalines. It would be like surrendering to the executioner; it was necessary, thus, to defend one's life, extenuated by privations, by misery; a life that, after all, was hanging by a mere thread.

Its sacrifice was already done! And anyway, what is life for the military? A glorious dream that a bullet often interrupts! The continuous presence of death had made us indifferent. At night, we kept vigil near the corpses; during the day, we counted the new gaps that had developed in our ranks. We felt great pleasure when we saw a comrade again; we would hug and give thanks to God; because, night after night, it was expected that we would not see each other on the next day.

It is necessary to live far away from one's fatherland, to know what the strength of friendship, of the fraternity which bonds men from the same country is like. In France no one has any idea of what this is like; friendship is just a word! They play with the word; they feign the sentiment; but only egoism reigns supreme.

Our last day had arrived! All hopes of receiving aid from [fellow] men seemed lost. Only a miracle could save us.

The miracle was granted.

The sun was rising for the twentieth-second time since we had been blockaded by the Negro army. The enemy must attack, we already knew it, and each one of us collected the little bit of strength we had left, to sell the rest of life we had left at a high cost.

Suddenly a scream of jubilation resounded in the air: "Sails on the horizon! Boats! Ships! A fleet! Could it be an enemy? We do not know; but, what does it matter! It is salvation! It is life!"

This was something to drive one crazy!

However, our eyes devoured the expanse! At last, with the help of field glasses, flags waving high on the masts were discerned. They were the [French] national flags!

We signaled and a greeting of twenty-one cannon shots let it be known to the fleet that Santo Domingo was occupied by the French.

This fortunate news, flying from mouth to mouth, soon reached the trenches; all discipline was interrupted. Officers, soldiers, colonists abandoned their posts and ran to the seashore, scaling the batteries to see those ships that brought us our salvation. Kneeling, yes, kneeling! With their arms stretched out, all of them cried, shouting: "We are saved! We are out of danger!"

That was a very imposing spectacle, to see those men, intoxicated with joy, laughing, crying, thanking God, while contemplating the French ships that gave us our lives back.

Rear Admiral Missiessy

The squadron, led by Rear Admiral Missiessy, had left Aix Island on the eleventh of January 1805, to sail the Antilles, inflicting considerable damage on the English colonies: Dominica, Montserrat, St. Kitts, where they landed and collected tributes. On that same voyage, the squadron had sunk and burned a large number of English ships; it had to make it to Havana and immediately return to France.

The whole fleet remained at sail; only the admiral came on land and confessed to the general his surprise to see so many people on the shore, and that he believed, for an instant, to be in the midst of a group of lunatics. And in reality, one could have believed that it was like that; reveille had been played in vain, the trenches were unguarded; everyone had gone to the seashore. "But—added the Admiral—why are you here?"

Ferrand then told him, how with a handful of men, he had sought refuge in Santo Domingo: he recounted his sufferings and the hunger that devoured the soldiers; finally, he asked the admiral for aid to sustain the struggle.

Supplying Santo Domingo

The Admiral dictated orders and boats loaded with food, ammunition, medications, and money soon arrived. Abundance suddenly reappeared, where the most frightful misery had reigned. Next, the admiral added two battalions to the city's garrison. These diverse arrangements took all day and on the following day the squadron left us to continue its cruise.

Our destiny was the result of a breath of wind. Certainly, the admiral did not have any special mission for Santo Domingo, and, if instead of surveying the southern coast of the island, he would have turned north, nothing would have prevented the capture of the city and no one would have escaped the fury of the Negroes.

It was probably believed in France that Santo Domingo had been abandoned: a year had passed since the report of General Ferrand about his rise to power and the departure of former Governor Kerverseau. The Emperor [Napoleon] was busy with his plan to invade England and could not think about a poor garrison located a few thousand leagues from France, abandoned, lost, in enemy territory. As he was leaving, the Admiral promised that he would give a complete report on the status of the garrison.

It seemed to us that the fortune that accompanied Napoleon had descended upon us. At that time, Jamaica had been very alarmed; only one ship defended it and our fleet could have caused great damage to it; unfortunately, his time was short and the leader could not change anything in his itinerary.

Lifting of the Siege

From his fortifications, Dessalines had seen the unexpected aid that had come to us; he had expected that hunger would force us to surrender; he thus doubted his success and, in consequence, made arrangements to lift the siege. If the leader of the Negroes had taken advantage of the abandonment of the trenches when the French fleet arrived and had attacked, he would, without any doubt, have taken the garrison; probably he did not think that discipline had been forgotten for a moment; it could also be that he feared that if his troops entered the city and were defeated, they would not have been able to reoccupy their positions, which constituted their main strength. The Negro army began its retreat that same day.

Ephemeral Independence

After Dessalines's retreat, the French occupation of Santo Domingo continued for several more years. A liberation struggle, led by Juan Sánchez Ramírez ensued, and in 1809, the French were finally defeated. Spanish troops from Puerto Rico, as well as the British Navy, participated in the "Reconquest War." Once liberated from French rule, the colony reverted back to Spain. The second Spanish colonial period (1809–1821) was a big disappointment for the people of Santo Domingo, who by now were already calling themselves Dominicans. However, Spain was at this time embroiled in the independence wars on the Latin American mainland and had neither the time nor resources to effectively administer Santo Domingo. The period of *España Boba* (Inane Spain), as it is known, was thus characterized by a lax administration and a return to the old race- and class-based policies of the past. In 1821, a group of prominent Dominicans, led by José Núñez de Cáceres, declared the independence of "Spanish Haiti" with the intention of merging the country with Simón Bolívar's Gran Colombia. At about the same time, villages in the interior, particularly near the borderland, issued proclamations expressing their wish to join Haiti, thus placing the independence plan of Santo Domingo's elites in jeopardy. The independence of Spanish Haiti was cut short when, in January 1822, Jean-Pierre Boyer, Haiti's president, took over the eastern part of the island. Núñez de Cáceres and his men realized the futility of opposing Boyer's huge army and peacefully capitulated. The "ephemeral" independence of 1821 lasted only five weeks. The following document is the declaration of independence drafted by the rebels.

DECLARATION OF INDEPENDENCE, 1821[23]

No more dependence, no more humiliation, no more subjection to the caprice and flightiness of Madrid's Cabinet. The resolution and will of the Dominican people,

---

23. Translated from Emilio Rodríguez Demorizi, *Santo Domingo y la Gran Colombia: Bolívar y Núñez de Cáceres* (Santo Domingo: Editora del Caribe, 1971), 45–53.

who today have sworn and proclaimed the compromise to support freedom, are summarized in these brief clauses that follow. Dominicans, as of this moment, are free forever. The links that had chained the Dominican people to the heavy and oppressive old wagon of the ancient Metropolis were just broken. And now, taking possession of its rights, the people reassume the dignity and energy of freedom and use it to protest, using the Supreme Being as a witness, so that it will be constituted an independent state where there will be no sacrifice that does not take place at the altar of the Homeland to carry out the heroic undertaking of becoming, and being admitted to the ranks and consideration of the other free peoples of the political world.

The 328 years of being disciples and servants to the Crown and of being loyal to the Kings of Spain have produced only disappointment for everyone, and have proven to be costly and unfruitful to the development of the island. With this false idol, sparked off by error, and sustained by political superstition, the spirit became drowsy, and fun was made of the credulity of a naturally simple and kind people. Being loyal to Spain, bearing with subdued patience Spain's contempt, not living, not moving, not belonging to us, but to Spain, was everything and the only thing on which we built our happiness, the fame of our virtues, and the recompense of the most distinguished services.

When, among us, we can still find dejected souls who, having sold themselves to servitude, dare to contradict the truth of the experience, we ask you to open your eyes for an instant and look at the devastated state, the ruin and desolation, in which the Spanish part of the *Primada* New World lies. We are not asking [them] to go back to the doleful epoch, when an order from the Spanish Cabinet was enough to demolish everything, because it [the Spanish Crown] could not keep the maritime plazas of Bayaha, Yaguana, Monte Cristi, and Puerto de Plata, where the Dutch and other foreigners went to supply them with merchandise, which the Metropolis did not provide. Get close to the recent events of our times, start your assessment with the furious hurricane of the cession [to France]: count, if you lack enough sensibility, the deluge of plagues this storm provoked, and that spread through the beautiful, fertile soil of Haiti, transforming its fields into deserts, and its rich, colorful cities into ruins and ashes. Still place, if you want, a dense veil over the melancholic history of the deaths, hunger, and other horrors of the last siege, which left it to the inhabitants of this capital to wrestle its ownership from the French, and look only at the eleventh of July 1809, a day forever memorable, in which the abandoned island, which had served as ransom for the peninsular provinces, was occupied by the victorious arms of the French Republic, and which saved in that raging crisis the unsteady throne of Carlos IV by its free and spontaneous will, ties once more the bonds dissolved by the Treaty of Basel, and is pleased with the most sincere and cordial jubilation by the close alliance that it renews with its former, disdainful Metropolis.

If Santo Domingo had committed an enormous fault of some sort since its discovery, or contracted a grave transgression to deserve the indignation and the grudge of Spain, it has earned forgiveness for its demerits with the valor and the joyous success of the reconquest [war], as well as the most affectionate demonstrations of gratitude. However, among the heroes of this trait who come to show off their loyalty in the arena, one does not find all the widows, the children, the parents of those who perished fighting to be subjects of a nation that cedes them, and hounds their guild

71

like a herd of lambs. Nor are there those who died of need, or are subject to the miserable sustenance of two or three copper reales: the ones who in the campaign occupied the front lines due to their bravery and ability as soon as the plaza was attacked, descending to the lower ranks, or ending up with nothing as a reward for their valor. Don Manuel Carvajal, the brave defender of Manganagua, second in command to Don Juan Sanches [. . .] is still waiting to receive acknowledgment that his services were pleasing. With the same pain died Don Pedro Vásquez, another champion of those who made the greatest efforts and fought to accomplish the reconquest, and after twelve years, the editor of the *Miscelánea* of the eleventh of November comes out saying that "for the satisfaction of those who might be interested, he has been authorized by the political Leader to publicize, that in an official letter dated the seventh of July of this year, directed to him by the Ministry of Overseas Government, among other things, His Excellency tells him, that the King has ordered to notify the War Minister what is needed in order to dispatch the ranks and decorations granted to these locals for the reconquest."

[. . .] But, why cloud with these sour memories the beautiful and clear day of the political regeneration of Santo Domingo? If the series of injustices, insults, abuses, humiliations, and neglect were the only cause of this auspicious move, it may be that no other people in the Americas could sketch a picture laden with darker shadows and more horrible specters than this unfortunate island. She [Hispaniola] was the first one in the order of settlements and is becoming the last one in advancement and progress which constitutes the peoples' well being. In spite of all that, to justify our cause, we need not to turn to the obnoxious numeration of the tempests and vicissitudes that we have been through: sentiments of honor, principles of justice, reasons of utility, and public convenience are the noble impulses that stimulate us to pronounce the divorce and emancipation from Spain forever.

[. . .] Santo Domingo has received in its midst the scholarly youth of Caracas, Puerto Rico, Cuba and Havana. It has adopted in the guild and senate of its University locals of all these towns and environs. It has ennobled them with degrees and prizes in all the sciences. Many of the heroes that are featured in the honorable arena of their revolution drank from the elements of knowledge here. And how honorable can it be, as one of the main centers of the American enlightenment, it is the last to recognize the eternal principles of the social order? The homeland of the Morfas, of the Minieles, of Don Juan Sánchez, and Marcos Torres, the one who has so many times shaken the yoke of the European powers in Sabana Real, in the mountains of Najayo, in Palo-Hincado, could it be insensible to the immortal glory of overthrowing and extinguishing forever the tyrannical empire of its Conquerors? Spain stripped us of everything, but the honor and strength of our fathers still remains.

We know with absolute certainty that men resigned to the independence of the natural state to enter into a civil society that secures their life, property, and liberty, in a stable and permanent way, which are three principal assets of which the nations' happiness consists. To enjoy these rights, governments are instituted and formed, deriving their just powers from the consent of the associates; from where it follows, that if the government does not correspond to these essential ends, that if far from looking for the conservation of society, it becomes oppressive, it is up to the people's faculties to alter or to abolish its form and to adopt a new one that seems more conducive to its security and future well being. It is our good fortune that governments, founded a long time ago, are not changed for petty motives and fleeting causes. Prudence dictates that ills are to be endured while they are bearable; but when they reach that last iota, when the same experience demonstrates that the aim is to reduce everything to an absolute despotism, then it would be degrading ourselves as rational and liberal beings. If men would not discard at the moment a government totally contrary to the high goals of its original institution, then who in light of these principles will not applaud as just the one which today adopts as its own the Spanish part of Haiti? As many blows, misfortunes, and disasters as the hydra of despotism can abort, so has Santo Domingo suffered during its shameful submission to Spain; thus it is our first obligation, and one of the most sacred rights that patriotic love imposes on us, to procure with efficiency and by whatever means are within our reach, the happiness that the Metropolis has not known, or has not been able to assure us in order to carry out its goals of despondency and tyranny.

We are truly convinced that to get it and augment it, there is no other way than our independence. With it, we will have laws made by us, analogous to the character, education and customs of the people, tailored to the climate and locality, and to our national representation over the numeric proportion will maintain a perfect equality among all the residents of these provinces, and it will not serve to feed discord between the various classes, as has happened with the foundations established by the Cadiz Constitution. We will fix the judiciary power in a way, that, while saving time and money, good administration of justice will not be lacking in the civic and criminal aspects, nor resources will be taken away from the territory. We will attend with special care to the education of our youth so abandoned until now, because without them all the wishes of public happiness are ineffectual. We will devote ourselves to the fostering of agriculture, of the arts and of commerce, as the sole and true sources of the people's wealth; we will fix our finances on the fundamental dogma of not spending more than what we have and it is compatible with the territorial wealth: all nations ready to provide for our needs and to give consideration and market the country's crops will come to our ports; instead of Spain which, besides lacking the principal articles of our consumption, has never known how to negotiate in a different way other than to benefit from exclusivity and with the deafness of monopoly which, like a legitimate child, is born and derived from that absurd principle. Finally, we will have everything at home and nothing will we have to go seek at a distance of thirteen hundred leagues, where our necessities are not seen, nor can there be an interest in remedying them to the extent of the urgency.

[. . .] Santo Domingo, on the contrary, in the midst of its decadence it is surviving from its own resources and would still have much more relief if it would have established its administrative system on the economic principles prescribed by its exhausted population, its agriculture and commerce; but it had to wash its hands of all good rule, to tend to the burdens that its ungrateful and unknown Metropolis has been piling up on it, as reward and to relieve the ills that overwhelm us since the ruinous blow of the cession. If the tariffs' law and the customs regulations had not been suspended and tempered to local circumstances, by now all the ports of the Island would have been closed once and forever, because when Spanish liberty is most pondered, it is exactly when it has sought to bolt down with more vigor the chains of monopoly and the exclusivity of commerce. Even the mail carriers of these precious regulations will not honor themselves to touch the maritime points of the Island as they were used to, forcing us to pay for someone to go and bring us the death sentences in order to have the barbaric satisfaction of executing them on us, and with our own hands. Here is the sole thing on which we depend on Spain, and not so that it would assist, provide for, and help us during our predicaments and neediness: up to now we have lived enslaved and dependent by habit, but the deeds that persuade much more efficiently than routines demonstrate and convince us that we are free and emancipated.

Thus, we recognize and feel it from our own experience, and guided by it we declare and solemnly publicize, that the Spanish part of the Island of Haiti, is from this day forth constituted in a free and independent State: that the good Dominican people will not now, nor in the future, nor ever submit itself to the laws or the government of Spain, considering itself absolved of all obligation of fidelity and obedience: that armed with the dignity and character of a sovereign nation, it has full powers and faculties to establish the form of government that best suits it, to enter into alliances, to declare war, to arrange peace, to negotiate commercial treaties, and to celebrate the other acts, transactions, and agreements that other free peoples have the right to; and that if Spain recognizes and approves this declaration, it will be reputed and regarded as a friend; but if it challenges it or if by any other way and means it pretends to hinder our institutions or the affairs of the new government into which we will enter, we will know how to defend it with our lives, fortune, and honor. Long live the Homeland, long live independence, long live the Union of Colombia!

Issued in the city of Santo Domingo of the Spanish part of Haiti on the first of December 1821. First year of the independence.— José Núñez de Cáceres, President, Manuel Carvajal, Juan Vicente Moscoso, Antonio Martínez Valdés, L. Juan Nepomuceno de Arredondo, Juan Ruiz, Vicente Mancebo, Manuel López de Umeres, Secretary.

The Haitian Annexation

Jean-Pierre Boyer was received amidst applause as he entered the former Spanish colony of Santo Domingo in 1822. For most common Dominicans, Haiti was a progressive nation. After all, Haiti had a presidential system and an elective Congress, and had abolished slavery and race-based privileges—a far cry from Spain's colonial rule. Upon taking power in Santo Domingo, Boyer again abolished slavery (which had been reestablished by the French in 1802) and extended Haitian citizenship to its inhabitants. For the next twenty-two years, the island of Hispaniola was a single political entity: the Republic of Haiti. Boyer's rule was egalitarian, if lax. Dominicans served in Haiti's army and some prominent local citizens even served as senators for the eastern *départements* (provinces). The political honeymoon did not last long, though. Boyer's ineffectual rule extended over a long period of gradual economic decline. In order to obtain diplomatic recognition from France, Haiti agreed to pay a large indemnity for damages caused by the revolution. This debt became a heavy burden on Haiti's treasury and a major element in its long-term economic woes. Economic malaise, coupled with cultural differences, further complicate things. The Dominican people—even two decades after the annexation—still saw themselves as fundamentally different from the Haitians and the latter still referred to them as "Spaniards." Dominicans still communicated in Spanish, attended Catholic services, and persisted in their local customs as usual. Thus, irreconcilable cultural differences still existed as late as the early 1840s. The following document is Boyer's 1822 proclamation to the (Haitian) people, in which he addresses the people of the East and welcomes them into the Haitian nation.

Liberty   *Equality*

REPUBLIC OF HAITI—PROCLAMATION TO THE PEOPLE.
JEAN-PIERRE BOYER, PRESIDENT OF HAITI.[24]

Haitians—The national flag flies over all points of the Island we inhabit! On this soil of liberty there are no more slaves, and we are but one family, whose members are united among themselves forever by a unanimous will which stems from the concordance of the same interests; and thereby articles 40 and 41 of our Constitution are fully implemented.

The reunion of the children of Haiti, begun to develop in a definitive way three years ago and concluded by my entry into Santo Domingo, has not cost tears to anyone. Who may disregard, in this fortunate revolution, the power of God that determines the destinies of the people? After having being separated, I mean, opposed to each other by the policies of the enemies of our rights, after many years of intense pain and wars, his hand unites us and pours on our hearts the healthy balsam of friendship and harmony. Let us give him thanks, my fellow citizens, for the singular protection that he has not ceased to dispense us, and let us make ourselves increasingly worthy of so many benefits for our fidelity to the oath that we have taken of always living united, free, and independent.

But in order to make the labor of our reunion durable and to consolidate the independence of our country, it is necessary to learn from the lessons of past experience

24. Translated from Charles Mackenzie, *Notes on Haiti: Made during a Residence in that Republic* (London: Henry Colburn and Richard Bentley, 1830), vol. 2, 241–244.

that will teach you to avoid the obstacles that were only surpassed by valor and heroic sacrifices; conscious in twenty-five years of vicissitudes that it is the private and
public virtues of the good citizen, of the zealous patriot that form the foundation of
the building you have raised to guarantee the existence of your posterity and you
must conserve without alterations; that your love for the Republic, your respect for
laws, your obedience toward the magistrates, who are its organs, constantly become
the triumphant response in opposition to the sophisms of our detractors, and the justification of the philanthropists who have defended and still defend our cause.

Owners of a soil with amazing fertility, your agricultural industry, as it receives
the impetus it needs, will open vast channels to the speculations of foreign trade, will
guarantee lucrative results, and will increase in this way your resources, as well as
the profits of the nations that have requested and established relations with us: to that
[nation] which knows best how to pay homage to our principles, we will concede, by
natural inclination, access to our consumption with more amplitude, and to purchase
the largest share of the rich production of our territory.

Citizens, you who were the first columns with which the immortal Pétion[25] built
the Republic, consider now the immense distance that you have traveled since the day
when you, renouncing to foreign domination, determined not to suffer it anymore,
until today. Contemplate without pride the triumph of your efforts and your perseverance: you were always docile to the voice of your leader and ready to sacrifice
your all for the homeland; keep on making yourselves worthy of what you have been.

And you, citizens of the eastern part, you have been unfortunate for a long time:
arbitrary and prohibitive laws have forced you to live with privations and in a state
of torpor; against all you had combated to recover your rights; but those in charge of
leading you put you again under the dependency of the metropolis, which had
expelled you from its heart by trafficking with your submission. Finally you have
moved spontaneously, you wanted to be free and Haitians like us, and you have
achieved it. Thus forget your former condition, think only but about the one which
you are going to enjoy; open your hearts to happiness; your trust on the Government
will not be betrayed; it will heal the deep wounds an anti-liberal system has formed
in you: that from now on no dark clouds will obscure the beautiful days that will
illuminate our homeland.

Haitians, in vain did our enemies try to alarm foreign powers about the reunion of
all of our territory! The principles established by articles 40 and 41 of our Constitution, which give us the ocean as limits, are as generally known as those designated in
article 5 of the same document, and by which we have bound ourselves never to carry
out an enterprise aimed at disturbing our neighbors' peace.

A farming and warring people, the Haitians will only occupy themselves with the
interests of the homeland; they will not use their arms except to defend their national independence, if the injustice of an attack against it should occur; always generous, always compassionate, they will continue to act in good faith with the foreigners who living among them respect the country's laws.

My destiny was, without a doubt, being the instrument used by Divinity to make

25. Alexandre Pétion, president of Haiti (1807–1818) and Boyer's mentor.

our sacred cause triumphant: only to its protection do I attribute the events that have accompanied my administration, since the reigns of State were placed in my hands. In doing whatever has depended on my person, I have constantly sought to be worthy of it; my days will in equal measure be dedicated to religiously fulfilling the obligations that the glory and prosperity of Haiti impose on me. I have the right to count on the cooperation of all my fellow citizens and I will count on it to elevate the nation to the rank it must occupy in the civilized world.

Long Live the Independence! Long Live Liberty! Long Live the Republic!
Boyer.
By order of the President the Secretary General,
B. Inginac.
Given in the national Palace of Santo Domingo on the ninth of February 1822. Year 19 of the Independence of Haiti.

CHAPTER THREE

Endangered Independence

The acquisition of Dominican independence was far easier done than maintained. After the declaration of independence on February 27, 1844 —which took the Haitian garrison in Santo Domingo by surprise—the Dominican people had to fight bloody, protracted wars against invading Haitian armies. The fear of a Haitian invasion, plus the lack of a democratic political culture, created a fertile ground for authoritarian regimes. Thus, the Dominican Republic, not unlike its sister republics in Latin America, came under control of a long succession of military caudillos. Some, like Pedro Santana and Buenaventura Báez, became archenemies who agreed on one vital issue: the need to seek the protection of a foreign power through protectorate agreements or outright annexation. This anti-national mentality led to such ill-fated attempts as the establishment of a third Spanish colonial administration in Santo Domingo, and later attempts to annex the country to the United States. Even the failure of these schemes did not deter the ambition of other nineteenth-century caudillos who, like Ulises Heureaux, mortgaged the country's future to foreign interests.

The nineteenth century was also a period of intense economic changes for the Dominican people. The semi-feudal cattle ranching economy gave way to a dynamic agro-exporting economy, characterized by tobacco production in the central Cibao region and sugar plantations in the East. These new economic activities would further immerse the country, and even ordinary Dominicans, into the global capitalist system, bringing in an increase in trade and new products, ideas, and people. Railroad building was hailed as a sign of progress. People marveled at the variety of products created by the industrial revolution, now available in the Dominican Republic. On the other hand, these economic changes were uneven and unequal, and they framed the country's progress on a dependent development mode. The main agricultural products were to be exported in order to gather the necessary hard currency to purchase much-needed manufactured imports. Moreover, many of these new industries—particularly sugar—were in the hands of foreigners, and eventually, powerful, faceless multinational corporations. Dominican governments would become extremely pliable to foreign interests, which bankrolled their administrations through loans, credits, and opportunities for graft. The nineteenth century finally ended for the Dominican people as it had begun—in bloodshed. In 1899, dictator Ulises Heureaux was assassinated and once again the country was engulfed in caudillo infighting.

A Declaration of Independence

The Haitian annexation of Santo Domingo (1822–1844) failed in the vital task of establishing one nation with one culture. After two decades of political incorporation into Haiti, the Dominican people felt—and were treated—as fundamentally different from the Haitians. Sporadic conspiracies developed during this period, but all were crushed by the authorities—often with local support. In the late 1830s, Juan Pablo Duarte, the son of a well-to-do family of Spanish origin who was educated in Spain, decided to organize a conspiratorial movement to topple the Haitian government and declare the independence of a country to be know as the Dominican Republic. His group, "La Trinitaria" (from the Holy Trinity), began as a small, mostly upper-class conspiracy made up of young men from prominent families. Over the years the movement expanded, bringing in individuals from other classes and racial strata. The Trinitarios took advantage of Haiti's political crisis in 1843—when Jean-Pierre Boyer was overthrown by the "Reform" movement—to further enlarge their conspiratorial activities. Although the Haitian government eventually persecuted the conspirators, forcing Duarte to go into exile and others to go underground, the Trinitarios had firmly established a plan for freeing the country.

This manifesto or declaration of principles issued by the Trinitarios and their allies on January 16, 1844, is the Dominican Republic's equivalent of a declaration of independence. Unfortunately, although it was the Trinitarios' hard and patient conspiratorial work that led to the country's independence, they were quickly ousted from the nation's administration by more conservative and authoritarian sectors, whose help the Trinitarios had originally enlisted in order to broaden the base of the pro-independence struggle.

MANIFESTATION OF THE COMMUNITIES ON THE EASTERN PART
OF THE ISLAND, FORMERLY KNOWN AS SPANISH SANTO DOMINGO,
CONCERNING THE CLAUSES OF ITS SEPARATION
FROM THE HAITIAN REPUBLIC.[1]

Sixteenth of January 1844
The respect, decency, and attention that is owed to the opinion of all men and to the civilized nations demand that when a group of people that has been joined to another decides to resume its rights, vindicate them, and dissolve its political ties, it shall frankly declare and with good will so as not to give rise to the belief that its cause is either ambition or the spirit of novelty. We believe to have demonstrated, with heroic constancy, that the ills of a government should be suffered as long as they are bearable. But when a long series of injustices, violations and humiliations, continuing to the same end, denote the design of reducing everything to despotism and to the most absolute tyranny, rather than seeking justice in abolishing the forms, it is up to the most sacred right of the people, and its obligation, to shake the yoke of such government and to provide new guarantees, assuring its future stability and prosperity. Because, gathered together, men in society with the sole purpose of conspiring for their conservation, which is the supreme law, receive from nature the right to propose and solicit the means to attain it; and for the same reason, such principles authorize them to guard themselves from whatever may deprive them of that right,

---

1. Translated from Javier Malagón, ed., *Las actas de independencia de América*, 2nd edition. (Washington, D. C.: Organization of America States, 1973), 126–128.

81

after society finds itself threatened.

This is why the communities of the eastern part of the island, formerly known as Hispaniola, or of Santo Domingo, using their own [right], goaded by twenty-two years of oppression, and hearing from everywhere the clamors of the Homeland, have taken the firm resolution to separate themselves from the Republic of Haiti forever, and constitute themselves as a free and sovereign state.

It has been twenty-two years since the Dominican People, due to one of those fatalities of chance, have been suffering the most ignominious oppression . . . whether it was that their downfall depended on the ignorance of their true national interest, or whether they allowed themselves to be swept by the torrent of individual passions, the fact is that a heavier and more degrading yoke than that of its ancient Metropolis was imposed upon the Dominican people. It has been twenty-two years since Dominicans and their towns have been deprived by violent measures of all their rights as well as those benefits to which they were entitled, if they were considered as aggregated parts of a Republic. And little was needed to make them lose their desire to free themselves from such humiliating slavery!!!

When in February 1822, the eastern part of the Island, ceding only to the force of circumstance, did not refuse to receive the army of General Boyer, who as a friend overran the boundaries of one place after another, the Dominican Spaniards did not believe that, with disguised perfidy, he would not keep the promises that had served him as an excuse to occupy the towns, and without which he would have had to overcome immense difficulties and maybe walk over our dead bodies if luck had favored them.

All Dominicans received Boyer then with open arms and a desire to demonstrate favor to the citizens of their neighbors: the simplest class of the towns he was occupying came out to meet him, believing to find in the one who had just received in the north the title of Peacemaker, the protection that so hypocritically he had promised. But soon, through the disguise that hid his sinister visions, everyone noticed that they were in the hands of an oppressor, of a tyrannical beast!

Upon entering the city of Santo Domingo, the disorders and the vices entered in a rush with him! Perfidy, divisions, defamations, violence, denunciations, usurpations, hate, and individualism up to then uncommon among those innocent peoples. His decrees and dispositions were the beginning of discord and the signal of destruction. By means of his disorganizing and Machiavellian system, he forced the most prominent and wealthiest families to emigrate, and with them the talents, richness, the commerce and agriculture, and the primary sources of jobs for our people. He sent away from their counsel and from their organizations and everyday life all the men he thought might organize and represent the people and the rights of all men. He reduced the families to poverty, taking away their properties and possessions in order to use them as a way to control the Republic, and in order to make single individuals of the western part become powerful and rich, or to sell them at negligible prices. He devastated the countryside, destroyed the agriculture, and trade, dispossessed churches of their riches, outraged and roughened with vilification the ministers of religion, he took away their rents and rights and because of his abandonment, he let public buildings fall into total disrepair, so that his functionaries would take advantage of the spoils and in that way satisfied the avarice that they brought with them from the west.

Later on, to give his injustices the appearance of legitimacy, he dictated a law, transferring the property of the absentees, whose brothers and immediate relatives were still alive and immersed in misery, to the State. His avarice still not satisfied, he seized the properties of the sons of the east with a sacrilegious hand; he authorized theft and fraud by the law of the eighth of July 1824; he prohibited tenure of common lands which, by virtue of agreements and for the utility and necessity of the families, had been conserved since the discovery of the Island, to take advantage of them in favor of his State, to finish ruining the raising of animals and to impoverish a multitude of heads of households. Little did it matter to him! To destroy everything, to ruin it! This was the objective of his insatiable avarice!

[. . .]

Our persecuted and violated Homeland could only find refuge from the fury of the tyranny in the arms of an afflicted and strong group of young people who, with a pure soul and a sincere desire, knew that, in order to succeed, they had to hide their sacrosanct principles from the oppressors in order to carry out their propaganda in a more appropriate time so that they could animate the struggle among those who felt without energy.

[. . .]

This was the sad picture of this part, when on the twenty-seventh of January of last year, the cry of reform was raised in Les Cayes[2] in the South of the Island. With the speed of light, the towns ignited; they adhered to the principles of a manifest on the 1st of September 1842, and the Eastern part flattered itself, but in vain!, of a happier future. To such an extent did their goodwill go! Commander Rivier proclaimed himself Chief of Execution, interpreter of the sovereign people's will. He dictated laws at will. He established a government without any legal from, without counting for it, with any of the inhabitants of this part, which had already pronounced itself in favor of his revolution; he toured the Island, and in the department of Santiago, without legal basis, he brought back with sorrow the memory of the sad times of Toussaint and Dessalines by bringing with him a monstrous general staff, which demoralized [the people] everywhere; he sold positions, dispossessed the churches; he destroyed the elections that the towns had organized to give themselves representatives who would defend their rights, and this was to leave this part always in misery and in the same fortuity and to provide himself with candidates who would elevate him to the Presidency without the special mandate of his constituents; and that is how it was, he threatened the constituent assembly and through strange communications made by him to the army under his command, he became President of the Republic.

[. . .]

Our condition has not experienced any changes. The same abuses, the same treatment of the prior administration, the same or greater taxes, the same monetary system without any guarantees that fosters the ruin of the people and a petty Constitution that will never achieve the country's happiness, has put the seal on the ignominy, depriving us against natural rights, even of the only Spanish thing that remained in us: the native tongue!, and throwing aside our solemn religion, so that it will disap-

---

2. town on Haiti's southern coast

pear from within us: because if that State religion, when it was protected, its ministers and itself, were despised and vilified, what would not it be now surrounded by sectarians and enemies?

The violations of our rights, customs, and privileges, and the many humiliations we have experienced have awakened us. We are now in a position of self-realization. We have come to realize that we are servants and we have decided to put an end to it, and to fight for our Fatherland, defending the matters that favor the well-being of our people and of our nations, as it was decided in favor of the Low Countries against Philip II in 1581. Under the authority of these principles, who would dare vituperate the resolution of the people of Les Cayes, when it raised itself against Boyer and declared him a traitor to the Homeland?

[. . .]

If the Eastern part had considered itself, voluntarily, incorporated into the Republic of Haiti, it should have enjoyed the same benefits as those with whom it had united; and if, by virtue of that union, we were obliged to sustain its integrity, it [Haiti] should have been obliged, on the other hand, to give us the means to comply with it; it failed on that by violating our rights, we [failed] to the obligation. If it [the eastern part] considered itself subject to the Republic, then even more so should it have enjoyed, without restrictions, all the rights and prerogatives that had been agreed on or promised to it, and lacking the sole and necessary condition of its subjugation, it becomes free from any obligation or duties toward itself, but obliged to provide for its own conservation by other means.

If we paused to reflect on the Haitian Constitution, we would see that more than the originality of the case of giving to an alien country a bastard Constitution, which was neither needed nor given a chance to be discussed among its local Deputies, there is also a usurpation, and a very scandalous one. The Haitians have never been in possession of this part of the island. Not when the French were expelled from the French part, nor later or before. The French could never give them this one [the Spanish part], because it was not theirs. By the Treaty of Basel, this part was ceded to France, and afterwards, reinstated or returned to Spain by the Peace of Paris. Then the Spaniards re-occupied this part in 1809, an act that lasted until the thirtieth of November 1821, when the eastern part was separated from the metropolis.

When the children of the west revised the Constitution in 1816, this part belonged neither to Haiti nor to France. The Spanish flag fluttered above its fortress by virtue of a perfect right; and that the Island of Santo Domingo was called by its locals, Haiti, it does not follow, that the western part that first constituted itself as a sovereign state giving itself the name of Republic of Haiti, referred to the eastern part, as an integral part of it, when the former belonged to the French and the latter to the Spanish. Very true is that if the eastern part belongs to any domination other than that of its own children, it would be to France or Spain, and not Haiti, because the easterners have more rights to dominate the westerners, than the other way around, if we go back to the early years of the discovery of the immortal Columbus.

Consequently, considering the established supposition, there is a usurpation that does not legitimize rights to anyone in a case like ours. If finally this part is considered as a conquest by force, then force will decide the matter, if necessary. Thus, considering that the humiliations and aggressions committed for twenty-two years against the Spanish part have reduced it to the greatest misery and completed its ruin, that the duty of its own conservation and of its future welfare oblige it to provide for its security by convenient means, being rightful: that a community that has voluntarily constituted itself as dependent on another, with the end of attaining its protection, is liberated from its obligations, at the moment when it lacks this, even if impossible [to gain] from the protector. Considering that a people that is forced to obey and does obey, does good, and that later on when it can resist and resists, does better. Considering, lastly, that because of the difference in customs and the rivalry that exists between one and the other, there will never be a perfect union nor harmony: The communities of the former Spanish part of the Island of Santo Domingo, satisfied that in twenty-two years of annexation to the Republic of Haiti, they have not been able to gain any advantages; quite to the contrary, they have been ruined, impoverished, and degraded, and they have been treated in the lowest and most contemptible way. They have resolved to separate forever from the Republic of Haiti, to provide for their security and conservation, by constituting themselves under their former limits into a free and sovereign state, in which, and under whose fundamental laws, it will protect and guarantee the democratic system; the freedom of its citizens abolishing slavery forever; the equality of civil and political rights without minding to distinctions neither of origin nor of birth; properties will be inviolable and sacred; the Roman Catholic and Apostolic Religion will be protected in all its splendor as the state's, but no one will be persecuted or punished for his religious beliefs; freedom of the press will be protected; the responsibility of public functionaries will be assured; there will be no confiscations of possessions due to crimes or offenses; public education will be promoted and protected at the state's expense; taxes will be reduced to the minimum possible; there will be a total forgiveness for loyalties and political opinions emitted to this date, so that individuals will adhere in good faith to the new system. Military ranks and jobs will be maintained under the rules to be established. Agriculture, commerce, the sciences, and the arts will be equally promoted and protected, as well as the status of those persons born on our soil, or that of the foreigners who come to live on it in accordance with the law. Finally, we will issue, as soon as possible, a currency with a real and true guarantee, without the public losing the one with Haiti's seal.

This is the goal we intend [to pursue] with our separation and we have resolved to show the entire world the spectacle of a people that will sacrifice itself in defense of its rights and will reduce itself to ashes and debris, if its suppressors, who pride themselves on being free and civilized, want to impose upon us conditions harsher than death. If against reason and justice they want us to transmit to our children and to posterity a shameful slavery then, facing all dangers with a persevering firmness, we solemnly swear before God and all men that we will employ our arms in defense of our freedom and of our rights, trusting in the mercy of the Omnipotent who will happily protect us, turning our contraries to bow to a just and rational reconciliation, avoiding the shedding of blood and the calamities of a horrible war that we will not provoke, but that will become one of extermination if needed.

Dominicans! (Comprised under this name all the children of the eastern part and those who wish to follow our destiny). The national interest calls us to union! By a firm resolution let us show ourselves as the honorable defenders of liberty: let us sacrifice before the altar of the Homeland the hatred and the individualism that the sentiments of public interest be the motive that decide us for the just cause of freedom and of *Separation*; with it, we do not diminish the happiness of the Eastern Republic, and we forge ours.

Our cause is holy; resources we do not lack, besides those that we have in our own soil, because, if necessary, we will employ them in case foreigners [investors] will aid us. Dividing the territory of the Dominican Republic into four provinces, namely: Santo Domingo, Santiago or Cibao, Azua from the border to Ocoa, and Seibo, the Government will be composed of a certain number of members from each of these so that they will proportionately participate in their sovereignty.

The Provisional Government will be composed of a Junta of eleven members elected in the same order. This Junta will summarize in itself all the powers until the Constitution of the State is formed, and it will determine the means that it deems most convenient, to maintain the acquired freedom, and finally will appoint one of the most distinguished patriots to the supreme command of the army, which must protect our borders adding to it the subordinates that are needed, etc.

Dominicans Unite! The opportune moment is presented to us from Neiba to Samaná, from Azua to Monte Cristi, opinions are in agreement and there is no Dominican who does not exclaim with enthusiasm: Separation, God, Country, and Liberty.

Santo Domingo, sixteenth of January 1844, and first year of the Homeland.

Tomás Bobadilla, M. R. Mella, F. Sánchez, M. Jimenes, Feliz Mercenario, José M. Perez Jr., Juan Arriaga, Carlos Moreno, Ldo. Valverde, Pedro Bonilla, P. de Castro y Castro, Manuel Cabral, Silvano Puyol, José M. Caminero, Mariano Echavarría, Ramon Echavarría, Angel Perdomo, Bernardo Santin, Juan Santin, Pedro Mena, Juan Ruiz, F. Sosa, Manuel Guerrero, W. Guerrero, Tomás Concha, Jacinto Concha, J. N. Ravelo, P. Valverde, Joaquín Puello, Gavino Puello, W. Concha, J. de la Cruz García, J. Pichardo, Pablo Pichardo, Gabriel J. de Luna, Luis Betances, Joaquín Lluveres, Domingo Rodríguez, C. Rodríguez, J. G. Brea, Jacinto Brea, Antonio Brea, Juan Pina, M. Leguisamon, Narciso Sánchez, Antonio Volta, Ignacio Padua, Pedro M. Mena, M. Aybar, José Piñeyro, Ramón Alonso, Hipólito Billin, E. Billin, José Billin, Fermín González, P. A. Bobea, Felipe Alfau, A. Alfau, Julián Alfau, D. Rocha, Nicolás Henriquez, Francisco Contino, Tomás Troncoso, Benito Peres, Nicomedo Peres, Francisco Santelis, Santiago Barriento, Juan Barriento, Manuel Antonio Rosas, Ramón González, Juan Alvares, Félix María Ruiz, José María Leyba, José María Serra, Fernando Serra, Fernando Herrera, Ignacio Bona, Carlos Gatón, Víctor Herrera, Emeterio Arredondo, Carlos Castillo, Joaquín Gómez, Gregorio Coatiu, Leonardo Contín, José María Silberio, Gregorio Ramires, Carlos García, Manuel Franco, Manuel María Bello, Narciso Carbonell, Manuel Galván, Emil Palmantier, José Ramón Alvares, Diego Hernandes, José María García, Ramón Ocumares, Antonio Moreno, Alejandro Bonilla, Juan Francisco María Acevedo, Teodoro Acosta, Edoit Lagard, Blas Ballejo, Ysidro Abreu, Juan Vicioso, Justiniano Bobea, Nicolás Lugo, Pedro Díaz, Marcos Rojas, Eusebio Puello, Rafael Rodríguez, Román Bidor, Juan Luis Bidor, Miguel Rojas, Jacinto Fabelo, Manuel Castillo, Ildefonso Mella, Juan Puvbert, Manuel Morillo, Juan Ariza, Pedro Pérez, José Valverde, Baltazar

Paulino, José Peña, José Nazario Brea, Toribio Villanueva Villanueva Padre, Narciso Castillo, Eusebio Pereyra, Juan Alvares, Esteban Roca, Nolasco Brea, Lorenzo Mañón, Manuel de Regla Mota, José Heredia, Francisco Soñé, Damián Ortis, Valentín Sánchez, Pedro Herrera, Rosendo Herrera, Narciso Ramires Peralta, Pedro Santana, Norverto Linares, Ramón Santana, Juan Contrera, Pedro Brea, Tito del Castillo, Bernabé Sandoval, Juan Rodríguez Pacheco, Jacinto de Castro, José Joaquín Bernal, José del Carmen García, Domingo Báez, Francisco Romero, P. Serón.

Santo Domingo, National Printing Office

Spanish Colony for a Third Time

On the night of February 27, 1844, a group of rebels declared the independence of the Dominican Republic and surrounded the Haitian garrison in Santo Domingo. Taken by surprise, the Haitians surrendered the next morning. The Dominican Republic was born. Independence had been achieved quite easily; its maintenance would prove to be a far more difficult task. Almost from the beginning, the country was beset by two significant issues: Haiti's attempts to recover its erstwhile provinces and the deep rifts between the country's political elites; military might eventually triumphed over ideals, and Juan Pablo Duarte and his liberal followers were displaced by conservative forces led by General Pedro Santana. The latter became a brilliant military commander, saving the young republic from annihilation by the far more powerful Haitian armies on more than one occasion. The Haitian-Dominican wars were brutal, bloody campaigns in which often nothing more than luck and valor seems to have saved the outnumbered Dominican armies. Santana then used his military power and his popularity as the nation's savior to entrench himself in power and rule as a despot. As such, Dominican independence came at a very heavy price.

Santana, like many other members of the Dominican upper classes, did not believe in the nation's viability as a sovereign entity. In spite of the success of Dominican arms in keeping the Haitian armies at bay, many upperclass Dominicans believed that the Dominican people could only be saved from re-annexation by Haiti under the protection of a foreign power. Moreover, these elites saw foreign powers as agents of civilization, who could contribute greatly toward uplifting the Dominican people in economic, cultural, and even racial terms. Santana, who initially had supported annexation to the United States, inclined toward Spain by the late 1850s. He forced the Spanish colonial status on the Dominican people, for which he was well rewarded by the Spanish Crown.

This is Santana's official proclamation, dated March 18, 1861, to the Dominican people of their new colonial status. The Dominican Republic lasted only seventeen years.

SANTANA'S PROCLAMATION OF MARCH 18, 1861[3]

Dominicans! It has not been many years since my voice, when presenting to you the reform of our political constitution, always loyal and always consequential, reminded you of our national glories, inherited from the grand and noble race to which we owe our origin.

When I made such a lively manifestation of my emotions at that time, I believed to have interpreted your desires in a faithful manner, and know now that I was not mistaken. My behavior has been forever marked; but yours has surpassed my hopes.

Numerous, and spontaneous, popular manifestations have come to my attention; and if yesterday you had invested me with extraordinary powers, today your wish, driven by your loyal desires, becomes a reality.

We still conserve with purity the religion, language, beliefs, and customs notwithstanding those who have tried to seize from us such precious gifts, and the nation that has bequeathed to us so much, is the same one that today has opened its arms to us like a loving mother who recovers her son she thought lost in the shipwreck in which his brothers perished.

Dominicans! Only the ambition and the resentment of a man separated us from the motherland; days later, the Haitians dominated our territory; our valor has expelled them. The years that have passed since then have been very eloquent for all!

Will we permit the loss of the elements on which we count on nowadays, so dear for us, but not as strong as to secure our future and that of our children?

Before that occurs, before we find ourselves, like those other unfortunate republics, continuously embroiled in civil wars, sacrificing in their course valiant generals, statesmen, large families, considerable fortunes, and a multitude of miserable citizens, without finding some way of constituting themselves soundly and strongly; before a similar day arrives, I, who always watched over your security; I, who, helped by your valor, defended inch by inch the soil that we step on; I, who know the urgency of your needs, see what I show you in the Spanish nation, see what it concedes us.

It gives us the civil liberty that its towns enjoy, it guarantees us natural liberty, and forever removes the possibility of losing it; it assures us our properties, recognizing as valid all the acts of the Republic; it offers to consider and reward merit, and it will keep in mind all the services rendered to the nation; finally, it brings peace to this embattled land, and with peace its beneficial consequences.

---

3. Translated from Gregorio Luperón, *Notas autobiográficas y apuntes históricos*, 2nd edition. (Santiago: Editorial El Diario, 1939), vol. 1, 49–51.

Yes, Dominicans, as of today, you shall rest from the fatigue of war, and you shall occupy yourselves with ceaseless eagerness in forging the future of your children.

Spain protects us, its flag covers us, its weapons will defeat foreigners; it recognizes our liberties and together, we will defend them, becoming just one people, just one family, as we always were. Together we will kneel before the altars that this very nation built, before those altars it will find today as it left them, unscathed, and still crowned with its coat of arms, its castles and lions, the first banner that Columbus planted next to the cross in these unknown lands in the name of Isabel I, the grand, the noble, the Catholic; a noble name that, when inherited by the current sovereign of Castile, inherited her love for the settlers of Hispaniola. Let us raise the flag of her monarchy and proclaim her as our queen and sovereign!

Long live Doña Isabel II! Long Live Liberty! Long Live Religion! Long Live the Dominican people! Long Live the Spanish Nation!

Pedro Santana

The Restoration of the Republic

Pedro Santana's treacherous move did not go unchallenged. Right from the annexation proclamation, the political opposition to Santana saw a new opportunity to challenge the caudillo. Annexing the Dominican Republic to Spain certainly created many new enemies for Santana, and they, in turn, organized several attempts to restore the nation's sovereignty. For example, former Trinitario and revered patriot Francisco Sánchez rebelled against Santana's plan. He was captured near San Juan de la Maguana in July of 1861 and executed, creating a powerful symbol of martyrdom for the cause of independence. But it was not until August 16, 1863, when a broad-based movement arose to seriously challenge the status quo. On that day, a Dominican military force crossed the border from Haiti into Dominican territory and declared the restoration of the country's sovereignty. Haiti had vehemently opposed Spain's annexation of the Dominican Republic, as it feared Spain's power next door and the potential restoration of slavery in its new colony. Therefore, in a complete reversal of previous policies, Haiti became an ardent defender of Dominican independence and provided refuge, funds, supplies, and weapons to the Dominican rebels.

After weeks of bloody fighting, the Dominican rebels were able to capture Santiago de los Caballeros, the country's second largest city and unofficial capital of the Cibao region. There, the rebels organized a provisional government in "liberated" Dominican territory and issued the independence act reproduced below.

ACT OF INDEPENDENCE OF THE RESTORATION[4]

We, the inhabitants of the Spanish part of the Island of Santo Domingo, manifest by means of the current Independence Act, before God, the entire world and the Spanish throne, the just and legal motives that have forced us to take up arms to restore the Dominican Republic and re-conquer our freedom, the first, the most precious of the rights with which man was favored by the Supreme Maker of the Universe, justifying in this way our determined conduct and our indispensable actions, since other soft and persuasive means, one of them very eloquent, our unhappiness, opportunely employed, have not been enough to persuade the Throne of Castile: that our annexation to the Crown was not the result of our spontaneous will, but of the treacherous fancy of general Pedro Santana and his followers, who, in the desperation of their inevitable fall from power, took on the desperate plan of relinquishing the Republic, a deed of great and bloody sacrifices, under the pretext of annexation to the power of Spain, allowing the crossed flag,[5] raised at the cost of the blood of the Dominican people and with a thousand gallows of dreary memories, to descend.

However magnanimous the intentions and reception of Her Highness Queen Doña Isabel II (may God save Her) regarding the Dominican people had been, when crossing the Atlantic to be implemented by her subaltern rulers, they have transformed in barbaric and tyrannical measures that these people cannot nor should not endure. As proof, it is enough to say that we have been governed by a Buceta and a Campillo, whose deeds are quite notorious. The annexation of the Dominican Republic to the Spanish Crown has been the will of one man who has subdued it; our most sacred rights, conquered in eighteen years of immense sacrifices, have been betrayed and sold; the cabinet of the Spanish nation has been deceived, and so have been many Dominicans of value and influence, with promises that were not kept, with offers later retracted.

Pronouncements, manifestations of towns, extracted by coercion, sometimes moral, sometimes physical by our oppressor and the henchmen who surrounded him, remitted to the Spanish government, made it falsely believe in our spontaneity of seeking annexation; however very soon, convinced of the deception and perfidy, the towns raised their heads and started making glorious efforts, though unfortunately useless, when they awoke from the surprise that such a monstrous act caused on them, to recover their lost independence, their stupefied freedom. If not, ask the victims of Moca, San Juan, Las Matas, El Cercado, Santiago, Guayubín, Montecristi, Sabaneta and Puerto Plata. And how has Spain exercised the control that it improperly acquired over a free people? Oppression of all sorts, restrictions and the imposition of unknown and unwarranted taxes, were later put in place. Has it observed, by

---

4. Translated from Emilio Rodríguez Demorizi, *Actos y doctrina del Gobierno de la Restauración* (Santo Domingo: Editora del Caribe, 1963), 23–28.

5. Refers to the white cross in the center of the Dominican flag.

any chance, with a people that grudgingly submitted to it, the laws of cultured and civilized nations, keeping and respecting, as it should, the conveniences, the customs, the character and the natural rights of every man in society? Far from it, the habits, the customs of a people, free for many years, have been upset, not with a life-giving and enlightening light, but with a burning and exterminating fire.

Derision, disdain, marked arrogance, persecutions, and unwarranted and scandalous gallows are the only results we obtained, as lambs of the subalterns of the Spanish throne into whose hands our fate was entrusted. The burning, the devastation of our towns, the wives without their husbands, the children without their parents, the loss of all our interests and the misery, all in all, here are the hazards we have obtained from our forced and false annexation to the Spanish throne. We have lost everything, but we still have our Independence and Freedom, for which we are willing to shed our last drop of blood. If the Spanish government is politically savvy, if it consults its interests, and also ours, it will persuade itself that it is not possible to subdue a people that for some time has tasted and enjoyed its freedom without the extermination of the last one of their men. The August Sovereign Doña Isabel II, whose noble soul we know, and whose philanthropic feelings we share and respect, must persuade herself of that; but Her Majesty has been deceived by the perfidy of the one who was our President, General Pedro Santana, and that of his followers; whatever has had a vitiated origin cannot become valid with the passing of time.

Here are the *legal reasons* and the very just motives that have forced us to take up arms and defend ourselves, as we will always do, against the domination that oppresses us and that violates our sacrosanct rights, as well as the oppressing laws that should not have been imposed on us.

The Spanish government must also know them, respect them, and act accordingly.

Santiago, fourteenth of September 1863.

Signed: Benigno F. de Rojas, Gaspar Polanco, A. Deetjen, P. Pujols, José A. Salcedo, Benito Monción, Manuel Rodríguez, Pedro A. Pimentel, Juan A. Polanco, Gregorio Luperón, Genaro Perpiñán, Pedro Francisco Bonó, Máximo Grullón, J. Belisario Curiel, H. S. Riobé, Esteban Almánzar, Ulises Espaillat, C. Castellanos, Juan Valentín Curiel, F. Scherffmberg, Juan A. Vila, F. A. Bordas, J. Jiménez, A. Benes, Ramón Almonte, Manuel Ponce de León, F. Casado, J. E. Márquez, J. Alva, Dionisio Troncoso, R. Martínez, presbyter Miguel Quezada, L. Perelló, R. Velázquez, P. Pimentel, Gabino Crespo, J. A. Sánchez, M. de J. Jiménez, Rufino García, Juan Riva.

[More signatures follow. It is an exact copy.]

The main officer of the Commission of Foreign Relations, Francisco Du Breil.

The Restoration War

The Puerto Rican intellectual and long-time exile in the Dominican Republic Eugenio María de Hostos called the Restoration War (1863–1865) "the real war of independence of the Dominican people." Hostos was not only referring to the fact that in 1844 the Dominican people really *separated* from Haiti, breaking away from a twenty-two-year annexation, but also to the fact that while the 1844 coup was the result of a plan carried out by Dominican elites, the Restoration War was a struggle that cut across class and racial lines. Resistance to Santana's policies began almost immediately by a broad-based political opposition from various political sectors, geographical regions, and even clashing personalities who would fight together against a common enemy. The Dominican lower classes were from the start active participants in the war against the Spanish, whom they considered—after decades of separation from Spain—as foreign. Thus, very few Dominicans shared Santana's public view that Spain was the *Madre Patria* (Motherland) and fought bitterly and gallantly during two years for the restoration of the Republic.

Gregorio Luperón was one of the most distinguished heroes of the Restoration War. A black man of humble origins, Luperón quickly rose through the ranks to become the war's leading military figure, particularly after defeating Pedro Santana in battle. After the war, Luperón became one of the country's leading liberal politicians and a beloved figure. His autobiographical notes are an excellent source for understanding the popular nature of the Restoration War. In this selection, he examines the motives behind the war and the Spanish military leadership, particularly the figure of General José de la Gándara, whose wartime memoirs are another excellent source on the war.

FROM GREGORIO LUPERÓN'S AUTOBIOGRAPHICAL NOTES[6]

When he could not defeat the revolution by force nor demoralize it with his pernicious maneuvers, this General [La Gándara] resorted to the most ignominious and terrible intrigues to prolong the war and stain it with blood. And with his vain presumptions, he sparked new conflicts between Spain and Santo Domingo, making impossible any arrangements that would have avoided great ruins and many dis-

---

6. Translated from Gregorio Luperón, *Notas autobiográficas y apuntes históricos*, 2nd edition. (Santiago: Editorial El Diario, 1939), 332–337.

graces to both peoples. He assured that Santo Domingo kept the memories of his final wanton orders: anger and revenge among the parties. As a coward and evil [person], he fostered revenge worsening the travails of a ruined people, and making its political existence difficult and distressing.

General La Gándara, with senseless malice, proclaimed to the world that the Dominican Republic was a barbaric, selfish, and murderous country, that it was responsible for its own disgrace and for those that necessarily had to come, when he knew the authors of so many calamities and the unforgivable lack of foresight of O'Donnell and Serrano in accepting the annexation, hypocritically planned by General Santana and his party to seek revenge for their enemies' offenses and to serve their interests, for no other reason than the satisfaction of political passions. It was, therefore, natural that the consequence of so much clumsiness would be the abandonment of Santo Domingo. By destroying the artillery and taking the archives of Puerto Plata as well as many hostages, La Gándara wanted to defame the Dominican people because he resented [the fact] that Dominicans did not want to accept the humiliating conditions the Spanish general sought to impose on them, trying to blame on the patriots, with a noticeable lack of truth and justice, the responsibility for the fires of Guayubín, Barahona, Santiago, Moca, Puerto Plata, Baní and San Cristóbal, when with justice, the Dominican people defended their national independence, for which their sacrifices did not and could not have limits. He forgot that he had assumed the position of Lieutenant General of Santo Domingo on the thirty-first March 1864, and that on the nineteenth of April of the same year, he sent two columns: One from the Capital under the command of General Villar, and the other from Azua under the command of General Puello, to San Cristóbal, to burn and destroy the town and its countryside. This force, made up of four thousand men, carried out its horrible mission.

General La Gándara called the Dominican people ungrateful, because they did not want to be slaves under the Spanish colonial system, already condemned by the inflexible logic of history. He believed that with his government, we could promise ourselves days of placid fortune and of eternal bliss, with mandarins like him, like Buceta and Campillo.

General La Gándara seemed to ignore that this oppressive domination, with its worries, with a ruinous and depressive economic system for all the guilds and public interests, that terrorized all the inhabitants with old religious intolerance now vanishing in the crucible of experience, without a reasonable basis, without a free press or freedom of thought, was not a claim of sympathies in favor of Spanish domination. It was just a ghost collapsing due to its own weight. Because the milieu of the people is the law; and modern civilization consists of independence in all aspects. Just as there is no insect without protection from the earth, it is not fair for citizens to be without the right to be equal in the homeland, and before other nations.

In his book about the history of the war of Santo Domingo, after slandering the Dominican people so much, it seems that moved by some remorse, he says the following, which was the only truth stated by his venomous pen in that work.

The Dominican, though of admirable aptitude toward fatigue, for his strength, agility, and robustness, and although brave and skilled in the use of the machete, shined above all in personal combat, and that is why he was a terrible adversary, but since he lacked the qualities that discipline confers, since he lacked the soundness that unity confers and the faith that comrades in arms inspire, even though he may feel courageous, he did not know if his comrades were going to feel likewise at the same time in the precise occasion and to the degree required, he doubted, he hesitated and he got confused when he could not encompass with his own sight the total extension of the danger, the total field of the enemy's actions, in a word, he was a great soldier only when he could assure his own security.

This is true, because almost all of the disciplined military men were in the Spanish army, and the Dominican people's patriotism had to organize its heroic defense in the midst of the fighting, under bullets and shrapnel.

Generals Rivero and Vargas thought and wrote about the war very differently than General La Gándara. These noble and polite gentlemen, distinguished soldiers, able leaders, and farsighted politicians, who preceded General La Gándara in the command of Santo Domingo with unquestionable honesty and noticeable morality and who previously held the highest public positions in Spain had very advantageous conditions for the superior Government of the Spanish part of the island due to their good sense and maturity in public affairs; they wanted neither to deceive Spain, nor gamble with the misfortunes of the Dominican people, nor shed blood with injustice and against their conscience. Before they resigned the positions they occupied as captain generals, they declared, with much good sense and noble honesty, to their Government that the continuation of the war in Santo Domingo was unjust, because *the annexation was not the result of the will of the Dominican people, but the work and the desire of a party that imposed it through terror, and that, afraid of the future, negotiated it with exclusive advantages.* It was convenient for Spain's good name, for its proverbial nobility, to leave Santo Domingo in an amicable way, and to protect it, so that it would not fall into the hands of other conquering nations. Before the annexation could be consolidated, for which the country was not prepared, events came to efface that deceptive appearance called the people's will. That two revolutions flared one after the other, the first one was defeated; the second one extended throughout the entire territory, attracting the majority of Dominicans, which justifies that the Dominican people did not want the Spanish domination. This was the truth, and one cannot find a more noble or just language.

[. . .]

The Dominican people were proud of their own heroism, and they preferred to wallow in misery and die of hunger rather than be enslaved under any dominator. Fortunately, General Narváez not only had the good sense to avoid for Spain the grave hazards of continuing the war, but also the great ability of leaving to the main author of the annexation, General O'Donnell, who was his successor in the ministry, the obligation of carrying out the abandonment of Santo Domingo. This cabinet disapproved of the last unforeseen, wicked, anti-patriotic, and anti-political measures and proposals of General La Gándara on leaving Santo Domingo, and his threats of violence, disappeared like the delirium of a dream.

Statehood for the Dominican Republic

Although many thought that Santana's ill-fated annexation scheme had been the last time that Dominican national sovereignty was in peril, events soon proved that the dreams of annexation were still very much alive among Dominican elites. President-dictator Buenaventura Báez, who rivaled Santana in his thirst for power, produced an annexationist scheme of his own: to make of the Dominican Republic a state of the United States of America. Early in his career, Báez had been an *afrancesado*, a Francophile who sought a French protectorate in exchange for the Bay of Samaná. By the late 1860s, he had shifted his position to favor U.S. interests in the region. After sparking the interest of U.S. President Ulysses Grant in his project, Báez fabricated a plebiscite in which the Dominican people supposedly gave their overwhelming approval to his plan. Grant was surrounded and lobbied by speculators who wanted to invest in the Dominican Republic—investments that would dramatically rise in value after statehood, such as land for U.S. military bases. Báez, on the other hand, was in dire straits with the fully armed political opposition in rebellion and desperately strapped for cash. Statehood would have offered him protection by the U.S. forces and a US $1.5 million payment to settle the country's debts.

The statehood treaty, reproduced below, was signed on November 29, 1869 and debated in the U.S. Senate during the summer of 1870. On June 30, 1870, the treaty was rejected after a twenty-eight to twenty-eight tie, thus falling short of the required two-thirds of the votes. After the treaty's rejection, a lease for the bay and peninsula of Samaná was also entertained, but it was shelved without the U.S. Senate voting on it.

TREATY CELEBRATED BETWEEN THE UNITED STATES
OF AMERICA AND THE DOMINICAN REPUBLIC FOR THE
INCORPORATION OF THE SECOND WITH THE FIRST[7]

The people of the Dominican Republic having, through their government, expressed their desire to be incorporated into the United States as one of the Territories thereof, in order to provide more effectually for their security and prosperity; and the

7. From U.S. Congress, Senate, *Senate Executive Documents, 1869–1871*, 41st Congress, 3rd session, 17 (January 16, 1871): 98–100.

United States being desirous of meeting the wishes of the people and the government of that republic, the high contracting parties have determined to accomplish by treaty an object so important to their mutual and permanent welfare.

For this purpose the President of the United States has given full powers to Mr. Raymond H. Perry, United States commercial agent in the city of Santo Domingo, in the Dominican Republic, and the president of the Dominican Republic has given powers to Mr. Manuel Maria Gautier, secretary of state for foreign affairs of the said Dominican Republic; and the said plenipotentiaries, after having communicated to each other their respective full powers, found in good and due form, have agreed upon and concluded the following articles:

ARTICLE I

The Dominican Republic, acting subject to the wishes of its people, to be expressed in the shortest possible time, renounces all rights of sovereignty as an independent sovereign nation, and cedes these rights to the United States to be incorporated by them as an integral portion of the Union, subject to the same constitutional provisions as their other Territories. It also cedes to the United States the absolute fee and property in all the custom-houses, fortifications, barracks, ports, harbors, navy and navy yards, magazines, arms, armaments, and accouterments, archives, and public documents of the said Dominican Republic, of which a schedule is annexed to this treaty; public lands and other property not specified excepted.

ARTICLE II

The citizens of the Dominican Republic shall be incorporated into the United States as citizens thereof, inhabiting one of its Territories, and shall be maintained and protected in the free enjoyment of their liberty and property as such citizens, and may be admitted into the Union as a State, upon such terms and conditions and at such time as Congress shall provide by law.

ARTICLE III

The public lands and property belonging to the Dominican Republic, not herein specifically ceded to the United States, are pledged to the payment of all the public debt, liquidated or unliquidated, which shall remain after the payment provided for in this treaty.

ARTICLE IV

The people of the Dominican Republic shall, in the shortest possible time, express in a manner conformable to their laws, their will concerning the cession herein provided for; and the United States shall, until such expression shall be had, protect the Dominican Republic against foreign interposition, in order that the national expression may be free.

ARTICLE V

The United States shall pay to the Dominican Republic, for the property hereby ceded, the sum of one million five hundred thousand dollars in the gold coin of the United States, such payment not to be made until the Senate of the United States shall have given its advice and consent to the making of this treaty, and an appropriation for the payment shall have been made by Congress, and until delivery of all the property ceded shall be made to the persons authorized to receive the same.

ARTICLE VI

The Dominican Republic engages to apply the amount so paid by the United States, through a commission to be appointed by the present actual Dominican government, toward the redemption of its public debt, in a manner conformable to the laws of said republic—this commission to be respected and protected by the United States while in the legal performance of its duties; and the said republic shall hold its public lands as a security for the payment of any part thereof, liquidated or unliquidated, which may remain unpaid after such application, and after the execution hereof to make no grants or concessions of lands or rights in lands and to contract no further debts until Congress shall assume jurisdiction over the Territory and officers shall be appointed to administer the affairs thereof. The United States are in no event to be liable for the payment of any part of such debt, or of the interest thereon, or of any obligation of the Dominican Republic.

ARTICLE VII

Until provision shall be made by law for the government, as a Territory of the United States, of the domain hereby ceded, the laws of the Dominican Republic, which are not in conflict with the Constitution and laws of the United States, shall remain in force, and the executive and other public officers of the republic shall retain their offices until Congress shall enact laws for the government of the Territory, and until persons shall be appointed to office pursuant thereto.

ARTICLE VIII

Immediately after the exchange of the ratifications of this treaty, the President of the United States shall appoint a commissioner to proceed to the Dominican Republic and receive the transfer of the domains and the property hereby ceded, subject to the foregoing provisions.

ARTICLE IX

The present treaty shall be ratified by the contracting parties, it being understood that it must receive the constitutional advice and consent of the Senate of the United States, before it can be ratified on the part of the United States, and the ratification shall be exchanged at Washington within four months from the date hereof, or sooner, if possible.

ARTICLE X

In case of the rejection of this treaty the United States of America shall have the right to acquire the Peninsula and Bay of Samaná at any time prior to the expiration of a period of fifty years by paying to the Dominican Republic the sum of two million dollars in the gold coin of the United States.

ARTICLE XI

It is understood that upon the ratification of this treaty the sum of one hundred and forty-seven thousand two hundred and twenty-nine dollars and ninety-one cents, paid by the United States to the Dominican Republic on account of the rent of Samaná, shall be deducted from the sum specified in Article V of this treaty.

In witness whereof, the respective plenipotentiaries have signed this treaty, and thereto affixed their respective seals.

Done in duplicate and good faith, in the English and Spanish languages, at the city of Santo Domingo, the twenty-ninth day of November, in the year of Our Lord one thousand eight hundred and sixty-nine.

[SEAL.] Raymond H. Perry

[SEAL.] Manuel Maria Gautier

Schedule of the property mentioned in Article 1, to wit:

The stronghold of the city of Santo Domingo, which comprehends its walls, sixteen forts and small redoubts, two heavy batteries, various quarters, two powder magazines, the fortress called Homenage, and a park of artillery, with a full armament of cannon and mortars, iron and brass; shells, grenades, grape, muskets, and various other utensils and instruments indispensable to a fortified place.

The Castle of San Jerónimo

The Castle of Jaina, on the river of that name

The Fort San Louis, at Santiago de los Caballeros

The Castle of San Felipe, at Puerto Plata

The Fort of San Francisco, at Monte Christi

The Fort of Santa Bárbara, at Samaná

The Fort of Los Cacaos, at the same place

The Custom-house at Santo Domingo and its dependencies

The Custom-house at Samaná, built of timber

The ports of Santo Domingo, Macoris, Azua, Samaná, Puerto Plata, and Monte Christi, are licensed for commerce with foreigners. There are, moreover, endless numbers of ports, bays, and coves which could be applied to similar use, especially Barahona, Puerto Viejo de Azua, La Caldera, La Romana, Chavón, Matanzas, and Manzanillo. Various other points intended for fortifications, military stations, which have either been removed or not yet been erected.

Witness the hands of the said plenipotentiaries, at the city of Santo Domingo, the twenty-ninth day of November, A.D. 1869.

Raymond H. Perry   Manuel Maria Gautier

CONVENTION CELEBRATED BETWEEN THE UNITED STATES OF AMERICA AND THE DOMINICAN REPUBLIC FOR A LEASE OF THE BAY AND PENINSULA OF SAMANÁ[8]

For this purpose the President of the United States has invested with full powers Mr. Raymond H. Perry, commercial agent of the United States to the Dominican Republic, and the President of the Dominican Republic has invested with full powers Mr. Manuel Maria Gautier, secretary of state of the Dominican Republic, who, after exchanging their said full powers, found in good and due form, have agreed upon, concluded, and signed the following articles:

ARTICLE I

The Dominican Republic grants immediate possession and occupation, in the form of a lease, to the United States of America, all the territory comprised in the peninsula and bay of Samaná, extending from Cape Samaná or Rezon to the R. Grand Estero, which begins at the mouth of the said Grand Estero on the north, and terminates at the mouth of the Trujillo, at the western end of the bay of Samaná, as appears on the map of the island of Santo Domingo, executed by Sir Robert H. Schomburg, and published in 1858 by order of his excellency President Buenaventura Báez.

The United States shall possess and occupy the above-described territory during a period of 50 years from this date, and the Dominican Republic cedes by this net to the United States the eminent domain of said territory during the above-described term of occupation.

It is understood that the Dominican Republic does not cede its right of free navigation of the waters of said bay.

ARTICLE II

During the above-named term of occupation of the said territory, the United States shall pay, as an annual rent, to the Dominican Republic, on the first day of January of each year, in Washington, D.C., or in the City of New York, the sum of one hundred and fifty thousand dollars in gold coin of the United States. The Dominican Republic hereby acknowledges to have received the sum of one hundred and forty-seven thousand two hundred and twenty-nine dollars and ninety-one cents on account of the first payment under this convention.

ARTICLE III

In case the United States shall establish a naval and military station, or either, on any part of the tract hereinabove described, the Dominican Republic shall, on demand of the chief officer in command thereof, arrest and surrender to the United States all deserters from the army or navy of the United States found within the said territory of the Dominican Republic, but the expense of such arrest and surrender shall be borne by the United States.

---

8. From U. S. Congress, Senate, Senate Executive Documents, 1869–1971, 41st Congress, 3rd session, 17 (January 16, 1871): 101–102.

ARTICLE IV

This convention shall be ratified by both parties, it being understood that it cannot be ratified by the United States until it has received the advice and consent of the Senate of the United States; and the ratification shall take place at Washington, D.C., as soon as possible within four months from the date hereof.

The United States shall protect the Dominican Republic against foreign intervention during the time agreed upon for exchange of the above ratification.

Done in duplicate and good faith in the English and Spanish languages, in the city of Santo Domingo, the twenty-ninth day of the month of November, in the year of our Lord one thousand eight hundred and sixty-nine.

[SEAL.]   Raymond H. Perry
[SEAL.]   Manuel Maria Gautier

A Nineteenth-Century Snapshot of the Country and Its People

As part of Báez's plans to incorporate the Dominican Republic into the Union or, failing that, to lease the bay and peninsula of Samaná, a Commission of Inquiry was sent by the U.S. government to study local conditions. Besides rendering a voluminous report to the U.S. Congress, one of the Commission's members, Samuel Hazard, published a travel account of his travels in Hispaniola entitled *Santo Domingo, Past and Present, with a Glance at Hayti*. With its detailed descriptions, numerous illustrations, and ample coverage, Hazard's book represents a veritable snapshot of Dominican society in the 1870s. He crisscrossed the country, visited most major towns, and even ventured into neighboring Haiti. His book describes an impoverished, but potentially very productive terrain. He decries the laxity of its inhabitants and laments the lack of industriousness of its authorities—problems that a U.S. administration and U.S. investments could certainly solve, according to him.

The following brief selection describes several towns in the Dominican Republic and its people as well as local economic activities. Notice Hazard's penchant for exalting the potential riches of the land if only U.S. businessmen were in charge.

THE CRADLE OF THE NEW WORLD[9]

Puerto Plata, like the few towns still left in the island of Santo Domingo, is old only so far as its location is concerned; for the buildings were utterly destroyed by the Spaniards when they evacuated the island in 1865. The town, however, has been rebuilt after a fashion, with moderate-sized houses of wood, and in the outskirts with small cabins made of strips of the palm and withes, and roofed with thatch. That it had at one time been a place of very great importance and solid structures is evident from the ruins of many of the warehouses and buildings still standing, which are composed of stone and the material of the country known as *mamposteria*, a sort of concrete.

The town is finely situated at the foot of a high mountain, fronting a crescent-shaped bay, on the right of which a narrow peninsula projects itself into the harbor. On this strip of land stands an antiquated fortress, a straggling range of dilapidated stone buildings and works, built ages and ages ago for protection to the town. Now they are dismantled, crumbling ruins, overgrown with moss and vines and grass, and form as pretty a study of ruins as any artist could desire. Twelve men and one musket, and several rusty pieces of ordnance that cannot be fired, comprise the garrison and equipment of the post.

The town itself is irregularly built. Most of the houses are of wood, are generally two stories high, with balconies to the second floor. The streets are narrow and badly paved. The port is capable of being made into a safe and important harbor. The population of the town is variously estimated at from two to three thousand souls, chiefly "colored people," a phrase meaning any complexion not pure white, from the lightest shade to jet-black. The prevailing religion is the Roman Catholic; but freedom of worship exists there, and a Methodist church has been established in the town.

Labor is cheap, ranging from $1 to $3 per day, according to circumstances; by the month, all are willing to work for $10 and $12. The women earn their living chiefly by washing, and, as a rule, are more industrious than the men. Strolling outside the town, our author came upon a group of forty or fifty of these washerwomen standing in the river, hard at work. Some were entirely nude, some with only a cloth about the waist; but all were busy, and chattering away like parrots.

From Puerto Plata the party proceeded by sea to Samaná. The cape was rounded at daybreak. This bold headland is generally spoken of as the beginning of the bay shore, the southern point being at Cape Rafael; but Samaná Bay proper commences at that point of the peninsula known as Balandra Head. This is a remarkable red cliff, lying at the foot of Mount Diablo, which rises to the height of 1300 feet. Between the base of Balandra Head and the shore lies a most attractive sloping levee covered with vegetation, and which would be most charming sites for coffee and sugar estates, to say nothing of their beauty and value as places of marine residence for the inhabitants of the future city of Samaná.

A glance at the map of Samaná Bay will give the reader an idea of the form and extent of this superb sheet of water, the coveted prize of many governments. In imag-

9. From Samuel Hazard, "The Cradle of the New World," *Harper's New Monthly Magazine*, 46, 275 (April 1873): 649–656.

ination clothe the sides of this bay with bold, high hills, varying from 200 to 2000 feet high, from which slope gently to the sea charming valleys covered with trees and vegetation; indent the shore with coves, or here and there small harbors, whose white sandy shores glisten in the tropic sun, and you have some idea of this beautiful bay that Columbus himself has named the "Bay of Arrows," being the place, it is said, where the blood of the children of the New World was first shed by those of the Old. Here resided the subjects of the Cazique Cayacoa, whose widow was afterward baptized in the Catholic faith as Doña Inez Cayacoa.

The country around Samaná is comparatively unsettled. One sees here and there the simple huts of the natives, whose chief occupation appears to be "killing time." This is varied now and then by a little manual labor in the small gardens, where every thing seems to grow of its own accord. The women, with very scanty clothing, gain their livelihood by taking in washing; but the household expenses are very light, and they work only when it suits them. The climate is both hot and wet, there being the usual rainy season, with frequent showers in the dry season, while the thermometer ranges at mid-day as high as 90 degrees in the shade, though at night and early in the morning throughout the year it descends as low as 70 degrees. This temperature is, however, always rendered more bearable by the constantly prevailing breezes.

From Samaná, Mr. Hazard proceeded to the City of Santo Domingo. A queer old place it must be. Bright colored walls, with dirty Negroes sunning themselves against them; narrow streets, with solid-built houses, whose immense doors and spacious windows contrast forcibly with their limited height of only one or two stories; horsemen with broad-rimmed hats on small, compact, quick-moving horses, contrast with the dusky urchin who, naked of every thing but a shirt, bestrides an immense straw saddle on the back of a very diminutive donkey—all serve, with hundreds of other noticeable things, to strike the stranger, and impress upon him the fact that he has exchanged his Saxon associations of order, cleanliness, and precision for the peculiarities of Spanish tropical life.

Knots of men and women, mostly colored, and busy in talk, are scattered about the quay, or in the small open places called "plazas;" odd-looking stores, with still more odd-looking assortments of goods, are entirely open to the gaze of the passerby; while in the market-place are noticed the same peculiarities observed at Puerto Plata, only on a more extended scale. Go where one will, however, every one is cheerful, polite, and communicative, while the dusky "fair ones" presiding over piles of strange, unknown tropical productions are merry and obliging. Such are the sights that today first greet the traveler in the city that at one time was famous for its magnificence.

The outskirts of the city are composed of unattractive frame or clay huts; while in the interior of the town many of the houses are solid and imposing. They are built in the old Spanish style, usually one story in height, seldom over two. A wide entrance with immense folding doors opens into the hall, leading into the patio, or courtyard around which are the quarters and offices. The same lack of glass in the windows, and the use of iron bars, seen in Cuba are universal here; while the quietness of many of the old streets in the upper part of the town reminds one of a city of sleepers. In the streets leading up from the wharf, and in the vicinity of the marketplace, more life is seen, and the architecture of the stores and houses, if not so imposing, is more modern.

The general business of the city appears to be very limited, there being, indeed, only one or two large stores in the place. But there is always a certain amount of amusement to be obtained when trading in these old Spanish towns. The easy, leisurely way of conducting business, the amount of chaff and compliment exchanged even in the most ordinary transactions, are astonishing to people of the Anglo-Saxon race; and it becomes quite a pleasant amusement to have a seller name an extravagant price for an article, and gradually descend to moderation and cheapness.

In a small village near the city, Mr. Hazard found a schoolhouse. It was simply a thatched hut with earthen floor. A number of boys and girls, white and colored, were seated on rude wooden stools arranged at the sides of the room. Fastened to a perch by the side of every pupil was a game cock, and in reply to Mr. Hazard's inquiry he was told, "Oh, they belong to the school-master, who fights them Sundays." In this sport, he was always joined by the village priest, education and religion standing on equal levels in Santo Domingo.

Near Santo Domingo city are the celebrated caves of Santana, reputed to be a place where the early natives assembled for the worship of their gods. The entrance to the cave is a double archway, the division being formed by grotesquely shaped pillars of corallaceous rock, one of the arches permitting ingress of mounted visitors. Around these grow the thick tropical vegetation, the parasitical plants pendent from the branches of the trees giving to the entrance an exceedingly graceful appearance. Passing through the archway, the visitor finds himself in a spacious amphitheater, open to the sky, which has all the appearance of having once been flooded with water. At the base of the walls, around the entire circle, are caves. From the upper edge of the amphitheater depend graceful vines, masses of luxuriant moss, long naked roots of towering trees, in strange relief against the dark recesses. The fact that idols have been found in these caves is cited as authority for their having been used by the natives as a place of worship. They may have been used as a place of burial; for when a Cazique died, his people opened and dried him by the fire, that he might be preserved entire. The body was then laid in some cave, together with his arms, and frequently his favorite wife attended him.

From the city of Santo Domingo, Mr. Hazard made the trip across to the north coast, in company with Commissioner White and two other gentlemen. Horses were fitted out with M'Clellan saddles and equipments for riding, while others were prepared with immense straw panniers for carrying supplies, hammocks for sleeping, and other necessities for the journey. With the servants the party made a gay cavalcade. They left early one morning in February, and, after some miles of riding, came upon broad and beautiful savannas, which, though somewhat more rolling, yet bear the generic name of "llanos," or prairies; and which would seem to have been designed by nature as natural farms, for the land was of the very best deep black soil, covered with long rich grass, while here and there were belts of timber. The country resembles that of the Minnesota bottom lands, except that here the horizon is bounded by beautiful views of cloud-capped mountains, to whose very feet roll the magnificent plains, all ready for the hand of the husbandman.

Toward evening of the second day of their ride the party reached their resting-place for the night. The proprietor received them with courteous hospitality, and at once placed sleeping apartments at their disposal. A glance at the illustration will show the character of the "apartments." In that delightful climate it is the custom to sleep in the open air, with only a roof above one, except during the most violent period of the rainy season.

Near the village of La Vega Mr. Hazard found the remains of a steam engine, said to be the only one ever put up in the island. It lies, broken and useless, on the bank of a little river, whither it had been brought out from the United States by the village priest, who used it to run a saw-mill. When the Spaniards left the island they wantonly destroyed both mill and engine, and no one has had the energy to repair the damage.

Six miles from La Vega rises the famous hill, the "Santo Cerro" of Columbus, from whose summit may be had a splendid view of the "Royal Plain." The hill derives its name from the tradition that Columbus having erected a cross there, the Indians attempted in vain to cut it down. While struck with amazement by their failure, they perceived the Virgin sitting on one of the arms of the cross, and were still more demoralized when the arrows they shot at her returned to pierce their own bodies! Every Spaniard in the island was eager to have a piece of this wonderful cross, and as long as there were applicants the wood held out. The place where it is supposed to have stood is now marked by a rude wooden cross, shown in the foreground of the illustration. The Vega Real, or Royal Plain, is a broad expanse of level country, many leagues in extent, bounded by lofty mountains, well watered by streams, and covered with the magnificent vegetation of the tropics. Modern enterprise may not be able to improve the picturesque aspects of this superb stretch of country, but, to the practical Anglo-Saxon vision, it does seem a pity that it should go to waste. Land is exceedingly cheap at present in the most fertile portions of the island. In the vicinity of Mocha [*sic*] Mr. Hazard visited a sugar plantation, which, with house and out-buildings, and over a thousand acres of good cleared land, capable of raising cane, coffee, cocoa, cotton, and fruits, could be bought for about $5,000 in gold. The soil in that part of the island is of the richest, blackest loam, similar to that of our Western bottom lands, but, owing to the lack of systematic agriculture and enterprise, the resources of the island remain almost totally undeveloped.

Some distance out from Santiago, the famous city of the "Cibao," or stony country, the party was met by the commander of the military district, who was accompanied by no end of governors, commandants, and generals, who came out to receive Commissioner White with due honors. Presentations and congratulations over, the cavalcade wended its way toward the city, along the banks of the wide, swift-running, but now rather shallow, Yaqui [del Norte] River, the famous gold river of Columbus, which, running through the heart of the island, drains some of its most fertile plains, the limits of which end abruptly, and in many cases precipitously, on the Yaqui. This river, known also by the names of Yaquey and Yacki Grande, takes its rise in the mountains near the Peak of Yaqui, and in its course extends some 200 miles, emptying finally into Manzanillo Bay. Having a number of tributaries, it waters and fertilizes a vast extent of country, and from the nature of its banks could easily be formed into a vast canal. So winding is its course that Columbus, crossing it several times, believed he had met with as many different streams, and accordingly bestowed various names upon it.

"Santiago de los Caballeros," the "City of Gentlemen," is one of the most ancient towns in the island and is today in every respect the most important. It was founded in 1504, and received its name in honor of an order of knights in Spain. In early times it suffered frequently from the attacks of the buccaneers; great fires have laid its streets in ruin; earthquakes have leveled it; it was sacked by Dessalines, and only a few years ago was again destroyed by the vindictive Spaniards when they left the island. For this reason it possesses no architectural attractions. It is built, as is usual with Spanish towns, around a large plaza, or square, in which is held the market. The streets are straight and regular, crossing at right angles. In the main part of the town the houses are of stone, while those in the outskirts are generally of framework.

Santiago lies in the heart of the finest agricultural region of the island, the chief product being tobacco. It is also the center of the mining interests, for which the island has been famous ever since its discovery, but which have never been fully developed. Gold is found scattered over a large part of the north flank of the central range of mountains (south side of Cibao), and also on the upper waters of the Jaina River. The gravel is rich in quality, but the quantity is too small over any given area to make it of great value. It might be placed on a par with the class of mines known in California as Chinese diggings, and will not pay a white man's labor.

Gold quartz veins abound higher up the mountains, above all these "placer" deposits, but their quality has yet to be ascertained. That they bear gold has been proved by direct examination, and by the inferential proof that the gravel deposits derive their gold from them. Iron occurs in paying quantities only in one place, the Maimon River, a south branch of the Yuna, about a hundred miles from Samaná Bay. It is superb in quality, and only enterprise and capital are needed to make it serviceable.

In early times the gold mines of the Cibao and Buenaventura were worked with great success. In 1502 there were minted at the old town of La Vega 240,000 crowns of gold. Santiago, it is said, was at one time mainly inhabited by goldsmiths. It is related by Oviedo that in 1502 an Indian woman, working in the service of two men named Garay and Diaz, found a lump of gold in the Buenaventura mines weighing 200 ounces, valued at 3,600 dollars of the time. The men were so delighted with the discovery that they feasted their friends upon roast pig, serving it up on this same "grain" of gold for a dish, of which they boasted that their majesties had never dined off so rich a one. The nugget was shipped to Spain, but was lost with the vessel in a storm.

That part of Santo Domingo lying contiguous to the Haytian frontier comprises some of the finest land in the island. The soil is rich enough to grow sugar, rice, coffee, and tobacco on all its levels; the hills are well wooded, while in the savannas cattle could be raised in large numbers, grass being abundant, and growing as high as a man's shoulder. Yet, owing to the long border warfare, this rich territory is known as the "despoblado" (uninhabited). The mountain range running through this district furnishes abundance of mahogany of the finest kind, together with fustic, lignum vitae, ebony, and many other valuable woods. Our hardy lumbermen from the Middle and New England States, with their experience and sawmills, would find a mine of gold in all these timbered lands of Santo Domingo, some of the most precious and choice logs having at times sold in England as high as 500 dollars.

The present mode of getting out this timber is very rude. A merchant, for exam-

105

ple, buys the right, at a trifling sum, to cut down in certain tracts all the mahogany he can find. Then with a party he penetrates into the forest, and at the most accessible point selects his trees, which are cut down, and divided into various pieces, according to the mode of transportation, which in every case is exceedingly difficult. If by water, then the logs are larger; but most generally oxen are used to haul the small pieces through the woods, and even then it often has to be cut into smaller pieces, easy to carry on mule-back. It is no uncommon sight to see trains of these diminutive animals, each with a small square piece of mahogany in the straw panniers carried on each side.

Tobacco and the Cibao

Pedro Francisco Bonó is considered the best interpreter of Dominican society in the late nineteenth century. His writings show a deep preoccupation with the plight of the common man, particularly the peasant. This selection from his writings describes the role that tobacco played as a cash crop for peasants in the northern Cibao region, the center of the Dominican Republic's tobacco industry. While tobacco began to develop as a cash crop destined for European markets in the early nineteenth century, by the end of that century, tobacco consolidated itself as the country's premier peasant-produced cash crop. Only sugar, which was produced on plantations requiring heavy capital investments, was a more important export crop than tobacco.

Peasants in the Cibao region preferred tobacco to other crops for several reasons: tobacco was easy to grow, good land was still available in the Cibao, and peasants could count on credit from tobacco middlemen. By the same token, these financial relations also tied the peasants into a web of debt and obligations in which—more often than not—they would end up on the losing side. Still, tobacco provided the peasants in the Cibao with a comparatively higher standard of living than peasants in other parts of the nation. These *Cibaeño* peasants usually owned their own land and there were no large socioeconomic disparities among them—as in the case of sugar production on plantations. This characteristic did not go unnoticed by Bonó, who called tobacco "the true Father of the Nation," for the progress and opportunities that it brought to the Dominican people.

FROM PEDRO FRANCISCO BONÓ'S
WRITINGS ON THE DOMINICAN ECONOMY[10]

The Dominican economy consists of cattle ranching and agriculture. [. . .] Since we are in the midst of the tobacco harvest, I will first deal with agriculture as an actual experimental case from which to glean lengthy details. Everywhere are piles, serones,[11] and packs of tobacco are being hauled; everywhere are warehouses full of this leaf and swarms of workers of both sexes, selecting, tying, weighing, and packing. Stores are packed with customers, supplies come and go, in a word there is an exchange of goods thrice that of the rest of the year.

In the past, farmers from the Cibao were advised not to limit themselves just to the planting of tobacco . . . [because] it is a precarious crop, very dependent on dry or rainy spells; and the consumer markets are flooded with this crop more than any other product, so that its price is subject to violent ups and downs. These recommendations are inane since there is no product that is not more or less subject to the same vicissitudes. After long struggles, supported by the Government . . . that conceded franchises, privileges, and exceptions to other crops, countless farmers devoted themselves exclusively to growing coffee, cocoa, and sugar cane, and the result of all this was many years of misery, of scarcity of export, and subsistence crops. The basis of the peasant's labor was not studied, nor were the details of the proposed crops, and we all collected very bitter fruits for the hurried style used in such a grave matter as that of ousting an important group, such as farmers, out of their traditional occupation, of their resources, and the means of their work.

[. . .]

The first thing to be considered in tobacco production in the Cibao is the capital that pays for the labor force, its origin and its ways of distribution; next, the tobacco leaf, its preparation, the diverse industries it activates, and finally, the locomotive industry, which gives the last push by dispatching to the shipping point.

In a previous article, we already said what provided the capital, that is, the certainty of the capitalist that there was in the Conucos an easily sold surplus commercial wealth that in four or six months would be at his disposal. But having summarily stated its consequences we ought not delve now in its main details.

After obtaining the advance in St. Thomas [the port of transfer] to England, Germany, or some other place, each retail merchant, on his own or through brokers, establishes himself close to the farmers to perform a service similar to the one described by Courcelle Seneuil about Scottish Banks. He gives money, linen goods, hardware goods, or other valuables to the peasant, through a consensual speculative contract and the latter uses this money and the other goods for his personal necessities and those of his crops with more or less judgment, more or less luck. It is difficult to enumerate the advantages of these advances, the relief they provide to works of all sorts in which the population in general can be maintained. Since [this commerce] is based on the freedom of exchange, it absorbs its benefits as well as its dis-

---

10. Translated from Emilio Rodríguez Demorizi, ed., *Papeles de Pedro F. Bonó* (Santo Domingo: Editora del Caribe, 1964), 193–199.
11. bags or bales of palm leaves.

asters. Every lender personally sees to the guarantee of his debtor on a weekly basis and extends the loan to the uppermost extent of the product's value. It is a pity, though, that the pattern does not have the regularity essential to this operation and that the habits are so deplorable regarding the most elementary precautions in credit contracts. None of the signators provides safeguards to avoid or punish reciprocal bad faith. There are no mortgages or chirographic titles. Everything is reduced to current accounts, very poorly managed by the merchant who does not even provide the peasant with either a duplicate or a copy. This lack of mutual safeguards, places tobacco advance operations in the category of gross loans, which usually account for a high interest on the advanced valuables, make the peasant very audacious and incline him to excessive expenditures which in the end are his and the retail trade's ruin. The military dictatorships that with rare intermissions have been the owners of the country, have introduced a remedy worthy of their system. Based on the merchant's word, the peasant is considered a debtor of any amount and if he does not pay, he goes to jail without further investigations. To my understanding, since the civil and commercial laws, as excellent as they are, have not been able to improve the tobacco advance operation, the Government is left with the empirical remedy of the stamps, and the business sector is left with lending banks.

In spite of many defects, progress gives an extraordinary impetus to tobacco cultivation and to the other industries related to its harvesting; it [tobacco] is the great engine that puts into motion small-scale agriculture, and has gained the interest of the more enlightened class which now presides over its classification, selection, and packaging.

Until now, the harvester had to do the classifying himself, thereby contributing ignorance, and greed to the already deficient coordination methods of a nascent industry. As a result of a *Juntas gratuitas,*[12] the lazy, playful, unskilled, and famished devoured in two or three days a harvester's family food of several months and produced a tobacco that was badly classified, poorly packed, very humid, very dirty, fraudulent and that discredited itself in the end when reaching Europe. This is now being corrected in big strides by the direct involvement of those who have suffered its disastrous consequences the most, and a labor decision is silently taking place, which is one more proof of the precision of economic formulas in free markets.

The veteran trader now buys tobacco in piles and the harvester delivers them wrapped in *yaguas* [palm tree bark] to his warehouse under his direct inspection. Urban laborers, most of them women, proceed to classify it as in a regulated professional workshop. This new combination produces surprisingly unexpected and fruitful results. [This industry] employs groups formerly idle for lack of labor demand appropriate to their skills and who thus offer their services for low wages. This has increased the peasant's free time, which he uses for other types of work. [The employment] of a more disciplined, intelligent labor force . . . with knowledge of the tastes or demands of the European consumer and who carry out stringent inspection of the waste of defective products and of those for wrapping, of the fermentations or remedies needed after ordinary fermentation, of fake expenditures, of the suscepti-

---

12. literally free juntas—a system of communal or shared labor

bility of the leaf, and so on. Under this inspection procedure, the hands or bundles are tied with one of its leaves. They are not allowed to get wet and are divided into purer, more complete classes. Finally they require more powerful pressure than the fork lever of the bagger, who is introducing vertical presses of great ease and hygiene.

As this procedure becomes generalized and improved upon, tobacco from the Cibao will acquire in the trading markets the high esteem it previously had. If it does not reach its former price level due to powerful competition from similar products by more developed countries, at least it will not deteriorate from the precious natural qualities the soil of its meadows graces it with.

The government's actions in this process have been counterproductive and it could only boast of the ill-advised patriotism that dictated them but not of its prevision and ability. It should be counseled not to disturb, as did its predecessors, the labor guilds, and to give more protection. [. . .] [Tobacco] has been, is, and will be the veritable *Father of the Nation* for those who preserve it in its economic, civil, and political effects. The success of our nascent democracy lies in the equilibrium in which [the government] keeps individual fortunes. This will become the most effective obstacle to potential oligarchies. It also was and still is the firmest support of our autonomy. And last, it maintains, to a large extent, the domestic trade of the Republic with the industries it promotes and needs.

Ulises Heureaux: The Ultimate Caudillo

The dictatorial rule of Ulises Heureaux (popularly nicknamed Lilís) during the last decade of the nineteenth century was, in many ways, unlike that of any other Dominican caudillo. Though Heureaux began his political career in the military like many of his predecessors, he established an iron-fisted, enduring dictatorship in an era characterized by spurious, short-lived governments. Starting in 1886, Heureaux broadened his power base and within a few years, he presided over a well-entrenched dictatorship. This despite the fact Ulises Heureaux was a black man of Haitian ancestry in a mulatto country with light-skinned economic elites, which had obtained its independence from Haiti. Still, Heureaux was able to outfox and defeat his enemies for more than a decade until he was assassinated in the streets of Moca in 1899.

Heureaux's dictatorship represents the zenith of trends that began in the period of the First Republic: despotism, praetorianism, personalism, political corruption, and clientelism. As such, his regime was no exception to the rule, but rather the culmination of deeply rooted historical currents and authoritarian political values. His contemporaries and biogra-

Ulises Heureaux,
commonly known as Lilís.

phers described him as a saga-
cious, cunning politician; a
man who knew the ins and outs
of the Dominican political
scene, important facts that
could explain his political
longevity. The following two
letters written by Heureaux
afford a glimpse into the Machiavellian nature of his regime
and attest to his relentless hold
on to power.

TWO LETTERS BY ULISES
HEUREAUX[13]
Santo Domingo, August 14, 1882
Mr. Don Jacobo Pereyra,
Dominican Consul, St. Thomas

My Dear Friend:
Your esteemed letters from the
eighth, ninth, and twelfth of the current [month] rest in my hands and I
have informed myself with proper
attention of their important contents.
I can guarantee you that nothing
about General Cesáreo's war prepa-
rations worries me and that you may
begin your trip whenever it suits you, guaranteeing to you beforehand that he will dis-
embark on any Coast he likes, because all are deserted and I will not order any ships
to enter into our waters, this is a big advantage for him and he may benefit from it.
I have news that Villanueva is going there probably to join Cesáreo, it is fine. The
more of these leaders of the usurper Army we encounter, the more of them will be
executed when the time comes. We are ready for word from the various landings to
start operations, it is just a matter of minutes before we mobilize our army.
I wish for the hostilities to start soon. Herein lies the true strength of the Government since there has never been in this Sacred land a better method of conquest than
the use of arms. I lament the means toward such triumphs, but I welcome the end,
which is to destroy with a strong arm the venom of the snakes who constantly stalk

13. Translated from Juan Daniel Balcácer, ed., *La correspondenica del Presidente Heureaux
(Lilís): 1882* (Santo Domingo, Editora Universitaria, 1987), 435–436.

peaceful men to destroy them.

In addition to the army, I have two great sources of support. First, I have you, my best friend, and advance sentinel, and, second, I have public opinion, which is the best support at all times and under all circumstances.

So far not even rumors of any disturbances are heard in the country, and maybe there will be no revolution. I know a conspiracy is brewing, but from the former to the latter is a long distance because the conspirators are men of such little significance that it would be an embarrassment for the government to call their attention, that would be granting them more importance than what they pretend to have, persuade yourself that our enemies will not be able to win, and count even less on the useless friends that they have in the country to consecrate the fact of the triumph, the enemies of the Government that are in the country are insignificant and impossible and at the time they try to raise their flag, they are completely destroyed and punished.

I am counting on your zeal and diligence, and as I await your first notice I close [this letter] as I have always done it. I will continue updating you of events by direct means.

Yours as always, your dearest friend, U. Heureaux

Yesterday I received letters from Luperón. He will be back soon.

Azua, December 22, 1893
Mr. General Wo. Figuereo, Vice President of the Republic in charge of the Presidency
Santo Domingo[14]

My Esteemed Brother:

This is to let you know and through your dignifying person the other members of the Government, what I have been forced to do to properly and exemplarily repress the assaults and crimes committed in this [provincial] seat.

Having considered the facts well and being fully convinced of the guilt of the accused of the aforementioned ambushes and murders, justly working and with the awareness of duty, that later imposes hard and painful measures, I ordered in La Clavellina, where General Joaquín Campo, delegate of the government, was cowardly assassinated, the execution of Messieurs Eugenio Go. Marchena, José Concha, Oliverio Reyes, José María Guzmán, José Reyes, and Carlos Baéz Figueroa.

In the town of Los Jovillos, where there was an ambush set to kill me on the way from Neyba to this City, I had José Pérez, Pablo Báez, and Lorenzo Brito executed.

In spite of playing an important role in these events, I did not execute Messieurs Alfredo Blandino, Abraham Ortiz, Antonio Romano, Manuel Mesa, Próspero Freites, Agapito Félis, and José Polini Reyes, considering the example sufficient, and I remit them to the jail of this capital, where they will stay, at least while I am president.

This morning I will hold a public audience, destined to show everyone the mag-

---

14. Translated from Juan Daniel Balcácer, ed., *Lilís: Cartas y comunicaciones* (Santo Domingo: Editora Cosmos, 1977), 55–56.

A sign of modernity. Train station in Santiago.

nitude of the criminal intentions developed in this town, and that I pursue ends of morality and the public good, by acting in this manner.

Please inform the delegates of the government and the governors of the provinces and districts outside of this region of these events.

In order to enforce, in a proper way, respect for the government and its representatives, I will stay in the area for a few more days, and before I can rejoin you, I recommend that you maintain constant vigilance particularly in your public duties.

I believe it is useless to send you and the government any guarantees concerning that by proceeding in the way I did, I have not been moved by any other force other than that of carrying out justice and of imposing a powerful and exemplary remedy for the despicable and anarchist ideas which some have wrongfully tried to introduce into this land in order to foster the decline of the nobility of our race.

This City's public opinion had been waiting for the current outcome and that, even though I may deplore it, strengthens the Government's action.

I will keep you constantly updated of everything that takes place.

Take good care of yourself and always think of me as yours, dear brother.

Ulises Heureaux

A Nation for Sale

The dictatorship of Ulises Heureaux was not only characterized by an authoritarian nature and exceptional longevity at a time of very brief regimes, but also by catastrophic and misguided economic policies. Even though Heureaux is sometimes credited with establishing the basis of a more modern nation through a capitalist economy (that is, the modern state), it is also true that Heureaux went to extreme lengths to stay in power and he relied on the resources of the state to accomplish that goal. Caudillos like Heureaux need money to run a state and its bureaucracy, to pay the army and buy the allegiance, or at least the neutrality, of dozens of regional caudillos. And when patronage did not work for Heureaux, he required emergency funds to combat the periodic rebellions challenging his regime. He followed in the footsteps of his predecessors by borrowing from local and, particularly, foreign lenders, taking this practice to previously unknown extremes. He borrowed heavily to stay in power, often forcing local merchants to grant him loans, issued worthless currency, and basically mortgaged the country to foreign speculators. Heureaux eventually sold whatever he could lay his hands on and even some intangible things, like the Dominican claim to territory lost to Haiti during the latter's revolution against the French armies.

In the following letter to a foreign banker an almost servile Heureaux pleads his case and asks for more funds.

LETTER BY ULISES HEUREAUX
TO MR. CHARLES I. WELLS, PARIS[15]
Santo Domingo, October 7, 1896
My Dear Mr. Wells:
Since my last letter of the fourteenth of July, I had the pleasure of receiving your favor of the eighteenth of August. I use this opportunity in order to give you some information about our general situation here. As far as politics are concerned everything is in very good condition which I had the opportunity to investigate personally during my last trip to the North, which was a very satisfactory one. Not the same can be said about the financial situation, chiefly as far as our mutual interests are concerned. Both Bank and Regie are in a very difficult and serious position and though I am always most perfectly willing to help even with prejudice to my own interest, I

---

15. From Cyrus R. Veeser, ed., "Cartas escogidas de los copiadores del Presidente Ulises Heureaux correspondientes a los años 1894–1898," unpublished manuscript, 1994, 157–159.

have come to the end of my resources and it is impossible for me to do more. At your request which was presented to me by Mr. den Tex, I once more accepted to guarantee your [draft] against the Regie for $25,000 gold in favor of the Drake & Stratton Co., but I repeat to you that this is really the last time that I can be of any material help to you.

The Bank has been constantly going back [sic], and notwithstanding the different combinations we have made in order to keep her running in a regular way it came so far, that last Monday, the 4th instant, only [6] were left to her in cash.

When M. Duvergé came to tell me so, I ordered him to close the Bank for that afternoon, promising him that I would try to find some silver money for him for the next day. So I did, and yesterday it opened again with some $10,000 oro mex. in cash. I do not expect that this amount will last a long time, as in this city nearly no drafts can be found, and the merchants who have to remit to the interior are obliged to ship silver coin even, paying the 6 percent export duty on this coin. The result is that there is a constant strain on the Bank and as soon as some silver is deposited, it is taken away by the commerce. As all this gives me great trouble, more so as that situation is very well known by the merchants, I have come to the conclusion that the only thing we can do to prevent these constant difficulties is to take up all the outstanding bills and retire the paper money from the circulation. To this end, I am studying a combination with Mr. Vicini that he will pay to the Bank a monthly sum of $20,000 memex, starting in December [18]96, which amount should be used to cover outstanding bills. In the mean time, Mr. Vicini will always be ready to assist the Bank when needed. The basis of this combination with Vicini is founded on the receipts of the Regie. This is the only solution that I see possible and through it we will greatly alleviate our daily troubles.

Whenever you come here in the next year, we will always have time to conclude some definitive arrangement, but meanwhile nothing else can be done.

As for the Regie, it too is in a very difficult position as your drafts for £15,000 gold and £4,000 were not taken up in the loan that Mr. Vicini and Mr. Lluberes made. At the behest of Mr. den Tex, I did all I could to persuade these gentlemen to bring these amounts into the general business, but Mr. Vicini and Mr. Lluberes explained to me, figures in hand, that at present they could do no more. So I had to beg Mr. den Tex not to make any difficulties and to sign the contract, promising him my help to find some arrangement for the payment of these drafts.

Before ending, I still want to tell you that in my opinion, in the present situation, which is so very strained and so very delicate and critical, I do not think that M. Duvergé is the right man in the right place. He is talking a great deal too much and is always in a state of excitement, which gives me great trouble and causes a prejudice against the Bank and our point interests. I, therefore, think it best if you recall him from here, giving him some position in your Bank in Paris, and the sooner you do so the better it will be. If it is possible without prejudices to you, call him by telegram. As for the first time to come [sic], the Bank will not do any transactions at all, the number of employees should be reduced also, and the Inspector, Mr. Amable [Gamirin], could easily take charge of the daily management, giving at the same time powers to Mr. den Tex for the general management and for all those questions that can arise in respect to our interests and yours. I hope that you will attend to this request as I think it necessary, and as until your arrival here no Bank operations will be made. I repeat once more to you that in the present circumstances in fact there is no use of having a Bank, and by the dispositions that I am taking I am only keeping up the institution in the hope that in a short time, the Bank will get its capital back in cash so that, at that time, through good management, it will be a source of great benefits to all of us and on [sic] order to prevent that by a general distrust of the public in the Bank [title], the possibility of issuing paper money should be lost for ever I have preferred to take these dispositions.

Still one more question.

I am studying the way to make a combination before the end of this year which will permit me to satisfy a great part of my outstanding obligations, and I suppose that I can succeed giving as a guarantee the 1-1/2 percent of War and Public Works, the 6 percent Recargo Adicional and the 3 percent Recargo Adicional. All these *apartados* are belonging to the Government and in the next session of the Congress on December another 1/2 percent more will be established which will make a total of 11 percent. Still in order to carry through this scheme I would be obliged to you if you would be good enough to send me a formal declaration from the San Domingo Improvement Co. that these *apartados* are not affected by any one of the loans under your control and that the San Domingo Improvement Company approves the direction I wish to give to them and agrees to this transaction.

Do not forget to do all you can to come to see me as soon as possible. We have a great deal to discuss and as my sympathy for you is so heartily meant I should like to see you out of your troubles, and I suppose that some serious talk between us could be of some moral help to you.

With best wishes, I am as ever

Your sincere friend,

Ulises Heureaux

CHAPTER FOUR

The United States Intervenes

The assassination of Ulises Heureaux on July 26, 1899, plunged the Dominican Republic once again into a state of chaos. It created a political vacuum that other caudillos were unable to fill. Moreover, the country was highly indebted to foreign lenders and its financial situation was calamitous. In consequence, the next decade and a half witnessed the country's unraveling. In 1905 the Republic lost its economic sovereignty, and in 1916 it lost its political independence. Except for the presidency of Ramón Cáceres (1905–1911), governments during this period were remarkably short-lived, often lasting just a few months.

In 1905, the country signed several humiliating agreements granting control of the Dominican custom houses to U.S. government agents, which was modified in 1907. Incensed by the country's inability to meet its financial obligations, and concerned about European meddling in Dominican affairs, the United States assumed control of the Dominican debt, guaranteeing its collection and severely limiting the government's economic power. As political infighting was exacerbated by Cáceres's assassination in 1911, the United States took the next logical step as part

Dominican military caudillos (or "generals") posing for the camera.

of its Caribbean policy: it ended the Second Republic by putting the Dominican Republic under U.S. military control. For eight years (1916–1924) the U.S. Marines governed the country. They transformed and modernized it, but at a very heavy cost in terms of repression and violation of individual freedoms. By the time the U.S. Marines left in 1924, the Dominican Republic was completely altered and thoroughly pacified. Modern roads, a professional bureaucracy, and a well-trained, capable military force to keep order had been introduced. U.S. capital took increasing control of the most profitable sector of the Dominican economy: its sugar industry. Large, powerful U.S. corporations, attracted by favorable laws, invested heavily in the Dominican Republic and exercised considerable leverage over the Dominican economy and its government. Finally, the U.S. government, always trying to safeguard its perceived national interest in the Caribbean region, played an important role in the signing of a border treaty between the Dominican Republic and Haiti (then under U.S. military occupation) in 1929.

Even though the U.S. military occupation modernized the Dominican Republic, it failed to transform its authoritarian political culture. The third republic was born with essentially the same cast of characters that had doomed the second one. With the occupation over, President Horacio Vásquez extended his term in office and sought reelection, while others conspired to replace him. The U.S. military occupation also created a practically unchallengeable Dominican military. So, unlike in the case of the nineteenth-century caudillos, whoever controlled the Dominican military now had the power to control the nation's destiny. Not surprisingly, it was precisely from this U.S.-trained Dominican military that the next great dictator emerged after Vásquez's overthrow in 1930— General Rafael L. Trujillo.

The Loss of Economic Sovereignty

In 1905 the Dominican Republic was obliged to sign an agreement with the United States regarding its outstanding external debt. The U.S. government, which now had new security interests in the region after the 1898 Cuban-Spanish-American War and the ongoing construction of the Panama Canal, felt threatened by the Europeans' use of warships in Caribbean waters to enforce payment on outstanding debts. The Theodore Roosevelt administration, therefore, considered establishing a protectorate in the Dominican Republic. The end result was the 1905 modus vivendi which relinquished Dominican control over its custom houses to U.S. agents, who from then on were in charge of collecting customs duties and making sure that the country's debts were paid.

The modus vivendi was rendered official in 1907 as the Dominican-American Convention. The U.S. government facilitated a large loan to pay off the country's debt to European creditors and, as mentioned, U.S. agents were in charge of collecting customs duties—the government's main source of revenue. Fifty percent of the amount collected were applied to the debt, 45 percent were handed over to the Dominican government, and the remaining 5 percent were used for administrative expenses. As a result of the 1907 Convention, the Dominican Republic was now fully within the economic orbit of the United States. Not only was the totality of the country's external debt now owed to the United States, but U.S. agents also were entrusted with its collection. Moreover, the Dominican government had lost effective control over its internal finances, as the United States government could deny funds to administrations that it did not recognize as legitimate. President Ramón Cáceres —like Carlos Morales Languasco before him—benefited from this close partnership with the United States that gave an air of stability to his administration. Thus, his comparatively lengthy tenure in power can be attributed in part to the economic and diplomatic support his administration received from the United States. The country, on the other hand, suffered the ignominious loss of its economic sovereignty. The 1907 Dominican-American Convention is reproduced below.

CONVENTION BETWEEN THE UNITED STATES OF AMERICA AND THE DOMINICAN REPUBLIC PROVIDING FOR THE ASSISTANCE OF THE UNITED STATES IN THE COLLECTION AND APPLICATION OF THE CUSTOMS REVENUES OF THE DOMINICAN REPUBLIC, THE ENABLING ACT, AND OTHER CORRESPONDENCE RELATIVE TO THE INTERPRETATION AND ENFORCEMENT OF THE TREATY.[1]

Convention concluded February 8, 1907. Ratification advised by Senate February 25, 1907. Ratified by President June 22, 1907. Ratified by President of the Dominican Republic June 18, 1907. Ratifications exchanged at Washington July 8, 1907. Proclaimed July 25, 1907.

By the President of the United States of America
A PROCLAMATION
Whereas a convention between the United States of America and the Dominican Republic providing for the assistance of the United States in the collection and application of the customs revenues of the Dominican Republic was concluded and signed by their respective plenipotentiaries at the city of Santo Domingo, on the eighth day of February, one thousand nine hundred and seven, the original of which convention, being in the English and Spanish languages, is word for word as follows:
Whereas during disturbed political conditions in the Dominican Republic debts and claims have been created, some by regular and some by revolutionary governments, many of doubtful validity in whole or in part, and amounting in all to over $30,000,000, nominal or face value;
And whereas the same conditions have prevented the peaceable and continuous

1. From U. S. Department of State, *Papers Relating to the Foreign Relations of the United States with the Annual Message of the President Transmitted to Congress, December 3, 1907* (Washington, D. C.: Government Printing Office, 1910), vol. 1, 307–310.

collection and application of national revenues for payment of interest or principal of such debts or for liquidation and settlement of such claims; and the said debts and claims continually increase by accretion of interest and are a grievous burden upon the people of the Dominican Republic and a barrier to their improvement and prosperity;

And whereas the Dominican Government has now effected a conditional adjustment and settlement of said debts and claims under which all its foreign creditors have agreed to accept about $12,407,000 for debts and claims amounting to about $21,184,000 of nominal or face value, and the holders of internal debts or claims of about $2,028,258 nominal or face value have agreed to accept about $645,827 therefore, and the remaining holders of internal debts or claims on the same basis as the assents already given will receive about $2,400,000 therefore, which sum the Dominican Government has fixed and determined as the amount which it will pay to such remaining internal debt holders; making the total payments under such adjustment and settlement, including interest as adjusted and claims not yet liquidated, amount to not more than about $17,000,000;

And whereas a part of such plan of settlement is the issue and sale of bonds of the Dominican Republic to the amount of $20,000,000, bearing five per cent interest, payable in fifty years, and redeemable after ten years at 102.5, and requiring payment of at least one per cent per annum, for amortization, the proceeds of said bonds, together with such funds as are now deposited for the benefit of creditors from customs revenues of the Dominican Republic heretofore received, after payment of the expenses of such adjustment, to be applied first to the payment of said debts and claims as adjusted, and, second, out of the balance remaining to the retirement and extinction of certain concessions and harbor monopolies which are a burden and hindrance to the commerce of the country, and, third, the entire balance still remaining to the construction of certain railroads and bridges and other public improvements necessary to the industrial development of the country;

And whereas the whole of said plan is conditioned and dependent upon the assistance of the United States in the collection of customs revenues of the Dominican Republic and the application thereof so far as necessary to the interest upon and the amortization and redemption of said bonds, and the Dominican Republic has requested the United States to give and the United States is willing to give such assistance:

The Dominican Government, represented by its minister of state for foreign relations, Emiliano Tejera, and its minister of state for finance and commerce, Federico Velásquez H., and the United States Government, represented by Thomas C. Dawson, minister resident and consul-general of the United States to the Dominican Republic, have agreed:

I. That the President of the United States shall appoint a general receiver of Dominican customs, who, with such assistant receivers and other employees of the receivership as shall be appointed by the President of the United States in his discretion, shall collect all the customs duties accruing at the several customs houses of the Dominican Republic until the payment or retirement of any and all bonds issued by the Dominican Government in accordance with the plan and under the limitations as to terms and amounts hereinbefore recited; and said general receiver shall apply the sums so collected, as follows:

First, to paying the expenses of the receivership; second, to the payment of interest upon said bonds; third, to the payment of the annual sums provided for amortization of said bonds, including interest upon all bonds held in sinking fund; fourth, to the purchase and cancellation or the retirement and cancellation, pursuant to the terms thereof, of any of said bonds as may be directed by the Dominican Government; fifth, the remainder to be paid to the Dominican Government.

The method of distributing the current collections of revenue in order to accomplish the application thereof as hereinbefore provided shall be as follows:

The expenses of the receivership shall be paid by the receiver as they arise. The allowances to the general receiver and his assistants for the expenses of collecting the revenues shall not exceed five per cent unless by agreement between the two Governments.

On the first day of each calendar month the sum of $100,000 shall be paid over by the receiver to the fiscal agent of the loan, and the remaining collection of the last preceding month shall be paid over to the Dominican Government, or applied to the sinking fund for the purchase or redemption of bonds, as the Dominican government shall direct.

Provided, That in case the customs revenues collected by the general receiver shall in any year exceed the sum of $3,000,000, one-half of the surplus above such sum of $3,000,000 shall be applied to the sinking fund for the redemption of bonds.

II. The Dominican Government will provide by law for the payment of all customs duties to the general receiver and his assistants, and will give to them all needful aid and assistance and full protection to the extent of its powers. The Government of the United States will give to the general receiver and his assistants such protection as it may find to be requisite for the performance of their duties.

III. Until the Dominican Republic has paid the whole amount of the bonds of the debt its public debt shall not be increased except by previous agreement, between the Dominican Government and the United States. A like agreement shall be necessary to modify the import duties, it being an indispensable condition for the modification of such duties that the Dominican Executive demonstrate and that the President of the United States recognize that, on the basis of exportations and importations to the like amount and the like character during the two years preceding that in which it is desired to make such modification, the total net customs receipts would at such altered rates of duties have been for each of such two years in excess of the sum of $2,000,000 United States gold.

IV. The accounts of the general receiver shall be rendered monthly to the *contaduria* general of the Dominican Republic and to the State Department of the United States and shall be subject to examination and verification by the appropriate officers of the Dominican and the United States Governments.

V. This agreement shall take effect after its approval by the Senate of the United States and the Congress of the Dominican Republic.

Done in four originals, two being in the English language, and two in the Spanish, and the representatives of the high contracting parties signing them in the city or Santo Domingo this 8th day of February, in the year of our Lord 1907.

Thomas C. Dawson   Emiliano Tejera   Federico Velázquez H.

Attracting Foreign Investment

After 1898, and particularly after 1907, new political and economic realities operated in the Caribbean in general and the Dominican Republic in particular. The United States was not only the political hegemon of the region—whose power could not be contested by the weak Caribbean nations—but also an increasingly powerful economic presence. Since the late nineteenth century, U.S. investors had been bringing their capital, technology, and business skills to the Dominican Republic. Moreover, Dominican governments slowly came to realize that the country's future was in its agro-exporting sector. Sugar, tobacco, coffee, and cacao dominated the economic picture of the Dominican Republic for close to a century (1870s to 1970s). The government tried to develop the country's infrastructure and to encourage foreign investment. Obviously, the Dominican upper classes neither had the capital nor the technology nor the business contacts to modernize the country by themselves, so foreign investment was considered a must.

Two laws enacted in 1911 by the Cáceres administration stand out in this context. The first one, the "Law for the Division of Communal Lands," did away with large tracts of common or communal lands, that is, lands that for centuries had been used by communities or groups of individuals without necessarily having titles. Many of these lands had been handed down from royal or state-owned properties and had been the basis for the development of the cattle ranching sector in the past. Now, these lands were quickly seized by legal or semi-legal means and sold to prospective foreign investors who needed them for the developing large sugar plantations. Particularly in the east, the vast expanses of land where planted with sugar cane. The second law, the "Law for Agricultural Exemptions," conceded ample facilities to foreign investors for the establishment of agricultural enterprises in the Dominican Republic, particularly regarding their use of, and access to, lands and waterways, and favorable tax exemptions for investors in the new key sectors of the Dominican economy. Both laws were part of Cáceres's economic program based on agricultural exports and the attraction of foreign, though mostly U.S., investment.

LAW FOR THE DIVISION OF COMMUNAL LANDS[2]

Article 1. The measurement, demarcation, and partition of communal lands is declared as in the nation's best interest. Those are understood to be those whose property is held by stocks and belong to two or more persons.

Article 2. The Tribunals or Courts of First Instance, in the case that one or more of the co-proprietors request it, through an official request with the titles justifying their rights, will order the measurement and partition of the indicated place, and will commission a Notary or someone in his place so that he may, with receipt, become the custodian of the titles, and in whose office those interested could inspect them. This functionary will give faith of whatever belongs to each stockholder at the end of the operation, which will be carried out, under the requirements of the Surveying Law, by the Surveyor who, for the lowest price, will carry out the operation, unless three-fourths of the co-proprietors had not designated another one by common agreement.

In the former case, the Tribunal will commission the one who within two months of the publication of the sentence's summary dealt with below, deposits with the Secretariat the best proposals, and declares to be satisfied with each stockholder, having the option for the required payment, whether in cash or in a given amount of land, which may not exceed one-fourth of his portion.

The Surveyor will grant each stockholder, as feasible, and keeping in mind the land's quality, the part that belongs to him, in the place that he has occupied with farms or crops, without being understood that in any manner he is required to complete the definitive portion of a co-owner, giving him the rest of that portion immediately following his possession.

Article 3. In the case referred to in the previous article, the requesters will designate all co-proprietors known to them, and their residence, if there are any absentee owners or minors without a tutor, or if they ignore it. The public ministry, in lieu of these facts, will let the interested party know that the terrain's partition has been ordered, by mailing them the printed issues containing the sentence's summary; and it will require, if necessary, the naming of the legal representatives dealt with in articles 112 through 114 and 405 and following of the Civil Code.

Article 4. The parties involved must make public in the press the sentence's summary and distribute it among neighbors and co-proprietors of the place through ads in fliers, for which they will deliver them to the Public Prosecutor Magistrate, so that this functionary has them distributed through rural officials. Three months after these publications, the Surveyor will start with the operation, unless an opposition lawsuit is filed, in which case he will wait until the rendered verdict becomes irrevocable.

Article 5. The co-proprietors, who may have reasons to oppose the operation or the validity or amount represented by some title, will sue the requesters of the operation or those who deposited the questioned titles, in the Tribunal of First Instance, without previous conciliation, in the ordinary manner for summons. The Tribunal and the Court, in case of an appeal, upon hearing the prosecutor's verdict, will render judgment within fifteen days, except in those cases in which it is necessary to order

2. Translated from *Gaceta Oficial*, no. 2187, April 29, 1911.

some preparatory measure.

Article 6. In the case that a co-proprietor occupied more land than entitled to, according to the rights granted by his title, he will be under the obligation of purchasing the excess from the rightful owner, or to sell him the improvements [on the land]; but if they cannot reach an agreement, the more diligent party can request from the President of the Tribunal the appointment of three experts to separately rate the portion of occupied land and the value of the improvements, and to, in case that after this they still cannot reach an agreement, authorize to proceed with the Notary commissioned to sell in public auction the portion of land, and once this is done, and paying for the notary's expenses approved by a Judge, if they are in conformity, to distribute them [the proceeds] among the interested parties according to their fair value.

Article 7. The negligent co-proprietor who failed to register his titles or rights before a commissioned Notary, can make a rectification of the operation at his expense, through an authorization from the Tribunal, proving his status of legitimate co-proprietor, as long as he makes use of this right within three years, after the date in which the sentence's summary ordering the surveying was published in some newspaper. Once this period is over, his rights will have expired in favor of those who attended the division and it will become irrevocable.

Article 8. Once the operations ordered by the sentence dealt with in Article 2 are finished, the Surveyor will deposit in the Tribunal's Secretariat copies of the acts of the aforementioned operations with the assignations and the liquidations of the proportional part that corresponds to each stockholder in the divided lands and in the common expenses of the landowners, for them to be examined and approved, if in conformity, or modified if that were not the case, by the President and the Prosecutor.

A similar report, and for the same purposes, shall be presented by the commissioned Notary, for the corresponding honoraria for the acts dealt with in the said article.

Article 9. When it is a case solely of a place-to-place demarcation, according to Article 646, of the Civil Code, any co-owner may request a Surveyor to do it, under the formalities established by the Surveying Law, the expenses being paid by the requester; but if there is opposition or if the co-owners enter into a legal action, the operation will be carried out as common expenses between those who intervene as plaintiffs or defendants, whether the case is taken to the Mayor, if it is under his jurisdiction, or to the Tribunal of First Instance, if a determined portion of land is being discussed, or if the titles are being questioned.

Article 10. The current Law does not oppose in anything the faculties granted by Article 819, of the Civil Code to adults, if they are present and are capable, to divide it [the land] in the manner and through the document that they deem convenient.

Article 11. The Law of June 22, 1907, is repealed, which banned Notaries or those who do their work, to prepare an act of sale or transfer of communal lands; being able to prepare them without determining limits indicating only important actions, and including the customary rebate note in the seller's documents; everything under a two hundred pesos fine payable to the Municipality's communal treasury where the functionary works; and in case of missing the payment a month after the Attorney General's request, as well as in cases of recidivism, to their suspension and disqualification from their duties.

Article 12. The current Law repeals all other laws contrary to it and it will be sent to the Executive Branch for constitutional purposes.

Given in the Sessions' Room of the Senate on the seventeenth day of the month of April of 1909; sixty-sixth year of the Independence and forty-sixth of the Restoration.

The President of the Senate: F. L. Vasquez, The Secretaries: Carlos Ginebra, Ramón O. Lovatón.

Given in the Sessions' Room of the House of Deputies on the seventeenth day of the month of April of 1911; sixty-eighth year of the Independence and forty-eighth of the Restoration.

The President, A. Acevedo, The Secretaries, Tancredo Castellanos, I. A. Cernuda

Implement it, communicate it through the corresponding State Secretaryship, and publish it throughout the territory of the Republic to ensure its compliance.

Given in Santo Domingo, Capital of the Republic, on the twenty-first day of the month of April of 1911; sixty-eighth year of the Independence and forty-eighth of the Restoration.

Ramón Cáceres

Countersigned: Manuel de Jesús Troncoso de la Concha, Secretary of State of the Bureaus of Justice and Public Instruction

Countersigned: E. Tejera Bonetti, Interim Secretary of State of Agriculture and Immigration

LAW FOR AGRICULTURAL EXEMPTIONS[3]

The National Congress in the Name of the Republic, after having declared the urgency, has approved the following law:

Article 1. Agricultural enterprises are defined as: all establishments that are or will be destined to land cultivation.

Article 2. All natural or legal entities that own an enterprise of this kind will enjoy the following exemptions:

a) The right to plant, cultivate, prepare, manufacture, refine, distill, store, utilize, buy, sell, transport and export all products in their natural state, such as firewood, cabinetmaking and construction lumber, railroad ties, sugar cane, nuts, fibers, coffee, cotton, cacao, tobacco, resins, and others derived from them through manufactures such as sugar, molasses, turpentine, and similar ones.

b) The right to build, maintain, use, and operate any kind of mills, factories or plants to elaborate, preserve, dry, manufacture, refine, distill, or prepare for their own use or for the market any goods from the land whatsoever produced in the Republic, as well as [the right to] build works, buildings, machinery and necessary tools, for the use of the said mills, factories or plants and for the disposition and handling of their products including pipes, conductors, transporters, siphons, ponds, and other machinery to handle, store, ship and steer waters and products from such establishments.

c) The right to build tracks and to build and extend, maintain, use, and operate

3. Translated from *Gaceta Oficial*, no. 2207, July 8, 1911.

with any engines, private railroads of any kind and size to be used solely for the transportation of the goods and properties of the establishment that owns it and to build detours, forks and indispensable stations, as well as all appropriate works and convenient connections to other railroads.

d) The right to build, maintain, use, and operate bridges and piers, as long as they do not make difficult or impede free navigation in the waters where they are established, in navigable rivers or in estuaries, for the particular use of these enterprises, of any class and size, with their corresponding accesses and entrances, landfills, buildings, depots, warehouses, pools, machinery, and convenient works.

e) The right to deepen, widen, dredge, improve in any other way the ports and rivers where the piers of these enterprises are built according to this law.

f) The right to use foreign ships, tugboats, and ferries for the exportation of the products of these enterprises and the importation of the goods that they need from overseas, considering together each tugboat with the ferries that it carries in each trip as just one ship.

g) The right to extract and distribute through pumps, gravity, or other means water from the ocean, from any port, river, and public waters whatsoever, in amounts necessary or convenient to irrigate lands owned, leased, or occupied by these enterprises and to use it for any railroad, factories, or other works related to them, and for any agricultural or industrial purposes whatsoever, and to build, maintain, and use where they deem convenient wells, dams, depots, canals, ditches, pipes, aqueducts, pumps, and any other kind of irrigation and distribution works that they deem necessary to collect, raise, channel, distribute and use said waters.

h) The right to build, maintain, use, and operate, for the exclusive use of these enterprises, radiotelegraphs for the reception and transmission of telegrams to and from any place and distance, as well as private telegraph or telephone lines within the lands owned, leased, or occupied by these enterprises.

i) The right to establish, maintain, use, and operate stations and machinery for the production of electricity and lines with poles for its transmission in any place, in piers, or in lands owned, leased or occupied by these enterprises or over any railroad lines exploited by them whatsoever; and to use and dispose of electric power for any purpose of these enterprises.

Article 3. The exemptions agreed to in article 2 will have the following limitations:

1st—regarding exports by the cotton, fibers, tobacco, resins, sugar cane, firewood, and railroad ties industries, referred to in section (a), they will be duty free for a term of no less than eight years, after the publication of this law, though after this period, they could be prohibited by Congress or taxed with a duty and regarding the other products mentioned in the same section (a), their export will be regulated by the current laws in place, and their current duties cannot be increased for a term of no less than twenty-five years, after the publication of this Law.

In the case that anytime during those periods, agreed to in this article, local interests required the taxation in some manner of the products referred to in section (a) of article 2, any duty that is levied, whether fiscal or municipal, or fiscal and municipal, will not exceed in part or in total, the 2 percent ad valorem, according to domestic market estimates.

2nd—those referred to in section (b) will have no other limitations than those specified in the laws to guarantee the rights of third parties; and regarding those products whose exploitation or storage is governed by special laws, they will continue under the authority of those same laws.

3rd—those comprised in sections (c) and (d) will be governed by the policies decreed by the Executive Branch and to its approval of the works' blueprints.

4th—those that refer to section (e) cannot be enjoyed without previous authorization from the Executive Branch in each case.

5th—those in section (f) concerning the ships of these enterprises will be subject to the payment of port duties whenever they bring cargo directly for their development, in the proportion of 50 percent of the established or to be established [duties] for the other ships in general and referring to exports, whenever they are articles exported by the enterprises themselves and whose value does not exceed $5 per ton, they will pay 1 percent ad valorem, and 50 percent of the tariff established or to be established, when it exceeds that value.

6th—those related to section (g), regarding the use of waters, the enterprises must present to the Executive Branch, whenever it is not seawater, an account of the water volume required with a list of the rivers or lakes in which the intakes should be established, so that, if the Executive Branch finds that these do not harm neighboring properties or neighborhoods, it will authorize them, prescribing the amount of water that these enterprises will have for their service, which they could always use, as long as they have the same need that originated the request, motivating the authorization.

No dam can be constructed in public waters and no hydraulic work can be done on public domain lands without the authorization of the Executive Branch and without its authorization of the blueprints prepared for the work.

7th—the exemptions agreed to in section (h) are subject to the prohibition of using for public service the radiotelegraphic stations, the telegraph and telephone lines. At the same time, they are in the obligation to put these communication tools at the service of the State, if they shall be needed, in cases of emergency.

8th—those agreed to in section (i) are limited to not utilizing the electric power produced by the enterprises, except for their own needs, unless the Executive Branch grants them a special permission to extend it to others.

Article 4. The fiscal stationery used in the payment of import duties for machinery imported by the enterprises and in those of export and port [duties], as well as in the dispatching of their ships will have 50 percent of the value established by the fiscal stationary law used for these cases.

Article 5. Each person, society or national or foreign company, that wanted to establish farms in the Dominican Republic, according to this law, must, in order to obtain the authorization to settle, present to the Executive Branch:

a) Name, marital status, place of residence, names of associates, if any, the place where the enterprise is to be established, the kind of crops to be grown, the amount of personal or social capital and the main place of business.

In the case of a corporation or society organized under the laws of a Foreign State, place selected for residence in the Republic, as well as the name and place of residence of an adult person duly authorized to represent it.

b) Authentic titles justifying the ownership of the land or its leasing, or the right to its benefits for a period of no less than ten years, and for an amount of no less than 50 hectares, if it is devoted to nuts, coffee, cacao, tobacco, fruits, and minor crops, and 100 hectares if it is devoted to cotton and other fibers, sugar cane, rice, and similar ones.

Article 6. Granted the permission referred to in the previous article, businessmen may start immediately their works, an operation that gives them the right to start enjoying the exemptions guaranteed by this Law, given previous compliance with its policies.

Article 7. The exemptions granted by this law expire:

1st—for not having begun work within a year, after the date of the authorization granted by the Executive Branch.

2nd—for not having cultivated within a two-year term, after the date of the authorization, the amount of land set as a minimum for each kind of crop.

3rd—for the cessation or abandonment of the works during two consecutive years.

Article 8. In the case that any of these enterprises may need to build a railroad line or road; whether to connect two zones under cultivation that are separated by someone else's land, or to facilitate the communication of any of these zones with other roads or waterways needed for the transportation of their products, the construction of these ways, as well as of the piers and warehouses necessary for storage; the public interest as well as the legitimate need of these business for these constructions will be examined prior to granting permission for any of the aforementioned works.

Article 9. The agricultural enterprises may not bring in, for their development, immigrants workers who are not of the white race, as all immigration coming in for these enterprises must be in agreement with the laws in place in the country or with policies to be decreed.

Only when it is evident that the crops or harvests of a given year could be harmed by a lack of workers, will the Executive Branch be able to allow the immigration of persons of other races from the neighboring islands, or from another origin, and only for the crops or harvests of that year.

Article 10. The exemptions that this law agrees to do not include taxes on permits, which could be imposed according to the appropriate law, on the establishments created by these enterprises in the same manner and in the same form than to any other establishments whatsoever.

Article 11. The agricultural enterprises that currently exist in the Republic may enjoy the exemptions in this law if within a year, after its publication date, they comply with its terms, following all its indications and they obtain from the Executive Branch the corresponding authorization to start enjoying said exemptions.

Article 12. This law repeals all others that are contrary to it.

Please send to the Executive Branch for constitutional purposes. Given in the Sessions' Room of the Senate of the Republic, on the twenty-seventh day of the month of April of 1911; sixty-eighth year of the Independence and forty-eighth of the Restoration.

The President: Ramón O. Lovatón, The Secretaries: José R. López, E. Victoria.

Given in the Sessions' Room of the House of Deputies on the eleventh day of the month of May of 1911; sixty-eighth year of the Independence and forty-eighth of the Restoration.

The President: A. Acevedo, The Secretaries: I. A. Cernuda.

Implement it, communicate it through the corresponding State Secretaryship, and publish it throughout the territory of the Republic to ensure its compliance.

Given in Santo Domingo, Capital of the Dominican Republic, on the twenty-sixth day of the month of June 1911; sixty-eighth year of the Independence and forty-eighth of the Restoration.

Ramón Cáceres, President of the Republic

Countersigned: Federico Velázquez H., Secretary of State of Treasury and Commerce, Rafael Díaz, Secretary of State of Agriculture and Immigration

The United States Lands the Marines

After Cáceres was assassinated in late 1911, political turmoil returned. Over the next five years, the Dominican Republic had one short-lived government after another. The United States, concerned about its security interests in the region and the safekeeping of the Panama Canal, witnessed this political chaos with increasing apprehension. In 1915, similar concerns had led to the U.S. military occupation of Haiti. In the Dominican Republic, the United States already controlled that nation's finances, so a military takeover seemed like the next logical step. Moreover, the 1907 Convention, though it guaranteed the payment of the nation's debt, could not do anything to stop political infighting. Desiderio Arias, a regional caudillo from the Northwest, threatened the administration of Juan Isidro Jimenes for months until the latter finally resigned on May 7, 1916. Arias was considered a threat by the United States and his pro-German sympathies exacerbated U.S. wartime fears of German influence in the Caribbean region.

On May 16, 1916, U.S. Marines landed and quickly took control over most of the country, facing some resistance from Arias's troops. An interim government, headed by Francisco Henríquez y Carvajal, was not recognized by the U.S. government and was notified that it would not receive funds from the U.S.-operated customs receivership. In a show of defiance, a facade of sovereignty was maintained for several months: a penniless Dominican government continued to operate while U.S. Marines controlled the country's strategic points. Finally, unable to break the deadlock and barter an agreement to set up a Dominican puppet administration, U.S. President Woodrow Wilson ordered his military

130

forces to take over the country's administration. On November 29, 1916, U.S. Navy Captain Harry S. Knapp issued a proclamation officially announcing the U.S. military occupation of the Dominican Republic, which is reproduced below.

PROCLAMATION[4]

Whereas, a treaty was concluded between the United States of America and the Republic of Santo Domingo on February 8, 1907, Article III of which reads:

Until the Dominican Republic has paid the whole amount of the bonds of the debt its public debt shall not be increased except by previous agreement between the Dominican Government and the United States. A like agreement shall be necessary to modify the import duties, it being an indispensable condition for the modification of such duties that the Dominican Executive demonstrate and that the President of the United States recognize that, on the basis of exportations and importations of the like amount and the like character during the two years preceding that in which it is desired to make such modification, the total net customs receipts would at such altered rates of duties have been for each of such two years in excess of the sum of $2,000,000 United States gold;

and,

Whereas, the Government of Santo Domingo has violated the said Article III on more than one occasion; and

Whereas, the Government of Santo Domingo has from time to time explained such violation by the necessity of incurring expenses incident to the repression of revolution; and

Whereas, the United Sates Government, with great forbearance and with a friendly desire to enable Santo Domingo to maintain domestic tranquility and observe the terms of the aforesaid treaty, has urged upon the Government of Santo Domingo certain necessary measures which that Government has been unwilling or unable to adopt; and

Whereas, in consequence domestic tranquility has been disturbed and is not now established, nor is the future observance of the treaty by the Government of Santo Domingo assured; and

Whereas, the Government of the United States is determined that the time has come to take measures to insure the observance of the provisions of the aforesaid treaty by the Republic of Santo Domingo and to maintain the domestic tranquility in the said Republic of Santo Domingo necessary thereto;

Now, therefore, I, H. S. Knapp, Captain, United States Navy, commanding the Cruiser Force of the United States Atlantic Fleet, and the armed forces of the United

4. From U. S. Department of State, *Papers Relating to the Foreign Relations of the United States with the Address of the President to Congress, December 5, 1916* (Washington, D. C.: Government Printing Office, 1925), 246–247.

States stationed in various places within the territory of the Republic of Santo Domingo, acting under the authority and by the direction of the Government of the United States, declare and announce to all concerned that the Republic of Santo Domingo is hereby placed in a state of Military Occupation by the forces under my command, and is made subject to Military Government and to the exercise of military law applicable to such occupation.

This military occupation is undertaken with no immediate or ulterior object of destroying the sovereignty of the Republic of Santo Domingo, but, on the contrary, is designed to give aid to that country in returning to a condition of internal order that will enable it to observe the terms of the treaty aforesaid, and the obligations resting upon it as one of the family of nations.

Dominican statutes, therefore, will continue in effect in so far as they do not conflict with the objects of the Occupation or necessary regulations established there under, and their lawful administration will continue in the hands of such duly authorized Dominican officials as may be necessary, all under the oversight and control of the United States Forces exercising Military Government.

The ordinary administration of justice, both in civil and criminal matters, through the regularly constituted Dominican courts will not be interfered with by the Military Government herein established; but cases to which a member of the United States Forces in Occupation is a party, or in which are involved contempt or defiance of the authority of the Military Government, will be tried by tribunals set up by the Military Government.

All revenue accruing to the Dominican Government, including revenues hitherto accrued and unpaid, whether from customs duties under the terms of the Treaty concluded on February 8, 1907, the Receivership established by which remains in effect, or from internal revenue, shall be paid to the Military Government herein established, which will, in trust for the Republic of Santo Domingo, hold such revenue and will make all the proper legal disbursements there from necessary for the administration of the Dominican Government, and for the purposes of the Occupation.

I call upon the citizens of, and residents and sojourners in, Santo Domingo to cooperate with the Forces of the United States in Occupation to the end that the purposes thereof may promptly be attained, and that the country may be restored to domestic order and tranquility and to the prosperity that can be attained only under such conditions.

The Forces of the United States in Occupation will act in accordance with military law governing their conduct, with due respect for the personal and property rights of citizens of, and residents and sojourners in, Santo Domingo, upholding Dominican laws in so far as they do not conflict with the purposes for which the Occupation is undertaken.

H. S. Knapp, *Captain, U. S. Navy, Commander Cruiser Force, U. S. Atlantic Fleet*
U. S. S. *Olympia* Flagship
Santo Domingo City, R. D., November 29, 1916

The Dominican Constabulary

A major goal of U.S. military forces in the Dominican Republic—as elsewhere in the Caribbean—was the creation of a professional, apolitical, domestic military force. Up to then, countries like the Dominican Republic had been ravaged by the infighting of regional caudillos who by raising a large peasant army eventually took over the government, only to lose power after a few months in office. This vicious cycle was ended by the Marines who, first disarmed most of the population, and then started building the country's first modern army. The intention of the U.S. military authorities—who knew that at some point the occupation would end—was to organize a domestic military force capable of guaranteeing order and meeting any armed challenges after the Marines' departure. Ideally, this force would be well trained and armed, professional, and would refrain from engaging in politics, acting just as the guardian of constitutional order. By the nature of its main mission, the Dominican military would become a constabulary force, that is, a corps with a military structure but with essentially police functions.

Dominican National Guardsman

Unfortunately for the U.S. Marines, they did not get much cooperation from the Dominican upper classes; the children of the Dominican elites would not join the new constabulary. Therefore, when the Marines began organizing this corps, they had to accept individuals from middle-class backgrounds who had less than desirable qualifications. Such was the case of Rafael L. Trujillo from the town of San Cristóbal. Trujillo had little education, and in spite of what he claimed in the letter reproduced below, he had been in trouble with the law in the past. The Marines, who were short on candidates, accepted him. Trujillo became an officer in the newly-established Dominican National Guard and later quickly rose to commander of the army, from were it was just a short step to assuming the presidency and total power. The Dominican constabulary, which the U.S. Marines had naively intended to be the guarantor of constitutional order, instead became the launching pad for the political aspirations of new dictators.

LETTER BY RAFAEL L. TRUJILLO[5]

Santo Domingo, December 9, 1918
Mr. C. F. Williams, Commanding Colonel, G.N.D.
The City
Sir: The undersigned, through your honorable medium, requests a position as Officer in the honorable institution of the Dominican National Guard.

Begging your pardon for the inconvenience, I must let you know, that I do not have any vices of consuming alcoholic beverages nor of smoking and that I have not been subpoenaed to Court, not even for simple Police matters.

In my home town, San Cristóbal, 30 kilometers from this city, I belonged and belong to the upper class and my age is twenty-seven, of married status.

In San Cristóbal, honorable people can give faith of my manners and behavior, and in this capital, Messieurs Rafael A. Perdomo, Examining Magistrate of the 1st District, Eugenio A. Alvarez, Secretary of the Court of First Instance, and Licentiate Armando Rodríguez, Legal Consultant of the State Secretaryship of Justice and Public Instruction.

Sincerely yours, (signed) Rafael L. Trujillo

A Dominican's Assessment of the U.S. Military Occupation

Resistance to the U.S. military occupation of the Dominican Republic took various forms: from refusal by the political elites to the establishment of puppet regimes to armed struggle of peasant rebels in the East. Elite Dominicans would not cooperate with the U.S. military authorities

---

5. Translated from Ernesto Vega y Pagán, *Biografía militar del Generalísimo Doctor Rafael Leónidas Trujillo Molina, Benefactor de la Patria y Padre de la Patria Nueva* (Ciudad Trujillo: Editorial Atenas, 1957), 19.

and instead organized political movements to lobby for the end of the occupation. In particular, the Latin American republics stood firmly behind the Dominican people in denouncing the illegal nature of the U.S. military government. Moreover, many upperclass Dominicans, like poet Fabio Fiallo, ended up in jail for their public criticism of the U.S. military occupation. The U.S. military also responded by imposing strict press censorship on any news piece deemed critical. Often, entire sections of Dominican newspapers were published blank, so as to show the people the effects of censorship. Other Dominicans openly resisted with force. Particularly in the country's eastern region, groups of peasants organized guerrilla armies which forced the Marines into protracted, unpopular anti-guerrilla military campaigns. It took the Marines several years to finally crush the rebellion of the *gavilleros* (road bandits), as the U.S. military authorities preferred to call them.

In essence, the U.S. military authorities trampled the rights of the Dominican people across the board. One of the major ironies of the U.S. military occupation was that it was led by the world's greatest democracy, yet these same democratic ideals did not seem to extend overseas. The Marines treated the Dominican people in a brutal, racist, and condescending manner. Many atrocities were committed, particularly against the peasantry, as is documented in the courts martial of officers and enlisted Marines who committed crimes while in the country. As was the case with other U.S. military occupations in the Caribbean, these events were becoming increasingly embarrassing for the U.S. government. Increasingly, all forms of resistance, peaceful or not, would bring a shortened end to what originally was intended to be a long-term military occupation. The U.S. Marines were stationed in the Dominican Republic just eight years, compared to nineteen in neighboring Haiti.

Monsignor Adolfo A. Nouel, Archbishop of Santo Domingo, was one of the most influential figures of his time. He even had briefly served as provisional president in 1912–1913 in a vain attempt to serve as a conciliatory figure while organizing new elections. Monsignor Nouel was also a known critic of the U.S. military occupation. So, when U.S. Minister William W. Russell sent him a letter asking for his impressions on the policies of the U.S. military government, Nouel responded in a sharp and caustic tone. His dignified stance represents well the feelings of the Dominican elites at the time: they felt powerless in the face of the overwhelming U.S. military presence, yet they would not budge from their peaceful, non-cooperative resistance to the occupation. His reply to Minister Russell is reproduced below.

LETTER BY MONSIGNOR ADOLFO R. NOUEL, ARCHBISHOP OF SANTO DOMINGO, TO U. S. MINISTER WILLIAM W. RUSSELL[6]

Santo Domingo, D.R., December 29, 1920
Mr. W. W. Russell, Minister of the United States
The City
Honorable Sir,

It is your wish to hear my impression of the current state of the nation. So I will tell you that I believe I am not mistaken when I say that the country is in a prosperous state. The individual efforts are intense. Nature has rewarded the land with good crops, and the fact that the exporting prices on our products are still high is so that the farmers may recover from the damage suffered in the previous years. Peace reigns throughout the country; and the people want to keep it and take advantage of it. But the people are also afraid that it will not be possible for them to continue in a state in which they cannot freely enjoy the fruits of their labor, and are therefore afraid to end up in a state of veritable slavery in the long term.

The people have suffered, not happily, but at least resigned, the embarrassment and the burden of an intervention. The people have suffered military sentences in purely civilian issues, when according to Admiral Knapp's decree, that tribunal could not judge but military issues. It has suffered (claim) court sentences issued in a sovereign manner without the right to appeal.

The people recognize the need of paying direct taxes over territorial property; but they cannot be satisfied with some unjust precepts from an almost incomprehensible law due to its complex and very difficult application in practice.

The people have patiently endured that, for some years, a part of the six million pesos that it was forced to sign for when the convention took place, supposedly to foster their wealth, has been invested in luxury salaries for employees and directors. The Public Works Office is considered by the people a veritable safety valve through which a great deal of the people's money, destined for roads, etc., has escaped and still escapes. As far as I know, that office was created because it was believed that in Santo Domingo there were neither professionals qualified to direct the works nor honest men for the administration of the funds; but in practice the result has been that the current scientific leadership of Public Works has less technical capacity than any of our master builders, and the administration of funds is equally or more endan-

---

6. Translated from Antonio Hoepelman and Juan A. Senior, eds., *Documentos históricos que se refieren a la intervención armada de los Estados Unidos de Norte América y la implantación de un gobierno militar americano en la República Dominicana* (Santo Domingo: Imprenta de J. R. vda. García, 1922), 17–19.

gered, as if it were in the hands of some of our speculators. And that status quo is maintained, according to some versions, because the system of rewards for services rendered in electoral foreign politics there in the United States supposedly requires it.

The people have endured for three years a Press censorship that is not only humiliating and demeaning, but also ridiculous and childish. I remember having seen a scientific article objected to by a censor, with his seal and signature, prohibiting its publication because the author of the article said: "Kant, the great German thinker, father of modern philosophy, cannot be considered inferior to Aristotle nor to Plato, etc." The war against Germany had already begun and that poor censor may have believed that the praise lavished on the great German philosopher could cause the defeat of the Allied armies.

A Spanish priest, of exemplary conduct, who worked saving souls in Sánchez, was jailed, kept isolated, and locked in Samaná in a dirty dungeon, where he spent close to six months, for the simple fact of having praised in an after-dinner conversation, in the hotel where he was staying, and well before the United States entered the war, the valor and the organization of the German army.

It is true that the Dominican people in their political commotions witnessed more than once unjust persecutions, violations of individual rights, summary executions, etc. . . ; but it never knew about the water torture, about the cremation of women and children, about the twist of the rope, about the hunting of men in the savannas as if they were savage animals, nor about the dragging of an old man in his seventies from the tail of a horse in broad daylight in the central square of Hato Mayor.

We, I do not deny it, knew about fraud in business and petty theft of public funds; but with the help and the lessons from some foreigners, we have perfected ourselves in the art of chicanery and in large-scale squandering.

An American Consul, around the year 1887, taught us to load ships with useless firewood as if they were shipments of good mahogany that were lost in our port without the slightest breeze roughing up the waters of the Caribbean Sea.

Banditry was among us an exotic plant; lately it has been implanted and patronized on several occasions by some foreigners that profited more easily in their businesses under our ancient Creole regime.

The National Guard still has neither a good composition nor a proper leadership. This institution, the sole guarantor of society, should be commanded by men of more prestige.

Fortunately the top leaders of the Military Government make the effort to rectify errors and to prevent the repetition of past horrors. I have known many American officers and employees who, for their correctness and enlightenment, honor their country. But you will understand that in the people's imagination the effects of an injustice and an outrage last longer than the consequences of a thousand good actions according to the law.

I do not doubt that if the three memoranda that the Consulting Board gave the Military Government are well studied; that if the American Government takes this people out of the uncertainty in which they live regarding their future destiny and speaks to them with full clarity regarding their present conditions, that if it is able to maintain within rational limits the aspirations of Capital and the unjust appetites of speculators without scruples nor conscience are moderated and if they are convinced that their sacrifices and heroism suffered seventy-five years ago to obtain their freedom and the right to independent government, as it was then obtained from all the civilized nations of the world, will not be unfruitful, that people will become sincere and grateful friends of the great people of Lincoln and Washington.

Adolfo A. Nouel, Archbishop of Santo Domingo

The Hughes-Peynado Plan

The opposition by Dominicans from all social strata to the U.S. military occupation shortened it drastically. As early as 1920, U.S. President Woodrow Wilson ordered the drafting of a plan to end the occupation. After several failed efforts, an agreement was reached by the Warren G. Harding administration and a group of Dominican political leaders led by the prominent lawyer Francisco J. Peynado. The plan, negotiated by Peynado and U.S. Secretary of State Charles Evans Hughes, and thus informally known as the "Hughes-Peynado Plan," eventually led to the departure of the U.S. forces in 1924.

The plan called for the establishment of a provisional government led by Dominicans, the drafting of a new constitution, and the scheduling of elections before U.S. troops left the country. From the standpoint of the United States, one of the plan's most important provisions was that the legal acts of the U.S. military government would be recognized by the new Dominican administration. Moreover, the 1907 Customs Receivership Agreement would remain in place until the Dominican Republic finally paid off its external debt. These two points guaranteed the defense of U.S. political and economic interests in the country.

When the occupation finally ended in 1924, the Dominican Republic had become a vastly different nation. Sovereignty had been restored, giving rise to the Third Republic. The foundations of a modern state had been laid by the U.S. military forces by the creation of a professional bureaucracy. Previously isolated regions of the country were now connected by a growing network of roads, and cars and trucks were also increasingly common. But more importantly, a modern military force effectively monopolized the means of coercion. Although not many politicians recognized it then, the era of the regional caudillos was over. Now, whoever controlled the military, also controlled the nation.

MEMORANDUM OF THE PLAN OF JUNE 30, 1922,
FOR THE WITHDRAWAL OF THE MILITARY GOVERNMENT,
SIGNED AT WASHINGTON, JULY 3, 1922 [7]

1. Announcement by the Military Government that a Provisional Government will be set up for the purpose of promulgating legislation to regulate the holding of elections, and to provide for the reorganization of the provincial and municipal governments, and to enable the Dominican people to make such amendments to the Constitution as they may deem appropriate and hold elections without the intervention of the Military Government. At the same time, the Military Government will announce that it will delegate to the Provisional Government administrative powers to carry out freely the aforesaid purposes.

2. Choice of a Provisional President and his Cabinet by a majority vote of a Commission composed of General Horacio Vásquez, Don Federico Velásquez, Don Elías Brache, Don Francisco J. Peynado and Monseñor Dr. Adolfo A. Nouel, upon the inclusion of whom the four above named representatives have agreed. The Commission, in determining upon the members of the Provisional Government, will determine the conditions placed upon the exercise of that Government, and the said Commission, by a majority vote, will fill the vacancies that may occur in that Government on account of death, resignation, or disability of any of its members. Upon the inauguration of the Provincial Government, the Executive Departments of the Dominican Republic shall be turned over to the members of the Cabinet thus designated. There shall be no change in the personnel of these Departments during the term of the Provisional Government, except for duly proved cause. Officials in charge of the Executive Departments of the Military Government will lend their assistance to the respective Secretaries of State of the Provisional Government. There shall be no payment made by the Department of Finance except in accordance with the Budget in force, nor will any payment be made otherwise than is customary. Any necessary items of expenditure not provided for in the Budget will be appropriated by the Provisional Government in accord with the Military Governor. Immediately upon the installation of the Provisional Government, the Military Government will deliver to that Government the National Palace, and at the same time, the Military Forces of the United States in the Dominican Republic will be concentrated at one, two, or three places, as may be determined by the Military Governor. From that date, peace and order will be maintained by the Dominican National Police under the orders of the Provisional Government, except in the case of serious disturbances which, in the opinion of the Provisional Government and of the Military Governor, cannot be suppressed by the Forces of the Dominican National Police.

3. The Provisional President will promulgate the legislation above referred to concerning the holding of elections and the reorganization of the Government of the Provinces and Communes.

4. The Provisional President will convene the Primary Assemblies in accordance with the provisions of the new election law and those assemblies will elect the electors as provided by Article 84 of the present Constitution.

7. From U.S. Department of State, *Papers Relating to the Foreign Relations of the United States, 1922* (Washington, D.C.: U.S. Government Printing Office, 1938), vol. 2, 33–35.

5. The Electoral Colleges so elected by the Primary Assemblies will elect the members of the Senate and of the Chamber of Deputies and will prepare the lists of the members of the Judiciary to be submitted to the National Senate.

6. The Congress will vote the necessary amendments to the Constitution and will issue the call for the election of the Constituent Assembly, to which the proposed amendments will be submitted.

7. The Provisional President will designate plenipotentiaries to negotiate a Convention of Ratification reading as follows:

I. The Dominican Government hereby recognizes the validity of all the Executive and Departmental Orders promulgated by the Military Government and published in the *Official Gazette*, which may have levied taxes, authorized expenditures, or established rights on behalf of third persons, of Administrative Regulations issued, and of the contracts which may have been entered into, in accordance with those Orders or with any law of the Republic. These Orders, Regulations, and contracts are those listed below:

The Dominican Government likewise recognizes the Orders above mentioned as having been laws of the Republic from the date of their promulgation and agrees that they shall remain in full force and effect unless and until they are severally and lawfully abrogated. The Dominican Government further agrees that neither the subsequent abrogation of these Orders, nor any law, executive order or other official act of the Dominican Government, shall affect the validity and security of rights acquired in accordance with those orders and contracts of the Military Government.

II. The Dominican Government, in accordance with the provisions of Article I, specifically recognizes the bond issue of 1918 and the twenty-year 52 percent Customs Administration Sinking Fund Gold Bond Issue authorized in 1922, as legal, binding, and irrevocable obligations of the Republic, and pledges its full faith and credit to the maintenance of the service of these bond issues, and to the complete execution of the contracts in accordance with which the bonds were issued.

III. The Dominican Government and the Government of the United States agree that the Convention signed on February 8, 1907, between the United States and the Dominican Republic, shall remain in force as long as any bonds of the issues of 1918 and 1922 shall remain unpaid, and that the duties of the General Receiver of Dominican Customs appointed in accordance with that Convention shall be extended to include the collection and application of the revenues pledged for the service of these bond issues in accordance with the terms of the Executive Orders and of the contracts under which the bonds were issued.

IV. This agreement shall take effect after its approval by the Senate of the United States and the Congress of the Dominican Republic.

This Convention will be referred to the Dominican Congress for its approval. The Congress will, in addition, pass a law recognizing, independently of the Convention of Ratification, the validity of the Orders, of the Administrative Regulations and of the contracts referred to in the said Convention.

8. The members of the Judicial Power will be elected in accordance with the

140

Constitution.

9. Immediately after all the steps specified in the foregoing articles have been taken, and after the Dominican Congress has approved the Convention and passed the law mentioned in Article 7, the members of the Executive Power will be elected in accordance with the Constitution. Immediately upon taking possession of his office, the President will sign the law ratifying the Executive Orders and the Convention, and the Military Forces of the United States, will then leave the Dominican Republic.

(Signed) Horacio Vásquez   Federico Velásquez   E. Brache, Hijo   Francisco J. Peynado

Haiti and a New Border Treaty

Since 1777, when the Treaty of Aranjuez called for the establishment of a fixed border between the French colony of Saint-Domingue and the Spanish colony of Santo Domingo, no new border treaties had been signed. Shortly thereafter, both colonies disappeared and were replaced by the independent states of Haiti and the Dominican Republic. Moreover, since its revolutionary war, Haiti had been occupying border territories formerly belonging to Spanish Santo Domingo. The Spanish and Dominican governments claimed these territories for decades, until President Ulises Heureaux renounced the Dominican claim in exchange for 400,000 pesos.

Although several attempts at mediation were made during the nineteenth century, it was not until the U.S. military occupation of Haiti (1915–1934) and the Dominican Republic (1916–1924) that the issue was revived, mostly at the behest of U.S. leaders. The United States, as part of its strategic concerns in the region, saw the lack of a defined Haitian-Dominican border as a potential source of conflict, and maybe war, between the two nations. Interested in preserving order within its new sphere of influence, the United States played an important role in getting the two parties to the negotiating table.

The border treaty was finally completed in 1929, under the administration of Dominican President Horacio Vásquez and with Haiti still under U.S. military occupation—though Haitian President Louis Borno ruled with restricted powers. A bi-national commission was set up to survey and clearly identify with cement markers the border line. Though the treaty was signed in 1929, it was not until 1936 that the surveying and agreements were finalized, thus establishing the fixed border that separates the two nations to this day.

TREATY BETWEEN THE DOMINICAN REPUBLIC AND HAITI ESTABLISHING A FIXED BORDER[8]

Santo Domingo, January 21, 1929

In the Name of Almighty God

The President of the Dominican Republic and the President of the Republic of Haiti;

Insofar as the Dominican Republic and the Republic of Haiti as sovereign, independent and Free States, share the territory of the Island where they are established;

Insofar as the Dominican people and the Haitian people, who have given, in the past, brilliant, glorious, and unforgettable proof of solidarity in the maintenance of their independence, remain indissolubly bound to the same Ideal of Peace, of Justice, and of Progress, and must unite their efforts to perpetuate this noble and lofty Ideal;

Insofar as in consonance with this Ideal the Dominican Republic and the Republic of Haiti must put a definitive end to the differences that have divided them in the past regarding the demarcation of the border line that separates their respective territories;

Insofar as to that end the Government of the Dominican Republic and the Government of the Republic of Haiti have proceeded to the study and careful consideration, from the legal, and historical, dual points of reference, of that issue, and taking into consideration the reciprocal interests, the equity and the local necessities of one and the other peoples, have come to establish which one is the line that separates the respective territories of the two Republics;

Insofar as for its legal existence and as the sole legal bond that is to unite the Dominican Republic and the Republic of Haiti regarding its borders that line must be described in a Treaty and its layout must be done in the field;

Insofar as the President of the Dominican Republic and the President of the Republic of Haiti have appointed their respective Plenipotentiaries namely:

The President of the Dominican Republic to Messieurs:

Dr. José D. Alfonseca, Vice President of the Republic, Dr. Manuel de J. Troncoso de la Concha, Professor at Universidad Central, Lic. Francisco J. Peynado; Lic. Angel Morales, Extraordinary Envoy and Plenipotentiary Minister of the Republic in the United States of America; Lic. M. A. Peña Batlle, Legal Counsel of the Dominican Legation in Port-au-Prince, and General José de J. Alvarez;

The President of the Republic of Haiti to:

Lic. León Dejean, Extraordinary Envoy and Plenipotentiary Minister of the Republic of Haiti in the Dominican Republic, who after having exchanged their full powers, have agreed on the following articles:

Article One: (A very detailed description of the border line from north to south follows here).

---

8. Translated from Vicente Tolentino Rojas, *Historia de la división territorial, 1494–1943* (Santiago: Editorial "La Nación" de L. Sánchez Andújar, 1944), 229–238.

Article Two: In order to determine with the required precision the dividing line described in the previous article and in order to establish on the ground, in the places, in the way and at the time specified below, markers showing the limits of both Republics, a Commission made up of six members, three for each Republic, will be organized.

Article Three: During the fifteen-day period after the exchange of the ratifications of the current Treaty, the Government of the Dominican Republic and the Government of the Republic of Haiti, will appoint the members of the Commission whose respective designation they have agreed to and in that same term they should officially notify each other.

1st—This Commission shall be organized within fifteen days after the exchange of ratifications of the current Treaty and it will meet and it will begin its work sixty days after the said exchange, except for unforeseen circumstances duly established and notified to both Governments; in this case the Undersigning High Parties will agree to establish a new date so that the tracing will take place as soon as possible.

2nd—The Commission thus organized will meet in the mouth of the Dajabón or Massacre River, in any of the banks of this river and will start right away its work and proceed without interruptions until its end. It must prepare an act every day and a chart of its operations that will be forwarded to the Dominican Government and the Haitian Government as soon as they are signed and sealed by the Commission.

3rd—It is understood that when in Article One it says that the line goes from one point to the other, this is a straight line, unless in the description it had been expressed in some other manner.

When the configuration of the terrain does not allow for the placement of markers, the Commission could alter the line as justly needed.

4th—In the places where the line goes over mountains, it shall always be understood that it follows the waters' dividing line.

5th—The decisions of the Delimitation Commission will be based on a voting majority, this majority consisting of at least two votes from each party.

6th—The acts as well as the charts should be made in two originals. The acts shall be written in Spanish and in French.

Article Four: In the case that difficulties may arise regarding the tracing of the line in some point and it were not possible for the two Undersigning High Parties to reach an agreement, an act will be prepared in the manner indicated in the previous article and it shall be forwarded to both Undersigning High Parties, so that it will be established as it is envisioned in Article Seven and those following it. The tracing operations shall continue after the next point on which there is no disagreement.

Article Five: In case of resignation, death or disqualification of any of the members of the Delimitation Commission, he shall be replaced within a fifteen-day period.

Article Six: The markers referred to in Article Two should have in the side facing the Dominican Republic the letters R.D. and in the side facing the Republic of Haiti R.H., and in both [sides] the numerals of the year of the current Treaty.

They will be placed every one thousand meters, unless the configuration of the terrain forces their placement at a greater distance.

Article Seven: In order to solve in a sovereign manner any differences that may emerge amongst the Delimitation Commission as a result of the tracing of the border line agreed to in Article One, and to determine in those places where the Delimitation Commission has not reached an agreement, the tracing of the line and its marking on the terrain according to the dispositions of Article Two of this Treaty, a Mixed Commission composed of five members elected in this manner will be organized: a Dominican one [chosen] by the President of the Dominican Republic, a Haitian one by the President of the Republic of Haiti, an American one by the President of the United States of America, a Brazilian one by the President of the United States of Brazil, and a Venezuelan one by the President of the United States of Venezuela, by requests made to them by the Undersigning Parties.

As soon as the first disagreement were to take place any of the two Governments will be able to request the other to jointly address the President of each one of the Republics designated in the current article so that the respective appointment is made. Immediately after being officially notified of the appointments made by the Presidents referred to in this article, the President of the Dominican Republic and the President of the Republic of Haiti will proceed to make the respective appointments of the Dominican and Haitian members of the Mixed Commission.

Article Eight: The members of the Mixed Commission will meet in the city of Santo Domingo sixty days after both Undersigning Parties are officially informed of the appointment of the three foreign members of the Commission, and their first duty will be to prepare and adopt regulations to which the procedures that they will observe in the performance of their task will be adjusted.

Article Nine: The Government of the Dominican Republic and the Government of the Republic of Haiti will submit to the Mixed Commission the issues that it will have to decide, clearly determining them.

Both Undersigning High Parties will provide the Commission, to the extent that each one of them deems convenient, with the necessary facilities for the full knowledge and exact appreciation of the facts that it must elucidate.

Article Ten: The issues will be solved by a strict majority of votes; it is to be understood that this majority will be made up of three votes in any case and under any circumstances.

Article Eleven: The decisions of the Commission will be final and therefore not subject to any appeals.

Article Twelve: Each one of the Undersigning High Parties may seek representation in the heart of the Delimitation Commission as well as in that of the Mixed Commission by one or several Delegates, who may deliberate, but do not vote.

Article Thirteen: Each Undersigning High Party will pay for the expenses of the Commissioners and Delegates that it respectively appoints. The expenses of the other Commissioners, of the placement of markers, and in general of the implementation of the current Treaty will be borne equally by both Undersigning High Parties.

Article Fourteen: A general chart of the tracing will be forwarded, as well as its description, by the Delimitation Commission to both Governments. This chart and, if need be, the one done by the Mixed Commission, will be considered as integral parts of the current Treaty.

Article Fifteen: Both Undersigning High Parties agree that the reconnaissance that they do of the line described in Article One as definitive and permanent border between the two countries is subjected, in an explicit manner, to the condition that the material tracing of the said line faithfully takes place within the provisions and stipulations contained in the body of this Treaty.

As soon as that condition is met, the agreed and traced line will be considered as the only one that at all times has separated the Dominican Republic and the Republic of Haiti.

Article Sixteen: Though there has never been any controversy regarding the ownership of the Adjacent Islands which are located near the mouth of the Dajabón or Massacre River and those of the Pedernales River; let the record show in the current Treaty that the following Islands, Islets and Keys are and have always been under the sovereignty of the Dominican Republic: from the North: Los Siete Hermanos and La Cabra; from the South: La Beata, Alta Vela or Alto Velo and Los Frailes.

Article Seventeen: The Government of the Dominican Republic and the Government of the Republic of Haiti renounce from now on and forever in the most formal, definitive, and solemn manner to any financial claim that the Dominican State has or could have had against the Haitian State or that the Haitian State has or could have had against the Dominican State.

However, the Government of the Republic of Haiti takes upon itself, the settlement of any indemnity to be paid to the Haitians whose properties were confiscated in 1844 in Dominican territory.

Article Eighteen: All difficulties, of any nature whatsoever, between the two Governments, in relation to the current Treaty, will be subjected to arbitration, without affecting all other conciliatory procedures, except those indicated in Article Seven and following ones.

Article Nineteen: The current Treaty will be approved and ratified by the Undersigning High Parties in accordance to their respective laws and the ratifications shall be exchanged in the City of Santo Domingo de Guzmán.

In witness thereof, the Plenipotentiaries sign and seal the current Treaty, in both originals, in the Spanish language and the French language, which have equal validity, in the City of Santo Domingo de Guzmán, on the twenty-ninth day of the month of January of the year of Grace of nineteen twenty-nine.

(Signed) Dr. José D. Alfonseca. M. de J. Troncoso de la Concha. Francisco J. Peynado. Angel Morales. M. A. Peña Batlle. J. de J. Alvarez. León Dejean. (Seals)

The 1930 "Revolution"

The old Dominican caudillos had now inherited a new country, and even though its face had been changed by the U.S. military occupation, the caudillos' old ways remained steadfast. For example, after President Vásquez assumed office in 1924, he extended his presidential term from four to six years, a move known as the "Prolongation." Vásquez and his followers argued that he had been elected under the old, 1908 constitution, which called for a six-year term. The opponents of the "Prolongation" argued that Vásquez had been sworn in after the implementation of the 1924 constitution, which called for a four-year term. This divisive issue led to the resurgence of factionalism and caudillo politics in Dominican politics. Vásquez was able to get away with extending his term until 1930, but when he decided to seek reelection, the opposition was galvanized into action. By that time, Vásquez was old and sick, and different political movements sought ways to get rid of him. In October 1929, he was flown to Baltimore for the removal of a kidney. The absence of the president set several conspiracies into motion. One of them involved the army's chief, General Rafael L. Trujillo, who had quickly risen through the ranks in no small measure thanks to the trust that Vásquez had placed in him. Trujillo conspired with members of the political opposition, in particular Rafael Estrella Ureña, a former member of Vásquez's government from Santiago, who now joined forces with some Jimenistas.

Vásquez returned to the country in January 1930, and on February 23, 1930, rebel forces attacked the San Luis army fortress in Santiago, taking it. The mock attack had been carefully coordinated by Estrella Ureña and Trujillo to give the impression of an all-out popular rebellion. Within three days, the rebels entered the capital, as the army did nothing to stop them. Vásquez, now fully aware of Trujillo's treachery, sought political asylum. By engaging in the old caudillo politics of the past, the first freely elected government of the Third Republic had brought about its own demise. The revolutionaries' manifesto, justifying their actions, is reproduced below.

MANIFESTO FROM THE SUPREME CHIEF OF THE REVOLUTION RAFAEL ESTRELLA UREÑA[9]

To the Nation

The Dominican people are worried about the serious situation that affects them at this hour. They, unanimously, demand a rapid and energetic action to stop the breakdown of the Republic. A solution that would save it from the economic collapse of The National Treasury that faces a crisis that will lead to the tremendous bankruptcy, which in the Institutional Order, as a denial to our purely democratic organization, inherited from the lofty principles of the French Revolution, is harming the traditions of the republican ideal.

9. Translated from *La Información* newspaper, Santiago, February 24, 1930.

As an interpreter of that unanimous longing, of that common aspiration, which is in all the spirits illuminating over the dark perspectives of our future the last rainbow of hope, I launch myself today to render viable the longing that is carried by all classes of the country in their torn hearts, raising again, with the soul at the same time embittered and convinced, the flag of the ideal that has found no medium in the field of civic-mindedness and that finds itself compelled to seek refuge in that other field of abnegation and rebelliousness where free men enforce their principles of civilization and democracy under the banners of armed protest.

I have been the first to proclaim in my political programs, as well as in the people's tribune, the need for keeping the peace that is so indispensable for the country's happiness. That is why, together with the other directors of the Alliance, I have requested, by all legal means, the reform of the current Electoral Law, which takes away from the act of suffrage all the guarantees and all the liberties required to become the truthful and free expression of the citizens' conscience. These efforts have been useless, given the stubbornness that men in power interpose to perpetuate themselves, making tenure in office elastic and tossing blots of ignominy over the white tunic of institutions.

We cannot cross our arms, in an attitude of indifference and cowardice, in view of the current situation fraught with dangers for the future of the Republic. The economic disaster provoked by the squandering of eighty-six million pesos in less than six years of administrative blunders; the ruin of commerce and national industry, due to the lack of a far-sighted regime that would put into practice a series of wise and energetic protective measures; the stagnation of agriculture; the reduction, increasingly alarming, of our export activity; the prostitution of justice; the corruption of education, in whose classrooms politics has entered with its entourage of shadows that negate the moral authority of the Dominican teacher; public disconcert; and as a banner of ridicule that floats over all this accumulation of betrayal, the moral anarchy planted in the country's heart for the scandalous impunity with which fraud thrives in all sectors of public administration and for the outrage which with each step the supreme law that governs the institutional life of the state is ignored every step of the way.

To place a retaining wall to that general disconcert, ruinous for the future of the teetering nation, I face the men in power with weapons in hand, since I cannot carry, unfortunately, the discredited codes of the laws mocked so many times. I am resolved to offer the country, under an oath of honor, economic stability, moral tranquility, protection of commerce and industry, now in ruins, judicial peace, electoral freedom, and to establish, finally, in the heart of Dominican society the rule of the democratic principles that today force us to travel once more to the dark paths of the past.

And now, may the national conscience, dispassionate and austere, condemn the real culprits and may posterity reserve for them the curse of history.

Rafael Estrella Ureña, Commanding General of the Revolutionary Troops

CHAPTER FIVE

The Trujillo Dictatorship

TRUJILLO PRESIDENTE INMEDIATAMENTE

891501

UN VOTO

UN VOTO

El Pueblo   Dominica

UN VOTO POR TRUJILLO

The thirty-one-year rule of Generalissimo Rafael L. Trujillo Molina (1930–1961) represents one of the darkest chapters in Dominican history. Renamed the "Trujillo Era" by the regime, this period was characterized by Trujillo's iron-fisted rule, widespread political repression, gross human rights violations, and large-scale corruption among the Trujillo family and their closest collaborators. Though Trujillo's rule has often been viewed as unique and exceptional, more objective analyses of his regime place it within the tradition of sultanistic regimes that prevailed in the Caribbean basin region throughout the twentieth century—alongside dictators like Fulgencio Batista of Cuba, Anastacio Somoza of Nicaragua, and François "Papa Doc" Duvalier of Haiti. To a certain extent, the Trujillo dictatorship was the culmination of trends dating back to the birth of the Dominican Republic. Despotism, praetorianism, nepotism, corruption, personality cult, and other political ills associated with authoritarian regimes were certainly nothing new to the Dominican people. The nineteenth-century despotic administrations of Pedro Santana, Buenaventura Báez, and Ulises Heureaux provide some sobering precedents. However,

Trujillo's rule happened to coincide with the post-U.S. occupation period and the dictator came to "inherit" a country that had been pacified, its population had been mostly disarmed, and a new professional army had been created. These modernizing twentieth-century developments, coupled with Trujillo's strong-willed, amoral personality, led inevitably to the establishment of a well-entrenched dictatorship.

The Trujillo dictatorship also benefited from pent-up feelings among the Dominican elites. For decades, the Dominican upper classes had decried their country's political and economic chaos and the lack of an effective leadership to impose order, conditions that had even led to a humiliating loss of sovereignty to the United States. In their quest for order, many members of the Dominican elites saw in Trujillo their redeemer. Trujillo, for his part, knew that he needed skilled men to rule the country and presented himself as the nation's savior and the bearer of a "new order." This symbiotic relationship, coupled with Trujillo's widespread use of coercion (thanks to his absolute control over the army), gave him virtually free reign over the country, which he ruled as his personal fiefdom.

No other leader before or after Trujillo held such absolute rule over the Dominican Republic for such a long time. Thousands of Dominicans were born, raised, and often died, knowing nothing else but Trujillo's rule. Intellectuals at his service even concocted a loose *Trujillista* ideology based on personality cult, ultra-nationalism, anti-Haitian scapegoating, Catholicism, and later, anti-communism. Not surprisingly, Trujillo's assassination on the night of May 30, 1961, caught the nation by surprise and sent the regime into a downward spiral. Trujillo had held onto power for so long, and in such an absolute manner that it was practically impossible for someone within the regime to replace him. The so-called Trujillo Era left an indelible imprint on the political culture and psyche of the Dominican people. The nation emerged from this dark period without any democratic institutions or experience, and with a political culture characterized by fear and distrust for the authorities and fellow citizens.

The Making of a Dictatorship

After the overthrow of President Horacio Vásquez—and even though he had made it public that he had no political ambitions—Rafael Trujillo ran for the presidency in the 1930 elections. The electoral contest was marred by widespread political repression conducted by the military and members of a gang at Trujillo's service known as "La 42." At one point, even the members of the Central Electoral Board, who were overseeing the elections, resigned. They were replaced with a rubber-stamp body loyal to Trujillo. The press, as well as the judicial branch, was also intimidated. As a result, Trujillo won the election easily and was inaugurated on August 16, 1930.

His inauguration was one of the most pompous ever. Trujillo, a megalomaniac who loved publicity and considered himself a predestined being, orchestrated an elaborate show for the people, capped by his first presidential speech, reproduced below. The central theme of his speech was the country's severe economic crisis—a result of the Great Depression that had started in 1929. Trujillo's regime thus began at a very difficult historical juncture, yet he was able to weather this crisis, and eventually, many others.

Trujillo's meteoric rise to power had proven what few Dominicans had realized: that whoever controlled the armed forces could now rule the country virtually unopposed. These same armed forces that the U.S. Marines had organized as an apolitical body had now become the perfect springboard for Trujillo's political aspirations.

TRUJILLO'S INAUGURAL ADDRESS[1]

Mr. President of the National Assembly, Messieurs Representatives:

I appear before you to take the constitutional oath that allows me to exercise the presidency with which I have been honored by the votes of my fellow citizens. The compromise I now make in respect of the constitution and the laws of the nation . . . has for me the transcendence it receives through the unique circumstance that it is formulated before you, who have been elected by the same votes as was I in the May elections. The same responsibilities, the same high national interest that inspired the supporters of our candidacies, bring us close together in facing the future, we carry

---

1. Translated from Rafael Leónidas Trujillo Molina, *Discursos, mensajes y proclamas* (Ciudad Trujillo: n.p., 1938), vol. 1, 17–23.

on our shoulders the weight of government. The same civic effort displayed, the same energy put into the service of the cause that we represent, will serve without doubt to promote the governmental agenda we initiate on this memorable day under the protection of the sacred spirits of our ancestors; those glorious champions who, on August 16, 1863, wrote in the pages of our history with blood the enduring journey begun at Capotillo.

In the brief, tumultuous national existence, frequently disturbed by acts as violent as they were unexpected, one may not be able to pinpoint any moment more interesting than this whose first stage culminates today. The national consciousness, lethargic under the weight of a government without ideals, seemed to have definitely acquired the immobility of the inert, and the hope that the people usually place in the work of their leaders had already disappeared from the heart of the Dominicans. [. . .] I do not want to, nor should I, analyze the facts to which I have referred, because they belong to the past and my greatest effort will be, from now on, to return to the Republic in lawful administrative acts the share of responsibility that falls on me in the agitation produced by them. Let history judge them in light of criteria rendered impartial by time, and for which, as a result of the work this government is about to initiate now, . . . the inexorable judgment of posterity will condemn or absolve us.

However, it is well to remember that the men who initiated and executed the movement that has completely changed the political physiognomy of the country in the short span between February and August of this year, could not, without betraying themselves, abandon the slogan that consecrated them in the first place to confront the men of the fallen regime, with weapons and with ballots, in the name of the democratic principles that are the soul of the Dominican nation.

The same cohesion, the same spirit of solidarity, which has presided over the work of the revolution in its dual aspect of an armed civic struggle and electoral campaign, will be the norm of the Government; and it is in the shadow of this ideal, backed by the people, where the prodigious work of national reconstruction will be realized.

I have spoken of national reconstruction and I should refer, even if just briefly, to the most urgent problem that the new government must solve: the financial crisis our Public Treasury is going through. A satisfactory solution of such a crisis to balance the Budget is indispensable. Even though the government of Licentiate Rafael Estrella Ureña, in his short term in power, ordered drastic radical measures in that respect, as it is demonstrated by the cuts that took place in several disbursement categories of the Law of Public Expenditures for the period comprised between the months of July through December of this year, it is evident that, in order to avoid the deficit that threatens to develop at the end of the year, it will be necessary to increase revenues through a better and stricter application of the laws that regulate the collection of internal revenue: in some cases, essentially modifying the method currently employed to collect it, and through the sale or leasing of some public utilities.

Various factors have contributed to the current crisis; but the main one among all is the considerable increase in the disbursements that will take place starting with the current month of August for the payment of interests and the amortization of the external debt, which represents a monthly disbursement, including customs collection costs, of 283,551.00 dollars against 115,218.33 dollars, that was being paid for the same item until February of this year. This situation has come to worsen even more due to the alarming diminution of the amounts budgeted as income.

The greatest pledge of the new government will be, therefore, that it will remedy, up to where it is possible under the present circumstances, the result of the mistakes of an administration renowned for its lack of foresight in matters related to the public treasury and by its evident lack of administrative organization. Every luxury, every unnecessary expense, every disbursement that is not of an indispensable nature, will have to be inflexibly discarded. We are a poor people and we cannot live like rich folk.

The salaries of public employees have already been reduced to the extreme limits compatible with the good functioning of public services and the high cost of subsistence; but the country needs, concurrently with those savings, energetic actions leading to repress fraud, to avoid filtrations in the collection of taxes, and to achieve the severe application, inexorably if need be, of the sanctions that the law has provided for such cases.

It is, however, undeniable that the current economic malaise is not exclusively the result of a lack of administrative foresight, but that it is due, in great part, to the crisis produced by the global readjustment that has affected all the nations of the world without even one that could take credit for escaping its disastrous consequences. Our main export products have suffered big reductions in the foreign markets, and, as a consequence, our imports have notably decreased, reducing, as a result, internal revenues in the same proportion. The actual crisis is not only one of the Dominican Republic, it is a global crisis that is equally worrying all the countries on the planet. From that stem the economic defense measures that are being proclaimed everywhere as one of the fundamental problems that governments need to confront, to such an extent, that the defense of the nation's integrity, instead of being assured with the creation of impregnable forts in strategic places, shields itself behind the walls of customs duties, in a policy frankly protectionist of native industries and products, reinforced with measures of strict and rigorous savings.

It is clear that our current tax system rests on an unjust and inadequate basis, as it does not establish an equitable relationship between taxes and the contributive capacity of the inhabitants. To carry out a scientific reform of our tax collection system, the new government will freely designate a commission of experts in the matter, advised by a world-renowned economist. Rather than being a labor of improvisation, this is the result of methodically organized studies and the scientific application and adaptation of the most advanced principles of economics in the Dominican milieu. This government tends toward a more equitable distribution, either by suppressing or reducing some that are considered onerous, or by modifying those that currently respond better to the special situation of the Dominican people and to the modern concept of political economy. Though the outlook may not be promising, it is far from desperate. Hard work and resolve; sacrifices and privations as the situation warrants; exploitation of the inexhaustible resources with which nature has endowed us, will no doubt assure that we shall emerge triumphant from the current crisis within a relatively short period of time.

For the national economy to develop so it meets our increasing demand, it is important not to neglect the basic factor of economic activity that human energy represents. Therefore, we must increase employment sources so that thousands of work-

153

ers whose fate deeply concerns the government can find opportunities to work, and also, we must protect those workers through appropriate laws and by following the rules of international organizations, but without creating conflicts that do not exist among ourselves and that are alien to our national mentality.

The new government will do whatever humanly possible to meet the necessities of our people and to assure the close cooperation of executive trusts without personal interest in the service of the national reconstruction. For my part, conscious as I am of the grave responsibilities I have assumed in accepting, under such difficult circumstances, the honorable position of President of the Dominican Republic, I solemnly declare that, by taking the oath required by the Constitution and facing the future, I consider myself irrevocably obligated to dedicate all my efforts to consolidating peace, and if necessary to punish, with all the severity prescribed by law, those who upset the public order; to blanket with effective guarantees the work of the courts of justice, so that no crime goes unpunished, and no offense goes without sanction; to guarantee the free exercise of civil rights within a policy of fraternal cordiality which closes its eyes to the past and welcomes with gratitude yesterday's adversaries; to strengthen the bond with those nations that favor us with their friendship and cordial exchanges of ideas and interests, so as to affirm the international stature of the Republic, and above all, to maintain in sound, integral, and immaculate fashion the dignity of the Homeland, whose ostensible symbol is the flag which in my hands will never be diminished in its glory nor stained in its honor.

Trujillo's Megalomania

If there was a personal characteristic that merits placing Trujillo in a class almost by himself, it was his megalomania. Though most dictators at some point suffer from it, in Trujillo's case it was extremely pathological, bordering on obsession. Trujillo loved adulation, whether it was in reference to his persona or to his achievements, and he was very self-conscious about his appearance. He always dressed in style, whether it was in a highly decorated military uniform or an expensive tailor-made business suit, of which he owned dozens. He was a light-skinned mulatto who relaxed his hair and resorted to using makeup to look more "European." As people learned of Trujillo's megalomaniac twists, they sought to feed his insatiable thirst for adulation. He received dozens of foreign decorations, thousands of gifts (including hundreds of ties, which he loved), several honorary degrees, and many titles, such as "Father of the New Homeland" and "Restorer of the Republic's Financial Independence." Hundreds of books, songs, and poems were written to please him, while countless speeches were delivered in his honor. Busts of Trujillo adorned

Trujillo's armed forces. Notice the Nazi-like attire.

every park—as well as many private residences—in the country. Two slogans from the period sum up well this phenomenon and portray the extent of this national adulatory campaign: "God and Trujillo" and "In this house Trujillo rules."

One of the most blatant examples of fawning to please Trujillo was the renaming of the city of Santo Domingo, capital of the Dominican Republic. In January 1936, the Dominican Congress approved its change of name to Ciudad Trujillo (Trujillo City). Trujillo, of course, publicly feigned opposition to the move, considering that Santo Domingo was the oldest city in the New World and that it had kept its name for over four hundred years—a fact that generated some debates in intellectual circles. Still, the change of name took place while Trujillo was traveling overseas and he used the opportunity to take notice of those who opposed the renaming of the capital.

THE NATIONAL CONGRESS[2]

In the Name of the Republic

NUMBER 1067.

CONSIDERING that the universality of the Dominican people have publicly manifested their legitimate desire that the city of Santo Domingo, capital of the Republic, be named CIUDAD TRUJILLO, as reverent expression of gratitude

2. Translated from *Gaceta Oficial*, no. 4867, January 11, 1936.

toward the remarkable Benefactor of the Homeland, Generalissimo Doctor Rafael Leonidas Trujillo Molina;

CONSIDERING that this unanimous manifestation of the Dominican people constitutes a plebiscite in which they have expressed their will to name the city of Santo Domingo, Ciudad Trujillo;

CONSIDERING that Generalissimo Doctor Rafael Leonidas Trujillo Molina, Benefactor of the Homeland, is worthy of the distinction that the Dominican people demand with patriotic fervor, due to his magnificent work of national reconstruction;

CONSIDERING that the City of Santo Domingo, destroyed by the hurricane of September 3, 1930, was rebuilt by the President of the Republic Generalissimo Doctor Rafael Leonidas Trujillo Molina, raising it, modern and beautiful, from its rubble;

CONSIDERING that the magnificent work of the Benefactor of the Homeland, Generalissimo Trujillo, has moved the national consciousness to grant him the glorious reward of giving his name to the city of Santo Domingo;

CONSIDERING that it is the duty of the National Congress to accept the manifestations of the people in the exercise of their sovereignty, as their worthy representative,

Having Declared the Urgency Has Issued the Following Law
Article 1.—From the publication of the current law on, the City of Santo Domingo, Capital of the Dominican Republic, will be named Ciudad Trujillo.

Article 2.—On a date to be set through a Resolution from the National Congress, an homage that the Nation will render to Generalissimo Doctor Rafael Leonidas Trujillo Molina, Benefactor of the Homeland, it is to be held in Ciudad Trujillo, for such a meritorious designation.

Article 3.—The Executive Branch will dictate the necessary dispositions regarding the use and value of postal and fiscal stamps, of documents and of any title or item bearing the name Santo Domingo, currently in circulation or in deposit in the State Offices.

GIVEN in the Sessions' Room of the Senate Palace, in Santo Domingo, D.N., Dominican Republic, on the eighth day of the month of January of the year nineteen hundred thirty-six; ninety-second year of Independence and seventy-third of the Restoration.

The President, Mario Fermín-Cabral
The Secretaries: Dr. Lorenzo E. Brea, Lic. Porfirio Herrera
GIVEN in the Sessions Room of the House of Deputies, in Santo Domingo, D.N., Dominican Republic, on the ninth day of the month of January of the year nineteen hundred thirty-six; ninety-second year of Independence and seventy-third of the Restoration

The President, Miguel Angel Roca
The Secretaries: J. M. Vidal V., Dr. José E. Aybar
PROMULGATED—In consequence, I rule and order that the current law be published in the Gaceta Oficial and in the newspapers Listín Diario and La Opinión for its diffusion, compliance and execution.

GIVEN in the Palace of the Executive Branch, in the city of Santo Domingo,

Capital of the Dominican Republic, on the eleventh day of the month of January of the year nineteen hundred thirty-six.

J. B. Peynado

The 1937 Massacre

The 1929 border treaty—and its subsequent amendments—solved a longstanding legal problem but did not have a major impact on life in the Haitian-Dominican borderlands. People there lived as they always did, moving freely, exchanging products across the now new border, and coexisting in a milieu where Spanish and Haitian Creole mixed to give rise to a border culture. For the power-hungry Trujillo dictatorship, this ill-defined cultural frontier presented a major challenge. The border was seen not only as the place where the homeland ended, but increasingly also as the place where it began. Trujillo needed to assert his power and control over this region that for so long had been isolated from the national mainstream. Moreover, the ultra-nationalist dictator would embark on an "ethnic cleansing" mission by trying to rid the Dominican Republic of Haitian migrants.

In early October 1937, Dominican troops, with the help of some locals recruited for this purpose, began the gruesome operation popularly known as "El Corte" (The Cutting Down). Trujillo ordered them to kill all Haitians within the borderland region, and as far away as the central Cibao valley and some of the eastern provinces. No guns were apparently used, only clubs and machetes, so as to give the impression that this had been an action carried out by local peasants driven to desperation over Haitian cattle rustling. There is no paper trail for this operation; orders were by word of mouth. Estimates about the number of dead Haitians—and of many black-skinned Dominicans—fluctuate considerably from about five thousand to as many as twenty-five thousand. The 1937 massacre is, without any doubt, the most horrific crime of the many carried out by the Trujillo dictatorship. The number of dead and the obvious intention of engaging in ethnic cleansing make of it a veritable genocide. Curiously, Haitians working in the sugar industry were not touched. Their labor was considered vital to the functioning of the industry; besides most plantations were owned by U.S. sugar companies. Years

157

later, as Trujillo began purchasing many of these sugar producing companies, he paradoxically became the largest employer of Haitians in the
country.

The following document is a secret report on the 1937 massacre prepared by the U.S. military. As is clearly obvious from the document, the
U.S. government was well aware of Trujillo's central role in ordering and
directing the massacre. Yet, the U.S. government maintained cordial relations with the dictator for the next two decades. This document was
declassified in 1989.

WAR DEPARTMENT
BUREAU OF INSULAR AFFAIRS
WASHINGTON[3]

December 22, 1937
Confidential
MEMORANDUM for the Chief, Military Intelligence Division, G-2.
Subject: Haitian-Dominican Incident.

The following information on the above subject was obtained during my recent
inspection of the Dominican Customs Receivership, December 7 to 14, 1937, from
Americans who have been long resident in the Dominican Republic and are well
informed regarding the local situation.

A large number of Haitians, estimated at sixty to seventy thousand, reside more or
less permanently in the Dominican Republic. Many live and work on foreign-owned
plantations, others in the towns, or as "squatters" on private or public land not otherwise utilized. Considerable numbers of laborers are brought in each year from Haiti
during the sugar-cane cutting season, their entry, transportation, pay, and subsistence
being taken care of by contractors under whom they work. In the past there appears
to have been no marked objection on the part of the Dominicans to the employment
of these Haitian laborers, as the wages they earn are too low and the work they do too
hard to offer sufficient inducement to Dominican peons to fill their places. Even the
public works program of President Trujillo has been carried out largely with Haitian
labor. The Haitians, both resident and transient, play an important part in the economic scheme of the Dominican Republic. Sugar interests directly, and the government indirectly, would be seriously crippled by cutting off this source of cheap and
reliable labor.

For many years there have been occasional minor clashes, mainly in Dominican
territory, between Haitians and Dominicans living near the frontier. These troubles
have been generally due to small-scale activities of Haitian bandits, differences
between Dominican and Haitian squatters and local feuds. Little if any official attention has been paid to these disturbances. It is reported, however, that during the cur-

3. From Lieutenant Colonel Howard Eager, Memorandum for the Chief, Military Intelligence
Division, "Haitian-Dominican Incident," G-2 Report, December 22, 1937, File 2657-387, Record
Group 165, National Archives, Washington, D.C.

rent year, Haitian banditry has materially increased. In the past, bandit activities usually have been restricted to thefts of a few cattle, pigs or chickens by individuals or small groups of Haitians; but recently bandit groups are reported to have been larger and their operations bolder and on a grater scale.

President Trujillo of the Dominican Republic is reliably reported to have made on Saturday, October 2, 1937, at Dajabon, a small town on the northern part of the frontier, a violent anti-Haitian speech, capitalizing on the Haitian bandits' activities, threatening the perpetrators with death and promising to rid the Dominican Republic of "dogs, hogs, and Haitians." Beginning on the following day and continuing until about October 10th the vicinity of Dajabon and Monte Cristi, a neighboring town near the northern coast, there was instituted by Dominican soldiers, local police and immigration inspectors, a quiet, systematic and thorough search for all Haitians in the area. Haitian individuals and families were brought into the towns where they were required to surrender the entry permits and identification cards issued them by the Dominican government. They were then confined pending deportation. It is reported that at Monte Cristi alone seventeen hundred cases of deportation were recorded. Following their detention, individuals and families were taken out by soldiers in groups to secluded places where they were massacred. The method almost invariably followed was by clubbing, bayoneting and machete slashing. It is reported that there were few if any shootings. Dominican civilians were not allowed to witness the killings. In fact they are believed to have had no inclination to do so since they were as terrified by the proceedings as the Haitians themselves. It was impossible for the Haitians to offer any resistance. Practically none escaped during their detention. In some places, native Dominicans who had sufficient disregard of their own safety are reported to have hidden out Haitian refugees, many of whom had lived among them peacefully for over a generation. No cases of destruction of huts or other property, and no cases of rape were reported. Such incidents might reasonably have been expected in that country if the massacres had been sporadic and uncontrolled. Victims included whole families, women and children being massacred indiscriminately along with their men.

At Monte Cristi, for three nights ending Tuesday, October 5th, groups of "deportees" were marched to the customs wharf, about three kilometers distant from the town proper, where they were killed and their bodies thrown in the ocean. The customs guard was ordered by the soldiers to clear out and keep his mouth shut. The method of disposing of bodies by throwing them into the ocean was abandoned when numbers of them began floating ashore. The bodies washed up were collected and thrown into an isolated pit not far from this dock where the bodies of other victims had been disposed of. Some bodies were buried in shallow graves, some were burned and others left unburied.

It is impossible to determine with any accuracy the number of Haitians massacred in the Dajabon-Monte Cristi area. It is reported that about five hundred were killed near Dajabon and seventeen hundred or more near Monte Cristi during the week October 3rd to 10th. On the latter date the massacres in that vicinity stopped, the last group of twenty-six Haitians having been put to death shortly after dark on Sunday evening, October10th.

Following the first massacres at Dajabon and Monte Cristi, beginning about

October 7th and continuing until about October 20th, the same systematic procedure was carried out at other points in the Dominican Republic distant from the frontier, namely at Puerto Plata, La Vega, Moca and Bonao. All these towns are in the Military District of the North, commanded by General Castillo. No killings are reported to have occurred after October 20th.

The total number of Haitians killed in the Dominican Republic during the entire period, October 3rd to 20th, has been variously estimated between three thousand and eighteen thousand. It is believed that a fairly reliable estimate is somewhere about five or six thousand.

It is reported that no Dominican civilians were involved in the massacres. The soldiers who carried out the work are said to have been sickened by their bloody task in many instances. A few are reported to have been summarily executed for refusing to carry out their orders, while many overcame their repugnance to their task by fortifying themselves with rum.

All circumstances point to President Trujillo as being directly responsible for the massacres. It is difficult to conceive that under a dictatorship such as exists in Santo Domingo a systematic massacre of the extent and duration of this one could have been carried out without his orders or against his will.

It is rumored that Trujillo, while on a prolonged drunken spree, ordered General Castillo to carry out the massacres, that the latter objected to doing so without written orders and that such orders signed by Trujillo were actually furnished to him; that later, when accounts of the massacre began to leak out abroad, Trujillo attempted to make General Castillo the scapegoat for the whole affair and ordered Castillo to report to him at Trujillo City, the capital, which orders the General refused to obey. He is reported to have remained at his headquarters in Santiago de los Caballeros where he has a force of some seven hundred soldiers loyal to him, which Trujillo is unwilling to attack for fear of stirring up a revolution.

It is generally agreed that Trujillo's action in the whole affair was stupid, utterly lacking in reason and likely to have most serious consequences for his government. It is believed that Trujillo now realizes this and is doing everything possible to suppress the facts, minimize the incident and avoid outside investigation and meditation. If his sole object had been to rid his country of Haitians, he could readily have done so at any time by less objectionable methods.

Through the efforts of the Haitian Minister to the Dominican Republic, several thousand Haitians have been repatriated since the massacre, without interference on the part of the Dominican government. Inspired articles in the Dominican press, which is absolutely government-controlled, claim that the repatriation of Haitians is an effort on the part of Haiti to embarrass the Dominican government and exaggerate the seriousness of the "minor border incidents." Sugar plantation managers are gravely concerned over possible labor shortage during the coming cane-cutting season as no adequate substitute for Haitian labor is readily available.

Since the beginning of the incidents, the strictest and most effective censorship has been exercised. Only brief mention has been made in the Dominican press of the "border incident," its extent and importance being minimized. Dominican "outs" in exile are being accused of spreading fantastic reports designed to discredit the Trujillo regime abroad.

160

Although many Dominicans are probably well aware of the extent of the massacres, the subject in never openly discussed. Americans who have business interests in the island are reluctant to discuss the affair, probably feeling that their best course is to mind their own business and ignore, at least openly, the whole situation. There seems to be a feeling among them that if Trujillo succeeds in weathering this storm undamaged, he will feel so strengthened that his future course of action may impair the security of foreign interests and investments in the Dominican Republic.

(Signed) Howard Eager, Lieutenant Colonel (FA), Bureau of Insular Affairs

Ideological Justifications

The 1937 massacre ended an era of cordial, friendly relations with Haiti. During the 1930–1937 period, Haiti and its government had been officially portrayed as friends of the Dominican people. Trujillo visited Haiti three times in the mid-1930s—the first Dominican president ever to do so—and Haitian President Sténio Vincent visited the Dominican Republic on several occasions. Trujillo even relinquished to Haiti disputed territories in the borderland in order to get the Haitians to finalize the border treaty. After the massacre, however, the regime's official stance on Haiti and Haitian migration to the Dominican Republic made a complete reversal. As part of an ultra-nationalist campaign, Haiti was portrayed as the perennial enemy of the Dominican people, and Haitian migrants as silent invaders bent on taking over and corrupting the racial and cultural makeup of Dominicans. Trujillo launched a propaganda barrage that fueled latent anti-Haitian historical feelings among the Dominican people by employing all the resources at the state's disposal: Trujillo's Dominican Party, the military, the Catholic Church, the state bureaucracy, and the media. This nationwide brainwashing campaign was accompanied by a program to "Dominicanize" the borderland by establishing colonies, building schools, improving socioeconomic conditions, and spreading official versions of Dominican culture through the use of state cultural agents.

Intellectuals at the service of the dictatorship played a valuable role in this campaign. Particularly Manuel A. Peña Batlle and Joaquín Balaguer became two of the most outspoken defenders and architects of the regime's ultra-nationalist, anti-Haitian policies. The document reproduced below is a speech delivered by Peña Batlle at the border town of Elías

161

Piña on November 16, 1942. This speech, by the clarity with which the regime's official views are expressed, is considered one of the pillars of Trujillo's anti-Haitian ideology.

A POLICY'S SENSE[4]

Gentlemen: The special extraordinary elections of the functionaries in the San Rafael Province, which will take place in the coming month of December, are a solemn motive for the settlers of this frontier region to contemplate the significance that Generalissimo Trujillo has wanted to attribute to his well-praised initiative of creating at the very end of our frontier a new provincial jurisdiction.

After long years of alternatives and constant labor we finally solved, thanks to the decisive intervention of the man who towers above our contemporary history, the oldest, most difficult and most complicated matter of State to ever occupy the minds and the attention of our leaders: I am referring to the delicate frontier issue that since 1844 divided us from Haiti.

When I judge that old matter in such a way, I do not reduce it, of course, to the demarcation of the frontier properly said, to the geometric demarcation of a dividing line of the two States, but instead I link into the problem the whole spectrum of our relations with the neighboring State, that makes use, together with us, of the marvelous and enchanted island where the genius of Columbus and constructive Spain of the sixteenth century began the conquest and the colonization of the American continent.

Just at the end of the one hundred years of independence have we been able to eliminate the promiscuity that rendered impossible the geometric limitation of our territory. Since 1777, when the monarchs of Spain and of France met in Aranjuez to recognize the existence of the colony that the adventurous genius of the latter established in the west of the island of Santo Domingo, as well as to demarcate the extension of their respective possessions in the island, it had not been possible to repeat the feats of Choiseul and Mr. Joaquín García.

In spite of its extraordinarily technical significance, the colonial division of 1777 was a failure. A few years after being accomplished it became dead letter. A decadent and stagnant Spain of the eighteenth century did not have the strength to either stop the penetration from the west or to give the economic, political, and social assistance the technical demarcation of Aranjuez required. Seventy-seven years after the accomplishment of this back-breaking task, the Dominican Republic, born into its own government, inherited a border situation much more complicated than the one that France created for Spain in the island and found much more to the east, at the same time, the impetus of the forces that the metropolis vainly sought to stop with the empty treaty of Aranjuez.

On only two occasions was it feasible to trace a border line in the island; in which more than three hundred years of negotiations and diplomacy were invested. The first

---

4. Translated from Manuel A. Peña Batlle, *Política de Trujillo* (Ciudad Trujillo: Impresora Dominicana, 1954), 61–72.

time the demarcation had neither a result nor a social sense; on the second occasion, if we Dominicans do not give them to it with the contribution of our own entrails, it will also lack them, because the penetration comes from west to east, and on the other side of the line there is not, nor will there ever be, a fundamental interest in containing or damming the flow of a social expansion biologically directed against us: every time that a new border is traced, it will be detrimental to the Spanish territory of the island and to the customs, sentiments, and memories of its Spanish settlers. Do not forget this warning!

We Dominicans have the duty to oppose to the failure of this demarcation, as the one of 1777 failed. To achieve this, we are obligated to make the greatest sacrifices and to put into play all the means of our collective vitality, our most hidden resources, and the last breath of our nationality. Do not forget that the situation has extraordinary peculiarities and that all of them conspire against our destiny: for Dominicans the border is an absolutely insurmountable social, ethnic, economic, and religious fence; for the neighbors, on the other hand, the border is a mirage all the more seductive as the development of progress and the collective level is greater in the eastern part.

The frontier, as defined by the most notable modern geographer, Ratzel, is a means of transformation formed by the conjugated influences of two opposing forces; an intermediary body that is constituted by the combined action of each one of them. The frontier is an organic product of vicinity. This explains its essentially variable character and its nature as a peculiar zone, animated by its own life, different from the interior and necessarily complex. The geometric demarcation line, as such, has no sense of reality whatsoever, it is a mere abstraction which only serves to initiate the complete process of the border formation, very diverse, very complicated, and very extensive.

Until now, Dominican governments have not focused on the frontier problem but as a simple matter of limits, absolutely lacking the essential sense of relations alien to all problems of vicinity and especially to the problem of vicinity that we Dominicans are faced with. The brilliant vision of President Trujillo was necessary so that the Dominican government would ponder the matter in all its consequences and would present it to the eyes of the world exactly as it should be presented, that is, with all its crushing social integrity. Generalissimo Trujillo understood that the mathematic outline of a border line only solved but one, the simplest, of our vicinity problems; he realized that such tracing of the line would mean nothing more than the start of a long and complicated work of social construction on the borderland, a work that he will not be able to finish as long as two opposing and unmistakable forces that struggle for the territorial surface in which destiny and the imperatives of history have placed them coexist in the natural territories of the island.

[. . .]

Until now our borderlands have been left to their own fate, without the manifestation in them of the effects of a well-concerted and intelligent governmental action, the only one capable of solidifying interests and creating an economy in territories that by themselves do not offer incentives to private activity; we have never worried about repopulating these uninhabitable regions on the magnitude required by circumstances; we still have not put real determination in creating and maintaining the public services of a sui generis kind that the border nature of these places requires; until Generalissimo Trujillo rose to power no one had worried about giving the frontier the essentially political character with which all civilized peoples of earth contemplate their problems of this kind. Before Trujillo, no Dominican leader understood the Haitian-Dominican border phenomenon as made up of roots thrice attached in the judicial, political, and economic life of the Dominican nation. The keen statesman has seen: from one side the desolation and traditional abandonment, the total negation of a frontier policy; that is the Dominican side. And from the other side, the hopeless reality of a people infiltrating, with slow, but sure, persistence, their negative influence to what was for them an ideal medium.

Generalissimo Trujillo has seen, with a statesman's vision, the alarming geometric progression with which the neighboring population multiplies, whose physiological power is, for various reasons, exceptional. He has seen the precarious economic movement of our neighbors and the evident lack of correlation that exists between the Haitian population and its means of subsistence; he has seen the disproportion that exists between the density of the extraordinarily growing population and the meagerness of the territory where that population resides. The renowned leader of the Dominican people has considered, in all their extent and intimate details, the difficulties that surround this population in a continuous struggle with a mountainous terrain, as well as the undeniable, mysterious influence that the environment in which they live and develop exercises over the psychic makeup of a people; the geographic determinism that unquestionably reveals the fatal influence of the land on the economy, which only ceases to increase when man, by defeating nature, creates a propitious artificial medium. Generalissimo Trujillo has been able to see the ancestral burdens, the primitivism, without possible evolution that maintains in a pristine state, unalterable, the old and negative customs of a great number of our neighbors, precisely those who stay in closer contact, due to their needs, with our frontier hubs. The Generalissimo had the good intuition to realize that the two social elements in the Haitian-Dominican border formation are very dissimilar in their origins, in their evolution, in their characteristic idiosyncrasy, and in their history to ever be able to combine in a unit favorable for civilization: he understood, with the eloquent lessons of Haiti's very own thinkers, that the ethnic peculiarities of the two peoples are not compatible, and he has decided to face the problem of the survival of both on the island, within the only feasible policy: for each one to make their life within the material limits of their possessions, without us being the ones called to suffer the consequences of the geographic and historical fatality of the dualism in which the island is divided on, that as one and indivisible Spain found and that as one and indivisible should had transmitted to us.

[. . .]

Generalissimo Trujillo, who was born to build and who lives building, does not desire anything else, nor is he looking for any ends but those of initiating the reconstruction of the Dominican borderland by putting in it all the factors of internal and international order that are at his disposal; if nature does not help him, he is willing to overcome nature to create an adequate means of livelihood for Dominicans in these regions. There are no obstacles that can, legally, block his path. No one can induce him nor induce the Dominican people to look on with resignation as the sources of our nationality are irreparably contaminated by elements foreign to their nature and their formation. Let us not forget that this Spanish, Christian, and Catholic nation that we Dominicans are, arose pure and homogeneous in the geographical unity of the island and that it would have conserved itself as that until now if it were not for the grafting that since the end of the seventeenth century fixed itself onto the pristine trunk to infuse its sap of agents profoundly and fatally different from those that in the beginning grew in La Española.

From then until now, the master trunk has been resisting the penetration, and our current program cannot be seen as anything but a new effort in the old struggle whose end no one is capable of predicting. We Dominicans put to the test in that battle the meaning of a civilization, of a central chapter of human history. The problem is not, therefore, all ours; with us the entire value of the ties of inter-American solidarity based on the identity of the origins of the peoples of the continent and in the homogeneous sense of their common civilization are compromised.

Our neighbors cannot become alarmed if finally Dominicans, incited by the spirit and action of a determined man, shake off an improper attitude and united agree to follow the only advisable and sensible path: opposition to penetration of the legitimate barrier of interests and economic and social creations to maintain the cognition of nationality. Otherwise, it is certain that in the long run we will diminish in our actual significance.

There is no feeling of humanity, nor is there a political reason or any convenient circumstance whatsoever that could force us to regard at the issue of Haitian penetration with indifference. The agent of that penetration is not and cannot be the select Haitian, the one who forms the social, intellectual, and economic elite of the neighboring nation. That type does not worry us because he does not create difficulties for us; he does not migrate. The Haitian who bothers and alarms us is the one who forms the last social expression beyond the frontier. That type is frankly undesirable. Of pure African race, he cannot represent for us any ethnic incentive. Dispossessed in his country of permanent means of subsistence, he is a burden over there, he does not have purchasing power and therefore cannot become an important factor in our economy. Poorly nourished and dressed even worse, he is weak, though very prolific due to his low living conditions. For that same reason the Haitian who enters [our land] lives afflicted by numerous and capital vices and is necessarily affected by diseases and physiological deficiencies that are endemic to the lowest levels of that society.

The religious sentiments of these people deserve a separate paragraph. I do not want to, nor should I, surpass the limits of an objective examination of our vital problem. I prefer that the most respected Haitian authors be the ones to describe the situation of what they themselves consider an irremediable calamity for their country. I would like to speak through the mouth of the Price-Mars, of the Dorsainvilles [sic], of the Bellegardes and of the Hollys.[5] In this case, not even the testimony of foreigners, who like Paul Morand and Seabrook have given themselves to the task of studying the social characteristics of what is for us an alarming threat, satisfies me.

All great Haitian writers agree that *vaudou,* or the Haitian popular cult, immemo-

---

5. Referring to Haitian scholars Jean Price-Mars, Justin-Chrysostome Dorsainvil, Dantès Bellegarde, and Arthur G. Holly.

rably professed by an immense majority of our neighbors, constitutes a racial *psychoneurosis* of a religious nature. The *vaudouist* is a paranoiac of the most dangerous type. Education is incapable of annihilating the power of inheritance and according to Dorsainville, vaudou "responds to a racial nervous habit established by belief, by secular practices of numerous Haitian families."

The cult of the dead is carried out by a guild of sorcerers and witches who practice incredible ceremonies with human cadavers according to Dr. Arthur G. Holly, an eminent Haitian doctor: "Those people are necromancers, who employ cadavers with magical ends." Dr. Price-Mars, prince of the Haitian men of science, teaches that *vaudou* is an undeniable remnant of African fetishism and animism, and that in Haiti an immense majority of the rural population practices it. According to Price-Mars's affirmations, "the *luá* or *misterio* preoccupies the Haitian people in an unexplainable way." For this most notable writer, the *vaudouist* crisis has all the characteristics of a hysterical crisis exempt of all simulation, that must be considered as a mystical state characterized by the delirium of theomaniac possession and the unfolding of personality. Doctor Price-Mars defines the constitutional mentality of the servers of *vaudou* as of an essentially hereditary nature that is transmitted from family to family. His book "Ainsi parla l'oncle" is a veritable quarry of teachings about the sui generis religious practices of the Haitian people.

Dantès Bellegarde, in his notable work "La Nation Haïtienne" also characterizes *vaudou* as a remnant of African animism among the Haitian people.

The quotes could prolong themselves indefinitely. George Sylvain, Hannibal Price, all the great Haitian thinkers, as affirmed above, concur in defining the popular religious practices of Haiti as mere detachments of the superstition and the fetishism of the tribes of Africa.

The length of this speech does not allow me to expand on a topic that requires volumes. Dorsainville agrees that the only way to abolish the cult worship so harmful to the healthy development of a country's religious sense is for a civilized governmental organization to apply most rigorously police laws against the rite's practices. To preserve us from western [that is, Haitian] religious paranoia, we, Dominicans must follow the advice of such eminent Haitians, deploying our police services as the circumstances warrant, with sternness and without sentimentality. Until twenty-five years ago, the Dominican people maintained unaltered the pure Catholic unity of their religious feelings. If we consider now the growing attraction the exercise of the monstrous fetishist practice of *vaudou* is gaining among our lower classes, we will conclude that if we do not act with a heavy hand and a strong spirit, the time will arrive when the malaise will be irremediable amongst us, just as it is on the other side. There is no government in this genuinely civilized world that will not take decisive measures against such a vital, serious threat. Is it possible for us Dominicans to be censured if, urged by a simple dictate of self-preservation, we dedicate ourselves to fighting elements subversive of our own national essence?

The Brooklings [sic] Institution, dedicated to public service through investigations and education in the social sciences and incorporated in the United States of America, recently conducted, under the direction of Mr. Dana G. Munro, Director of the School of International and Public Affairs of Princeton University, profound studies about the social conditions of the Dominican Republic. The results of these studies have been published in a voluminous report of which we Dominicans must make continuous use, if we decide to take a definitive attitude against the penetration of which we have been made victims.

The figures provided by the aforementioned study are desolating and cast a large shadow on any perspectives for the future of our country. From this study are the following paragraphs:

> Here is a wave of color that increases and that will cover any white colony that is not fully prepared and protected. In many of the old communities the darkening of the whites is almost total, and with rare exceptions the absorption and mixing of the races is changing the color of those white groups that still exist in the Caribbean region. Modern colonization continues to ignore this aspect of the problem of colonization.

As A. Grenfell Price points out, many of the most fertile regions of the tropics contain a high density of colored persons with low economic standards, and in the majority of the tropics colored persons with their low living and culture standards are absorbing the whites. He suggests the working of Gresham's racial law by which a people ready to accept a low living standard and the lack of comforts of large families, generally will expel or absorb persons of a higher level, unless the latter increase their numbers through immigration or protect themselves through political supremacy, social barriers or laws.

This is the path along which President Trujillo is leading us now, in what he refers to as the creation of social barriers and adequate legislation to save the indisputable origin of Dominican nationality from neighborly influence. We cannot lose sight of the fact that no other country in the Caribbean basin is as exposed to contamination or has suffered its effects as our country has, precisely due to the existence of this border that was unfortunately taken away due to Spain's weakness, carelessness, and lack of administrative vision.

No one should be surprised that we, warned by the force of truly shady acts, decide to combat the malaise in the manner observers and impartial and objective students advise us.

Our current viewpoint does not imply nor can it imply an appreciable change in the relationships with the constituted powers on the other side of the border, whose good friendship we will try to maintain through all possible means. The fact that Generalissimo Trujillo has decided to nationalize and reconstruct the borderlands of his country cannot directly or indirectly influence the maintenance of the political and international solidarity ties that the two governments that share the dominance of the island for the good and happiness of their respective peoples should maintain. We Dominicans do not foster any goals of penetration or of interference in the free unfolding of the institutions of the neighboring people, and if we have finally decided to preserve ours from uncontrolled penetration that we have been subjected to since we were born into the community of free nations, we have not been moved to adopt such an attitude for any reason but for preserving our future from the harmful effects of a policy clearly directed against us.

Only the creator of this new Dominican national attitude is authorized to delineate and specify the complete sense of his reconstruction program; my words are a mere marginal note to the goals that he seeks and advocates. But I do not hesitate to declare before the country's consciousness that when President Trujillo reaches the peak of his nationalist posture, he will have achieved total secular support for Dominican life.

Economic "Sovereignty" Restored

Since 1905, U.S. customs agents had been in control of the Dominican customhouses. Moreover, the country's financial options were limited because the Dominican government was required to obtain clearance from the U.S. government to get any new loans. In 1940, after several years of negotiations, Trujillo, serving as extraordinary ambassador for the Dominican Republic, and U.S. Secretary of State Cordell Hull signed an economic agreement informally known as the "Trujillo-Hull Treaty." The agreement was made possible thanks to the country's political stability since 1924 and its good record on the payment of its external debt. Even during the difficult years of the Great Depression, Trujillo negotiated reduced payments with the U.S. government, thus avoiding defaulting

Cordell Hull and Trujillo signing the convention that ended the Dominican Customs Receivership in 1940.

on the debt. The international context had also changed. World War II had started and U.S. President Franklin D. Roosevelt wanted to maintain cordial relations with Latin American nations in the face of Nazi expansionism. As part of his "Good Neighbor" policy, Roosevelt agreed to return control of the Dominican customhouses to his trusted ally Trujillo.

The agreement eliminated U.S. control over the Dominican customhouses and allowed the country to obtain foreign loans without U.S. approval. For the first time in decades, the Dominican Republic had some control over its finances and the ability to establish long-range economic development policies. In 1947, the Dominican government paid the balance of its long-standing debt to U.S. creditors, finally freeing the country from this ignominious burden. Trujillo seized the opportunity to project himself as the hero of the moment and restorer of the country's financial sovereignty. He declared the country free of debt, created a central bank, reinstated the Dominican peso as the nation's currency, and even built a monument to commemorate the country's new status.

TRUJILLO-HULL TREATY[6]

Convention

WHEREAS at the City of Washington, D.C. on the twenty-seventh day of December of 1924 a Convention was concluded and signed between the Plenipotentiaries of the United States of America and the Dominican Republic, providing for the assistance of the United States of America in the collection and application of the customs revenues of the Dominican Republic; and

WHEREAS the Government of the United States of America and the Government of the Dominican Republic have performed their obligations under the said Convention of 1924 in a manner satisfactory to both parties; and

WHEREAS the Government of the United States of America and the Government of the Dominican Republic are both desirous of modifying the said Convention to the advantage of both parties and at the same time of safeguarding the rights of the holders of the bonds of the issues of 1922 and 1926;

The President of the United States of America, represented by Cordell Hull, Secretary of State of the United States of America, and

The President of the Dominican Republic, represented by Generalissimo Rafael Leonidas Trujillo Molina, Benefactor of the Country, Ambassador Extraordinary on Special Mission,

Who, having communicated to each other their respective full powers, found to be

---

6. From Charles I. Bevans (compiler), *Treaties and other International Agreements of the United States of America, 1776–1949* (Washington, D.C.: U.S. Government Printing Office, 1968), vol. 7, 224–228.

in good and due form, have agreed upon the following Articles:

Article I: The Government of the Dominican Republic shall collect through its appropriate national officials the customs revenues of the Dominican Republic and all revenues pertaining to the customs duties. The General Receivership of the Dominican Customs provided for in the Convention of December 27, 1924, shall cease to operate on the day on which the Dominican Government undertakes the collection of customs revenues.

All property and funds of the General Receivership shall be turned over on that day to the Government of the Dominican Republic. No claim shall be advanced by either Government against the other on account of any act of the General Receivership.

Article II: The Government of the United States of America and the Government of the Dominican Republic, in common accord, shall designate a Bank, with establishment in the Dominican Republic, as sole depository of all revenues and public funds of whatsoever nature of the Dominican Government. They likewise shall designate, by common accord, an official who shall act in the said Bank as representative of the holders of the bonds of the external debt of 1922 and 1926, in all matters that concern the service of the said external debt. If at any time the Bank so designated ceases for any reason to function in this capacity or if either Government shall deem a change advisable, a successor shall be designated under the procedure stipulated above. If the representative of the holders of the bonds of the external debt of 1922 and 1926 shall, for any reason, be unable to continue in that capacity, or if either Government shall deem a change advisable, his successor shall be designated in accordance with the same procedure established for the original designation. In the event that it should become necessary to designate a successor to either the Bank or the official representing the holders of the bonds of the external debt of 1922 and 1926, and in the further event that the two Governments should be unable to reach mutual accord on such designation within a period of three months, the Foreign Bondholders Protective Council, Incorporated, shall be requested to nominate said successor, and in the event of its failure to make such nomination the President or a Vice President of the American Bankers Association, or his duly authorized representative, shall be requested to make the nomination; provided, however, that neither a Bank nor a person previously rejected by either Government may be so nominated. In the event that a Bank or person is nominated in accordance with this procedure, the two Governments shall designate such nominee.

The official representing the holders of the bonds of the external debt of 1922 and 1926 shall, with the approval of the two Governments, designate a deputy to serve in his stead in the event of his temporary absence or incapacity.

Article III: During the first ten days of each calendar month the representative of the holders of the bonds of the external debt of 1922 and 1926 or his deputy shall receive, by endorsement and orders of payment which shall be issued to the Depository Bank by the Dominican Government through the intermediary of the Secretary of State for Treasury and Commerce, the sum necessary to cover monthly payments as follows:

(1) the payment of one-twelfth of the annual interest charges of all of the outstanding bonds of the external debt of 1922 and 1926;

(2) the payment of one-twelfth of the annual amounts designated for the amortization of the said bonds, including the interest of all the bonds which are or may be retained in the sinking fund. The said amortization shall be computed and effected in accordance with the loan contracts as modified by the agreement between the Dominican Republic and the Foreign Bondholders Protective Council, Incorporated, concluded on August 16, 1934, and by the provisions of Article V of the present Convention;

(3) the payment of one-twelfth of the annual cost of the services rendered by the representative of the holders of the bonds of the external debt of 1922 and 1926, or his deputy, who shall receive salaries which are the subject of an exchange of notes attached hereto, which shall be given full force and effect as integral parts of this Convention, and a reasonable amount for expenses incurred in the performance of their duties, and the payment of one-twelfth of the annual amount agreed upon between the Dominican Government and the Depository Bank as the compensation for the services of the said Bank.

No disbursements of funds of the Dominican Government shall be made by the Depository Bank until the payments provided for in this Article shall have been made. The sums received by the above-mentioned representative for the service of the bonds shall be immediately transmitted by him to the Fiscal Agent or Agents of the loans.

Article IV: The Government of the Dominican Republic declares that the interest and amortization service of the bonds of the external debt of 1922 and 1926 as well as the payments stipulated in the third numbered paragraph of Article III of the present Convention, constitute an irrevocable first lien upon all of its revenues of whatsoever nature.

Article V: In case the total collections from all the revenues of whatsoever nature of the Dominican Government should in any calendar year exceed twelve million five hundred thousand dollars ($12,500,000) there shall be applied to the sinking fund for the redemption of bonds of the external debt of 1922 and 1926 which may be outstanding, ten percent (10%) of the excess above twelve million five hundred thousand dollars ($12,500,000) but less than thirteen million five hundred thousand dollars ($13,500,000), and in addition five percent (5%) of all sums exceeding thirteen million five hundred thousand dollars ($13,500,000).

Article VI: The representative of the holders of the bonds of the external debt of 1922 and 1926 shall have complete access to all records and books of the Depository Bank relating to the public revenues. The Secretary of State for Treasury and Commerce of the Dominican Government shall supply monthly to the representative of the holders of the bonds of the loans of 1922 and 1926 complete and detailed reports, duly certified, of all the revenues and disbursements and other fiscal operations of the Dominican Government.

Article VII: The system of deposit of all revenues of the Dominican Republic shall be carried out in accordance with the Dominican laws of accounting and of the Treasury now governing such matters, and these laws as well as the powers conferred by this Convention upon the representative of the holders of the bonds of the loans of 1922 and 1926, shall not be modified by the Dominican Government during the life of this Convention without the previous consent of both Governments.

Article VIII: Any controversy which may arise between the Government of the United States of America and the Government of the Dominican Republic in relation to the execution of the provisions of the present Convention shall, if possible, be settled through diplomatic channels. Upon notification by either the Government of the United States of America or the Government of the Dominican Republic that, in its opinion, possibilities of settlement by this means have been exhausted, such controversies shall be settled in accordance with the procedure stipulated in the Inter-American Arbitration Convention signed at Washington, January 5, 1929, notwithstanding the provisions of Article 2 (a) thereof.

Article IX: The Convention signed by the United States of America and the Dominican Republic on December 27, 1924, shall cease to have effect, and the present Convention shall enter into force upon the exchange of ratifications which shall take place in the City of Washington within thirty days following ratification by the Government which ratifies the later in point of time; provided, however, that Articles I, II and V of the said Convention of December 27, 1924 shall continue in full force and effect until the two Governments agree that there have been adopted and put into operation all the measures necessary for the execution of the present Convention.

The present Convention shall continue in full force and effect during the existence of the outstanding external bonds of 1922 and 1926. After the redemption or cancellation of the said bonds, the provisions of this Convention shall automatically cease to have effect.

IN WITNESS WHEREOF the respective Plenipotentiaries have signed the present Convention in duplicate in the English and Spanish languages, both texts being equally authoritative, and have hereunto affixed their seals.

Done in the City of Washington this twenty-fourth day of September 1940.

Cordell Hull   [SEAL]   Rafael L. Trujillo   [SEAL]

Trujillo's Fortune

The Trujillo regime was also a mighty economic emporium. The dictator managed the country as if it were his private estate, and actually, most of the country's wealth eventually came into his personal possession. Trujillo's ambition knew no bounds and his financial interests reached into practically every economic activity in the Dominican Republic. He backed up his financial grip with the power of the state, the military, and a pliable bureaucracy that would implement the most outrageous laws to protect and foster Trujillo's numerous enterprises. It was not uncommon for Trujillo to acquire businesses using governmental funds, or for him to intimidate and coerce the original owners into selling their companies at a loss. Moreover, if a business was not doing well, Trujillo would sell it to the state to recoup his loss, and later reacquire it from the state at a discount.

Sugar was one of his largest and riskiest investments. When Trujillo assumed power in 1930, most of the Dominican sugar industry was in the hands of U.S. and foreign investors. By the time of his death in 1961, only the Vicini family and the South Porto Rico Sugar Company still had sugar plantations in the Dominican Republic, and the latter was negotiating with Trujillo to sell. Using the state's power and resources, and a nationalistic discourse to justify it, Trujillo disguised his takeover of the sugar industry as the "Dominicanization" of this economic sector. He built large sugar plantations on his estates and pressured U.S. companies into selling their plantations to him while at the same time maintaining cordial relations with the U.S. government.

Trujillo also fostered the country's industrialization and the substitution of imports, a process in which he played a major economic role and which dramatically increased his personal fortune. It is estimated that toward the end of his regime, Trujillo controlled about 80 percent of the nation's wealth, including some virtual monopolies over raw materials and basic foodstuffs. After his death, these businesses and industries were confiscated by the Dominican government and became part of the state's public sector, one of the largest in Latin America.

The following selection is an annotated description of Trujillo's businesses prepared by Juan Bosch and originally published in the late 1950s.

TRUJILLO'S BUSINESS ENTERPRISES[7]

A list of the most important businesses that Trujillo exploits in Dominican territory can give us a good idea of how much his governmental regime is, as I have said, more of a capitalist enterprise than a political system. The situation is better understood if one realizes that very few of the firms mentioned on this list existed when Trujillo seized power in 1930; and that those in operation, like the Anonymous Tobacco Company, Read Hardware, and the Dominican National Brewery, became monopolies only after falling into the hands of the dictator.

Trujillo's enterprises provide employment for almost 45 percent of the country's active labor force, and since another 35 percent is made up of governmental positions, including those in the armed forces and the banking, electrical and hotel systems operated by the government, it results that almost 80 percent of salaried individuals in Santo Domingo depend for their livelihood on Rafael Leonidas Trujillo,

---

7. Translated from Juan Bosch, *La fortuna de Trujillo*, 4th ed. (Santo Domingo: Editora Alfa y Omega, 1997), 61–75. Reprinted by permission.

since nobody would dare offer employment in the bureaucracy or in the autonomous institutions of the State without the dictator's consent. Moreover, no operations involving lending, purchasing, selling, or the movement of personnel, in the banking, hotel and electric systems of the government can be performed unless they are authorized by Trujillo. The same happens with the government's own functions.

Any reader will easily understand that the remaining twenty percent (20%) of the active labor force in the Dominican Republic is occupied in less valuable establishments: petty trade such as pulperías, handicrafts, such as woodworking shops, carpentry shops, mechanic shops, barber shops, dressmakers, tailor shops, repair shops; small-scale transportation, such as taxis, small boats, private trucks; which lack, as a whole, political or economic power. To those should be added the independent professional sectors, members of a middle class with little economic power and almost no political power: physicians, dentists, lawyers, engineers, surveyors.

The gross of Dominican economic activities is in Trujillo's hands. This almost absolute control over a country's economy by one person is unheard of anywhere else within capitalist countries. Labor syndicates cannot function, not even with a minimum of freedom, in a place where the owner of the enterprises is also the one who proclaims the labor laws and who orders the public force to implement them; commerce is a slave in the land where it depends on an industrial production monopolized by the same person who rules the state and the repressive corps; even maritime and air transportation are in Trujillo's hands, so that just by delaying the loading of the merchandise for export belonging to a merchant who is not his supporter it is enough to ruin him.

The state's banking system is established to finance Trujillo's enterprises, not the country. As explained above, when one of his enterprises does not meet his expectations, Trujillo sells it to the state, either directly or through the state's banks, for amounts several times larger than its inventory, in order to buy it immediately for a fraction of its real value. The public institutions assigned to foster national economic development, such as the Commission for the Defense of Sugar and the Promotion of Cane and the Public Works Commission, only work for Trujillo, even though they are state institutions, paid by the state.

For now it is practically impossible to know how much is the dictator's net income from the enterprises he manages. The profits from these enterprises are direct or indirect, since almost all of them have personnel paid by the state, mostly through the armed forces, and very often, one way or the other, they are financed by the state. Frequently a Dominican ambassador is appointed just to carry out a business deal designed to increase the profits from some of these enterprises, and with a surprising unanimity, Dominican economic legislation is determined by the convenience of Trujillo's industrial, financial, and commercial complex.

Trujillo carries out a huge number of unorganized business deals on a daily basis which do not figure in my list, just as his real estate or personal properties do not figure on it either, nor his bank accounts. Neither am I listing the enterprises or the assets of his many relatives—siblings, in-laws, nephews, and nieces—all of whom are also into business.

Just as I have said several times, so that the reader will not forget it, the Dominican government is a legal servant of the commercial enterprises of Rafael Leonidas

Trujillo.

Here is the list of Trujillo's enterprises, grouped by category [. . .]:

Alcohol: A monopoly on production and sale by Trujillo, and, of course, a sub-product of his sugar business (see sugar, on this list). To ensure more consumption, the law establishes that gasoline for cars must be mixed with alcohol. The factory that produces alcohol, named Universal Distillery, Inc., is actually a state property, after having purchased it at a high price from Trujillo, but it is operated by Trujillo and it works with the molasses produced in the dictator's mills.

Food for cattle, hogs and poultry: Subproducts of the oil plants (see edible oils). As is the case for all other of Trujillo's monopolies on production, the import of competing products is prohibited.

Rice: Rice production is not monopolized, but the dictator is an important producer and his grains have preference in the foreign market, whenever there are purchasing requests from other countries. In the exportation of rice, he operates through Dominican Exporting, Inc., and in the national market, through Rice Husker, Inc.

Construction, hardware, and electrical items: Read Hardware, Inc., the only supplier to the state, and with privileges in the payment of all sorts of taxes, though not monopolistic, that controls the selling of these articles, is an old business of Trujillo managed by one of his brothers-in-law, Mr. Francisco Martínez. The firm continues under a name that already existed when Trujillo seized power.

Dockyards: Trujillo is the owner of Dominican Dockyards, Inc., an enterprise set up by the State. Dominican Dockyards, Inc., is currently expanding into building boats destined for other countries. Its biggest earnings come from repairing the State's warships, at disproportionate prices. As a business promoter for Dominican Dockyards, Inc., General Arturo Espaillat traveled throughout the Caribbean in 1958, proving that even the army's hierarchy is at the service of the dictator's industrial and commercial enterprises, even thought they get emoluments and travel expenses from public treasury funds.

Automobiles, spare parts and tires: The majority of American and European automobile brand names sold in Santo Domingo are sold by the following Trujillo organizations: Caribbean Motors Company, Inc., Dominican Motor, Inc., and Santo Domingo Motors, Inc. These firms also sell tires and spare parts for cars and trucks. They are not, however, monopolies in any of the sectors in which they operate, but just like all of Trujillo's businesses, they have privileges in the payment of customs duties and of benefits and in credits from official banks, which they use to establish an unfair competition.

Sugar: Trujillo is the largest producer of this product, which is also the most important item among Dominican exports. The domestic market is supplied with the production from Trujillo's mills, and all of the country's alcohol must be produced with the molasses from the dictator's mills. On the foreign markets, mainly European, Trujillo's sugar has privileges over his local competitors, reduced to a mere two. Trujillo began dabbling in the sugar business during the last world war; between 1944 and 1956, he became the owner of eighty percent (80%) of Dominican mills; one of them is the country's largest, and several have refineries. In alphabetical order, here are his factories: Amistad, Barahona, Boca Chica, Catarei, Consuelo, Esperanza, Monte Llano, Ozama, Porvenir, Río Haina, Santa Fe, Quisqueya.

Banking: Usurious loans are a Trujillista monopoly, managed by the Popular Credit Bank, Inc., whose loans are made at 3.5 percent monthly interest, plus commission and insurance fees. A very severe anti-usury law liquidated in the whole country even pawn shops and another law granted special permission to the Popular Credit Bank, Inc., to provide loans to all public employees with the guarantee that they will retain the amount lent by the official dependency in which the interested parties provide their services. The Popular Credit Bank, Inc., buys devalued public debt notes and liquidates them at par. Loans from this bank cannot exceed RD$500.00, so they cannot be used for productive purposes. This is certainly the most leonine business currently operating in the Americas.

Vehicle batteries and retreading: The manufacture and repair of car and truck batteries, as well as the operation of repairing auto and truck tires, which uses the same industrial installation built to manufacture the batteries' cases, is another Trujillista monopoly, operated through Dominican Battery Factory, Inc.

Bottles and other glass containers: Manufacture and sales are monopolized by the dictator. A law from the national Congress prohibits, under severe penalties, to reuse a glass container, which presupposes a minimum of production and a maximum of sales for the manufacturing firm. This firm is National Glass Industry, Inc.

Coffee: As in the case of rice, Trujillo competes in the production of coffee with obvious unfair advantages over other producers: labor extracted from garrisons and jails, tax evasion and preference in the national market. Regarding sales overseas, the dictator has the monopoly through the firm Dominican Coffee, Inc.

Beef: Another one of Trujillo's oldest businesses, organized under the name of Dominican Industrial Cattle, Inc., in combination with the Fundación Hacienda, a personal property of Trujillo, which buys and fattens cattle, the Industrial Slaughterhouse, the only slaughterhouse authorized to kill cattle for the consumption of the country's capital and for export, and the cannery Cami Products, Inc. The latter firm transforms the pork meat used by the Dominican Industrial Society, Inc., in the production of animal lard. Both monopolies—beef and animal or vegetable oil—are among the most energetically organized and are those with the heaviest weight in the popular economy. Whoever is caught bringing into the capital of the Republic a slice of meat that does not come from Dominican Industrial Cattle exposes himself to all sorts of abuses; and there are those who have paid for this crime with their lives.

Cement: A Trujillista monopoly, the Dominican Cement Factory, Inc. manufactures the product, and Dominican Distributor, Inc. is its sole distributor. Only cement manufactured by Trujillo can be sold in the country, and in case some extra amount needs to be imported, only Dominican Distributor, Inc., can do it (see the construction industry).

Beer: Production is monopolized through the Dominican National Brewery, Inc., one of the dictator's oldest businesses, who forced the original founders to sell him the company. It manufactures, among others, *Presidente* beer, given this name by the previous owners of the company in an effort to ingratiate themselves with Trujillo.

Cigarettes: Monopoly of production through the Anonymous Tobacco Company, Inc., an old firm that Trujillo forced its owners to transfer over to him. Simultaneously with the takeover of the Anonymous Tobacco Company, Inc., the dictator unceremoniously dissolved other cigarette-making private companies. The monopoly manufactures dark and Virginia tobacco cigarettes under several brands.

Cigars: Manufactured by the Anonymous Tobacco Company, Inc., this sector, however, is not monopolized by the dictator. There are small producers in the country's interior. Anyway, the market for cigars is mainly dominated by the name brands from the Trujillista industries.

Chocolate and cacao byproducts: All production of Dominican cacao, for the table or as candy, is monopolized by Industrial Chocolatier, Inc. It was established during the World War under the name of Sánchez Chocolatier in order to exploit the prestige of the Sánchez-type local cacao in the world market. Industrial Chocolatier, Inc., monopolizes the export of semi-manufactured cacao through the legal expedient of demanding that any company intending to export it, must have particular machinery that nobody else can install in the country.

Jams: Processor of Dominican Fruits, Inc., has the monopoly of sales to the state's dependencies of jams manufactured with national fruits. Processor of Dominican Fruits, Inc., is, of course, a Trujillista industry.

Industrial gases: A relatively recent business in Trujillo's hands, the production, importation, and consumption of oxygen, acetylene and medical oxygen are monopolized by his company Dominican Industrial Gases, Inc.

Edible oils: All edible oils consumed in Santo Domingo come from the factories of the Dominican Industrial Society, Inc., property of the dictator. The peasant producer of peanuts and hogs is forced to sell them at the price stipulated by the only factory, and the consumer has to buy the oils at the selling price determined by it [the factory]. Together with beef, this is a monopoly jealously defended by Trujillo, given the ease for the household production of beef and oils.

Construction industry: Besides the monopolization of cement, which is general, Trujillo retains the monopoly over governmental purchases in various categories of the construction industry, and this monopoly operates though the following companies: Dominican Pottery, Inc., a factory of pipes and glassy clay elbows, favored by a law that demands the construction of sewers in all of the cities in the country; Cement Asbestos, Inc., that manufactures panels for walls and ceilings in official constructions, as well as pipes of a larger diameter; Dominican Company of Hot Asphaltic Concrete, Inc., Dominican Concrete, Inc., Dominican Sand, Inc., and Dominican Gravel, Inc., which provide to the government the products that give them their names. All the above firms make up, with the Dominican Cement Factory, Inc., and with those that control marble and national lumber (see lumber and marble), as well as gypsum (see salt) and the materials imported through Read Hardware, Inc., a veritable industrial and commercial complex dominant in the private and public construction industry of Santo Domingo. This entire industrial complex is the property of the dictator.

Milk and dairy products: This monopoly of Trujillo is organized on two levels: the national one, controlled by the Dominican Milk Central, in which Trujillo only reserves for himself the monopoly over the manipulation and sale, but cattle ranchers provide the raw milk, and the monopoly of the capital city, in which Trujillo provides the raw milk and controls the manipulation and sale. The latter one is exercised through Industrial Milk, Inc., the only firm authorized, moreover, to export milk. With Industrial Milk, Inc., the dictator completes his absolute dominion over the market of the country's capital on all the products and sub-products from beef and milk cattle.

Lumber: This is probably the most extensive sector of Trujillo's businesses throughout the country. The enormous wealth of Santo Domingo in lumber of all kinds, for construction and fine furniture, was barely exploited by part of the national market when the dictator seized power. The global demand for lumber at the beginning of the Second World War catapulted Trujillo into this business. Sawing, drying, transporting, manufacturing of doors and windows, the building of furniture for governmental uses and the exportation of lumber have been under Trujillo's control for many years now. With the exception of the small woodworking shops, staffed by artisans with a local clientele, all of Dominican lumber for sale in the country and oversea is a tributary of Trujillo. A list of the dictator's lumber companies would make this account too long, but it can be affirmed that these businesses are centralized at Piña House, Inc.

Marble: Production is a Trujillista monopoly, founded to control the sale of marble to the state, as a result of the structures built to celebrate the centenary of the Republic in 1944. Currently buildings of certain value must use some percentage of marble, according to the law. The company that exploits this sector is named National Marble.

Medicines and medical supplies: Through Dominican Chemical Laboratory, Inc., Trujillo monopolizes the sale of nationally produced medicines to State dependencies, and through Caribbean Medical Supply, Inc., he monopolizes the sale of hospital and medical supplies to government hospitals and clinics.

Minerals: Extraction and exportation are totally monopolized by Trujillo through the Dominican Mineral Profiting Company, Inc. In the last few years this company has been exporting gold, iron, and manganese. The extraction is carried out using inmates and soldiers, and the transportation to the port with trucks from the armed forces.

Air transportation: The national routes are a monopoly of the dictator and are managed by Dominican Aviation Company, Inc. This company also travels overseas, but it alternates its overseas flights with Caribbean Atlantic Airlines, Inc., a bogus company, in order to avoid monopolistic appearances.

Maritime transportation: High-end transportation for import and export is mostly handled by two of Trujillo's companies: Dominican Merchant Fleet, Inc., and Dominican Shipping, Inc. The personnel for the ships in both lines comes from the Navy and is paid through this branch of the armed forces; the ships are repaired with funds from the Navy and it [the Navy] also pays for the petroleum and the lubricants that they consume. Cabotage transportation is not monopolized, and here the routes of the Lesser Antilles and the Caribbean are included as long as they are served by low-tonnage schooners and sloops.

Bread: In this item and all baked goods, Trujillo has had an important participation since the first days of his regime, through the biggest bakery in the country, Quico, Inc.

Newspapers, books, publishing: Several publishing companies are the property of Trujillo, among them the two most important in the country: El Caribe, Inc., publisher of the daily newspaper *El Caribe*, and *La Nación*, Inc., editor of the daily newspaper *La Nación*. All public functionaries and employees of the dictator's enterprises are forced to buy the newspapers that these two enterprises publish. In order to transform this business into a monopoly, Trujillo forced the disappearance of older newspapers, such as *La Opinión* and *Listín Diario*.

Seafood: The market of the capital city is monopolized through Dominican National Fishery, the only company, on the other hand, that may sell fish to hotels, hospitals and State garrisons. With the monopoly of the capital's market, Trujillo prevents that his beef monopoly in the city may be penetrated by free producers of fish.

Oil: For many years now, Trujillo has been concentrating all oil explorations and concessions in the hands of his company, Dominican Petroleum, Inc. This firm works in closely with official institutions, such as the Petroleum Section of the Geological Consultancy, a dependency of the Secretariat of Agriculture, for which it receives, without having to pay a cent, the studies performed by foreign companies and by government technicians. With Dominican Petroleum, Inc., Trujillo is ready to monopolize the country's oil production as soon as it starts.

Paints: A Trujillista monopoly, favored by a law that forces property owners around the country to paint their houses at least twice a year. The monopoly is exercised through Dominican Paints, Inc.

Politics: All public functionaries must become members of the Dominican Party, and as such, they must contribute 10 percent of their monthly salary to the party's leader, Rafael Leonidas Trujillo. The deduction is made at the General Accounts Office of the Nation and the total is handed over to the dictator. It is estimated that this sector represents a daily income of ten thousand pesos (equivalent to dollars) for Trujillo. From this amount one should deduct the office and bureaucratic personnel expenses of the Dominican Party, that probably amount to 20 percent of earnings. Summing up, besides being a political instrument, the Dominican Party is a source of income for the dictator, with a favorable balance of no less than two million dollars per year.

Radio and television: Through the Dominican Voice, Inc., that appears as property of his brother J. Arismendi Trujillo, the dictator monopolizes the country's radio business at the national level. Dominican Voice is well known in several American countries for its disturbing role. This same enterprise has the television monopoly. Free merchants are forced to advertise on the Dominican Voice's radio and television stations under threat of mistreatment and incarceration.

Bottled drinks: Produced by Industrialization of Dominican Fruits, Inc., Trópico brand sodas are the only ones consumed in the State's dependencies, though in the official hotels other brands are sold.

Rents (from rental property): It is difficult to know the number of houses for rent that Trujillo owns, but one must consider that he has been in this business since he was chief of the Army, before 1930. It is known that the majority of Dominican embassies in Europe are located in houses belonging to Trujillo, which must pay him a high rent, and that many of the houses rented to foreign diplomats in Santo Domingo belong to the dictator.

Bags, rope, and woven fibers: A Trujillo monopoly that reaches from the growing of the fibrous plants to the manufacture and sale of the items that cover the entire national market. The law severely punishes the use, on more than one occasion, of the bags manufactured by the dictator. Latifundia, dedicated to growing of fibrous plants that supply the factory, are worked by inmates and soldiers. It was in these latifundia where functionaries from the OIT [Organización Internacional del Trabajo] (International Labor Organization) confirmed in 1957 the presence of several hundred slave workers without salary or work schedule. The firm that handles this monopoly is Dominican Bags and Textiles, Inc., supported by subsidiary firms, such as the Dominican Rope Factory and the Dominican Wadding Factory.

Salt: One of the oldest and most voracious of Trujillo monopolies. In order to avoid some of the inconveniences related to production, the dictator transferred to the state, some years ago, the ownership of the salt mines and their operation, but he retained the monopoly over sales in the country and for export, which guarantees greater benefits for him, because if there are production losses they ought to be absorbed by the State. Currently the monopoly operates under the name Dominican Salt and Gypsum, Inc., whose name is misspelled. Gypsum is a byproduct of the rock salt mines from where salt is extracted.

Insurance: All insurance required by law for private and official workers, as well as maritime ones, are monopolized by San Rafael, Inc., an enterprise among the first ones established by Trujillo. Injured persons who are insured by San Rafael are attended to at State hospitals, including government employees and the military, though, in order to maintain appearances, there are medical practices at the enterprise's service; only basic care is provided in those practices. Indemnities for accidental deaths are rarely paid, and in order to avoid civil responsibilities it resorts to the procedure of not registering deaths in the official records. Life insurance is not monopolized by San Rafael, Inc.; some foreign firms are allowed to underwrite a few.

Cotton textiles: In its spun and stitched forms, and even with the product manufactured into clothing, shirts, socks, t-shirts, that of cotton textiles is another one of Trujillo's monopolies. It is handled by several firms: Cotton, Inc., that manufactures the textiles; several branches of Alma Shirts, that manufacture and sell shirts; and Miss America, that manufactures women's clothes.

Shoes: State purchases, the largest customer in the country, particularly through the Army and the Navy, are done exclusively with Fa-Doc, Inc. (Dominican Shoe Factory), also favored by a law that fines those who do not wear shoes. Fa-Doc is probably the oldest enterprise of the Trujillista cartel, and for thirty years it has annually been selling to the State a number of pairs of shoes destined for the country's inmates that have been systematically charged, but never delivered.

Surprised by the multiplicity of businesses belonging to Rafael Leonidas Trujillo, Daniel James, a U.S. journalist, said that in Santo Domingo "it is almost impossible to eat, drink, smoke or wear anything without benefiting the benefactor or his family in some way. Dominicans pay taxes to him from their cradles to their graves."

It is true. And there lies, precisely, the key to the control that the Dominican dictator has over his people: Rafael Leonidas Trujillo does not lead a political regime, he is the boss of an implacable, monolithic economic organization, whose voracity is equally stimulated by one dollar as by ten million; that organization has at its service a government and a sea, air, and land military; and for the shame of the legal system that links the countries of the Americas, it is received and treated as if it were the legitimate representation of the Dominican people.

Nepotism and Corruption

The Trujillo dictatorship was a family affair. Rafael L. Trujillo's brothers would become high-ranking officers in the Dominican army (and wealthy), while his sisters, in-laws, and other relatives and close friends would come to own or administer profitable business that had the full backing of the state. In the 1950s, his little brother Héctor Bienvenido (a.k.a. Negro) even became president of the Dominican Republic —while Rafael ruled from behind the throne. Another one, José Arismendi (a.k.a. Petán) would come to rule the little town of Bonao as his personal fiefdom, where he owned large tracts of land and the country's first radio station. His abuses of power were legendary, and parents scurried to get their young daughters out of town before they caught the eye of Petán.

Perhaps the greatest beneficiary of these practices was Rafael Trujillo Jr., the dictator's first-born son. Ramfis—as he was called—was born out of wedlock and it was not until years later that Trujillo married his mother, María Martínez. Trujillo adored Ramfis and catered to his every wish. As a result, Ramfis grew up amidst luxury and privilege, spoiled by his parents and a large côterie of adulators who realized that one of the best ways to get to the old dictator's heart was through his son. Trujillo intended to one day transfer power to Ramfis, but the latter never showed the leadership abilities of his father. Quite to the contrary, Ramfis spend most of his time partying, womanizing, and spending his father's fortune— which Trujillo had exacted from the Dominican people. The following piece details one example of Ramfis's typical behavior, but which this time made headlines in the U.S. press. Ramfis was sent to the U.S. Army High Command School, but instead he ended up in Hollywood, where he dined and wined some of the hottest actresses of the day. When the U.S. military refused to grant Ramfis a diploma–since he had barely been to classes—his father considered it a diplomatic incident and ordered home all Dominicans attending military courses in the United States in protest. Of course, Ramfis was never chastised by his father for his irresponsible behavior. Instead, the dictator dispatched the ship *Angelita*[8] to California to pick up Ramfis and his entourage.

---

8. The *Angelita* was a four-mast, 316 feet luxury yacht named for one of Trujillo's daughters.

THAT GENEROUS GENERAL[9]

Even for the son of a dictator, the military career of Rafael Trujillo Jr. has been nothing short of spectacular. At the age of three, he was a full colonel in the Dominican army; at the age of eight, he won the Military Merit Medal "for exceptional virtues," and at the age of twenty-three, despite the fact that he cannot fly an airplane, he became chief of staff of the air force.

Last year, young Trujillo (by then twenty-eight and a lieutenant general) was given an appointment to the U.S. Army Command and General Staff School at Fort Leavenworth, Kansas. He showed up with his wife, six children, an entourage including a male secretary and an aide-de-camp, and a $50,000-a-month allowance for incidental expenses.

A quiet, dark, solemn man, Trujillo settled down to live—by his standards—quietly. He rented a $450-a-month ranch house in Leavenworth itself, and took over the entire top (or ninth) floor of the Ambassador Hotel in Kansas City. A security guard of thirty men was set up, and the top floor of the Ambassador was turned into a fortress. Special drivers took Trujillo from Leavenworth to Kansas City (by Cadillac), and the drivers were instructed to "watch the high points and bluffs [for snipers]."

Going Hollywood: Two circumstances developed to upset his quiet way of life in Kansas. Last January, Trujillo took his wife and children back to the Dominican Republic, and a few weeks ago his adenoids were removed. Presumably in search of sunshine, he went to Hollywood to recuperate.

The general took a three-room suite at the Beverly Hilton Hotel, and rented a $2,500-a-month home in Bel Air. He met a number of motion-picture actresses, including two blondes in particular named Zsa Zsa Gabor and Kim Novak.

He became Miss Novak's steady escort, taking her to dinner three or four times a week at L'Escoffier, a swank restaurant on top of the Beverly Hilton Hotel and from there to the adjoining Star-on-the-Roof Room to sip champagne and liqueurs for hours; he sent Miss Novak a dozen roses every third day. "He was very much in love with Kim." Trujillo's friend and secretary, Victor Sued, told a reporter.

To show his affection for Miss Novak, Trujillo gave her an $8,400 Mercedes-Benz automobile; and lest Miss Gabor feel slighted, he gave her a $5,600 Mercedes, plus a mink coat.

Last week in Washington, these presents exploded in the House.

For instance, Rep. Charles O. Porter, Oregon Democrat, suggested that $1.3 million in foreign aid earmarked for the Dominican Republic be paid directly to Miss Novak and Zsa Zsa. That way, he said, the U.S. would be able to collect taxes on the grant.

General Trujillo proved that he knew one military lesson: Silence is the better part of valor. He refused to make one word of explanation.

At the weekend, it was disclosed that young Trujillo had instituted divorce proceedings against his wife in Chihuahua, Mexico; Trujillo's father, Generalissimo Rafael Trujillo, revealed the divorce action, but said it had nothing to do with either of the Hollywood actresses to whom his son had given presents.

9. From *Newsweek*, May 26, 1958. © Newsweek, Inc. All rights reserved. Reprinted with permission. Pages 36–37.

Macho Politics

An important characteristic of Trujillo's authoritarian personality was his machismo. In the tradition of the times, Trujillo considered himself a "real man." Politics in the Dominican Republic was then still the realm of men, and Trujillo sought to reign supreme over all of them. Thus, Trujillo was careful to cultivate an image that combined the characteristics of the perfect gentleman with those of the stern leader. For example, Trujillo thought of himself as a man of honor who paid his debts on time, who always kept his word, who was punctual, and who was socially suave and refined. But Trujillo also had no qualms about murdering his enemies, embezzling the state's resources, and periodically picking women to satisfy his sexual appetites.

Women played an important role in this scheme of domination. Since the 1920s, Dominican women had been mobilizing to demand legal equality with men. One of their most important organizations was Acción Feminista Dominicana (Dominican Feminist Action, or AFD), founded on May 14, 1931. Its first president was Abigaíl Mejía, one of the pillars of the country's feminist movement. The main goal of AFD, which was made up of upper and middle-class women, was the achievement of voting rights, but it also sought to educate lower-class women by establishing night schools. Its statement of principles (reproduced below) was in tune with then current feminist thought and was influenced by developments taking place in Europe and the United States. Trujillo, seeking to expand his social base, co-opted the movement. While some of the AFD leaders decided to retire or went into exile, others actively supported the dictatorship, which eventually integrated the organization into Trujillo's Partido Dominicano (Dominican Party, or PD). For the 1942 elections, Trujillo gave women the right to vote, though elections were rather meaningless during the dictatorship.

Trujillo's mask fell on November 25, 1960, when, by his direct orders, Patria, Minerva, and María Teresa Mirabal were assassinated along with their chauffeur. The sisters had become outspoken opponents of the Trujillo regime and, together with their husbands, had joined the underground resistance. On their return home from a visit to their husbands in a Puerto Plata jail, they were intercepted by Trujillo's henchmen, detained, murdered, and their car was pushed off a cliff to simulate an accident. The Dominican people, who did not believe the regime's official story, were horrified by the cold-blooded murder of these three defenseless women, as now no one felt safe from the dictator's wrath.

STATEMENT OF PRINCIPLES OF
ACCIÓN FEMINISTA DOMINICANA[10]

This group will be made up of women of good conduct, who have reached their eighteenth birthday and who know how to read and write. Its main goal is to tend to the betterment of the intellectual, social, moral, and legal condition of women, as well as to campaign for social defense against alcoholism, prostitution, and narcotic drugs, and the like, to fight for the passage of laws for the protection of mothers, children, adolescents, the aged, and the blue-collar workers. To advocate for the establishment of tribunals for children, to work to instill in women the understanding of the necessity to be frugal and to dissuade them from spending on unnecessary luxuries; to persuade Dominicans not to sell their land to foreigners; to fight so that our traditions are preserved and to sponsor every idea that would mean the advancement and welfare of the Republic.

[. . .]

The Acción Feminista aspires to enroll in its rank all their compatriots, so that a true feminist union will result, formed by ladies and young ladies who live, some by their rents and incomes, others by teaching, by industry, blue-collar work, students, and so on. One of its principal goals will be to accustom Dominican women to the agreement of thought and of mutual tolerance and protection at work. The Acción Feminista wishes to make mothers truly conscious of their mission; it wishes to prepare mothers to earn a livelihood in a dignified manner for themselves and their families, should the need arise; it wishes that even women with means to receive such training so they are prepared to administer their fortune and make them fit to sustain the moral and material equilibrium of the home, because lest we forget, whosoever says balance at home, says balance in the fatherland.

Feminism will tend to bring about the happiness of women by preparing them so that they always marry for love, and not of necessity and in a hurry with the first to come for fear of facing the demands of life; it will work so that laws are passed that would support marriage and the stability of the family.

Political Repression

The Trujillo dictatorship was characterized by high levels of violence in its early stages as the regime consolidated its power and eliminated all

---

10. From Daisy Cocco De Filippis, *Documents of Dissidence: Selected Writings by Dominican Women* (New York: CUNY Dominican Studies Institute, 2000), 61–62. Reprinted by permission.

political opponents, as well as toward its end as it began to unravel. Only in the middle stages was there an extended period of enforced "peace." Within a few years after assuming the presidency in 1930, Trujillo established a well-entrenched dictatorship backed by the Dominican military, sectors of the intelligentsia, the Catholic Church, and the United States. Trujillo's police state was based on the surveillance of individuals, networks of informants (or *caliés*), the brutal interrogation of detainees by using torture, the selective assassination or "disappearance" of political opponents, and the widespread use of intimidating terror. Though publicly Trujillo disavowed these brutal acts, he made of "peace and order" one of his main policy goals.

Trujillo's repression even extended overseas. Dominican political exiles were murdered by Trujillo's agents in Cuba and the United States, and he was involved in attempts to kill Presidents Carlos Castillo Armas of Guatemala and Rómulo Betancourt of Venezuela. One of Trujillo's most notorious murders was the case of Basque exile Jesús de Galíndez, who disappeared in 1956. Galíndez, a refugee from the Spanish Civil War, had lived for a few years in the Dominican Republic, and even worked for the Dominican government before leaving for the United States. In New York City, Galíndez became a doctoral student and part-time instructor at Columbia University, where he was writing his dissertation about the Trujillo dictatorship, an exposé of the regime's inner workings. Attempts by the Trujillo regime to dissuade or bribe Galíndez were unsuccessful, and in the evening of March 12, 1956, Galíndez disappeared on his way home. He was supposedly kidnapped, drugged, and flown to the Dominican Republic, where he was brutally tortured until he died. To this day, Galíndez's body has not been found, and several individuals linked to the case died in mysterious circumstances shortly after his disappearance. Galíndez's dissertation survived him, thanks to copies that he had left with friends and professors. It was published posthumously in Spanish and English, and to this day the "Galíndez Affair" is still considered one of the most brazen crimes carried out by the Trujillo dictatorship. A section of his work that deals with Trujillo's repression is reproduced below.

FROM THE DISSERTATION OF JESÚS DE GALÍNDEZ[11]

Political Freedoms

According to Paragraph 5, Article 6 of the Constitution, "the right to express thoughts without subjecting them to previous censorship" is inherent to human beings, restricted only by this limitation: "The law will establish penalties applicable to those who act against the honor of persons, the social order, or the public peace." According to Paragraph 6 of the same article, "freedom of association and of assembly for peaceful ends" is also inherent in human beings. And according to Article 103, "the organization of political parties and associations is free, in accordance with the principles established in the second article of this Constitution."

Let us note the application of these constitutional principles in detail.

The hard truth is that freedom of speech has not existed since May 1930; the last use of this freedom during the election campaign of that year was crushed by the terror of "the 42nd" and the post-electoral arrests of leaders of the National-Progressive Alliance. Reading the Dominican press during these twenty-five years would suffice to prove this, but perhaps it will be useful to analyze some concrete cases of relative freedom of public expression in order to evaluate its nuances; the exception proves the rule.

The author personally witnessed some of these cases during his stay in the Dominican Republic. In October 1942, the president of the Basque government-in-exile, José A. de Aguirre, visited the Dominican Republic for two days. His visa was requested and granted with difficulty. Then it was suggested that he give a lecture at the university; the president of the university favored the idea but he did not dare approve it without previous authorization by the president of the Republic, which was also granted. When the arrival of President Aguirre was announced in the press, the minister of Franco Spain made an oral protest to the Office of Foreign Relations, which relayed the protest to the organizers of the trip and warned them not to mention Aguirre's title as president and not to have him speak in public about Spanish politics. The Chamber of Deputies appointed a committee of three of its members to attend all functions honoring Aguirre, including the lecture in the university and a semi-private dinner. Not the slightest restrictions were imposed for the lecture on "The Spirit of Freedom in the Peoples of the World"; Dr. Troncoso de la Concha presided, and the room was full of people who enthusiastically applauded the lecturer. The Office of Foreign Relations only requested advance copies of the speeches to be delivered at the dinner by some refugees resident in the country. One can say with all justice that in this case a freedom prevailed which the Dominicans lack.

In the same way, Spanish refugees enjoyed freedom to hold political meetings in private places; they included, remarkably enough, the activities of the Communists through their front, Centro Democrático Español. This club was watched discreetly by the police, but its activities were not curtailed until 1945. Non-communist groups had no difficulties until 1947. Fascist Spaniards also had the same freedom to act during the period of the Spanish Civil War, and the local branch of the Falange Española

11. Excerpt from *The Era of Trujillo*, by Jesús de Galíndez and edited by Russell Fitzgibbon. © 1973 The Arizona Board of Regents. Reprinted by permission of the University of Arizona Press, 128–137.

was active until it disbanded of its own accord at the end of 1939.

Foreigners thus enjoyed in general a freedom of speech that the natives could not even dream about.

On the debit side of the record, one must point out that street demonstrations that the different national groups of exiles had planned in Ciudad Trujillo to celebrate the surrender of Germany were never allowed by the authorities, although they used delaying tactics instead of openly prohibiting them. It seems that in this case the government feared the fact of a public demonstration in which Dominicans might participate. On the other hand, the Americans in La Romana held a similar public demonstration in the streets after the surrender of Japan.

Concerning the Dominicans, the only variation from this silence, except to voice praise of the regime, was during the period in 1946 when, first, *La Opinión* for a few weeks, and, afterward, the Popular Socialist party (communist) and the Democratic Youth, for another short period, were able to carry on a moderate campaign of opposition. The political nuances of this period are worth analyzing.

Let us consider, first, the campaign of *La Opinión*. It started in January 1946, as suggested by the president. The secretary of the presidency himself visited the editor to request that campaign, adding that the government desired to direct it and was ready to subsidize the editor personally. The editor, a former Spanish refugee, did not accept those conditions and requested an interview with Trujillo himself. In this interview, Trujillo agreed to the requested freedom of action on condition that neither the president nor the army were attacked. The first evidence of the new stand was the printing, as authorized by Trujillo himself, of a letter signed by several Spanish non-Communist exiled leaders against the person hiding behind the generic pen name of "A Spanish Republican," attacking the new Venezuelan government of Acción Democrática and the ambassador of the Spanish Republican government-in-exile in Caracas; no name was mentioned at all, but it was generally known that he was the private secretary of Trujillo, José Almoina.

During the following weeks, *La Opinión* carried on an active campaign of criticism of social and labor problems, including the cost of living. Among other things, it published the stenographic record of the national committee on wages in which it was affirmed that some Dominican sugar cane workers were at that time making twenty-five cents a day without meals. When this campaign of *La Opinión* entered the political field by printing a letter saying that Trujillo was not the only possible presidential candidate, the government became alarmed because of the favorable reaction it produced among wide groups of students and others. The campaign was then stopped, and a short time later Trujillo bought the newspaper. A new editor amended its policy to conform to the usual Trujillista line, but finally the newspaper disappeared permanently.

With regard to the campaign of the Popular Socialist party, for several weeks the party was allowed to hold public meetings until that riotous one in Ciudad Trujillo that offered a pretext for repressive measures. The formation of the party and its first activities were encouraged by Trujillo's agents, who went to Cuba to discuss terms with Communist exiles; but a similar freedom of speech in favor of the majority of Dominicans who wanted a change in policies and abhorred communism was not permitted. The campaign was presented in these terms: the only enemies of the regime are the Communists, and Trujillo is saving the democratic and spiritual values of the Dominican people against the threat of a disturbing and atheistic communism.

During twenty-five years, these are the only known examples of free speech and political activities not exclusively concerned with mere praise of Trujillo and his work. The Trujillista party as well as the National Democratic and National Labor parties later, were no more than fronts organized and backed by the government to simulate an appearance of multiplicity of political parties during a period in which world events were moving towards wider democracy.

Not only is there no freedom of speech, on the contrary, it is possible to cite countless instances in which public opinion favorable to Trujillo and his regime is forcibly created. Instances include those public demonstrations in the streets in which public employees are asked to participate by departmental order; one of the best examples was the demonstration against the Venezuelan government held on November 10, 1945. But there are more concrete cases.

The blank that all public employees were forced to fill out and send to the "Purification Commission for Public Employees" in 1945 sought not only information about relatives and other people not friendly to the regime, but also the answers to such questions as the following: "11. What political work have you done? 12. Details about your cooperation with the present government: (a) meetings you attend; (b) meetings you do not attend; (c) propaganda you have carried on in favor of the Government; (d) how many nonpolitical articles have you written? (e) how many political articles? (f) how many talks, lectures, and speeches have you made on topics of interest for the Government? (g) what other demonstrations of loyalty have you given? (h) do you attend punctually the *Te Deums* on National Holidays, political-cultural meetings, agricultural meetings, assemblies of the Dominican Party, etc.? (i) what special work of a political character have you done during the current year? (j) which activities did you carry on before being a public employee? (k) before being a member of the Dominican Party, what were your political activities?"

In the second place, was the circular addressed by Trujillo himself to all public employees one year later, in which he said: "I want to know if you have had conversations with persons who are enemies, unfriendly or neutral towards the Government, and what efforts you made to influence those persons in its favor. If you did not, what was your reason?"

In the third place, a question was included in almost every government blank, including passports or permits for imports, requesting the number and date of registration in the Dominican Party.

Given these circumstances, it is not surprising in the Dominican Republic to see letters printed in the newspapers, in which a close relative, even a parent, repudiates those who have made statements abroad or have carried on activities of opposition to Trujillo's regime. These statements have also been occasionally forced from foreigners for different reasons.

Arrests without Indictment, and Murders
Despite the guarantees offered in Paragraph 12 of Article 6 of the Constitution, everybody in the Dominican Republic believes that he may be arrested by the police without due process and that his arrest may be prolonged indefinitely. In some cases

the arrest is brief, if there are only suspicions or it is in the nature of a warning; in other cases the arrest ends finally in a trial which legalizes the situation, although the alleged crime occurred many years before; and in still others, the individual just disappears.

It is difficult to prove this with documentary evidence but in the highest positions of the Dominican government there are persons who know these facts from personal experience, such as Dr. Manuel de Jesús Troncoso de la Concha, president of the Republic from 1940 to 1942 and president of the Senate from 1943 until his death in 1955, who had been arrested in 1930; or such as his successor as president of the Senate and holder of the same office from 1930 to 1938, Mario Fermín Cabral, who was arrested in 1941 after carrying out his duty of sending to jail and humiliating General José Estrella; or such as the editor of *El Caribe*, Germán Ornes Coiscou, who was arrested for a few days in 1945.

The best description of the prisons during the Era of Trujillo is the book *Una Gestapo en América* by Juan Isidro Jimenes-Grullón. He describes his own experiences from the time of his arrest on July 19, 1934, on suspicion of being implicated in the conspiracy of Santiago, until his pardon on October 31, 1935. During that year he was sent to the penitentiary of Nigua, so well known at the beginning of the regime, and to the solitary cells of Fortress Ozama in the capital. He suffered for a long time as a political prisoner at the mercy of General Fiallo and finally went through a trial and sentence; he was beaten and witnessed the more serious tortures suffered by other prisoners. He mentions by name and gives details of the cases of prisoners who were killed in prison. His book seems objective and at the same time dramatic; it has an authenticity stemming from direct sources of information.

The novel *Cementerio sin Cruces* by Andrés Requena is essentially true, but it cannot be mentioned as a source because the author was not an eyewitness and uses hearsay evidence. The events belong to a later period, when the young boys of the Popular Socialist party and the Democratic Youth were arrested after their activities in 1946–47. Requena was himself murdered a few months after the publication of this novel.

The author of this study had also occasion to speak with some persons who were in the penitentiary of Nigua during the first years of the regime, such as Lic. José A. Bonilla Atiles, and with others who were at Fortress Ozama in more recent years. He has also spoken with one of the survivors of the 1935 plot against Trujillo in the capital, Ing. J. C. Alfonseca.

The penitentiary of Nigua was closed in April 1938. Its disappearance marks the end of a period. Its prisoners were reportedly tortured in order to force confessions; most of the time they worked in the fields cutting grass with machetes. It is not surprising that some persons, after being there a few days, preferred to surrender unconditionally to the regime, and from the penitentiary, went on to occupy positions of great importance in the government; one among them was the nephew of the ousted President Horacio Vásquez.

This susceptibility to conversion may explain the relative benignity of the Trujillo regime. Hicks mentions 134 victims by name in his book; but that is a small number compared with the victims of that other vague terror to which we will refer later. Trujillo and his agents resort to extreme measures infrequently; it is more efficient to subdue the will, in order later to humiliate people by forcing them into collaboration.

However, there are also cases of presumed political murders. The best-known case was that of Virgilio Martínez Reyna and his wife in June 1930. *Listín Diario* denounced it at the time, but the best official confirmation of this crime was made public by the regime itself ten years later, when General Estrella was arrested in 1940 and tried because of that murder, which he admitted.

Detailed reference will be made to only one of the most notorious public murders during recent years. It is that of the businessman Porfirio Ramírez and seven other persons on the night of June 1, 1950. Porfirio Ramírez died because he was the brother of the chief of staff of the 1949 invasion. He was in the trucking business. That evening he departed from the capital in a truck loaded with flour, together with his driver Juan Rosario, an assistant driver, and three handymen; at the last moment, an old man and a woman requested that he take them also. About two miles from the city, they stopped at the usual military police post, and a sergeant ordered him to take six soldiers to the bridge of the Nizao River between San Cristóbal and Baní. This was the place chosen for the murder. When the truck arrived there, Lieutenant General Federico Fiallo in person (at that time chief of staff of the air force) and several officers stopped the truck, while the soldiers held the travelers at gunpoint. Ramírez was killed on the spot. The remaining persons were carried to a nearby curve to simulate an accident on the road, where they were beaten to death. But the driver, Juan Rosario, did not die then, although he pretended to be dead even when the criminals set the truck on fire; this time, a victim and witness survived for a few hours and could tell what had happened before he was finished off at the Baní hospital.

Murders Abroad

Enemies of Trujillo have also been murdered in foreign countries on at least three occasions; and in these three cases it is possible to prove the crime, although the authors still remain unpunished.

The first murder took place in New York City on April 28, 1935. That evening, an unknown person went to a modest rooming house at 87 Hamilton Place and asked for Dr. Angel Morales. Morales had been vice-presidential candidate for the Alliances in the 1930 elections and had been forced to escape into exile afterwards; he had been declared a traitor to the Fatherland because of his activities against Trujillo abroad. Morales was not at home, and his fellow roomer, Lic. Sergio Bencosme, appeared when the landlady told him that somebody was asking for Morales; Bencosme was shaving at the moment, and it seems that the murderer thought that it was Morales himself when he shot Bencosme to death. Ten months later the district attorney's office was able to get an indictment from the grand jury against Luis ("Chichí") de la Fuente Rubirosa as the murderer of Bencosme; when the required action was started to extradite him from the Dominican Republic, where he went after the murder, the official answer was that no such individual existed there.

The second case cannot yet be qualified officially as murder (because the body was never recovered) but its complete disappearance is doubtless evidence of what happened. This time the victim was Mauricio Báez, a labor leader who was given asylum in the Mexican embassy after the strike of 1946 and was later a leader of the Popular Socialist party, and who again went into exile in Cuba some time later (breaking with the party at the same time). On December 10, 1950, three individuals went to his home in Havana and persuaded him to go with them apparently to see Congressman Enrique C. Henríquez (a Dominican by birth and an enemy of Trujillo); it seems that Báez at the beginning suspected something and refused to go, but he finally agreed. He has never been found, dead or alive. The Dominican legation in Havana attempted to place the blame upon other exiles, because Báez was said to be in communication with the chargé d'affairs Felix W. Bernardino (appointed consul general in New York a few days before), so that he might be granted amnesty to return to the Dominican Republic.

The third murder was that of Andrés Requena in New York City. On the evening of October 2, 1952, Requena left his home about 9:00 p.m. after saying to his fiancée: "I'm going to see the people you know." About 10:30, he took a cab on the corner of Sixth Avenue and 57th Street; a man "in a raincoat" accompanied him, who later never gave himself up to the police. He gave the taxi driver the address of 243 Madison Avenue in the downtown section of the city, and as soon as he entered the hall he was killed with five bullets. Again in this case the Dominican consulate general attempted to blame Dominican exiles because Requena was in communication with the consul; but Requena himself had brought to the printing shop where an anti-Trujillo paper was published an article in which he told the whole story. Two months before, he had tried to get his mother and sister out of the Dominican Republic, and a travel agent had told him that Consul General Bernardino wanted to discuss the matter with him. They agreed that the Dominican government would allow the exit of the two women if Requena accepted the compromise of not writing any more articles against either Trujillo or the Bernardino family; Requena accepted the proposal, but at the same time he reported to his exiled friends that as soon as his relatives arrived in the United States, he would again start his campaign. Finally he lost all hope that the Dominican government would fulfill its promise, and decided to renew the fight without waiting longer. It seems that this article was read in the presence of too many persons. The murder of Requena continues officially unsolved.

Just at the time of closing this study, on August 8, 1955, another Dominican exile was murdered in Havana. He was Manuel de Jesús ("Pipí") Hernández Santana, who escaped from the Dominican Republic in 1931 and until his death was active in revolutionary groups.

The Catholic Church Takes Action

The Catholic Church has traditionally been a supporter of the status quo, and the case of the Dominican Republic under Trujillo was no exception. In an almost symbiotic relationship, the Church provided its moral backing to the dictator, while the Trujillo regime bestowed all sorts of privileges and economic favors on the Church. The good relations between the Catholic Church and the Trujillo regime reached their high point in 1954, when a Concordat was signed at the Vatican in a ceremony attended by Trujillo himself. However, within a few years these cordial relations soured. By late 1959, the Trujillo regime was unraveling and it had become more erratic and vicious in its repression. The June 14, 1959 invasion by political exiles sparked a wave of official repression throughout the country. Shortly thereafter, and emboldened by the invasion and the success of the Cuban Revolution against dictator Fulgencio Batista, a clandestine internal opposition movement developed. It was made up of young men and women, many of whom were from the elites or were related to known Trujillo supporters. This movement was uncovered by Trujillo's intelligence services and another wave of arrests and tortures ensued.

Finally, the Church took a stance against the seemingly limitless repression. This time it was not military invaders who were being killed on the field of battle, but young men and women from well-to-do families who were being imprisoned and savagely tortured by Trujillo's henchmen. On February 28, 1960, the day after Dominican Independence Day, all Catholic priests read to their congregations a pastoral letter (reproduced below) signed by the Church hierarchy. The Church called for the respect of the rights inherent to all human beings and mentioned in passing the case of the political detainees. The Church's stance infuriated Trujillo, who at one point even considered executing some outspoken priests and seminarians. The regime had lost another one of its support pillars.

PASTORAL LETTER BY THE DOMINICAN CHURCH
OF FEBRUARY 28, 1960[12]

To the Venerable Clergy and all the Faithful,

Venerable Brothers and Beloved Children in Christ:

Lent is the appropriate time of spiritual health, in which the Church, [like a] loving Mother invites all its children to repent, to the pain of their faults and to a proper reparation and expiation.

Also in this circumstance we address our beloved brothers and children, trusting that our voices as Pastors reach your ears and descend to the bottom of your hearts, as the word of our Divine Master reached the ears and hearts of the Apostles and dis-

---

12. Translated from *Documentos de la Conferencia del Episcopado Dominicano (1955–1990)* (Santo Domingo: Comisión Dominicana Permanente para la Celebración del Quinto Centenario del Descubrimiento y Evangelización de América, 1990), 49–54.

ciples in order to strengthen faith, hope, and charity, especially during the moment of trial.

We address everyone, but in a special way the weak, the humble, the troubled ones, the sick, because these are called in a particular way to be witnesses of the truth through the stigmas of suffering, of tribulation, and of pain.

With the strong voice of a herald of eternity the Liturgy of this time claims: *"Let us mend the faults we have committed due to ignorance, so that we do not, surprised by the day of death, seek a time of penitence and cannot find it"* (Blessing of Ashes).

In order to carry out in us this solemn invitation of the Holy Spirit and respond to the calling of the Church, there is no better way than to examine our lives together, and see which are the points that we must especially consider in order to realize the precepts of the New Testament, the conversion, the change of mentality, setting aside superficial, obsolete and obscure criteria, to cover ourselves in God's criteria, our supreme and definitive reality. That way we will purify our soul and we will live with integrity, dignity, and honor the robust and everlasting ideology of eternal life proposed to the world by God's Son, and we will be worthy of the Father who is in heaven.

First and foremost, there is no ideal for us so big and transcendental as that of charity in its aspect of fraternal love, being that we are children of a common Father who is in heaven. As St. John the Apostle wrote: *"If anyone says, 'I love God,' and abhors his brother, he is a liar; for whoever does not love his brother, whom he has seen, cannot love God, whom he has not seen. And this commandment we have received from Him: that whoever loves God must also love his brother"* (I John 4:20–21). We all have the same fundamental rights and over all rest the same obligations and we all walk toward the same goal. We all have the same nature, made by God, in which the dignity of being an image and resemblance of God talks higher than all the titles of nobility and all the demands of human conventions.

A wonderful example of universal charity comes to us from God *"who makes the sun shine over the good and the bad; and he lets rain fall over the fair and the unfair"* (Matthew 5:45).

On this earth, a valley of tears in effect, a place of transit and an arena of hard trials, we have plenty of opportunities to exercise that charity following the example of our Father in heaven, because just and sinner, wheat and weeds, coexist together.

God does not tend to suddenly punish sinners for committing their faults. He lets them live, because as long as there is life, there is hope of salvation and, above all, because the behavior of sinners serves *to keep alive the faith of the just, to exercise patience and to make charity fecund*.

a) *To keep faith awake:* There is no one so saintly that does not, at least, have a little fault to purge on this earth. It results, therefore, in a true blessing of God to undergo and suffer in this world in order to deserve the joys of heaven, because with reason Saint Paul exclaimed: *"The sufferings of the present life are not adequate to the future glory that will be revealed in us"* (Romans 8:18). That is why Saint Augustine prayed one day in a way very strange to human feelings: *"Here and now God, burn, cut, do not forgive me, so that I can be forgiven for all eternity."*

The opposite happens to the sinner. The temptation of many Christians of denying the lovely Providence of God, because so many sinners live and triumph on earth, has no real reason for being, for their fortune compared to the eternity is like *"the grass of the countryside that today exists and tomorrow is thrown into the fire"* (Matthew 6:30), such prosperity ends without remedy the day in which rigorous, detailed and complete justice will be made.

In reality there is no sinner that does not posses any small virtue and does not practice some good deeds, which God cannot leave without reward. But if the mystery of injustice in sinners surpasses mercy itself, then God, the infinite justice to those who have made themselves ineligible for eternal reward, indemnifies in this life for the good that they could have done, leaving for eternity just the punishment without limits of the city of pain.

b) *To exercise patience:* No one ignores that the coexistence of the just and sinners is also for the former a purifying exercise of patience; because there is nothing that can make a righteous soul suffer so much than to see the grace of God violated; nor is there a more pitiful ordeal than that inflicted by those that, to their own disgrace, poke fun at Religion and Faith, in one word of Christ's own labor. It is an ordeal that does not require less valor nor less patience that the rest of life's mortifications demand; but it helps us all, loving brothers and children, to climb with more merit, for being then more similar to Christ, the slope of our painful Calvary.

c) *To make fecund the charity of the good:* You must console yourselves with the strength of Christ, of whom you are members, since in the face of all the wrongs and slanders that the Christian suffers, the only vengeance worthy of a follower of Christ and according to the commandment of love is the constant pleading to God for the conversion of those who have lost the path that is Christ. Every Christian that perhaps secretly suffers and undergoes this major ordeal of anguish, should not forget the divine example of *forgiveness*. To forgive is charity. To forgive is love. To forgive is generosity.

In the light of the teachings of this holy period of Lent we also invite you to be always prepared for the last moment of life, "so that surprised by the day of death, we seek time for penitence and we are not be able to find it" (Blessing of Ashes). Jesus himself, good Master and solicitious Pastor, is who admonishes us describing the arrival of death "like a thief at nighttime," who could surprise us at any instant. And if we find ourselves in the love of God, why fear death, if this is then the beginning of our true life? Let us not forget that we were not created for the moment, but for eternity.

We must, therefore, wait for death with the spirit that the Church prays with in the Preface of the Mass of the Dead: "To your faithful, God, their lives are not taken but rather exchanged for a better one; and as the house gets rid of this earthly dwelling, an eternal room in heaven is acquired."

The imposition of the ashes, which initiates the period of Lent, reminds us of the old ceremony during which the Bishop moved away public sinners from the temple, who had to perform penitence at the entrance of churches during the period of Lent. Receive yourselves these ashes on your heads and carry in your hearts the spirit that such ritual instills; the austere, pious and mortified life.

Four things were similarly practiced in antiquity, in this time of Lent: a) charity; b) public penitence; c) fasting, with the privation and abstinence of certain delicacies; d) and as immediate preparation for the Easter period: expiations and a more intense

194

life of meditation and praying.

Therefore, making ours the slogan of Saint Paul: *"Compassion is useful for everything"* (1 Timothy 4:8), we urgently exhort you to persevere during the time of Lent in a fervent crusade of prayer and penitence, *"because the persevering prayer of the just is very valuable"* (James 5:16).

For the consolation of an afflicted and aching humanity, the loving Providence of God in his inscrutable designs over the great human family, healthily restless in the search of a lost good, opens a luminous angle of the heavens, shining with candor, with hope, with a happy life, with sacred aspirations: the Virgin Mary, Queen and Mother of all humanity. In her we deposit, with an unlimited and indestructible trust, our wishes, our hopes and our prayers.

A motive of new consolation to all of us is the message of blessing and paternal love that in these same days the Holy Father, giving us an additional proof of his affectionate solicitude for us, has directed to the Dominican people. This majestic message is for all a comforting balm. Moreover, the Supreme Pontiff, knowing your piety and your Marian devotion, has deigned himself to associate with it by offering a symbolic votive candle that will burn at the feet of Our Lady of Altagracia at her Sanctuary of Higüey, joining in this way before the miraculous image, the prayers of these people with his and those of the universal church.

With words of lively gratitude for the Vicar of Christ, we transmit his apostolic Blessing as a token of special celestial graces.

In finishing Our Pastoral Letter, we trust that it will be a motive of hope to everyone, the words with which the highest Authority of the Nation has well received Our recommendation, assuring us that the pleas that were directed to him in favor of the political detainees will be considered with particular attention and solicitude in a context of comprehension and clemency.

With the certainty that, in the holy period of Lent Our wishes and common efforts of peace and concordance are crowned by the desired success, we ask God Our Lord that you may all celebrate the glorious Resurrection of Christ in an environment of complete serenity and spiritual joy.

To this end, as a token of Our Pastoral request, we implore for you, for all those who are particularly dear to you, for the sick, and for the common intentions of our loved diocesans the most effusive Divine Blessing.

Ricardo Pittini, Metropolitan Archbishop of Santo Domingo; Octavio Antonio Beras, Archbishop of Eucaita; Hugo E. Polanco, Bishop of Santiago de los Caballeros; Francisco Panal, Bishop of La Vega Real; Juan F. Pepén, Bishop of La Altagracia; Tomás F. Reilly, Bishop of Temisonio—on February 28, 1960, Quinquagesima Sunday.

The End of the Dictator

On the night of May 30, 1961, a group of men in three cars intercepted Trujillo on the outskirts of the capital city and assassinated him.

Trujillo was accompanied only by his chauffeur, who was injured but survived to tell the story. The men who participated in the assassination plot were mostly disgruntled ex-supporters of Trujillo. Most of them had been in the military or had worked for the government, and most had suffered personal humiliations at the hands of Trujillo. In the particular case of Antonio de la Maza, Trujillo had ordered the murder of his brother and disguised it as a suicide. Although the plotters were successful in killing Trujillo, they were not able to take over the government. The assassination was quickly discovered by the authorities and within days most of the plotters had been captured or killed in firefights. Only two of them escaped arrest and outlived the dictatorship. Those who were captured, including one of Trujillo's sons-in-law, were brutally tortured and killed shortly before the Trujillos left the country.

Trujillo's death was short of a national catastrophe. Dominicans who had never known any other head of state but Trujillo suddenly found themselves without their leader. The regime staged elaborate funeral ceremonies and puppet president Joaquín Balaguer delivered the eulogy, reproduced below. Balaguer had been one of Trujillo's most trusted men for thirty-one years, slowly climbing the ranks of the bureaucracy until he achieved the presidency in 1960. After Trujillo's death, and given the lack of leadership skills and experience of Trujillo's eldest son, Ramfis, Balaguer was poised to inherit the country's governance.

FACING TRUJILLO'S COFFIN[13]

Here lies, gentlemen, smashed by the blow of a treacherous flash of gunfire, the powerful oak that for more than thirty years defied every bolt of lighting and emerged victorious from all storms. This horrendous act fills our spirit with dismay and shakes the national soul with the deafening thunder of a catastrophe. Never has the death of a man produced such a feeling of consternation in a people nor has it ever loomed over the collective consciousness with greater anguish. We all know that with this glorious deceased we lose the best guardian of public peace and the best defender of safety and peace of mind in Dominican homes. The event has been so overwhelming that we still refuse to believe it. The earth still trembles under our feet and the world seems to have collapsed over our heads!

Who would have told us that this extraordinary man, who left his National Palace office just two days ago with a smile on his face, was to return to it cowardly sacri-

---

13. Translated from Joaquín Balaguer, *La palabra encadenada* (Santo Domingo: Fuentes Impresores, 1975), 175–180.

ficed a few hours later! But there is the tremendous reality with all its terrifying eloquence. Silent is now the mouth that gave so many commands. Over the chest, where the heart has stopped beating, lie unmovable his hands that held the sword that symbolized during forty years all the physical force of the nation. Lifeless and vilely pierced by bullets, there lies the heroic chest where the tricolor sash proudly waved, as if it floated on its pole.

[. . .]

What a great man Trujillo was and how his stature of national hero projects itself over Dominican history! He was human, many times too human, but his own mistakes deserve our respect because they were a product of his utmost passion for order and the Messianic concept that he had of his mission as a public man and head of state. His strong character and monolithic willpower did not diminish whatsoever neither in the difficult conflicts in which he was constantly involved, nor in the indispensable deterioration that his forty years of public life and his intense participation in the debates that divided his fellow citizens during the last three decades implied for him. His religious faith, for example, remained unscathed in spite of all appearances, and the final thought that he left written by his own hand, and that he gave to one of his personal assistants on the day of his death for the preparation of a speech that he intended to deliver at the inaugural ceremony of an Adventist temple, clearly shows that inseparable condition of his character undoubtedly faithful to his cardinal feelings. That thought is conceived like this, and it reveals that on the day of the catastrophe the great man already had a tragic premonition about his destiny: "I am convinced that all Christians have the same opportunities and the same privileges before God. To confirm it I shall make reference to that phrase by Jesus: 'I am the Resurrection and the Life; he who believes in Me will live, even though he dies'."

I remember that on one unforgettable occasion he told me with a certain emotional tone of voice: "I always think a lot about the dead." With his thoughts devoted to his children, he used to say many times: "Work is what gets man the closest to God."

His enthusiasm for decorations and his penchant for titles and for everything that is theatrical pomp in the implacable struggles for power, did not respond deep down to a simple feeling of vanity, as many believed, rather it was one of the resources that this artist of politics employed, a profound connoisseur of mass psychology, to sway the masses and to influence the imagination of men with all the prestige of his strong and disconcerting personality.

At the same time as he was a man who had a blind faith in God and in destiny, Trujillo was fundamentally good. Under his steel chest beat an immensely magnanimous heart. Only a granite-like will such as his could resist, without falling into unforgivable excesses and useless revenges, the series of extraordinary traps, of infamous denunciations, and of perverse insinuations that arrived daily, through some of his collaborators, on the problem-laden desk of this dominator of fate. On his shoulders have been placed many debts that he never contracted and whose responsibility corresponds to the masters of adulation and intrigue which speculated on the good faith and the natural passions of a man who loved intensely life's sensualities.

[. . .]

Dear Boss: so long. Your spiritual children, veterans of the campaigns that you fought during more than thirty years to aggrandize the Republic and stabilize the

State, shall look to your tomb as to a towering symbol and we shall not omit means to impede that the flame that you lighted in the altars of the Republic and in the soul of all Dominicans is extinguished. You have come here, brought on the shoulders of this weeping multitude, to reintegrate yourself to the soil that saw you being born and where you will sleep on the same lap on which your ancestors rest. The soil of San Cristóbal, the same one on which you drank for the first time the water of your native rivers, will always be propitious for you and in it you will finally find the repose that life denied you, you tireless warrior who killed sleep and who did not know fatigue. You are no longer the belligerent champion that you were until yesterday. Now, transformed by the attributes conferred by the mystery to those chosen by the sleep from which there is no awakening, you are an example, a plume, an index that points to us the way to follow from the infinite remoteness of the unknown. May God receive you in his bosom and may your mortal remains, when transmuting beyond the tomb into spiritual vigor and into impalpable matter, contribute to invigorate the soil that you loved so much, so that the consciousness of the homeland could continue nourishing itself with the lime and with the energy of your bones in the vastness of time.

CHAPTER SIX

The Politics of Instability

The 1960s were troubled years for the Dominican people. After Trujillo's assassination on May 30, 1961, it did not take long for the regime that he had nourished for thirty-one years to teeter and fall. One of the greatest challenges for sultanistic regimes has always been the problem of succession. Trujillo, power-hungry dictator that he was, never prepared anyone to succeed him, except maybe his eldest son Ramfis, who never showed any leadership qualities. Moreover, the power of the sultanistic dictator is so overwhelming, and so concentrated in his persona, that usually no alternative forms of leadership exist to guide the country after the collapse of the regime. Institutions tend to be very weak and individuals who show leadership qualities are quickly swept away by the dictator's paranoia. As a result, transitions to democracy from a long-standing sultanistic dictatorship are quite rare and fraught with difficulties. The Dominican Republic was no exception.

During the next few months, the Trujillo regime collapsed rapidly, only to be replaced by short-lived administrations. Joaquín Balaguer tried to hold on to power, until he too was forced into exile. An interim government carried out the first free elections in decades in December 1962. The winner, former political exile Juan Bosch, was overthrown seven months after assuming office by a conspiracy involving the Dominican military, the oligarchy, and elements of the Catholic Church. The sudden ouster of a popular, democratically elected leader was an event that polarized Dominican society. Moreover, winds of change were sweeping the Caribbean. In Cuba, a revolution had ousted former dictator Fulgencio Batista in 1959, only to take a turn to the left and establish a socialist regime at odds with the region's superpower, the United States. The Cuban Revolution brought cold war politics to the forefront in the Caribbean region and its impact on the Dominican Republic was immediate. Right-wing elements, including former *Trujillistas,* gained the upper hand and justified from then on their authoritarian excesses in the name of anticommunism. Bosch himself was accused of communist sympathies and anticommunism was the rallying cry of the coup makers.

The polarization of Dominican society would lead to a countercoup several months later. On April 24, 1965, a group of pro-Bosch military officers, in alliance with civilian politicians, staged a coup to bring Bosch back from exile in Puerto Rico. The move further divided the Dominican military; within hours pro- and anti-Bosch forces were fighting each other in what now seemed to be a civil war. In the United States, the Lyndon B. Johnson administration, worried about instability on an island so close to Cuba, and with an exaggerated fear of Dominican communists taking advantage of the situation to usher in a socialist revolution, ordered U.S. military forces to invade the Dominican Republic. The U.S. military intervention restored peace, but also prevented Bosch from lawfully reassuming the presidency. Negotiations took place over several months, and new elections were scheduled for 1966. Bosch, who was forced to resign before his presidential term had expired, faced Joaquín Balaguer, who had organized a political movement, the Partido Reformista (Reformist Party, or PR), from exile in New York. With Bosch practically prevented from campaigning due to death threats, the Dominican people voted for the candidate who offered them peace and a respite from chaos, and who seemed to have the United States' blessing: Joaquín Balaguer. Moreover, the people also understood that only Balaguer would be accepted by the Dominican military; if Bosch were elected, the military would not have allowed him to serve his full term.

In this fashion, the Dominican Republic made it from the Trujillo dictatorship to a civilian, yet semi-authoritarian, administration. The road to an administration resembling a civilian, democratic government was fraught with difficulties, mostly stemming from Trujillo's authoritarian legacy, mainly represented by the Dominican military, and the cold war context in which the Bosch presidency and the 1965 civil war developed. If these events had happened at some other time, or in a different region, they would have gone mostly unnoticed by the U.S. government. The fact that they took place in the midst of the cold war and in the U.S. sphere of influence made all the difference. Unfortunately, the lesson was not lost on the new Dominican political leadership: instability and chaos were a fact, order had to be enforced.

The Decline of the Trujillos

As soon as he heard the news of his father's death, Ramfis Trujillo rushed back home from France where he was at the time. He immediately assumed the role of chief of staff of the armed forces, thus maintaining a strong presence of the Trujillo family in the military. However, civilian power remained in the hands of Joaquín Balaguer, puppet president at the time of Rafael Trujillo's assassination. A symbiotic relationship developed between the two. Given his incapacity, Ramfis needed Balaguer's administrative skills to run the country. Moreover, the Dominican Republic was still under sanctions imposed by the Organization of American States and Balaguer's presidency gave it at least a democratic facade. Balaguer, in turn, needed Ramfis to stay in power. Some members of the Trujillo family and Trujillo's henchmen hated Balaguer and envied his influence to a point where there was even talk about "getting rid" of him. Balaguer had to walk a delicate tightrope, realizing that he needed to loosen up the regime's grip in order to be acceptable to the international community, but without losing power or his life.

The next two documents are letters by Ramfis to Balaguer. In the first one, just a few days after his father's death, Ramfis pledges his support of the Balaguer administration as he assumed the office of chief of staff of the Dominican armed forces. Ramfis states for the record that he and the armed forces would not intrude into the formulation of the country's foreign policy, a message clearly intended for the international community. The next letter was a sign of the new times. After several massive, and often spontaneous, popular protests against the regime in which mobs destroyed effigies of Trujillo, Ramfis asked the country for a symbolic de-Trujilloization, that is, for the removal of his father's name from hundreds of streets, schools, roads, and countless other public places, including the capital. This concession to the people was a sure sign that the Trujillos were losing their grip on the country. Within a few weeks, they were all in exile.

LETTERS BY RAMFIS TRUJILLO TO JOAQUÍN BALAGUER FOR GENERAL DISSEMINATION[1]

Upon assuming the office of Major General Joint Chief of Staff of the Armed Forces, a position from which I take on the responsibility of maintaining the cohesion and the unity of the air, sea, and land services, for the preservation of order and the maintenance of peace, as well as the defense of national sovereignty, I publicly express my unbreakable decision to support the legitimately constituted institutions and to offer my strongest support to the Government that is presided by his Excellency Doctor Joaquín Balaguer.

The armed forces, whose command I assume in all of the Republic, are, according to our constitutional law, totally apolitical, and do not interfere nor will they interfere in international politics whose direction constitutionally pertains to the President of the Republic, nor in any of the activities that are the exclusive jurisdiction of the other authorities consecrated by the State's Organic Law.

Rafael L. Trujillo, Jr., General, Trujillo City, D.N., June 3, 1961

November 7, 1961
Dr. Joaquín Balaguer, Honorable President of the Republic, His Office.
Your Excellency:

I feel honored to address Your Excellency to request the issuing of the proper legal measures needed so that my father's name, given in the course of the last thirty-one years to a great number of avenues, streets, parks, libraries, academies, schools, casinos, colonies, roads, neighborhoods, hospitals, bridges, airports, stadiums, provinces, and the like, be substituted by that of national heroes and relevant events from Dominican history.

I appreciate in all its value the gestures of my father's friends who, inspired by a feeling of loyalty or moved by the emulating desire of making evident the national gratitude to the one that so many efforts and vigilance consecrated to the aggran-

---

1. Translated from José Rafael Vargas, *Trujillo: El final de una tiranía* (Santo Domingo: Editora Universitaria, 1985), 160 and 157–159.

dizement of the homeland and the well-being of its citizens, took the initiative of honoring my progenitor by giving his name to many of the works that he wisely left as an everlasting legacy to the Dominican people. I believe, however, that gone from the national stage the author of those realizations and of those works of progress, it is logical to let history be the one to impart justice on that extraordinary man, and to be the one to render a definite judgment over him when contemporary passions finally settle down and his figure as a patriot and as a statesman can be judged without the passions typical of the turbulent times through which the national consciousness is going today.

Allow me, your Excellency Mr. President, to refer to your own words, spoken in San Cristóbal: *"His enthusiasm for decorations and his penchant for titles and for everything that is theatrical pomp in the implacable struggles for power, did not respond deep down to a simple feeling of vanity, as many believed, rather it was one of the resources that this artist of politics employed, a profound connoisseur of mass psychology, to sway the masses and to influence the imagination of men with all the prestige of his strong and disconcerting personality."*

If I may, I would like to suggest that in those cases in which it may be recommendable, the places designated with my father's name should be restored to the appellation that they originally had, and that was consecrated by a long tradition or by some feature of a positive historical relevance.

I thank you in advance for the attention that you deign to give to this request, and I renew my feelings of consideration and friendship.

Dr. Rafael L. Trujillo, Jr.

Balaguer Tries to Hold On

Joaquín Balaguer managed to stay at the helm of government after Trujillo's death and even consolidated some power. Though he was seen as a puppet president working for the Trujillos, he at least could not be associated with the regime's bloody deeds. Balaguer resorted to that image to weaken the power of the Trujillos and steer the country toward a more liberal regime. The sanctions imposed by the international community, the incompetence of Trujillo's relatives, and their unpopularity among the people, certainly made Balaguer's task easier.

On October 2, 1961, Balaguer visited the United Nations in a desperate attempt to plead his country's case and to get the sanctions lifted so that the Dominican Republic could reintegrate itself into the international community. Balaguer's speech (reproduced below) severely criticized some of Trujillo's actions and policies, while stressing how things had changed for the better after he assumed "full" control of the country. This speech was a very dangerous gamble for Balaguer. He had publicly criticized Trujillo in an international forum without being sure of getting anything in return. The speech outraged many of the "hawks" within the Trujillo family, who believed that Balaguer was a traitor who had to be killed for desecrating Trujillo's memory. However, others realized that only by eliminating all vestiges of Trujillo and his policies, and by establishing a more open, quasi-democratic regime would the international sanctions be lifted. In the end, as is common with most weakening authoritarian regimes, sharing even a little bit of power brought about the collapse of the dictatorship. On November 19, 1961, under pressure from a newly created political opposition, popular manifestations, sectors of the Dominican military, and the U.S. government (the latter even sent some warships to the Dominican Republic), the last of the Trujillos left the country. Balaguer's gamble had paid off. He was now in charge, but not for long. In January 1962, after maneuvering to establish an interim government pliable to his interests, Balaguer was ousted by angry mobs. He sought political asylum and left for the United States.

BALAGUER'S SPEECH TO THE UNITED NATIONS
OF OCTOBER 2, 1961[2]

At the World Forum of the United Nations

Given at the headquarters of the United Nations, in New York City, in the Plenary Session held by the world organization on October 2, 1961.

Dear Delegates:

This is perhaps the first time in the history of the United Nations that a country of the American continent is reincorporated to this international organization after having reacquired all the titles that make it morally capable to form part of an institution that was founded to defend the rights of men to live in a world free of injustices and fears. The Dominican Republic has been part of the United Nations since its birth in 1945, but it is only now, after many long years of purely theoretical adherence to the principles of the San Francisco Charter, that it becomes part in reality, with complete awareness of its obligations and its duties, before this universal forum in which only the nations where international agreements are not myths and human rights are not a lie should be able to find a space.

After the fall of the man who personified the Dominican state for thirty-one years, a rule of law began in our country that has gradually modeled its institutions on the principles of representative democracy. Instead of a single party, as in the nations where political activity responds to just one directive of totalitarian inspiration, today

---

2. Translated from Joaquín Balaguer, *La palabra encadenada* (Santo Domingo: Fuentes Impresores, 1975), 111–127.

national opinion is divided into diverse oppositional groups among whom the ideals and the various aspirations of the Dominican soul have finally found expression. The fundamental civic rights, without which neither liberty nor civil order can be conceived, have been recognized, without moderation, for all citizens who for the first time, after thirty-one years of political obscurantism, freely exercise their constitutional prerogatives. The iron barrier that surrounded the island, and through which independent opinion could barely seep, has been abolished, and the right of free circulation has been reestablished for three million human beings who were detached from all contact with international political trade and with human civilization. Today no capricious requisite obstructs the free acquisition of passports and the necessary visas to enter and leave Dominican territory. That political reintegration of our country into the Free World is strengthened by the birth and organization of political factions carrying out, without arbitrary limitations, their proselytizing work, and making free use of the right of assembly for peaceful ends, and of the right to elect and be elected in clean elections, controlled internationally and conducted with exemplary impartiality, with the technical advice of specialists recommended by the Organization of American States. Together with these decisive steps in the process of our political reconstruction, we have taken other, no less important steps to benefit free enterprise and rescue our economy from all reactionary obstacles. The monopolies that existed to favor individuals, and the companies established to deviate for self-seeking ends a large part of the nations's economic activity, are being eliminated and once again the most absolute liberty in the field of business has been reestablished to private initiatives. A series of new laws, inspired by an ample spirit of fiscal justice, have been enacted to abolish all those taxes that costly gravitated over the consumer and made the lives of the poorer classes practically impossible. The basic products of our export trade have been submitted to a new tax regime that sacrifices most of the state's earnings in the exclusive interest of the farmer.

The country's institutional life has, in turn, been organized on a truly liberal legal basis. Honorable achievements that deserve mention in this field are those consecrated by the law that returns full administrative capacity to the city councils and establishes without restrictions the principle of the autonomy of municipal corporations; the law that institutes the university's autonomy and reestablishes the principle of academic freedom in the oldest house of learning of the American continent; the law, already submitted for legislative approval, that tends to make effective the constitutional principle of the separation of the branches of the state and consecrates the permanence of judgeships and the independence of the judiciary, the basis of all civil organization in any civilized country; and the laws, finally, that tend to structure the juridical order and to give the nation a political physiognomy of a fundamentally republican essence.

In the Dominican Republic, therefore, gentlemen, a democracy is being born. The edifice of the dictatorship has totally collapsed and on its ruins we have begun to build, with patience and without demagogic displays, a regime cast in the old mold passed down to us from the founders of the Republic which in content do not differ from any of the secular molds created by the genius of Bolívar, of San Martín, of Washington, of O'Higgins, of Morazán, of Juárez, of Martí, and of the other great heroes of American independence. That is why I occupy this platform without blush-

205

ing, and can raise my voice from it without any doubt in my mind and without fear of offending the revered ashes of the fathers of the homeland, rehabilitated in their majestic rights and in their everlasting legacy that now recovers the purity of the metal that has served to melt the bells of resurrections. The case of the Dominican Republic constitutes a heartening example that democracy in the Americas gains new ground everyday and that, in spite of the misery in which the majority of our peoples struggle, of the pain in which our irredeemable masses are consumed, and of the obstacles that our underdeveloped economies present to our evolution toward the great goals of justice, we advance with an unbreakable determination toward that ideal, seemingly unreachable, which only those few nations have reached who can proclaim that the lands of our continent are infertile grounds for oppression and for dictatorship.

[. . .]

A harsh sentence of proscription has been cast on the Dominican Republic for more than a year now, which condemns us, as if we were a plague-ridden country, to economic strangulation and diplomatic isolation. The VI Consultation Meeting of Chancellors that met in 1960 in San José, Costa Rica, imposed on us a punishment whose justice and origin is not proper to insist on at this instant. Nobody ignores that we were condemned on this occasion for having meddled in the domestic life of another sister nation, and for having carried out, against a distinguished statesman of America, an act of political delinquency. I do not deny that this violation of the non-intervention principle, the basis of inter-American relations, and this censurable act that almost cost the life of one of the leaders of continental democracy, were not deservingly sanctioned. But it is not fair for the punishment to survive the guilty party and that this institution, typical of the Stone Age, in which children responded for their parents' faults, and in which the doors of damned cities were marked with an eternal INRI, is transferred over to international law. The episode sanctioned in San José, Costa Rica, belongs to the past. All of the Americas repudiated it, but it has been forgotten that the sentence in which that personal act, product of the enmity between two political rivals, is reprehended, cannot be maintained over a people and entire generation, without any responsibility for an act whose executors rest today in the bosom of a tomb, awaiting the verdict of history.

[. . .]

I do believe this occasion is appropriate to solemnly declare that the episode for which we were condemned in San José is a page definitively closed in the history of our international relations. I can assure all the countries represented today in this assembly that the current Dominican government will not carry out any acts that could be seen as interference in the sphere reserved for the sovereignty of other American states. With the same irrevocable and solemn character, we declare facing this assembly that the new government that rules the Dominican Republic submits itself from this moment on to the jurisdiction of the Commission for Human Rights of the Organization of American States and that of the United Nations. Our unrestricted adhesion to these organizations and to the principles represented by them as guardians of the inalienable rights of the individual, and as a guarantee in America and in the world of the dignifying norms of human personality, is, of course, dependent on the events that have occurred or may occur in the Dominican Republic after

July 1, 1961, the moment when the rule of law for whose moral and judicial solvency we are responsible began functioning. After the tragedy of the thirtieth of May, there was a period of approximately one month during which the powers of the State were impotent to contain the wave of reprisals and violence unleashed under the cover of the disorder produced by that tremendous event in Dominican society. I should make one final declaration regarding this point, with the same accent of sincerity and with the same tone of firmness: with sanctions or without sanctions, with the injustice of San José of Costa Rica or without it, we will be a nation irrevocably faithful to the destiny of America, a destiny that is and will be identified with that of the United States while the United States continues to carry out the mission it has imposed on itself of defending the liberty of the world and safeguarding our civilization even at the risk of its own existence.

The political transformation of our country and the new ideology that now prevails, among its people and in its institutions, allow us to suggest what will be our position regarding the global problems on the agenda of this assembly, and on whose solution world peace primarily depends. On each one of these problems—the prohibition of nuclear weapons, German reunification, the extinction of the last remains of colonialism in the African countries, the aggressions in Asia, in Laos, in Cambodia, etc.—our position cannot be other than to support without reserve the criterion of Western democracies.

[. . .] Our country today is a riddle and its future is full of uncertainty. What is gestating there cannot be foreseen nor analyzed. A people subjected for thirty-one years to one of the harshest dictatorships known to the contemporary age anxiously seeks the path to its ultimate redemption. But numerous factors conspire against this intention in the midst of a particularly difficult and complex situation. The instincts of the masses who want liberty, but who confuse it with license and anarchy, clashes there with the obstacle of three decades of political barbarism. The precarious conditions in which our political stability unfolds are aggravated in time with the economic shortage that in our country, as elsewhere, is the great stimulus of social crises. The entire atmosphere is filled with explosive elements and revolutionary ferments. This is about a country that, like all Latin American countries, has been dragged down by an uncontrollable political inclination, and that aspires to a better life without having a clear notion as to what road to take to realize its destiny. An oppressed middle class, intelligent and ambitious, many of whose members have painfully ascended on the tough road of a university education and whose desire for improvement is often frustrated by the lack of employment or a profitable exercise of their professions, energetically denounces misery and economic injustice, but is afflicted with the same disorientation as the working masses. Add to this traumatic scene the amazing population growth and the lack of suitable positions for almost half a million workers, professionals, students, and farmers, who migrate to the city attracted by the mirages of its deceptive jaws.

All this social, political, and economic decomposition, the inheritance of an eminently constructive dictatorship, which in its last days saw itself undermined by moral corruption and by physical wear, can be exploited by communism to create a new branch of the Kremlin in the American Balkans. The parties and the political tendencies of the opposition have inclined toward intemperate demagoguery, which has been so far incapable of elaborating a program and of obeying the postulates of a constructive action, and the fragility itself of political power, shaken by the constant threat of the mutiny and of the coup d'état, create there a special psyche that prepares the whole island for an almost inevitable eruption. [. . .]

America, therefore, must observe what is going on today in the Dominican Republic; it is essential that the political phenomenon developing there is contemplated with objectivity, if it is desired to impede a new communist spear from penetrating that side of the Caribbean into the heart itself of America, of this America of ours that should keep in mind that it is this stormy sea, which Humboldt compared to a Mediterranean with many entrances, through which the new barbarians, the implacable enemies of American democracy, will reach our shores.

[. . .]

Please allow me to invoke from this stage the work and the word of those humble missionaries from the old Spanish island, so that the United Nations, guided by the example of this group of religious men to whom corresponds the honor of having been the first civilizers of the continent, continue the quest for universal harmony, fortified by the faith in God and inspired by the beautiful myth of human fraternity. Several centuries later, in his proclamation of January 1, 1863, eighty-seven years after the independence of the United States of America, an apostolic figure who symbolizes the equality of men and public freedoms, Abraham Lincoln, condemned violence, proclaimed reconciliation among his compatriots and also invoked, as supreme touchstone of all human conflicts, the upright judgment of humanity and the grace of Almighty God. May that lofty example and these apostolic words guide this General Assembly so that the vessel of peace, anchored today on the banks of the Hudson, could reach all the ports and all the continents, where the peoples wait for it with the message that will revive in the heart of the world this flower nowadays bared and withered: hope.

Free Elections

The Consejo de Estado (Council of State) that succeeded Balaguer was entrusted with the difficult task of organizing free elections in a country where none had been held in decades, and where democratic institutions were practically nonexistent. Still, the transitional government was able to carry out this task and elections were held in December 1962. This truly open electoral contest was a source of excitement for a people hungry for democracy as it pitted against each other two mighty candidates: Juan Bosch of the Partido Revolucionario Dominicano (Dominican Revolutionary Party, or PRD) and Viriato Fiallo of the Unión Cívica Nacional (National Civic Union, or UCN). Bosch and the PRD represented the liberal, anti-Trujillo opposition who had lived in exile, while Fiallo and the UCN represented the Dominican upper classes who became tired of Trujillo and organized to oppose him. As such, while Bosch was able to win the sympathy of the urban masses and the peasants with his simple, plain language, catchy slogans, and an agenda based on political equality, Fiallo's campaign style was aloof, elitist, and old-fashioned. Bosch won by a landslide with over 60 percent of the votes and was inaugurated on February 27, 1963.

Bosch's campaign style was a radical departure from traditional politics in the Dominican Republic. His down-to-earth approach appealed to lower-class Dominicans who, for the first time, felt empowered and mobilized to influence decision making in a system laden with authoritarianism. Bosch also employed radio and television to convey his message, and used a didactic style in his speeches, aimed at educating Dominicans and fostering a democratic political culture. One of his 1962 radio broadcast campaign speeches is reproduced below.

BOSCH REAFFIRMS POSITION[3]

Speech read at the Democratic Tribune on December 10, 1962.

We are descending into a quagmire; and if the political leaders do not halt the race of insults and infamy and lies in which the country is being submerged, we will open the door to the next dictator. Let no one have illusions; democracy cannot be established on such dirty and weak bases as the ones we are laying here. Democracy is a way of life, not only a system of government, and the moral foundation of democracy is mutual respect; respect among men, among parties, among social groups.

There are things that no one should do for any reason. For example, a political party is using two Cubans to create a campaign of mimeographed anonymous messages in which they even resort to naming the wife of one of the candidates for the presidency, accusing her of being an agent for Fidel Castro; and it happens that this lady has suffered in her own flesh the Cuban situation because her parents, two senior citizens, and her brothers and her nephews had to leave Cuba and leave everything they had there, even their clothes, and all the family is now in exile, struggling hard in order to live.

We know this case very well, much better than the two Cuban authors of the anonymous letter and much better than the political party that pays them for their work, because this lady is my wife and the two exiled senior citizens who had to abandon even their clothes in Cuba, are my in-laws, and after having a position that allowed them to live with security in Cuba, they live with us now, dependent on what we can give them, which is very sad for people with self-esteem. Besides that anony-

---

3. Translated from Juan Bosch, *Discursos políticos, 1961–1966*, edited and compiled by Orlando Inoa (Santo Domingo: Presidencia de la República Dominicana, 1998), 21–25.

mous letters' work, the two Cubans of which I speak about have recorded an audio tape to broadcast it in the evening on short wave radio to pretend that it comes from a Cuban station, and in that recording they ask the Dominican people to vote for us, with which they pretend to make the people believe that we are allies of Fidel Castro.

It is not moral to cheapen oneself so much to attain the Presidency of the Republic. Those who do this to attain the Presidency will do very ugly things when they reach power. If we had to spread anonymous letters in the streets, if we had to invent lies and slander, if we had to use a fake sound recording to deceive the people, we would not be struggling, because we would not accept the Presidency of the Republic at that price. The Presidency is not a war booty to be conquered by fire and blood.

The Presidency is a heavy burden, and whoever receives this burden cannot be tarnished by wickedness or hate or slander or lies or libel. Whoever wins the election has to seek forgiveness for the victory, because every winner leaves behind enraged people, and he cannot make himself forgiven if he did not use clean methods in the struggle. A Presidency won by ploys and without scruples will be the entrance door of a dictatorship, for whoever does anything, no matter how wrong it is, to become President, he will later do worse things to maintain himself in power.

While the fake audio tape is broadcast to make believe that it is coming from Cuba, here, in our country, the Popular Socialist Party distributes in the streets a leaflet entitled "Don't Vote!" in which they state the following words:

> The PRD's program does not offer a solution to any important matter . . .
> The revolutionaries should state clearly that the PRD does not struggle against imperialist domination, nor against latifundia, nor for secular and democratic education, nor is it in reality a leftist force . . . neither for the oligarchs of the UCN nor for the demagogues of the PRD. The way things are, the only correct stance is electoral abstinence. Do not vote for any candidate.

Up to here, what the Dominican Popular Socialist Party says, among other things. However, it so happens that this same party . . . is the one that has an hour dedicated to our country on Radio Havana; one radio hour in which the leaders of that party who are in Cuba speak. So that if the Popular Socialist Party here, where its leaders are, says one thing, how can it be that the leaders of that party exiled in Cuba say another? Someone might think that the popular socialists have changed their minds; but to that we respond by saying that the mimeographed leaflet we are referring to is not last month's but this month's, and it has a date: it is from December 8, 1962, that is to say, from the day before yesterday.

We dedicated many years, at least twenty-five years to fighting for democracy, not only in the Dominican Republic but in various countries in the Americas. We are too old to change. For years and years, we were cruelly attacked by Trujillo and the communists; and sometimes we did not know which attacks were the harshest, those of Trujillo or those of the communists. Whoever doubts it should browse a collection of *Claridad*, the newspaper the communists had until recently, or *Libertad*, López Molina's newspaper, or *El Popular*, the newspaper of the Popular Socialist Party.

But neither Trujillo nor the communists nor anyone else ever provoked us into responding to those attacks. Because everyone is the way they are, and we have an affirmative nature. We have always preached democracy and we have acted democratically, we have not crusaded against anything.

Our actions against Trujillo are clear: we never hurled an insult against the tyrant. Our democratic work took us to direct the Institute of Political Education of San José de Costa Rica, which is a political university, the only one in the Americas, devoted to scientific teaching what democracy is and how it should be. Our democratic struggle has made us friends, and not lightly but true friends, of men like Rómulo Betancourt and José Figueres, Víctor Raúl Haya de la Torre, and Luis Muñoz Marín, and all those men were accused everyday of being communists by Trujillo. "Tell me with whom you walk and I will tell you who you are." If we are communists, so too are Betancourt, Figueres, Haya de la Torre, and Muñoz Marín.

It happens in all parts of the world, whoever fights for the unfortunate, the needy, is accused of being a communist. This is a dangerous game since it amounts to propaganda for communism when, in an indirect manner, everything that upholds justice and redemption to exploiters is branded as communism and everyone who preaches justice and redemption is branded a communist.

Communism and democracy are two forces engaged in a struggle. Whoever propagates democracy is preventing the country from ever falling into communist hands; and whoever portrays the democrats as communist agents is serving communism since he is obstructing the establishment of democracy.

Wherever there is democracy, there cannot be communism. There will never be communism in Sweden, in Switzerland, in England, in Canada, in the United States, in New Zealand. A communist government has never developed in a democracy. Communism has only triumphed in countries where tyrannies existed, as in Russia, in China, in Yugoslavia, in Cuba; and it can emerge in countries where there is plenty of misery and social justice is not reached by democratic methods.

In Cuba, tyranny and corruption, scrupulous politicians and journalists and radio as well as television commentators, the destruction of all the country's values, which were discredited on a daily basis by the parties and by a portion of the press and the radio and the television, produced the crisis from which Fidel Castro emerged as master of that country and transformed him into the absolute owner of Cuban consciousness. The entire Cuban people, without exception, have kneeled down at Fidel Castro's feet, adoring him as if he were a god. Fidel Castro was a product of the lack of faith of Cubans, because Cubans had lost their faith in everything, and a people cannot live without faith. If we destroy the faith in democracy here, we will suffer the same fate as the Cubans. If we import Cubans to do in the Dominican Republic what they previously did in Cuba, we will wake up one day with a Fidel Castro on top of a hill.

Dominicans cannot even imagine what a democracy is; they do not realize, they cannot realize it, that in a democracy everyone is respected; that no one is forced or can be forced to do what one does not want to do or think in ways one does not want to; that real democracy is the only political system which truly guarantees the freedom of man: freedom to live without miseries, freedom to educate oneself, freedom to think how ever suits one best, freedom to practice the religion that one likes. A functioning democracy has never been seen here, and there are people who are so afraid of democracy that they want to kill it before it is born, as it is being done by the ones who are killing it by cheapening the current political struggle until they have placed it, as it is today, in a quagmire of insults, infamies, and lies.

And why do they want to kill democracy before it is born? Because they already know, they know it well, they are certain about it, that the democracy that will be born, on December 20 in the Dominican Republic will be a real democracy, a democracy that will not tolerate privileges, abuses, exploitation; and there are people who cannot live if their privileges, the right to abuse and the custom of exploiting the people are taken away.

El Caribe, December 11, 1962

A Feeble Democracy

Bosch's short-lived administration was one of the most democratic governments the Dominican Republic ever had. It respected civil liberties, refrained from using state repression, tolerated the political opposition, was largely free of corruption, and passed important pieces of legislation dealing with social issues, including a new constitution in 1963. The 1963 Constitution was the hallmark achievement of the Bosch administration, since in order to create a democracy, the country first needed a truly democratic constitution. Bosch's constitution was a very progressive document for the time. It guaranteed the basic liberties and respect for human rights found in other constitutions, plus it banned latifundia, monopolies, and foreign ownership of land, except when regulated by the Dominican state. Moreover, Dominicans had the right to work, to housing, to medical services, and to education. Individuals were to receive equal pay for equal work, regardless of their gender, age, or status. Finally, in one of its most controversial points, the 1963 Constitution gave legal equality to children born out of wedlock and instructed government functionaries not to disclose such information in official documents. This provision put the Bosch administration at odds with the powerful Catholic Church, who saw it as undermining the sacrament of marriage and challenging its authority, while the constitution's economic and labor provisions faced stiff opposition from the business sector and the upper classes.

The constitution was approved on April 29, 1963, thanks to the majority the PRD held in congress, yet its approval sparked an anti-Bosch campaign that did not end until he was overthrown some months later. Some key fragments of the 1963 Constitution are reproduced below.

EXCERPTS FROM THE 1963 CONSTITUTION[4]

Article 1.b To seek the elimination of obstacles of an economic and social nature that limit the equality and freedom of Dominicans and that oppose the development of the human being and the effective participation of all in the political, economic and social organization of the country.

Article 2.a The right of all individuals to work and the obligation of the State to foster and guarantee the indispensable conditions to render effective the exercise of this right are recognized.

Article 5. Declared as a crime against the people will be acts committed by those who, for their personal benefit steal public funds or, taking advantage of their positions within the State's institutions, its dependencies or autonomous entities, obtain illicit economic advantages.

Those individuals who, from the same positions, deliberately provide advantages to their associates, relatives, kin, friends, and contacts, will have incurred the same crimes.

Article 17. To equal work corresponds equal pay, without discrimination based on gender, age, or status.

Article 19. In every agricultural, industrial, commercial, or mining enterprise, the workers will have the right to participate in its benefits, while recognizing the legitimate interest of the entrepreneur and other factors of production.

Article 23. Declared as against the collective interest is the property or possession of land in an excessive amount by individuals or private entities. As a consequence, individually owned latifundia are prohibited, regardless of how they originated.

The law will determine the maximum extension of lands that can be owned or possessed by an individual or entity, while attending to agrological, social, and economic reasons.

Article 26. The establishment of each Dominican household in a lot and with improvements of their own is declared of high public interest.

Each Dominican family shall possess its own house, comfortable and hygienic, which, if its members lack economic resources, shall be provided by the State with the cooperation of the beneficiaries to the extent of their incomes and economic abilities, everything according to the plans drafted by the competent entities.

Article 30. Monopolies in favor of individuals are prohibited.

Will be persecuted and sanctioned according to the law:

a) Those who devote themselves to the stockpiling or concentration of articles of necessary consumption or essential goods, with the purpose of causing the rise or elevation of the prices of such articles;

b) The author or authors of all agreements, accords, maneuvers, or combination, in any way whatsoever, among producers, industrialists, merchants, or entrepreneurs

---

4. Translated from Ministerio de Educación, Bellas Artes y Cultos, *Constitución de la República Dominicana* (Santo Domingo: Campaña Nacional de Educación Cívica, 1963).

at the public's service, tending to fix prices over the norm, distribute markets, deny commercial deals to others, or link the sale or lease of a product or service to the sale or lease of another, or that in any way limit or impede, or try to limit or impede, free concurrence in industry, in internal or external trade, or in services to the public.

Article 49. Public officials or functionaries are prohibited to issue certifications related to the civil status of individuals where the condition of child born in or out of wedlock is noted and, in general, any judgment related to the nature and character of the filiation, except for those exceptions established by the law.

The Coup d'Etat

Bosch's popularity and his concern for the Dominican lower classes sparked the ire of conservative sectors within Dominican society. These sectors had supported the removal of Trujillo, not to democratize the country and empower the lower classes, but just to get a larger share of the economic pie while maintaining a strict social order in which they enjoyed considerable privileges. These aspirations were now jeopardized by Bosch's populist agenda. A plot to destabilize his government and oust him found the receptive ear of the Dominican oligarchy, the hierarchy of

Juan Bosch arriving in Puerto Rico just hours after his overthrow.

the Catholic Church, and the military. The Church was incensed by Bosch's secular style and his promotion of equal rights for children born out of wedlock. The military was soon convinced by these two sectors that Bosch was either a secret communist—as Fidel Castro had supposedly been—or he was just too soft on communism. So, a campaign was orchestrated to destabilize Bosch's government with strikes and marches, while the military kept a close eye out for any signs of communist influences in Bosch's government. After some grave incidents between Bosch and the François "Papa Doc" Duvalier dictatorial regime in Haiti—in which Dominican troops were mobilized along the border—the Dominican military leadership decided to oust Bosch.

In the early hours of September 25, 1963, Bosch was arrested in the National Palace and soon deported to Puerto Rico without a single shot being fired. The Dominican armed forces issued a joint communiqué (reproduced below) announcing Bosch's ouster, the dismissal of Congress, and the annulment of the 1963 Constitution. A Triumvirate of three businessmen was chosen to rule the country with the military acting as the power behind the throne. The coup was to a large extent the brainchild of Colonel Elías Wessin y Wessin, a devout Catholic, staunch anti-communist, and commander of the Centro de Enseñanza de las Fuerzas Armadas (Armed Forces Training Center, or CEFA), the military's most powerful unit, since it had most of the country's artillery, tanks, and war planes.

OFFICIAL COMMUNIQUÉ TO THE PEOPLE
BY THE ARMED FORCES AND THE NATIONAL POLICE[5]
People of the Dominican Republic:
The chaotic state in which the country lives, caused by administrative indecision, the abuse of power of the docile and indirect majorities of our legislative bodies, servile in all to the central power and without their own orientations; the entrenchment of incapacities in the Government's diverse branches; non-fulfillment of the electoral promises made to the people, which have taken us, contrary to what was expected, to the most acute unemployment and a hunger crisis; the attacks on freedom of speech; the dangerous fabrication of international incidents with internal political ends, which, more than compromising the prestige of the Republic, could have taken us into a grave and unnecessary international conflict of unforeseen con-

---

5. Translated from Centro de Enseñanza de las Fuerzas Armadas, *Libro blanco de las Fuerzas Armadas y de la Policía Nacional de la República Dominicana: Estudios y pruebas documentales de las causas del movimiento reivindicador del 25 de septiembre de 1963* (Santo Domingo: Editora del Caribe, 1964), 90–95.

sequences; the neglect of public education and the mistreatment of the dignity of the teaching profession and, the gravest of all, the consented and alarming maneuvers of the leaders of international and atheist communism, the one that, as *international*, does not acknowledge particular nationalisms, and as *atheist*, denies God, have taken the Nation to the edge of bankruptcy and its inhabitants to the limits of desperation, threatening to destroy the traditional democratic and republican essences that our Founding Fathers consecrated in the Manifest of January 16, 1844.

Anguish has overtaken the Dominican family to such an extent that our bishops, deeply concerned, saw the need to state, in a "Declaration" dated August 3rd of last year, that "there is no home in the Dominican Republic that enjoys full tranquility," because "the political events that are taking place, have not been able to establish the reign of true peace which embraces all men equally, whatever their position is in society."

In the face of such alarming events, and in the face of the precarious health status of the Nation, which aggravates by the hour, we have decided to intervene, to put order into this chaos, and to stop the disintegrating revolutionarism of communism which seeks to destroy through violence the slogan of our shield, in which "Country" has been placed between "God" and "Freedom."

It is obvious that, besides guarding public order, the Armed Forces and the National Police have a social function to uphold, extraneous to their ordinary functions, especially when this order is evidently threatened, and the institutions society has created to accomplish its ends are so seriously compromised that they are incapable of achieving the general well-being. Moreover, when these institutions are so deeply affected and the environment is threatened by a violent dislocation of its national strata, it is necessary to admit that such grave problems cannot be solved within the framework of a strict constitutionality. The Constitution, made for the safeguarding of peace and of the people's rights, cannot be an impassable dike when it cannot suffice itself for the preservation of peace and of such rights. Especially now, when the henchmen of supine communism shield themselves behind the Government and in the political parties, using the faculties their own doctrine rejects from now on, and their system will deny later, to their proselytes, who will stop being free citizens to become enslaved proletarians. The Constitution is invoked in order to knock it down later. That is the trick and the Government allows it.

The regime that governed us used to say that it was a "State of Law." We want to transform it into a "State of Duties," which would not be a fiction, and would convert the false into true, something that the indifference and the leniency of the prevailing regime, facing international communism, cannot give us. We want, therefore, a veritable *State of Law* to emerge from our fulfilled duties. Consequently, our purpose will never be punitive, but constructive and preventive, and we hope that the citizenry will help us in the task of preserving order and achieving national unity. We do not want to use the authority of force, but the authority of reason, propitiating the empire of distributive justice.

For all that: GIVEN the constitutional duty that commands us to preserve public order, in an active form, when it has been altered, as well as in preventive form, if there are evidences that this is going to happen;

IN THE SAFEKEEPING of the basic norms of the Dominican State that is the

Nation politically organized into a free, independent and sovereign entity; with an essentially civil, republican, democratic and representative Government; divided into Executive Power, Legislative Power and Judicial Power, independent in their respective functions;

BY VIRTUE of that international communism intends, by violent means, to destroy that organization, and that the Republic, as a result, is on the brink of a fratricidal struggle as a consequence of a state of latent, but permanent, subversion, evidenced by the different pronouncements of the leaders of that group, issued by the press, as well as radio, television, speeches, and public manifestations, all of which has taken place under the indifferent eye of the current Government, which has ignored the friendly and reiterated warnings made by the people, as well as by their foremost notables, and, very especially, by the Armed Institutes of the Republic;

We declare: 1st—OUTLAWED, the communist, Marxist-Leninist, Castroite doctrine, or however one would like to call it, as well as the political parties that covertly or openly profess it, and placed under a state of prevention all the members of such parties, and, very especially, their leaders and visible heads;

2nd—DEPOSED the current Government of the Republic, for propitiating the attempts against the Constitution regarding the essences of the State; regarding the destruction of public trust, and regarding the violation of the fundamental and citizen's rights, as well as for having become incapable of channeling the Country through the roads of order, respect for the law, general security, peace, progress, and the common good;

3rd—NONEXISTENT the latest Constitution of the Republic, voted by the Constituent Assembly arisen from the last general elections, as well as the acts carried out in accordance with it, since it was by an insufficient majority in light of universal parliamentary principles, and, very especially, in view of that disposed by art.113 of the Constitution of September 17, 1962.

4th—That, from this moment on, *the current Legislative Chambers should be considered dissolved*, and without the faculty to carry out any function of power, since it is obvious, by public consensus, that they no longer represent the occasional majority that they obtained in the elections of last December.

5th—That, accordingly, is DECLARED IN VIGOR the Constitution of September 17, 1962, under whose empire the last elections were carried out, except in what is contrary to the purposes of the present pronouncements;

6th—That we shall FORM, in the briefest possible term, a PROVISIONAL GOVERNMENT, presided over by an eminent citizen, extraneous to the militant political parties, and, while this is being done, the Armed Forces, represented by the undersigned, will assume the executive functions and will dictate all those dispositions demanded by the urgency and the good handling of public affairs;

7th—That we will RESPECT, in an absolute way, all the international commitments, that validly have been contracted by the Dominican Republic, especially the Resolutions voted in the Tenth Inter-American Conference, of Caracas, against *international communism*, and in the Eighth Meeting of Consultation of Ministers of Foreign Relations, of Punta del Este (Uruguay), against so-called "Castroism";

8th—That we will GUARANTEE human and citizen's rights, civil as well as political, and, among them, the right to property and of free enterprise, and analogous

217

rights, so that trade, industry, banking and national and foreign capitals, may contribute, without the fear of expropriations and spoliations, to the development of our wealth and to the prosperity of the country, and, equally, we will guarantee all the social rights and labor conquests, as well as the right to request and to obtain work and justified help from the State.

We have taken this transcendent, historical step, aside from the aforementioned reasons, by uniting these with President Bosch's refusals, when on reiterated occasions the Armed Forces requested of him, for the security of the Republic and the well-being of the Dominican people, a radical break with communism, and any tendency originating from that perverse and unhealthy ideology.

Santo Domingo, D.N., September 25, 1963.

Signed: Victor Elby Viñas Román, Army Major General, Secretary of State for the Armed Forces; Renato Hungría Morel, Army Brigadier General, Army Chief of Staff; Atila Luna Pérez, Pilot Brigadier General, Air Force Chief of Staff; Julio Alberto Rib Santamaría, Navy Chief of Staff; Belisario Peguero Guerrero, Chief of the National Police; Félix Hermida Jr., Army Brigadier General, President of the Superior War Council of the Armed Forces and the National Police; Manuel García Urbáez, Army's Brigadier General, Inspector at the Service of the Secretaryship of the Armed Forces; Antonio Imbert Barreras, Army Brigadier General; Luis Amiama Tió, Army Brigadier General; Salvador A. Montás Guerrero, Army Brigadier General, Inspector of the Army Northern Zone; Marcos A. Rivera Cuesta, Army Colonel, Deputy Secretary of State for the Armed Forces; Ramón Eduardo Cruzado Piña, Pilot Air Force Colonel, Deputy Secretary of State for the Armed Forces; Librado Andújar Matos, Navy Captain, Deputy Secretary of State for the Armed Forces; Elías Wessin y Wessin, Air Force Colonel, Director of the Armed Forces Training Center; Manuel Ramón Pagán Montás, Army Colonel, Army General Intendant; Braulio Álvarez Sánchez, Army Colonel, Commander of the Army Transportation Battalion; Neit Rafael Nivar Seijas, Army Colonel, Director of Army Military Training; Juan N. Folch Pérez, Pilot Air Force Colonel; Andrés Gerónimo Sanz Torres, Navy Captain, Inspector of the Navy; José María Sánchez Pérez, Pilot Air Force Colonel; Carlos María Paulino Asiático, Army Lieutenant Colonel, Assistant to the Secretary of the Armed Forces; Rafael E. Saldaña J., Lawyer Lieutenant Colonel, Legal Consultant of the Secretaryship of State for the Armed Forces; Rubén Ant. Tapia Cesse, Army Colonel, Deputy Chief of Staff; Sergio de Js. Díaz Toribio, Navy Commander, Deputy Chief of Staff; Ismael Emilio Román Carbuccia, Pilot Air Force Colonel, Deputy Chief of Staff.

The People Take to the Streets

Although the international community, including the United States, condemned Bosch's ouster, there was little that could or would be done. The U.S. government was concerned about the coup d'état, but it was

218

much more concerned about maintaining political stability in the region and containing the spread of communism. As such, the illegal actions of the Dominican military were tolerated since their anticommunist credentials were well established and they could maintain order. For example, in December 1963, the leftist Fourteenth of June Revolutionary Movement staged an uprising in the mountains protesting the coup d'état against Bosch. The uprising, which tried to emulate Fidel Castro's guerrilla campaign in Cuba's Sierra Maestra mountains, was quickly crushed by the Dominican military. Most of the rebels were actually captured alive and murdered by the military.

These events served to further deteriorate the credibility of the Triumvirate, which was soon reduced to a one-man administration, led by businessman Donald Reid Cabral. On April 24, 1965, some pro-Bosch members of the Dominican military, acting in accordance with civilian cadres of Bosch's PRD, staged a countercoup against Reid Cabral. The "Constitutionalists" quickly seized the capital and ousted Reid Cabral, which led to an enthusiastic outpouring of lower-class Dominicans into the streets. One young PRD leader, José F. Peña Gómez, went into a radio station and broadcast the news, asking the people to mobilize and take to the streets to defend the 1963 Constitution from right-wing, reactionary elements.

JOSÉ F. PEÑA GÓMEZ'S RADIO BROADCAST[6]

On September 25, 1963, the national oligarchy, in collaboration with the worst forces, overthrew the constitutional government of the Dominican Republic and installed a government of corruption, of abuses, of arbitrariness, and of despotism. The Dominican people were misled on that occasion by lies and deceptive propaganda by paid spokespersons of the reactionary forces, so that they [the people] were left paralyzed by terror when the Armed Forces, tricked by a small group of men without honor, went to the streets and deposed the democratic government. By a rare coincidence, today, the twenty-fifth of April, the Dominican Armed Forces, acting sparked by the heroism and the valor of the noncommissioned officers and enlisted men of the Sixteenth of August camp and the High Command of the Army, and led victoriously by a group of honest young men, have initiated a liberalizing movement that will culminate with the reinstatement of the constitutional government that was elected by the people, in the pure and clean elections of December 20 [1962].

It has been many years since the Dominican people have demonstrated such a

---

6. Translated from Diómedes Remigio, *Peña Gómez: Su pensamiento político* (Santo Domingo: Editora Victorama, 1994), 54–60.

high degree of patriotism and valor. It is a moving spectacle to see the roofs packed with citizens raising their machine guns and their rifles to the skies, watching the steel birds of the enemies of freedom.

It is gratifying to see the crowds, enthusiastic and frenzied, surrounding the National Palace like a living wall of compatriots ready to sacrifice themselves, if necessary, for the freedom of the Dominican people. It is gratifying to see those soldiers, those sergeants, those corporals, those honest officers, showing at this moment, that the Dominican Armed Forces, though they were tricked on September 25, are now firmly committed to let the flag of the Constitution and freedom wave victoriously on the top of balconies and monuments, proclaiming to the wind that the Dominican Republic is ready to be free or die.

Comrade Dr. José Rafael Molina Ureña has just informed me that he, as well as the officers who initiated this movement, will not relinquish their objectives, not even in favor of a military junta that would organize a plebiscite within a month; and that the position of the officers, noncommissioned officers, and enlisted men who initiated this movement is to achieve a return to constitutional order, regardless of the cost.

People of the Dominican Republic! Foreign and antipatriotic forces are mobilizing to snatch this resounding victory from the people. A military junta is about to be imposed. But those who are trying to impose that sham on the people do not know that the national majority has already chosen one path: the road that leads to the return of constitutional order. On that road we shall die rather than allow this flag to be thrashed by the exploitative reactionary forces that dismissed the popular will with the treacherous coup of September 25. People of the Dominican Republic: the victory is yours: this time victory will not be denied to us. All the revolutionaries must concentrate on the National Palace, on the Duarte Bridge, and on the bridge that leads to Villa Mella, so that the enemies of liberty and democracy know that facing their tanks or their cannons there is a wall of Dominican hearts, ready to sacrifice themselves for the definitive liberation of the Dominican homeland.

[. . .]

People of the Dominican Republic, this is the hour of unity, of patriotism, and of Dominicanness. This morning, while we were at the Army's High Command, in the company of that national hero named Captain Peña Taveras, the initiator of this revolutionary and patriotic movement, we were informed that some police vehicles and civilian mobs were looting some businesses and houses belonging to members of the overthrown regime.

People of the Dominican Republic: nations show their greatness in victory, in the hour of triumph. It is necessary that you, valiant and heroic people, show your greatness and your generosity in this moment, by not destroying the national patrimony, by respecting private property, and by leaving to the men of the revolutionary government who are already leading the national destinies, the task of delivering justice to these people tricked countless times. The Americas as a whole have their eyes fixed upon this half-island. They are watching what we, the revolutionaries, do; looting and burning are barbaric acts that will discredit us in the world's eyes.

[…]

Dominicans! Have faith in the Dominican Revolutionary Party, have faith in the Social Christian Revolutionary Party, have faith in the democratic parties; because it is important to say that this will not be the government of one party, but the government of all Dominicans of good will, regardless of their flag's color. The hour in which all Dominicans must construct a new nationality has arrived. It is also necessary that all the hemispheric nations, which contemplate us with surprise and admiration at this moment, know that this is a drama being written by the Dominican people with their own hands, without the interference of any foreign power, neither from the East nor from the West. This is a revolution of the meek, of the enlisted men and noncommissioned officers of the Armed Forces, of the honest officers of the Armed Forces, of the men of the people, of the Dominican revolutionaries, who are willing to ensure that the flag of the white cross waves with pride on the peak of victory forever.

Another U.S. Military Intervention

Shortly after the Constitutionalists deposed Reid Cabral, the situation began to deteriorate. Worried about this fissure in the Dominican military, some attempts were made to reach an understanding among comrades-in-arms, but talks collapsed over the issue of Bosch's eventual return to the presidency. Within hours, planes from the CEFA began strafing the city of Santo Domingo, while people from the capital's lower-class neighborhoods, incited by Peña Gómez's speech, took to the streets to defend the

U.S. troops frisking Dominicans during the 1965 military intervention.

city. The Constitutionalists began distributing small arms among the people in an attempt to bolster their ranks, while the CEFA was preparing a tank assault on the city. On April 27, 1965, tanks and troops from the CEFA were badly beaten back as they attempted to cross the Duarte Bridge into Santo Domingo. This defeat at the hands of a lightly armed group of civilians and some Constitutionalist soldiers almost caused the collapse of the right-wing Dominican military leadership, which at this point formally requested U.S. military intervention to stop the civil war.

The Lyndon B. Johnson administration worried about the crisis that was taking place in Santo Domingo. It was the zenith of the cold war, with the unnerving experiences of the failed Bay of Pigs invasion of Cuba and the Missile Crisis still fresh on the minds of U.S. policymakers. Moreover, the U.S. military was also getting deeply involved in the Vietnam War, in an effort to "contain" communist expansion in the region. Within this context, Johnson quickly decided to defuse the Dominican crisis. Having "lost" Cuba to the communists, Johnson was bent on preventing a second socialist revolution in the region. Though nothing seemed to indicate that this would certainly be the case in the Dominican Republic, the U.S. government felt that communists might take advantage of the ongoing civil war in Santo Domingo and of the collapse of the Dominican military to derail the conflict into a full-fledged socialist revolution. On April 28, 1965, the first U.S. troops landed in Santo Domingo, presumably to protect U.S. citizens and other foreigners. Very quickly, however, their role changed to that of peacekeepers. The U.S. military separated the warring parties, imposed order, and sought a mediated solution to the conflict. However, it became very clear that the Johnson administration supported the CEFA camp. The Constitutionalists were contained in the old part of the city, with their backs to the sea, while the CEFA was given free reign over the rest of the country. Moreover, the U.S. military was in close contact with the CEFA leadership at all times and even used its facilities at the San Isidro military base. From the perspective of the Johnson administration, the presence of some communists in the Constitutionalist camp and the latter's decision to arm the civilian population made them a threat to U.S. interests in the region. Eventually, more than twenty-three thousand U.S. troops landed in the Dominican Republic.

Below are two documents related to the 1965 U.S. military intervention. The first one is the telegram by William T. Bennett, U.S. ambassador to the Dominican Republic, to the State Department, recommending the immediate landing of U.S. troops. The second one is a speech by President Johnson defending his Dominican policy and explaining the objectives of the U.S. military intervention as preventing "a second Cuba."

WILLIAM T. BENNETT TO THE STATE DEPARTMENT[7]
CRITIC, CRITIC, CRITIC.

Regret report situation deteriorating rapidly. San Isidro pilts [sic; pilots] tired and discouraged. [Police Chief] Despradel says cannot control situation. MAAG chief went to San Isidro, found [former Police Chief] Belisario Peguero there in an hysterical mood, urging "retreat," number of officers weeping. Benoit[8] requests U.S. troops formally. The country team is unanimous that the time has come to land the marines. American lives are in danger. Proposes marine beachhead at Embajador Hotel. If Washington wishes, they can be landed for the purpose of protecting evacuation of American citizens. I recommend immediate landing.

William Tapley Bennett, telegram, 28 April 1965, 5:16 P.M.

STATEMENT BY PRESIDENT JOHNSON, MAY 2, 1965[9]
White House Press Release, dated May 2

Good evening, ladies and gentlemen: I have just come from a meeting with the leaders of both parties in the Congress, which was held in the Cabinet Room of the White House. I briefed them on the facts of the situation in the Dominican Republic. I want to make those same facts known to all the American people and to all the world.

There are times in the affairs of nations when great principles are tested in an ordeal of conflict and danger. This is such a time for the American nations.

At stake are the lives of thousands, the liberty of a nation, and the principles and the values of all the American Republics.

That is why the hopes and the concern of this entire hemisphere are on this Sabbath Sunday focused on the Dominican Republic.

In the dark mist of conflict and violence, revolution and confusion, it is not easy to find clear and unclouded truths.

But certain things are clear. And they require equally clear action. To understand, I think it is necessary to begin with the events of eight or nine days ago.

---

7. From Piero Gleijeses, *The Dominican Crisis: The 1965 Constitutionalist Revolt and American Intervention* (Baltimore: Johns Hopkins University Press, 1978), 254.

8. Dominican Air Force colonel Pedro Bartolomé Benoit

9. From *The Department of State Bulletin*, vol. 52, no. 1351 (May 17, 1965), 744–748.

Last week our observers warned of an approaching political storm in the Dominican Republic. I immediately asked our Ambassador [W. Tapley Bennett, Jr.] to return to Washington at once so that we might discuss the situation and might plan a course of conduct. But events soon outran our hopes for peace.

Saturday, April 24—eight days ago—while Ambassador Bennett was conferring with the highest officials of your Government, revolution erupted in the Dominican Republic. Elements of the military forces of that country overthrew their government. However, the rebels themselves were divided. Some wanted to restore former President Juan Bosch. Others opposed his restoration. President Bosch, elected after the fall of Trujillo and his assassination, had been driven from office by an earlier revolution in the Dominican Republic.

Those who opposed Mr. Bosch's return formed a military committee in an effort to control that country. The others took to the street, and they began to lead a revolt on behalf of President Bosch. Control and effective government dissolved in conflict and confusion.

Meanwhile the United States was making a constant effort to restore peace. From Saturday afternoon onward, our Embassy urged a cease-fire, and I, and all the officials of the American Government, worked with every weapon at our command to achieve it.

On Tuesday the situation of turmoil was presented to the Peace Committee of the Organization of American States.

On Wednesday the entire Council of the Organization of American States received a full report from the Dominican Ambassador.

Meanwhile, all this time, from Saturday to Wednesday, the danger was mounting. Even though we were deeply saddened by bloodshed and violence in a close and friendly neighbor, we had no desire to interfere in the affairs of a sister Republic.

On Wednesday afternoon there was no longer any choice for the man who is your President. I was sitting in my little office reviewing the world situation with Secretary Rusk, Secretary McNamara, and Mr. McGeorge Bundy. Shortly after 3 o'clock, I received a cable from our Ambassador, and he said that things were in danger; he had been informed the chief of police and governmental authorities could no longer protect us. We immediately started the necessary conference calls to be prepared.

At 5:14, almost 2 hours later, we received a cable that was labeled "critic," a word that is reserved for only the most urgent and immediate matters of national security.

The cable reported that Dominican law enforcement and military officials had informed our Embassy that the situation was completely out of control and that the police and the government could no longer give any guarantee concerning the safety of Americans or any foreign nationals.

Ambassador Bennett, who is one of our most experienced Foreign Service officers, went on in that cable to say that only an immediate landing of American forces could safeguard and protect the lives of thousands of Americans and thousands of other citizens of some 30 other countries. Ambassador Bennett urged your President to order an immediate landing.

In this situation hesitation and vacillation could mean death for many of our people, as well as many of the citizens of other lands.

I thought that we could not and we did not hesitate. Our forces, American forces, were ordered in immediately to protect American lives. They have done that. They have attacked no one, and although some of our servicemen gave their lives, not a single American civilian or the civilian of any other nation, as a result of this protection, lost their lives.

There may be those in our own country who say that such action was good but we should have waited, or we should have delayed, or we should have consulted further, or we should have called a meeting. But from the very beginning, the United States, at my instructions, had worked for a cease-fire beginning the Saturday the revolution took place. The matter was before the OAS Peace Committee on Tuesday, at our suggestion. It was before the full Council on Wednesday, and when I made my announcement to the American people that evening, I announced then I was notifying the Council.

When that cable arrived, when our entire country team in the Dominican Republic, made up of nine men—one from the Army, Navy, and Air Force, our Ambassador, our AID[10] man, and others—said to your President unanimously: Mr. President, if you do not send forces immediately, men and women—Americans and those of other lands—will die in the streets—well, I knew there was no time to talk, to consult, or to delay. For in this situation delay itself would be decision—the decision to risk and to lose the lives of thousands of Americans and thousands of innocent people from all lands.

I want you to know that it is not a light or an easy matter to send our American boys to another country, but I do not think that the American people expect their President to hesitate or to vacillate in the face of danger, just because the decision is hard when life is in peril.

The revolutionary movement took a tragic turn. Communist leaders, many of them trained in Cuba, seeing a chance to increase disorder, to gain a foothold, joined the revolution. They took increasing control. And what began as a popular democratic revolution, committed to democracy and social justice, very shortly moved and was taken over and really seized and placed into the hands of a band of communist conspirators.

Many of the original leaders of the rebellion, the followers of President Bosch, took refuge in foreign embassies because they had been superseded by other evil forces, and the Secretary General of the rebel government, Martínez Francisco, appealed for a cease-fire. But he was ignored. The revolution was now in other and dangerous hands.

When these new and ominous developments emerged, the OAS met again, and it met at the request of the United States. I am glad to say they responded wisely and decisively. A five-nation OAS team is now in the Dominican Republic, acting to achieve a cease-fire to insure the safety of innocent people, to restore normal conditions, and to open a path to democratic progress.

This is the situation now.

I plead, therefore, with every person and every country in this hemisphere that would choose to do so, to contact their ambassador in the Dominican Republic direct-

10. U.S. Agency for International Development

ly and to get firsthand evidence of the horrors and the hardship, the violence and the terror, and the international conspiracy from which United States servicemen have rescued the people of more than 30 nations from that war-torn land.

Earlier today I ordered two additional battalions—2,000 extra men—to proceed immediately to the Dominican Republic. In the meeting that I have just concluded with the congressional leaders—following that meeting—I directed the Secretary of Defense and the Chairman of the Joint Chiefs of Staff to issue instructions to land an additional 4,500 men at the earliest possible moment. The distribution of food to people who have not eaten for days, the need of medical supplies and attention for the sick and wounded, the health requirements to avoid an epidemic because there are hundreds that have been dead for days that are now in the streets, and other protection and security of each individual that is caught on that island require the attention of the additional forces which I have ordered to proceed to the Dominican Republic.

In addition, our servicemen have already, since they landed on Wednesday night, evacuated three thousand persons from thirty countries in the world from this little island. But more than five thousand people, fifteen hundred of whom are Americans —the others are foreign nationals—are tonight awaiting evacuation as I speak. We just must get on with that job immediately.

The evidence that we have on the revolutionary movement indicates that it took a very tragic turn. Many of them trained in Cuba, seeing a chance to increase disorder and to gain a foothold, joined the revolution. They took increasing control. What began as a popular democratic revolution that was committed to democracy and social justice moved into the hands of a band of communist conspirators. Many of the original leaders of the rebellion, the followers of President Bosch, took refuge in foreign embassies and they are there tonight.

The American nations cannot, must not, and will not permit the establishment of another Communist government in the Western Hemisphere. This was the unanimous view of all the American nations when, in January 1962, they declared, and I quote: "The principles of communism are incompatible with the principles of the Inter-American system."

This is what our beloved President John F. Kennedy meant when, less than a week before his death, he told us: "We, in this hemisphere, must also use every resource at our command to prevent the establishment of another Cuba in this hemisphere."

This is and this will be the common action and the common purpose of the democratic forces of the hemisphere. For the danger is also a common danger, and the principles are common principles.

So we have acted to summon the resources of this entire hemisphere to this task. We have sent, on my instructions the night before last, special emissaries such as Ambassador [Teodoro] Moscoso of Puerto Rico, our very able Ambassador Averill Harriman, and others to Latin America to explain the situation, to tell them the truth, and to warn them that joint action is necessary. We are in contact with such distinguished Latin American statesmen as Rómulo Betancourt [former President of Venezuela] and José Figueres [former President of Costa Rica]. We are seeking their wisdom and their counsel and their advice. We have also maintained communication with President Bosch, who has chosen to remain in Puerto Rico.

We have been consulting with the Organization of American States, and our distinguished Ambassador—of whom there is no better—Ambassador Bunker, has been reporting to them at great length all the actions of this Government, and we have been acting in conformity with their decisions.

We know that many who are now in revolt do not seek a Communist tyranny. We think it is tragic indeed that their high motives have been misused by a small band of conspirators who receive their directions from abroad.

To those who fight only for liberty and justice and progress I want to join with the Organization of American States in saying—in appealing to you tonight to lay down your arms and to assure you there is nothing to fear. The road is open for you to share in building a Dominican democracy, and we in America are ready and anxious and willing to help you. Your courage and your dedication are qualities that your country and all the hemisphere need for the future. You are needed to help shape that future. And neither we nor any other nation in this hemisphere can or should take it upon itself to ever interfere with the affairs of your country or any other country.

We believe that change comes, and we are glad it does, and it should come through peaceful process. But revolution in any country is a matter for that country to deal with. It becomes a matter calling for hemispheric action only—repeat, only—when the object is the establishment of a Communist dictatorship.

Let me also make clear tonight that we support no single man or any single group of men in the Dominican Republic. Our goal is a simple one. We are there to save the lives of our citizens and to save the lives of all people. Our goal, in keeping with the great principles of the inter-American system, is to help prevent another Communist state in this hemisphere. And we would like to do this without bloodshed or without large-scale fighting.

The form and the nature of the free Dominican government, I assure you, is solely a matter for the Dominican people, but we do know what kind of government we hope to see in the Dominican Republic. For that is carefully spelled out in the treaties and the agreements which make up the fabric of the inter-American system. It is expressed, time and time again, in the words of our statesmen and the values and hopes which bind us all together.

We hope to see a government freely chosen by the will of all the people.

We hope to see a government dedicated to social justice for every citizen.

We hope to see a government working, every hour of every day, to feeding the hungry, to educating the ignorant, to healing the sick—a government whose only concern is the progress and the elevation and the welfare of all the people.

For more than three decades the people of that tragic little island suffered under the weight of one of the most brutal and despotic dictatorships of the Americas. We enthusiastically supported condemnation of that government by the Organization of American States. We joined in applying sanctions, and, when Trujillo was assassinated by his fellow citizens, we immediately acted to protect freedom and to prevent a new tyranny, and since that time we have taken the resources from all of our people at some sacrifice to many, and we have helped them with food and with other resources, with the Peace Corps volunteers, with the AID technicians; we have helped them in the effort to build a new order of progress.

How sad it is tonight that a people so long oppressed should once again be the targets of the forces of tyranny. Their long misery must weigh heavily on the heart of every citizen of this hemisphere. So I think it is our mutual responsibility to help the people of the Dominican Republic toward the day when they can freely choose the path of liberty and justice and progress. This is required of us by the agreements that we are party to and that we have signed. This is required of us by the values that bind us together.

Simón Bolívar once wrote from exile: "The veil has been torn asunder. We have already seen the light and it is not our desire to be thrust back into the darkness."

Well, after decades of night, the Dominican people have seen a more hopeful light, and I know that the nations of this hemisphere will not let them be thrust back into the darkness.

And before I leave you, my fellow Americans, I want to say this personal word: I know that no American serviceman wants to kill anyone. I know that no American President wants to give an order that brings shooting and casualties and death. I want you to know, and I want the world to know, that as long as I am President of this country, we are going to defend ourselves. We will defend our soldiers against attackers. We will honor our treaties. We will keep our commitments. We will defend our nation against all those who seek to destroy not only the United States but every free country of this hemisphere. We do not want to bury anyone, as I have said so many times before. But we do not intend to be buried.

Thank you. God bless you. Good night.

The Constitutionalist Perspective

The four days that the so-called Dominican "Revolution" lasted, helped define new leaders. As the situation deteriorated, many PRD and Constitutionalist leaders sought political asylum in foreign embassies. Others decided to fight it out to the end. Among the latter was Colonel Francisco A. Caamaño Deñó, who rushed to the Duarte Bridge to organize the defenses against the CEFA's tank attack. The victory of the people over the tanks catapulted Caamaño's leadership in the Constitutionalist movement. As the Constitutionalists were later surrounded and contained within the old city, Caamaño emerged as a figure of resistance to U.S. imperial designs and as an outspoken supporter of the return to constitutional order and the restoration of Juan Bosch's presidency.

On May 5, 1965, Caamaño was named president of the Dominican Republic. Juan Bosch, prevented by the U.S. authorities from returning to the country, resigned so that Caamaño could succeed him and a de jure president would thus be in the country. The CEFA camp organized its own parallel government, and for the next few months both camps claimed to be the legitimate rulers of the Dominican Republic. In this speech, Caamaño resigned as president shortly after a peace agreement was reached after months of negotiations. The speech recounts the democratic struggles of the Dominican people and concludes that even though the Constitutionalists did not win, they were also not defeated.

CAAMAÑO'S SPEECH DELIVERED ON SEPTEMBER 3, 1965, AT THE PLAZA OF THE CONSTITUTION[11]

Dear Members of the National Congress, Dominican People:

Because the people gave me the power, I come to the people to return what belongs to them. There is no legitimate power if it is not given by the people, whose sovereign will is the source of all public mandate. On May 5, 1965, the National Congress honored me by choosing me as the Constitutional President of the Dominican Republic. Only in that way could I accept such a high-ranking position, because I have always believed that the right to govern cannot emanate from anyone but the people themselves.

Very legitimate was that right, forged by our large national majorities in the cleanest elections in our entire history, and deposited in my hands at a time in which the Dominican people were struggling, with great violence, to conquer their democratic institutions. Those institutions, which came out of the electoral consultation of December 20, 1962, were devoured by the infamy and the ambition of a minority that has always disregarded the popular will.

Dominicans struggled with great violence because that minority took away their freedoms on September 25, 1963. That minority is the one that has always stolen, imprisoned, deported, and assassinated our people. And that minority, represented by the Triumvirate that Donald Reid presided, even thought that this country belonged to them and that its inhabitants were their slaves.

All those vices and mistakes meant greater pains and misery for the people. Life was becoming unbearable. There was not a shred of hope in the souls of Dominicans while the usurpers of power were governing. In order for that hope to be reborn, it was necessary to return to the freely-elected government, that is, to the Democracy of the 1963 Constitution. Everything indicated that the governing minority, which thought and acted as if they were the owners of the nation, would remain in power even against the most vigorous popular claims, directed toward the rescuing of the democratic regime.

Armed rebellion against the illegitimacy of their mandate then became an urgent social need. Out of that need and of the determination of Dominicans to be free, without caring about the extent of the price, the glorious movement of April 24th exploded.

That movement, inspired by the noblest democratic spirit, was not just one more military uprising. Professor Juan Bosch was right when he said, during the first days

11. Translated from Francisco A. Caamaño Deñó, *¡A golpes de heroísmo! Discursos pronunciados durante su mandato constitucional* (Santo Domingo: Editora MIROX, 1978), 21–30.

of the struggle from his forced exile in Puerto Rico, that Dominicans were making a social revolution. It was like that because the democratic sectors of the people, after a lot of suffering and major frustrations, had assumed a profound consciousness of their historical role and in brotherhood with the military men, who respected the oath of defending the majesty of the laws, took to the streets in search of their lost freedom.

Heroically, with more faith than arms, and with an immense abundance of digni-ty, the Dominican people opened wide the doors of history to build their future. Deep, very profound were the roots of that struggle. Since Independence, since the Restoration, the people sought their right of being free, dying and winning. April 24th was a gigantic step toward the achievement of that right and toward the democracy that fully consecrated it.

The enemies of the people, those who put their own interest before the interest of the Fatherland in a useless attempt to stay in power, made generous blood run like rivers. But over our dead bodies we always rose up with more strength. The Revo-lution advanced triumphantly. America as a whole looked at this land with admira-tion, anxiously waiting for our triumph, because in it [America] saw a victory for democracy over the oppressive minorities that lashed, like pests, the entire American Continent.

Unfortunately, on April 28th, four days after revolution began, when freedom was being victoriously reborn, when a whole people fervently moved themselves to the encounter of Democracy, the government of the United States of America, violating the sovereignty of our Independent State, and scoffing the fundamental principles that sustain international coexistence, militarily invaded and militarily occupied our soil.

What right could the North American leaders invoke to trample the freedom of a sovereign nation in this way? NONE! They were guilty of a serious crime, a crime against our nation, against America, and against the rest of the world. The principle of nonintervention, fundamental basis of the relationships among civilized nations, was so brutally unrecognized, that the echo of the harshest repulse against the invaders is still heard throughout the vastness of the planet.

[. . .]

The humiliation the government of the United States made the Dominican Republic go through, militarily invaded, also means a painful humiliation for all of America. What norms, what principles can be of service to the American Nations to render valid their vocation and their right to independence, when the North American leaders decide with vain excuses and supported by the force of their cannons, to impose a political destiny on them? Where to go to claim the recognition of the right of a nation to be independent and master of its own life? What organisms, what insti-tutions will be capable of defending those rights and of encouraging the people to exercise them, without fear of the intrusion of those who have made themselves into arbiters of the determination of others?

For the misfortune of the Dominican Republic and for the misfortune of America, the Organization of American States instead of assuming the defense of our sover-eignty, instead of severely sanctioning the military intervention in order to make valid in this way the honor of the principles that it is said to sustain, not only turned its back on its own constitutive charter, but it also pushed, even more, the dagger that today is stuck in the heart of our Fatherland.

Four days after the North American military intervention, the Organization of American States decided to do "everything that is possible to seek the restoration of peace and normality in the Dominican Republic." In the text of the resolution, which expresses the aforementioned, nothing was said about the violation of our sovereignty. NOTHING! Not a single word makes reference to the monstrous crime of April 28, 1965, that for a long time will shake the fragile foundation of the Inter-American judicial order. Quite the opposite, the Organization of American States was then bent on, ignoring and twisting the principles, into justifying and validating the North American military intervention. And thus it thought to do it by creating the Inter-American Force. The resolution that consecrates this disastrous measure, registered as document Rev. 2 of the Tenth Meeting of Consultation of American Ministers, reveals very clearly the attitude of the regional organism in that respect. In effect, the following is in it: "That the integration of an Inter-American Force will signify, ipso facto, the transformation of the forces currently in Dominican territory into another force that will not be from a State but from an interstate organism."

Transformation! This is the word that reveals the connivance of the OAS with the invaders. The Marines were being transformed into an Inter-American Force. That was the institutionalization of political crime as a norm of the international relations in our continent.

The North American intervention thus came to halt the triumph of Dominican Democracy and to prop up the minority that denies and disputes their rights to our peoples. Behind the so-called Government of National Reconstruction, the work of the functionaries of the foreign intervention, the disdain of the people was heard, corruption was strengthened, and crime extended throughout the entire country.

In spite of the momentary frustration the Revolution suffered in those tragic days, the constitutional government naturally decided to defend its rights, in the face of the violence and strength of North American might, represented by more than forty thousand soldiers, the armed triumph of the Dominican democratic movement was no longer possible. We had to negotiate with the invaders in order to preserve the treasure of Democracy that we had started to create.

At the negotiating table we always defended the principles. If we abandoned some of the conquests for which the Dominican people launched the struggle, it was not because the negotiators of the Organization of American States brought forward proposals with a greater democratic content than the ones we followed in our initial objectives. We only relented in the face of the reality that the North American intervention imposed. The corridor that the foreign troops established, arbitrarily and unjustifiably, dividing the city in two, had no other reason but to prevent the spread of the struggle, from this glorious city, to the rest of the country.

The desire for democracy had turned the entire Republic around. The cause that the people of Santo Domingo defended with arms in hand was the National cause. This four times centenary city was the vanguard and from it we threw ourselves, victorious against the local oppressors. The victory of the democratic arms was already forthcoming, and when we were about to fully obtain it, the United States of America interfered, invading us to preserve the worst interests and the most despicable ambitions.

It was then when we had to give up some of our objectives, because we could not win with arms. But in spite of all the force and all the violence of the North American military might, we did not give up for fear of being defeated. The world is a witness to the struggle we fought, of the courage and the bravery of these people in the realm of honor and in the field of battle.

It is adequate for me to stop here to give homage to the heroes who gave their lives fighting for democracy and national sovereignty. That Unknown Fighter, who rests in this plaza of the Constitution, is the symbol of the sacrifice and of the love of Dominicans for their freedom. Like him, thousands died. From this breeding ground of heroes the future of the Fatherland will grow vigorously. Because heroes are those who gave their lives trying to halt the creation of the international corridor that stopped our victorious march. Because heroes are those who, with stones in their hands, stopped the steel tanks at the Duarte Bridge.

Heroes, those who defended, with their last breath, the northern zone of the city; heroes those who impassively received the aerial attacks on the National Palace; heroes those who on the fifteenth and sixteenth of June, bravely received the foreign fire; heroes those of the twenty-ninth of August; also heroes those who have died on all our fronts, in rural areas and cities, defending the national integrity.

Maybe never in the lives of Dominicans had we struggled with so much heroism against an enemy so superior in arms and numbers. We fought like this, with the bravery of legends because we were blazing with reason the path of history.

We could not win, but were not defeated either. The truth championed by our cause was the greatest strength and the greatest inspiration to resist. AND WE RESISTED! That is our triumph, because without the tenacious resistance we put up, today we could not boast about the objectives achieved.

We gave in, it is true, but they, the invaders who came to prevent our revolution, to destroy our cause, had to give in as well in the face of the revolutionary spirit of our people.

There they are, speaking for themselves, the conquests achieved and that are stated, magnified by the blood of the dead, in the Institutional Act and in the Act of Dominican Reconciliation. Multiple economic and social rights have been recognized for us. We have achieved the scheduling of free elections within a brief term. We have conquered public freedoms, the respect for human rights, the return of political exiles, the right of every Dominican to live in his homeland without the fear of being deported. But above all, we have achieved an appreciable conquest, of fertile future projections: Democratic Consciousness! Consciousness against military coups, against administrative corruption, against nepotism, against exploitation, against interventionism. We have achieved consciousness of our own historical destiny. In sum, consciousness of the people of their strength, which on April 24th served them to defeat the civilian and military oligarchies, and which today, nourished by this wonderful experience and this astonishing struggle, will allow them to forge, in peace or in war, their freedom and their independence. The people awoke, because their consciousness awoke!

[. . .]

I firmly believe that the Dominican people will end up achieving their happiness, and April 24th will always be an inspiring symbol of its definitive realization.

[. . .]

Before the Dominican people, before their worthy representatives, here embodied by the honorable National Congress, I resign as Constitutional President of the Republic. God willing, and may the people achieve it, this will be the last time in our history that a legitimate government has to abandon power under the pressure of national or foreign forces. I have faith that it will be like that.

Finally I invite the people gathered here to take the following oath:

On behalf of the ideals of the Trinitarios and Restorers who forged the Dominican Republic. Inspired by the generous sacrifice of our civilian and military brothers fallen in the constitutional struggle. Interpreting the feelings of the Dominican People.

WE SWEAR to fight for the withdrawal of the foreign troops that are in the territory of our country.

WE SWEAR to fight for the validity of democratic freedoms and human rights and not to allow any attempt to reestablish tyranny.

WE SWEAR to fight for the unity of all patriotic sectors to make our nation fully sovereign, FULLY DEMOCRATIC.

Peace Restored

Negotiations dragged on for several months as the U.S. authorities and the Organization of American States, which had taken symbolic control of the military intervention, tried different solutions acceptable to both camps. Several interim governments were proposed and discarded, until finally, on August 31, 1965, the "Act of Dominican Reconciliation" was signed (reproduced below). According to its provisions, Héctor García Godoy was appointed provisional president of the Dominican Republic, and entrusted with organizing new elections by mid-1966. A full amnesty was granted, civilians were to be disarmed, and the Constitutionalists were to dispose of their arms and be reintegrated into the Dominican armed forces, a stipulation that was only partially carried out. On the side, U.S. authorities encouraged the leaders from both camps to leave the country, so as to defuse the highly-polarized Dominican political scene. Both Caamaño and Wessin y Wessin, as well as many other Constitutionalist and CEFA officers, were sent to diplomatic posts overseas. Moreover, other former combatants were granted emigration visas to the United States.

ACT OF DOMINICAN RECONCILIATION
AND INSTITUTIONAL ACT[12]

Santo Domingo, August 31 and September 3, 1965

Convinced of the urgent need to restore the peace and unity of the Dominican family, to foster the economic recuperation of the Nation and to reestablish its democratic institutions;

Determined to reach the aforementioned to assure a climate of peace and conciliation in which all Dominicans can live in a regimen of liberty and social justice.

The undersigning Parties, who respectively declare to fill the positions indicated in the "Constitutional Government" and the Provisional Government of the Dominican Republic, declare that they have reached the following accord as a result of the negotiations by the Ad Hoc Commission of the Tenth Meeting of Consultation of Ministers of Foreign Relations, whose members also sign the current Act to affirm that the Parties have agreed to accept its dispositions:

1. The "Constitutional Government" accepts the Provisional Government presided by Dr. Héctor García Godoy as the sole and sovereign government of the Dominican Republic. The members of the "Constitutional Government" will lend their maximum cooperation to the Provisional Government for the establishment and consolidation of political peace as well as for the rehabilitation of the national economy.

2. The parties accept the Institutional Act that results from this accord as a constitutional instrument according to which the Provisional Government will exercise its functions. No prior constitution shall be effective during the tenure of the aforementioned Institutional Act, whose text is added to the current accord.

3. On the day of its installation, the Provisional Government will decree the general amnesty that Article 11 of the Institutional Act dictates and will take the necessary measures to set free all political prisoners.

4. Immediately following the installation of the Provisional Government, the contending forces will start the process of retiring their defenses from the zones currently under their control.

The Inter-American Peace Force will return to its camps, leaving in the current lines only the wire fences and reduced surveillance posts.

The demilitarization and disarmament of civilians will start immediately in the constitutionalist zone.

The current check points will be operated during the disarmament phase by elements from the Inter-American Peace Force.

The current surveillance posts and check points of the Inter-American Peace Force will be withdrawn as soon as the demilitarization of the zone and the disarmament of civilians have been verified by the Provisional Government.

The Provisional Government will take the necessary measures in order to verify compliance with what was stipulated in this article.

The Provisional President will indicate the places to which the Inter-American Peace Force will move to until the date of its departure from the country is determined.

12. Translated from *Gaceta Oficial*, no. 8944, 4 September 1965, 3–19.

234

5. The maintenance of public order in all of the national territory will be the responsibility of the Provisional Government, and it will take all measures deemed necessary for that purpose.

6. As soon as it is installed, the Provisional Government will establish special posts for the retrieval of weapons in the hands of the civilian population. These posts will be filled with persons appointed by the Provisional Government. The Provisional Government will decide when the recovered weapons shall be returned to the arsenals of the Nation.

7. The current "Constitutional Government" will take all the necessary measures so that, in a prudent period after the installation of the Provisional Government, the weapons currently in the hands of the civilian population under its jurisdiction are returned to the posts established in conformity with the preceding article. The Provisional Government will take the necessary measures to retrieve weapons that are not returned voluntarily.

8. Once the Provisional Government is installed, the Armed Forces will return to their bases and will place themselves under the orders of their Commander in Chief, the Provisional President. Those military men who participated in the current conflict will be reintegrated into the Armed Forces, without discrimination or reprisals.

9. According to the declaration of general amnesty, no officer, noncommissioned officer, or enlisted member of the Armed Forces will be subjected to court-martial or will be punished for acts committed after the twenty-third of April, 1965, with the exception of common crimes. Any member of the Armed Forces who wishes to retire, can do so in conformity with the procedures established by the Organic Law of the Armed Forces, and with the corresponding pensions. Any member of the Armed Forces who wishes to leave the country, can do so with the guarantees and the help of the Provisional Government.

10. The Provisional Government will immediately begin negotiations with the Tenth Meeting of Consultation of Ministers of Foreign Relations regarding the procedure and the date for the withdrawal of the Inter-American Peace Force from the national territory.

IN FAITH OF THIS, two copies of this document are signed, which will be known with the name of "Act of Dominican Reconciliation," one of those will be destined for the archives of the Dominican Republic, and the other one will be deposited in the General Secretaryship of the Organization of American States.

The Secretary General of the Organization of American States will forward certified copies to each member State.

Signed on this thirty-first day of August of nineteen hundred sixty-five.

For the Constitutional Government:

Francisco A. Caamaño Deñó, President; Aníbal Campagna, President of the Senate; Jottin Cury, Minister of Foreign Relations; Héctor Aristy, Minister of the Presidency; Salvador Jorge Blanco, Attorney General of the Republic; S. Antonio Guzmán, Member of the Negotiating Commission

For the Provisional Government:

Hector García Godoy, President

For the Ad Hoc Commission of the Tenth Meeting of Consultation of Ministers of Foreign Relations:

Ilmar Penna Marinho, Ambassador of Brazil; Ramón de Clairmont Dueñas, Ambassador of El Salvador; Ellsworth Bunker, U. S. Ambassador

The 1966 Elections

As instructed, the administration of García Godoy scheduled presidential elections for June 1966. From the beginning, two main candidates emerged: Juan Bosch and Joaquín Balaguer. After resigning the presidency, Bosch was eventually allowed to return to the Dominican Republic and to participate in the election. However, he was unable to campaign effectively and rarely left his home, as he had received numerous death threats. Moreover, dozens of PRD activists were murdered and intimidated by the Dominican military, who had made it very clear that they would not accept another Bosch presidency. Thus, Bosch had to limit himself to campaigning through radio broadcasts from home. Balaguer, on the other hand, had cultivated excellent relations with the U.S. government. Since his exile in 1962, Balaguer had been promoting himself as the candidate of conciliation and as a moderate in a highly polarized political environment. Balaguer's anti-communist credentials were well known, and the fact that he had not been involved in the 1965 conflict helped his self-promotion. Besides, even though Balaguer was not a military man but a conservative politician, he was acceptable both to the conservative Dominican military and to U.S. interests. As such, Balaguer would become the clear choice of the Johnson administration. He was allowed to campaign all over the country and he received the open backing of a military establishment that still fondly remembered the Trujillo regime where Balaguer had played a prominent role.

The Dominican people—many of whom supported Bosch—got the message: a victory by Bosch would mean a renewal of the conflict, while a victory by Balaguer would mean a return to peace and some sense of normalcy. Not surprisingly, Balaguer won the election with ease. Bosch left for Spain—where he spent the next three years—while Balaguer was inaugurated as U.S. troops were preparing to leave the country. In the meantime, dozens of former Constitutionalists and leftist sympathizers were being murdered by paramilitary forces in an attempt to head off the

Dominican Left.

One of Balaguer's 1966 campaign speeches is reproduced below. Notice his references to the divisive 1965 civil war and how he presents himself to the Dominican electorate as the candidate of conciliation; the only one who could get the country out of the political morass that it was stuck in.

THE ONLY WAY OUT[13]

Delivered at the popular concentration celebrated in the city of Dajabón, on April 23, 1966.

Agents paid by international communism, as well as by the leftist parties that support the political tendency that will confront the Reformist Party in the elections of June 1st have spread in the past months, mainly in Dajabón and all the towns of the border region, the idea that the elections of June 1st will have no practical result, and that it would be preferable, before resorting to that formula to solve the Dominican problem, to simply and purely reestablish the regime overthrown through military action on September 25, 1963.

I think, gentlemen, that the experience gained by the country from the coup of September 25th should bring us to diametrically distinct conclusions from those stated by the ones who oppose a new democratic consultation, which is scheduled to take place on June 1st at the ballot boxes.

It is notorious that the main share of difficulties the country faces, not only in the institutional realm but also in the development of its economic activities, is due to the interruption of the democratic process that was initiated with the election of the first government imposed by the popular will in the last forty years. Military coups have plagued all Latin American democracies. But those periodic crises represent, in each one of our countries, the natural expression of a process of accommodation of the institutions to a regime of democratic coexistence that only rules halfway, even in many already-mature nations of the civilized world. But the Dominican case was different. Our people, despite their educational deficiencies, gave a moving demonstration of civic spirit in the elections of December 20th. Moreover, the civic revolution that culminated with the expulsion of the Trujillo family was made, according to the commitment assumed with the country by all those who intervened in those massive mobilizations, in the name of democracy. As a consequence, the old dictatorial structures were swept away to be replaced, as everyone believed, with liberal systems and institutions.

The balance of the military adventure of September 25th has been terrifying not only for the future of national democracy, a thing in which very few currently believe, but also for the goals that the country had the ability to reach, when the coup d'état took place, in the field of material achievements. The results have been terrible in all areas. The authors of the civil-military coup of September 25th, have politically

13. Translated from Joaquín Balaguer, *La marcha hacia el Capitolio* (Santo Domingo: n.p., 1973), 209–216.

transformed the country into a can of worms; socially, into a Pandora's box, and economically, into a bottomless barrel, like the one of the Danaïdes, where not only the stability of the currency disappeared but also the dignity on which it rests, as its only moral support, Dominican sovereignty.

Why then another coups d'état, once the Constitution had been reestablished in the Dominican Republic? A monstrosity of that kind can only be justified in the presence of a dictatorial government that capriciously suppresses individual rights and restricts civil liberties for no reason. Popular contempt toward the instigators of the coup is not due to the fact that the constitutional order has been subverted, but that this subversion took place against a regime in which the political rights of the citizenry were to a certain extent respected. If it was believed that the deposed government really constituted a threat to the principles on which our society has been organized, or that it tended to drag the nation, with measures of a revolutionary nature, toward a situation incompatible with its Christian essence, it is obvious that it could have been toppled with the same procedures that democracy puts within reach of public opinion in every regime in which the right to disagree is respected by the authorities. It is an indisputable fact that the government deposed on September 25th did not restrain in any way the free activity of the political parties of the opposition nor did it impose any kind of limitations on the fundamental freedoms of the Dominican citizen. Back in those days the shameful woodworm of the detractors of all political situations that dared to enter, broom in hand, in the mansions where privilege intransigently maintains its semi-feudal charters, could walk freely in the streets.

With acts that were named "Manifestations of Christian Affirmation," they were able to shake a government consecrated by the support of five hundred thirty thousand voters. Public opinion proved, on that occasion, the might of its demolishing strength with flying colors. It is evidenced by the fact that the deposed administration could not impose any of its reforms with a revolutionary content. Its most hopeful initiatives in the social field were reduced to mere threats, because they were paralyzed by the action of public opinion thanks to the freedom with which the Government itself surrounded the flag bearers of intrepid diatribe and subversive opposition. It was useless to the Government to have an overwhelming majority in Congress. The 1963 constitution itself was the object of substantial modifications under the pressure of public opinion, mobilized by reactionary sectors as well as by groups with a moderately conservative ideology. The experienced lived by the country in the scarce seven months in which it was democratically governed, shows that the fears of those who believe that a people can be dragged into lamentable situations under a government in which public freedoms are respected and in which public opinion conserves the right to manifest itself with all the amplitude of its unsuspected energies are imaginary.

That is why the act of September 25th was so unjustified. An uprising of that kind can only be explained as a natural reaction, or as an act of legitimate defense, when the prevailing regime arbitrarily suppresses civil rights, when it transforms the right to assemble for peaceful purposes into a myth, when freedom of the press or of radio suffer capricious restrictions for politically related motives, when the robe of justice is treaded on by intrusive boots, and when in public life the principle of separation of powers ceases to be a working reality.

The nature of the regime matters little in the final analysis. A de facto government, in spite of its unconstitutional origin, can make itself as deserving of public esteem as a government freely born out of the electoral ballot boxes, if it abides by the law and does not commit unnecessary excesses in its task of custodian of public order and guardian of the national institutions. On the contrary, a government triumphant in an electoral contest can make itself hated and deserving of being repudiated through illegal means if it betrays the popular trust, establishing itself as the predator of the public finances or the henchman of civil liberties.

The perfect weapon for overthrowing a bad government is, therefore, that of public opinion. When that method can be employed, as it could had been and was under the regime overthrown on September 25th, resorting to the coup d'état becomes one of the gravest errors that can be committed against a nation eager for just laws and civilized institutions. This is the only positive benefit the country has acquired from the last military coup: thanks to that error, we know now that a constitutional government should not be overthrown except in the case it creates in the country a situation in which public opinion could not be used, as a weapon a thousand times more prolific and more effective for the defense of the Fatherland and for the safekeeping of its fundamental liberties than machine guns.

After this simple analysis of the national situation, made without partisan enthusiasm or sectarian prejudice, we can come to the conclusion that the crisis this country is going through cannot be satisfactorily resolved by either the reestablishment of the regime of 1963 or the establishment of a government sustained by the Armed Forces or imposed by foreign intervention. To exit the dead end into which the ambitions and the follies of the parties, which have ruled of late, have taken us, it is necessary for us to resort to a radical solution that will decide the destiny of the Dominican people once and for all. That solution can be no other than one of absolutely free and absolutely pure elections in which the country chooses between two paths: that of a just and balanced social revolution and that of a violent and disrupting social revolution.

The social revolution is inevitable in itself. It is imposed by the times and demanded by the majority of the Dominican people who desire to be emancipated, just as they emancipated themselves from the dictatorship of Trujillo, from the triple tyranny of poverty, privilege, and economic exploitation. But that revolution cannot take place as Juan Bosch tried to do it; with demagogic promises that have no sense nor with follies such as those tending to dissolve the immutable principles on which free enterprise and the right to private property are based. Neither can we undergo this transformation without regard to the realities of our milieu, the conditions on which our economy operates, and the circumstances of an environmental nature in which Dominican life develops socially. We need, in other words, a social revolution of autochthonous origin, not a bookish revolution brought from Cuba or imported from Venezuela.

In the next electoral contest, the three tendencies into which the opinion of the Dominican people is presently divided will face each other in a duel to the death: first, that of the oligarchy, represented by one of those vengeful and choleric leaders who annihilates without contemplation or who carries five whips, one on each finger

239

of the hand that is resting on the helm; second, that of the revolutionary left, headed in turn by one of those demagogues who transforms the social revolution into a war machine, ready to blaze a path with bombs and with incendiary torches; and third, that of the moderate tendency, inclined to the left like the heart, but conscious of its commitment which is not to concentrate all the blood on just outside of the body but to carry it through the arteries to the entire organism.

From the results of those elections, the system according to which the people want to be governed will be inferred: whether with the whip, with the steamroller, or simply with the scales of justice and the sword of the law. But one thing can be anticipated right now without fear of missing the prediction: the only thing that can bring back to the country the lost equilibrium is the triumph of the intermediate tendency in between the two extremes. For the Republic to advance without stumbling in the midst of a truly fruitful climate of peace, it is necessary for the next government to be a government capable of initiating and of carrying out a vast program of social demands. We may ask ourselves here: could those reforms be realized, to the extent that the circumstances make it necessary, by a government that represents in power the interests of the ultra-conservative class? Lenin used to say, and he said it with reason even from the point of view of his revolutionary radicalism, that "capitalists cannot renounce their interests just as a man cannot pull himself up by his own hair." But similar reforms cannot be realized, with a truly constructive spirit, by an extremist government, because then we would run the risk that invariably runs through all regimes of a communist physiognomy: that in which the wealth-producing class, which is precisely the most useful class for the growth of the nation, is sacrificed through counterproductive measures or social laws with negative effects.

Just one notable objection has been made to the initiative of those who clamor for a new electoral contest: if we admit the coup of September 25th, who will guarantee that the government coming out of these new elections will not also be overthrown by a military coup? It is true. But the same can be said about a new Constitution: if the one of 1963 was abolished, what do we need a new constitutional law for? So that it can be abolished too? But the same can be said about the father whose son is taken away by death at the wrong time: if that son was taken away at the wrong time, why have others? So that he will be born exposed to dying when he least expects it? Juridical solutions, on the other hand, are not always the most constructive or the healthiest. Nothing is achieved with a just solution if that solution is not capable of offering the country what the country needs most: peace.

People of Dajabón: this is not a partisan message. This is a cry of anguish. It is also an appeal to your good sense so that you do not become an instrument of demagoguery or a toy for ambition. The choice of the Dominican people as a whole is clear: to save themselves or to resign themselves to have on their walls a sign similar to the one that Cromwell ordered placed on the ruins of the British parliament, in the house that had been up to then the symbol of English freedoms: "Gentlemen: this country is for rent."

CHAPTER SEVEN

Contemporary Politics

Joaquín Balaguer's inauguration in 1966 marked a new chapter in Dominican history; one characterized by the birth and evolution of a democratization process, but also by the still incomplete nature of democratic government. Politics did not revert to the autocratic style of the Trujillo dictatorship, yet Dominican democracy was still far from institutionalized. A centralizing, authoritarian political culture still permeates the system—a legacy of the thirty-one years of Trujillo's rule and centuries of oppressive, dictatorial administrations. Dominican presidents are like little monarchs, as all other authorities and branches of the state pale in contrast to the power of the Executive—a phenomenon known as presidentialism.

Balaguer kept a tight grip on power. He eliminated threats from the radical Left and the extreme Right and had himself reelected in 1970 and 1974, while most of the opposition abstained in face of state-led military and paramilitary repression. It was not until 1978 that the political opposition, led by the PRD, gathered enough momentum to defeat Balaguer at the polls, and even then the Dominican military staged a short-lived internal coup in an attempt to stop the vote counting process. From 1978 to 1986, the PRD occupied the presidency, though Bosch had left the party in 1973 in disgust over its electoral strategy. The PRD administrations coincided with the 1980s economic crisis which, coupled with the PRD's blunders and mismanagement of the economy, facilitated Balaguer's unexpected comeback in 1986. The "new," less authoritarian, Balaguer again had himself reelected on two occasions (1990 and 1994) by dividing the opposition and using fraudulent tactics at the polls. In 1990 he defeated Juan Bosch, while in 1994 he defeated José F. Peña Gómez in questionable electoral contests. The latter led to a prolonged post-electoral crisis that was eventually resolved by a "gentlemen's agreement" bartered by the leadership of the three major political parties: Balaguer's term was reduced to two years and new elections were to take place in 1996. Additionally, the constitution was modified to ban consecutive presidential reelection and to implement the majority runoff electoral format in case of no clear winner in the presidential election—meaning that if no candidate obtains more than 50 percent of the valid votes in the first round, the two candidates with the most votes had to face each other in a runoff election.

Some of these constitutional modifications would come back to haunt the political opposition that had initially suggested them. For example, though Balaguer was prevented from running in the 1996 presidential election, he backed the second runner-up, Leonel Fernández, who then went on to easily defeat Peña Gómez in the runoff election. More recently, with the PRD back in the presidency in the year 2000, its legislators rescinded the ban on consecutive presidential reelection in 2002.

The Dominican political system has certainly come a long way since the troubled years of the early to mid 1960s. It is, by most accounts, an electoral democracy, with some shortcomings in the areas of justice, institutionalization, and the rule of law; but with major accomplishments in the spheres of basic civil liberties, freedom of the press, and increasingly transparent and regularized electoral contests. Though the outlook for the future is hopeful, whether Dominican democracy will proceed further on the road toward its institutionalization still remains to be seen.

Balaguer's Twelve Years

With the election of Joaquín Balaguer in 1966 began twelve years of a semi-authoritarian government. While Balaguer maintained a modicum of democracy and held elections, violations of human rights and political repression were commonplace. For example, in 1970 and 1974 Balaguer was easily reelected after most of the opposition abstained from participating in an electoral campaign marred by state coercion and where the military and the police openly voiced their support for Balaguer. Moreover, his administration unleashed a "dirty war" against known or suspected leftists, in which the military, the police, and right-wing death squads (for example, La Banda) acted with impunity. More than three thousand Dominicans died or "disappeared" in this low-intensity cold war conflict, while dozens took the road of exile or became political prisoners. During this time, Balaguer also received the support of the United States, which still wanted to prevent a "second Cuba" and thus tried to uproot any leftist movements. The Dominican Republic received high levels of military and economic aid, which, coupled with good sugar prices, led to high economic growth rates during 1966–1972. Balaguer

Government repression during Balaguer's "twelve years" (1966–1978).

243

also developed an ambitious public works program that created jobs and changed the face of a country torn by years of political instability and official idleness. Balaguer's "economic miracle" won him the favor of the upper and middle classes, who saw in him a stabilizing factor in a polarized society, and the lesser evil in a world sharply divided into two ideological camps. For the U.S. government, Balaguer and the Dominican Republic were a showcase of democracy in the Caribbean, in sharp contrast to Fidel Castro's communist Cuba.

The following selection is from the memoirs of one of those participants in the "dirty war." Rafael Chaljub Mejía was an active member of the radical Left of the 1970s who spent time in jail and was periodically persecuted by the Dominican authorities for political offenses. In this selection, he describes the repressive tactics of the Balaguer administration at the height of the 1970s "dirty war."

THE APOGEE OF THE DIRTY WAR BY RAFAEL CHALJUB MEJÍA[1]
Nineteen-hundred seventy, the year of Balaguer's reelection, closed with the bloody tally of two hundred sixteen dead on account of terrorism.

Meanwhile, the attempts of the government to gag the press and honest journalists by way of terror continued. The twenty-eighth of October of that tragic year, Arcadio Emilio Mañán Paniagua, informant of the Police's Secret Service, publicly revealed, in an act of apparent repentance, that for more than a month he had been following the journalist Juan Bolívar Díaz, in preparation of an attempt, whose direct execution had been entrusted to two agents of the said police department.

Besides the planned assassination of journalist Díaz, these two officials, named Lizardo and Cabrera, respectively, had the mission of blowing up with explosives the installations of Radio Comercial, principal broadcasting station of Noti-Tiempo; according to the denunciation of Mañán Paniagua, who involved the Chief of the Secret Service, Colonel Luis Arzeno Regalado, in the criminal conspiracy.

Juan Bolívar Díaz, whose vehicle had already been destroyed by a bomb, seven months earlier, opted to leave the country.

"Those who dynamited my car now intended to dynamite my head" said the professional, in a temporary goodbye note, as he left on a plane for Mexico, on November 3, 1970.

Among the gloomy deeds of the terrorism that characterized the year 1970, there were also disappearances as mysterious as those of the aviation technician Leonel Lagranje, and the Puerto Rican citizen Anarda Casanova; lost forever on the eleventh of November, when, on route to the Airport of the Americas, toward the Capital, their

---

1. Translated from Rafael Chaljub Mejía, *Cuesta Arriba: Memorias* (Santo Domingo: Editora Taller, 1997), 187–192. Reprinted by permission.

244

vehicle was hit by another that carried official plates and apparently had been chasing them.

Terrorism intensified even more and acquired new and crueler methods with the coming of 1971, and the appointment of General Enrique Pérez y Pérez as Chief of Police.

The declarations of the Police acquired thereafter a more injurious and more offensive, more insolent and more menacing tone than ever, as part of a psychological warfare strategy, which, at the same time, inculcated the troops with a clear predisposition for the use of weapons and for shooting to kill; and the hysteria, dominating the patrols sent out into the streets, provoked tragedies like the one that took place on the evening of January 12, 1971, when police units shot dead the five occupants of a vehicle that had departed from the environs of the Mercado Modelo.

In the wake of the crime, General Pérez y Pérez said the dead were five thieves who, after committing an armed robbery, opened fire on a patrol and the latter returned the fire in self-defense, with the end result of victims: on one side only, of course! This shameless lie immediately collapsed under its own weight when it was proven that among the murdered were several known crop merchants who, after traveling from their native Constanza and San José de Ocoa, and after leaving their vehicle, loaded with agricultural products, properly parked in the area of the Market, were on their way to the place where they would spend the night.

On the thirteenth, police troops searching the neighborhoods of the upper part of the Capital, detained, on the street Projecto 7 of the Ensanche Luperón, the leaders of our Party, Moisés Blanco Genao, Julio de Peña Valdez, Rafael Báez Pérez, Edgar Erickson, Onelio Espaillat, and Luis Sosa. What saved them from summary execution was the fact that the Police established the identity of the captured when they already were at the General Headquarters and had been seen alive by numerous eyewitnesses, including journalists.

The following day, the Police captured seven top leaders of the PCD,[2] who were at a reunion in the house of Asdrúbal Domínguez, the preeminent leader of that group, in the José Gabriel García street of the Ciudad Nueva sector. Besides Asdrúbal, José Israel Cuello, Mario Sánchez Córdova, Julián Peña, Alfredo Conde Sturla, Alfredo Pierret González and Osvaldo Domínguez were detained.

On these PCD leaders immediately fell the injurious accusation of forming an Association of Criminals, though four days later they were taken to the Attorney's Office, where their freedom was ordered and a court date was set for the following twenty-seventh, changing the original accusation to violation of laws 6, 70, and 71, which penalized communist ideas and practices.

On the other hand, the deeply rooted hatred that the authorities reserved for the MPD[3] was dumped on the leaders of our Party. The Chief of Police hurled at them the dirtiest and most unlikely criminal accusations. Among those accusations a plan to kidnap Father Agripino Núñez Collado, Rector of the UCAMAIMA;[4] and another high authority of the Catholic Church, as well as a North American diplomatic rep-

---

2. Partido Comunista Dominicano (Dominican Communist Party).
3. Movimiento Popular Dominicano (Dominican Popular Movement)
4. Universidad Católica Madre y Maestra (Mater of Magistas Catholic University)

resentative; without failing to mention in the litany of injurious accusations, those of criminal association, use of false documentation, bearing of arms of war, conspiring against the security of the State, and practicing terrorism.

Mr. Alberto Dacosta Gómez, the owner of the house where the leaders were captured was imprisoned together with the comrades.

Although in an interview with relatives of the detained comrades, the Attorney General of the Republic, Marino Ariza Hernández, guaranteed that they would not be mistreated, and that on the following day they could be visited at La Victoria,[5] this did not go beyond an empty promise from a bureaucrat without authority or capacity to back up his words with deeds. Because the Chief of Police had already ordered the six leaders of our Party, and Mr. Dacosta, buried in the isolation of the solitary cells of the Police Headquarters; where the government expected that the slow passing of the months would take its toll on the health and the life itself of the detainees, as well as on the tranquility of their relatives.

On Sunday, January 16th, the Chief of the Secret Service, Colonel Arseno Regalado, ordered units of that Department to enter [house] number 53 on the Padre Billini street, because in that place the overthrow of the government was being planned. In spite of the presence of the interim Papal Nuncio at the place, twenty-five youths were detained, and taken to the General Headquarters, although since the beginning it was established that they were members of a Catholic group called Legionnaires of Christ and Mary, who were practicing religious songs.

"We had information that they were armed and that they were MPD members", said Colonel Regalado, attempting to justify that abusive mass arrest.

Police operations again touched our Party, when on February 8th Carlos Tomás Fernández, Vladimiro Blanco, Gerardo Taveras were detained, as well as Nelson Enrique Figuereo, the journalist Aleyda Fernández, owner of the house where the arrests took place; and a sister of Aleyda's, called Eva, and Carmen Santos Peña, who worked in the house as a domestic servant.

In this same repressive plan and as part of the assault against our organization, Gladys Gutiérrez, Carmen Mazara, the latter the wife of Maximiliano Gómez, were arrested on March 10th, when they went to the Moscoso Puello Hospital to request the delivery of the body of Rafael Emilio Estrella (Cabeza), a member of the party, felled that day, in a confusing incident in which Judge Rafael Arias Mota was attacked by gunfire. Gladys, Carmen, as well as Nereyda Sánchez Reyes and Juana Mojica, arrested with them, were taken to the infernal prison of La Victoria.

In March 1971, a new form of massive terror began, when known antisocial elements with proper names such as Constantino Félix, Ignacio Arias Peña, Wilfredo Vargas Nova, Julio César Hernández, Salomón Soriano Martínez, Alejandro de León, among others; but using nicknames such as Carabina, Come Hierro, El Nacional, Patato, started to commit abuses throughout the neighborhoods of the city, alleging to be part of a so-called Front of the Democratic Anti-Communist and Reformist Youth; a Gang that acted as an instrument of the Police itself.

In one of their first actions, on the night of April 12, 1971, the criminals kidnapped young Santiago Manuel Hernández (Mangá), who was in the Padre Billini Hospital,

5. state penitentiary

after receiving a bullet wound caused by police agents who chased him to the patio of his mother's house, located in the San Miguel neighborhood. With the complicit passivity of the patient's police guard, the assassins kidnapped Mangá, who, still wearing his hospital pajamas, was found the following day, shot to death, in Punta Pescadora, on the outskirts of San Pedro de Macorís.

From the beginning, Balaguer took care to define what would be the complicit tolerance of himself and his government, faced by the crimes and abuses of *La Banda*.[6] That way, facing this brutal assassination of someone practically a boy, the President said that the horrendous death of Mangá was the product of rivalries between leftist groups and that he totally discarded the claim that the Police could commit such a crime.

On April 20th, Alejandro Félix Liriano (Nariz), one of the leaders of La Banda, sought asylum in the Mexican Embassy, with four of his crime companions. Nariz confessed that he was repentant, that he feared for his life, and offered a long list of telephone numbers, contact locations, names of officers, license plates of vehicles, and other data proving that the leaders of La Banda were really in the Police, that its direct ringleader was one of the trusted men of Pérez y Pérez, Lieutenant Oscar Núñez Peña, whom Nariz denounced as the principal author of the kidnapping and eventual assassination of Mangá.

The chief of police insisted that the institution under his orders had nothing to do with the criminals, in spite of the fact that groups of these individuals were seen entering and leaving the General Headquarters on a daily basis, meeting with officers of the Secret Service and on occasions with uniformed officers, acting with police neighborhood patrols, detaining persons, and taking them to police stations.

On May 12, Balaguer was again questioned by the press about the abuses of La Banda, and as a convincing example of the quality of the man who exercised power during those ominous times, here is his cynical response word-for-word:

"What Banda are you talking about?" he asked, in a tone feigning a bad temper; "no one has seen it; this is becoming something like a ghost, like the time when it was said that in the neighborhood of Gazcue a tiger was wandering, but no one saw it. Tell me which are the crimes committed by this said Banda, I do not know which are the abuses and the anguish that the Banda has sown in the country."

Under the stimulus such a presidential attitude gives, the terrorists continued scourging our nation, sowing mourning in the capital, extending their bloody acts to towns in the interior; and, when it was a matter of persecuting and killing members of our Party, even reaching peaceful regions of the cordillera, such as Las Auyamas in Constanza, where on the night of May 6, 1971, the anonymous claw of terror cut short the life of Comrade Máximo Castro, a young worker from La Vega, a professional cadre of our party.

The shadow of tragedy darkened the country, and in the midst of this tragic situation, when a strong and active revolutionary party was needed the most, our Party suffered increasingly severe blows and losses so costly, that it was impossible to even think about replacing them in a short time.

One of the dead was our Secretary General, Maximiliano Gómez (El Moreno).

6. "The Gang," paramilitary group mentioned above.

Threats from the Right

During his twelve-year rule, Balaguer faced not only the revolutionary left, but also threats from right-wing military extremists with personal ambitions. Such was the case of former general Elías Wessin y Wessin. After the 1965 civil war, Wessin y Wessin was sent overseas for a few years. He later returned to participate in the 1970 elections as the presidential candidate of his own party, the Partido Quisqueyano Democrático (Dominican Party of Quisqueya, or PQD). Being soundly defeated by Balaguer in the elections, which were marred by the boycott of most of the opposition's parties, Wessin y Wessin alleged fraud and started conspiring against the government. Intense speculation reigned during the next few months, until the evening of June 30, 1971, when Balaguer appeared on television surrounded by his top military officers and with Wessin y Wessin sitting by his side. Balaguer made the surprising announcement that a plot led by Wessin y Wessin, and with the complicity of active military personnel, had been foiled and the conspirators arrested. Balaguer then went on to play a taped message which Wessin y Wessin had intended to broadcast upon assuming power. With that undeniable evidence in hand, Balaguer confronted Wessin y Wessin, who remained silent. Balaguer then proceeded to hand Wessin y Wessin over to his military commanders, who were entrusted with deciding the latter's fate. Wessin y Wessin was placed under house arrest and exiled to Spain a few days later.

In a theatrical, yet masterful move, Balaguer dealt with the extreme right by, first, presenting Wessin y Wessin as an impenitent conspirator and a threat to peace and order, and then by handing over the problem of what to do with him to his former comrades-in-arms, who now rushed to get rid of Wessin y Wessin and make a public showing of support for Balaguer. After the Wessin y Wessin fiasco, the Dominican armed forces stood solidly behind Balaguer, who deftly manipulated and divided, but also pampered, them. The day after Wessin y Wessin's arrest, the armed forces' leadership submitted a memorandum to Balaguer recommending Wessin y Wessin's deportation and pledging their unconditional support to his administration. It is reproduced below.

MEMORANDUM OF THE DOMINICAN
ARMED FORCES TO BALAGUER[7]

Dr. Joaquín Balaguer
President of the Dominican Republic

1. The High Command of the Armed Forces and the National Police very respectfully address Your Excellency to let you know that, aware of the fact that it has been established conclusively that retired National Army Brigadier General Elías Wessin y Wessin has devoted himself to conspiratorial activities, geared toward overthrowing the legally constituted regime, by trying to gain adepts for such a nefarious goal within the ranks of our armed forces and the National Police, is endangering our democratic institutions, the tranquility of the Dominican family, and the destiny of the Fatherland, which today proceeds through safe routes toward economic, political, and social rehabilitation.

2. That such behavior, which places him on the margins of the dispositions of our Penal Code that sanctions crimes against the internal security of the State, makes him unworthy of continuing to reside in the national territory, since his presence in it disturbs order and social peace.

3. By virtue of that, the said High Command, with the same respect, allow ourselves to recommend to Your Excellency, taking into account humanitarian reasons, that, under the prerogatives conferred to you by the Constitution and the law, retired National Army Brigadier General Elías Wessin y Wessin be deported from the country, even though the acts committed by him make him liable to prosecution by repressive justice.

4. This is a propitious opportunity to ratify to the Honorable President of the Republic, Commander in Chief of the Armed Forces and the National Police, the unconditional loyalty of uniformed men to him and to the government that he presides with such a sense of Dominicanness.

Major General Joaquín Abraham Méndez Lara, Secretary of State for the Armed Forces; Major General Enrique Pérez y Pérez, Chief of the National Police; Brigadier General Juan René Beauchamps Javier, Secretary of State for Interior and Police; Brigadier General Braulio Alvarez Sánchez, Commodore Francisco A. Amiama Castillo, General Juan de los Santos Céspedes, Deputy Secretaries for the Armed Forces; General Rafael Adriano Valdez Hilario, Chief of Staff of the Army; General Salvador Lluberes Montás, Chief of Staff of the Air Force; Commodore Ramón Emilio Jiménez, Jr., Chief of Staff of the Navy; General Juan E. Pérez Guillén, Supervisor of the Armed Forces; General Anselmo Pilarte, Chief of the Military Aides-de-Camp of the President of the Republic; Commodore Francisco Javier Rivera Caminero, Naval Advisor to the President of the Republic; Brigadier General Neit Rafael Nivar Seijas, Commander of the First Brigade of the Army; Brigadier General Elio Osiris Perdomo, Commander of the Second Brigade of the Army; Colonel Francisco Medina Sánchez, Commander of the Third Brigade of the Army; Colonel Rafael de Jesús Checo, Deputy Chief of Staff of the Army; Captain Manuel A. Logroño Contín, Deputy Chief of Staff of the Navy; Marco Antonio Jorge Moreno, Commander of the Support Command of the Combat Service of the Army;

7. Translated from *El Caribe* newspaper (Santo Domingo), July 2, 1971.

Colonel Robinson Brea Garó, Deputy Chief of the National Police; Colonel Manuel A. Cuervo Gómez, Commander of the Combat Support Command and the Artillery Battalion of the Army; Pilot Colonel Antonio Alvarez Albizu, Aviation Advisor to the President of the Republic

Caamaño Returns

On February 2, 1973, years of wild speculation came to an end. Since his disappearance in 1967, it had been rumored that Colonel Francisco A. Caamaño Deñó, the Constitutionalist hero of the 1965 civil war, had been secretly training in Cuba for an invasion of the Dominican Republic. On that day, Caamaño landed in a small boat with eight men. They made it to the heights of the central cordillera, from where they were unable to wage an effective campaign against Balaguer's government. Caamaño's small guerrilla unit was quickly discovered and the Dominican armed forces were ordered to crush it before it could develop into a bigger threat. The government also immediately unleashed a wave of arrests, rounding up dozens of leftists and their potential supporters, while others were forced underground. As a result, Caamaño's group was effectively isolated and cut off from any sources of support in the cities. There were a few skirmishes between the guerrillas and the Dominican military, ultimately leading to Caamaño's death on February 16, 1973, and the destruction of the group. Only two of the guerrillas survived: one was captured and the other made it into a foreign embassy, where he obtained political asylum.

The death of Caamaño was the end of the left's military options. Unlike Cuba years before, a rural guerrilla insurgency was not feasible in the Dominican Republic of the 1970s. First, the country did not offer the geographical conditions needed for a prolonged guerrilla struggle. Second, the Dominican left had been dismembered after years of state-led repression. Third, the democratic political parties were in disarray. And fourth, Balaguer, thanks to his impeccable anti-communist credentials, enjoyed the full support of the Dominican military and the U.S. government. The following selection is from Hamlet Hermann, one of the surviving participants in Caamaño's group. He analyzes the fate of the expedition and ponders its influence on the course of events in the Dominican Republic.

FROM HAMLET HERMANN'S MEMOIRS[8]

The events at Playa Caracoles[9] left a deep impression on participants and spectators. We should take advantage of the great value of that which, in the end, was considered a military defeat. The responsibility we now assume is one of transforming
the military action into political action so that whatever success there was can be
maximized. There is still a long way to go on the road toward the definitive emancipation of the Dominican people and these lessons can be useful to us.

The armed episode at Playa Caracoles ended in a military victory for Balaguer's
government. A very important circumstantial success for the regime then because it
eliminated a great political reserve of the Dominican people: Colonel Francisco
Caamaño Deñó. After that, the Dominican people were left without a charismatic figure of moral integrity and with the qualifications to achieve revolutionary unity.
Since his death, North American imperialists and the reformist governing circles bask
in their transitory victory until the Dominican people forge the necessary leadership
and organization for their emancipation.

The military outcome of Playa Caracoles should be analyzed in light of our own
historical experiences in a retrospective manner. As in 1973, in April of 1965 we
Dominicans were defeated by the massive North American invasion. Similarly, the
insurgent groups of the "Fourteenth of June" Political Organization were defeated in
1963. A similar thing happened in the memorable upsets of Constanza, Maimón, and
Estero Hondo in 1959 and successively up to the origins of the Dominican nationality where, apparently, the people have been losing every single battle to acquire
power. All these events represented victories for the leaders in power at the time but,
at the same time, they were landmarks that registered the deterioration of each one of
the regimes which, in the end, were displaced from power.

Our guerilla uprising could not link itself sufficiently with the development of the
country's social struggles, either due to the intense military opposition, or because
revolutionary armed struggle did not develop as the direct extension of the national
political struggle. Our attempt in 1973 was an effort made "from the outside" when
the situation required a movement "from within." But, given the inaction and conformity of some of the political leadership within the country, we considered that our
action could not be postponed any further, even at the risk of our own lives. For years,
the Balaguer regime used, in an implacable way, a preventive war against the patriots and revolutionaries. He forced many into exile, into corrupting themselves, or
into becoming victims of the selective or indiscriminate repression being applied.

The Caamaño option in 1973, although complex, had no revolutionary alternative.
He ignored the siren songs of those who sought to seduce him to turn him into a pro-
pagandistic instrument and he ignored those who, with neither moral nor political
experience, wanted to assume positions for which they would never be qualified.
Those "allies" of Caamaño always politically underestimated him and believed they
could fool him one more time with offers that would mean a great deal of propagan-
distic publicity, but did not contain solutions for the Dominican people. So we have

---

8. Translated from Hamlet Hermann, *Caracoles: La guerrilla de Caamaño*, 3rd ed. (Santo
Domingo: Editora Tele-3, 1993), 241–247. Reprinted by permission.
9. Caracoles Beach, the landing place of the insurgents

the cruel paradox that both Caamaño's "friends" as well as his enemies wanted him to stay out of the country; so that his personality and actions would not disturb the tranquility they enjoyed as a result of the suffering of the Dominican people.

Traditionally, the Dominican left, and our group in particular as part of it, had been organizing a struggle of cadres without applying cadre politics. We have been too much of a vanguard for the small rear guard that we have. The secret to the lack of continuity in our struggle lies in that we have not given enough attention to the formation of revolutionary cadres, an indispensable instrument for the reproduction of a militancy. We did not have the patience and capacity sufficient enough to carry out such a difficult and complex job. We were too strategic and not very tactical, when the political situation demanded the opposite. We lacked originality in the interpretation of the national issues, and guided ourselves by continental historical generalities.

We understand now that we never achieved the level of an "organization." We identified ourselves so much with our leader, Colonel Caamaño, that his death led to the practical disappearance of the group. For various reasons, the men linked to us, started to walk away from politics or began looking for excuses to justify their timid behavior in 1973. We were not able to forge a veritable organization, one that replenishes its forces, one that survives the greatest blows. More than an error on our part, it is a historical "disgrace" Latin America has been enduring since the sixties.

The development of a revolutionary war does not depend, on most occasions, on vanguard organizations. It is the dominant violence that starts eliminating alternatives until there is no other option but insurrection. In Caamaño there was no spontaneous enthusiasm about organizing the repatriation; that grave decision was seriously considered, without being frivolous, and without ignoring the suffering of the Dominican people at the time.

Caamaño would have liked to have North American imperialism and Balaguer as his only enemies, but it could not be like that. Since 1966, he had encountered enemies within the leadership of a complacent petty bourgeoisie that became accustomed to and was satisfied with the scarce liberties that Balaguer offered. One of our errors, maybe the biggest one, was to trust in that certain political leaders would react favorably to our actions and would be willing to make small sacrifices to their personal positions. It did not occur to us that they would refuse to make a small sacrifice, much less oppose us causing disarray and confusion. We had to live through Playa Caracoles to realize we cannot choose our enemies. We were unable to see from a distance that Caamaño's 1965 allies had accommodated, enjoying it, to the equilibrium of forces violently established by Balaguer and they did not want it to be altered. They did not want to disturb that tranquility, a very exclusive one I should say, and rather fortified the equilibrium of forces that, obviously, hurt the Dominican people.

Our attempt to modify the terms of that political equilibrium through revolutionary violence would be qualified with the strongest political epithets. They ignored, deliberately, that Caamaño tried to work with them on several occasions and he was always arrogantly ignored. It was hidden from the Dominican people that the attitude of refusal toward Caamaño and the passivity vis-à-vis the regime were the main complicity elements that allowed the North American invaders to place and sustain Balaguer in power when patriotism was at its height in the nation. If Caamaño had to act on his own account and risk in 1973 with a reduced number of men it was because, since 1966, the passive and complacent attitude of some political leaders allowed for the recovery of the repressive apparatus that had been destroyed by the Dominican people in the 1965 battles.

Only now has it become evident that the leadership of the liberal petty bourgeoisie and some pseudo-revolutionaries are not willing to participate in a truly liberating national revolution. Though they pride themselves on being democrats, they are anti-communists and in these times that only means to comply with the most retrograde policies of the U.S. political circles. For those, Caamaño was just a very convenient auxiliary mechanism to feign patriotism and independence when negotiating some political patronage. It was no wonder that those revolutionary spectators were so unmerciful regarding our actions at Playa Caracoles. The farther they were from the main stage of the struggle, the cruder were their remarks.

For many it is now evident that the democratic-bourgeois "revolution" is not feasible in the Dominican Republic because it is not part of the historical order of the day. Humanity has advanced too much and has recognized its main enemies to settle for halfway solutions. Moreover, North American imperialism, in its obvious decline, will not allow among its liberal allies attitudes that weaken the ties of dependency. From there the only possible alternative for the future is the transformation of our current society through a new economic order in which each citizen is rewarded according to his work: socialism.

While the guerilla uprising lasted, we verified an important thing. We could sense the enormous honest potential that exists in the lower ranks of the armed forces. The schemes that identify all military men as politically homogeneous and unconditional servants of the powerful sectors are somewhat deceiving. Military and civilians all have, definitively, a common enemy; it is just a matter of time for the necessary consciousness to develop in them and we can join forces against the foreign power on which we depend. In the last twenty years, U.S. strategy has considered the military as the only trustworthy force capable of maintaining internal stability. This strategy has been designed, exclusively, to guarantee the uninterrupted stability of U.S. investments, a steady supply of raw materials, cheap labor, and access to military markets, all of which are essential to the survival of the U.S. system at the expense of our misery and backwardness. We need to stop the groups in power, U.S. and Dominican, from widening the breach they have created to isolate the military from their civilian brothers. We must fight to prevent the Dominican military from being involved in other repressive activities against the Dominican people, actions that have only contributed to create differences among Dominicans for the benefit of the Americans.

It is not by serving as a parapet for dictatorships and tyrannies that a nation is made; it is not by impeding the exercise of civil liberties that the people are being served; it is not by supporting the surrender of natural resources how sovereignty is being defended. To die little by little is an unacceptable situation and the Dominican people will continue to struggle until they are liberated from misery and backwardness.

One aspect that greatly hurt our action was the felony and disloyalty of some individuals trusted by Colonel Caamaño. Elements, who to his face would appear to be, either patriots, or stern and incorruptible revolutionaries, began transforming in the proximity of the enemy until they became informants. Sent to establish the basis for the linkages of the guerilla group with its logical rear guard, they became paralyzed with fear upon seeing, just seeing closely, the repressive mechanisms of the regime. Fear transformed into panic and, without any pressures, they voluntarily denounced Colonel Caamaño and all the mechanisms that served as support for the start and development of the struggle. From intransigent militants they turned into pacifist sheep, finding themselves after having deceived themselves for so long. They found again their ideological and political truth, finding that which deep inside they had never ceased to be. It will always be difficult to measure the extent of their betrayal, to quantify the amount of anonymous lives lost to the enemy, just because of the cowardice of men with no morals.

Nevertheless, the immediate results of Playa Caracoles, its effects, have been gradually and increasingly leaving their mark on the Dominican political situation. It was during that February 1973, when the Balaguer regime lost the initiative in its political action for the first time. It was able to recover it later, but already in a situation of ever-increasing deterioration, until its political-military structure cracked, losing the fundamental support of its U.S. sponsors. Playa Caracoles marked the transition point toward the demise of Balaguer's dictatorship which culminated in a change of government.

How many of the events after February 1973 were the result of Playa Caracoles? This is impossible to quantify just as it is impossible to evaluate the influence of other kinds of political activities. Beyond discussion is the fact that the Dominican people, who are overall free and interested detractors, remember Caamaño, Playa Caracoles, and its participants with love, respect, and admiration because they were able to represent then the hopes and needs of a people. Our people, just and intelligent, have included Playa Caracoles among their heroic feats due to Colonel Caamaño's great personality, for the inequality of that struggle, for the rebellious spirit it represented, and for the courage it demonstrated. The time that has elapsed has shown us that the Dominican people feel represented by Caamaño, Lalane, Galán, Pérez Vargas, Holguín, and Payero, not by the detractors and enemies of then or now.

The more time passes, the greater figures those martyrs will become, just as it will decline in the eyes of the people the images of those who betrayed or did not assume at the precise moment the responsibilities that corresponded to them and did not fulfill the moral promises they had made . . . on the Duarte Bridge, on the fifteenth and sixteenth of June, on the northern part, in the trench of Santa Bárbara, on the Pasteur . . . in 1965.

The moment when Dominican and Latin American patriots and revolutionaries will have again the need to confront events, to harmonize methods, to support each other, to achieve the necessary unity, is rapidly approaching. I hope this book will help so that, in spite of how intense the struggle promises to be, the final decision will be quickly favorable to the interest of the peoples.

THERE WILL BE A NATION

The Radicalization of Juan Bosch

The 1966 elections left Juan Bosch bitterly disappointed. He was over-thrown by the Dominican military in 1963 and was prevented from returning to the presidency by the government of the world's greatest democracy. Moreover, later he had to resign the presidency and agree to participate in a new election in which his followers were intimidated and repressed by the Dominican military. After his defeat in 1966, Bosch left for exile in Spain, only to return a few years later in time for the 1970 elections. However, renewed government persecution forced his party, the PRD, to withdraw from the race. His prolonged absence and the outcome of the 1970 elections further distanced Bosch from his party. While in exile, he also began embracing Marxism—though not Leninism—and his political thought moved farther to the left during the late 1960s and early 1970s. The suppression of Caamaño's guerrilla group brought about bitter recriminations within the PRD due to its lack of action in support of the expedition. Finally, Bosch held a dispute with other PRD leaders, including José F. Peña Gómez, regarding electoral strategy. Bosch believed it made no sense to participate in elections organized by Bala-guer, while others believed that the PRD could defeat Balaguer at his own game. Bosch's belief in electoral democracy had waned to the point that he called elections under Balaguer "an electoral slaughterhouse." In 1973, Bosch left the PRD, and with a group of faithful followers, found-ed the Partido de la Liberación Dominicana (Dominican Liberation Party, or PLD), a small, elitist, leftist party based on the principles of national liberation that coalesced around Bosch's political thought and his charis-matic figure.

One of the best examples of Bosch's radicalization is "Dictatorship with Popular Support," an essay first published in 1969. After studying Marxism for years, and carefully examining the socioeconomic situation of the Dominican Republic, Bosch concluded that the Dominican people were not ready for democracy. Democracy could certainly flourish in more advanced countries, but not in countries like the Dominican Repub-lic, so Bosch called for an enlightened one-man rule that he called "dic-tatorship with popular support," since it would be accountable to the peo-ple and rule in their best interest. A selection from this work is presented below.

255

FROM BOSCH'S ESSAY
"DICTATORSHIP WITH POPULAR SUPPORT"[10]

What will Dictatorship with Popular Support Be?
Dictatorship with Popular Support will be a new type of state that will dedicate itself to:
1. the guarantee of work, health, and education to all those who currently do not have these attributes;
2. the absolute guarantee of all the fundamental human rights; the suppression of hunger and its dreadful social consequences; of the exploitation of some men for the benefit of others who control the means of production; of governmental, police, or any other kind of terror;
3. the guarantee of the true equality of all citizens, not only in the eyes of the laws of the state, but also in the eyes of those which are not written and still manage to keep human beings divided because of race, religion, social status, culture, and gender, and those which push them to fight each other to seize, or to defend from seizure, food, positions and rights.

Dictatorship with Popular Support will not be the so-called representative democracy, the political system of bourgeois society, which has been failing in Latin America for over one and a half centuries. It will not be it, because representative democracy, in the best of cases, cannot guarantee work, health, and education for everybody; it cannot guarantee the fundamental rights of human beings and it cannot guarantee true equality, given the fact that it is a fundamentally unjust social and political system, that it is organized and sustained by the principle that there are men with the right to exploit others and there are those with the duty of letting themselves be exploited.

In order to guarantee not only respect of freedoms of all, but also the rights of each one and those of each class or social sector to enjoy, under conditions of equality with everyone else, the benefits that society may provide, in the government of Dictatorship with Popular Support there will be representation, through people chosen freely by them, of all the organizations of the people, political, economic, cultural, scientific, religious, unions, sports groups, the army, the police, public employees, and any other organization of any kind. The representatives of these organizations will work at the level of all State institutions, from villages or rural sections, urban neighborhoods, provinces or states, up to the national government, and in none of those levels will measures be carried out without being freely approved by the majority of those representatives.

In order to establish a state that is capable of achieving these goals, Dictatorship with Popular Support will start out by affirming the full independence of the nation, and therefore will take the appropriate measures to cut all foreign influence exercised over institutions, enterprises or individuals, regardless of where it comes from or what its ideology is.

For the purpose of dismantling the oligarchic front, the Dictatorship with Popular

10. Translated from Juan Bosch, *Dictadura con repaldo popular*, 4th ed. (Santo Domingo: Editora Alfa y Omega, 1991), 61–70. Reprinted by permission.

Support will first proceed to nationalize enterprises that belong to foreigners, or the share that foreign companies might have in national enterprises, and will pay them with a percentage of the benefits from these companies or share of these companies; but it will not nationalize personal dwellings or farms or other small establishments that belong to foreigners nor will it allow foreigners to be persecuted just for being such; it will also proceed to nationalize national latifundia, and will adequately compensate those property owners who have fought for the establishment of the new regime. Latifundia will be declared social property and shall be given to the peasants so that they can work them under the cooperative system; it will also proceed to nationalize the banking sector, which will continue to be administered by those working in it, but it will be declared a social property; and it will proceed to nationalize export-import commerce, whose administration will remain in the hands of the employees and operatives who work there at the moment when the new political system is implemented, but under the supervision of the State, and with its participation in the benefits. In the case of the banking sector, of export commerce and of other enterprises, the national or foreign owners who struggled for the establishment of the Dictatorship with Popular Support will be adequately compensated.

Dictatorship with Popular Support will not be an anti-bourgeois regime, and therefore it will only be able to nationalize the enterprises of those national bourgeois [elements] who oppose its establishment or after its establishment try to overthrow it; but neither will it establish a bourgeois society, and for that reason precautions will be taken to prevent bourgeois enterprises from expanding in number or in political and social power. No one will have his capital confiscated, but investment will be regulated by law.

All owners of bourgeois enterprises, whether rural or urban, agricultural, ranching, industrial, or commercial—with the exception of import and export—will be able to remain in charge of them, in association with their workers and the state, without fear of being economically, politically, or socially persecuted, and their organizations will have representation before the state just as any other organization.

The agricultural or urban properties of the petty bourgeoisie will be scrupulously respected as long as their benefits are not based on the exploitation of the work of others. Peasants who own small and mid-size properties will receive all the benefits that peasant cooperatives can provide, but only in the case in which they want to voluntarily associate themselves to the cooperatives, since the law will not be able to force anyone to participate in the peasant or urban cooperatives if they do not want to do it. Every company founded by the state will be social property, administered by those who work in it.

Dictatorship with Popular Support will maintain in their positions those public employees who do not conspire or act against it, and in the case of the latter, as in all those of this sort in which accusations of conspiracy or acts against the new regime are presented, they will have to be proven in a public trial, because all citizens should live without fear of being unjustly persecuted.

Dictatorship with Popular Support will proceed to guarantee every child and youngster a totally free education, including books, school supplies, transportation, medical attention, and medicines and nutrition, and it will organize all types of schools for adults who want to learn any trade or career, or for those who want to expand their knowledge.

Dictatorship with Popular Support will establish as fundamental rights, that of peasants to have land, that of all men and women to work, that of all children and youngsters to education, that of all the people to health, to equality, and to the integral respect of their freedom, their dignity and the attributes of the human personality of each citizen.

The leadership of the armed forces and the police corps will be entrusted to those of their members, whether they are officers, sergeants, corporals, or privates, who have shown that they defend and enforce respect for the principles of the Dictatorship with Popular Support.

No person shall be persecuted in any form for having belonged to the oligarchic fronts, unless they act against the Dictatorship with Popular Support during the time of the rise to power of the new regime or after its establishment.

The laws that will regulate the functioning of the Dictatorship with Popular Support will be elaborated by the people, through all of their organizations, by decisions made freely and democratically.

On Whom Should We Rely?

Dictatorship with Popular Support is a regime that will benefit almost the entire population, but not everyone will fight for it. There will be some members of the oligarchy who will do it, too, because in all social classes there are men and women willing to sacrifice their privileges for the greater good, but it must be expected that the oligarchy and the bourgeoisie will fight the idea of the Dictatorship with Popular Support; the former, because it is an anti-oligarchic revolution, and the latter, because U.S. propaganda has convinced them that any change that occurs in our countries will be detrimental to them.

It goes without saying that among the petty bourgeoisie, a part of the upper sector will oppose the Dictatorship with Popular Support with more vigor than even the bourgeoisie, because their inclination to insert themselves into the world of the oligarchy will take them down this path. But the same cannot be said for the mid-petty bourgeoisie; in that stratum the idea of the Dictatorship with Popular Support will find numerous defenders and some activists, especially among intellectuals, artists, and professionals.

The number of defenders and activists will be even greater among the lower-level petty bourgeoisie, particularly those who verge on the proletariat, where we find those who can be designated as the upper semi-proletariat, since there is another semi-proletariat, which we may call lower, and that is situated between the workers and the unemployed. The wing of the lower petty bourgeoisie that has renounced the dream of making it to the mid and upper, who has become disillusioned with so-called representative democracy, will be supportive of the Dictatorship with Popular Support.

In the mid as well as in the lower petty bourgeoisie, we will also find irreconcilable enemies of Dictatorship with Popular Support, and probably in greater number, relatively, than in the upper. One must keep in mind that, as said before, the petty bourgeoisie wants reforms that facilitate its movement into bourgeois society, and that there is in it a reactionary part which plans, fights, works, and conspires in favor of the oligarchic fronts because the oligarchies are at the same time the model that attracts it and the business sector where it can obtain power and money with the greatest ease and speed; one must also keep in mind what was said regarding a part of the lower petty bourgeoisie that in order to avoid descending to the level of the proletariat and even that of the unemployed or underemployed [its members] are willing to commit all sorts of immoral deeds, to become spies and paid assassins. Therefore, the activists of the Dictatorship with Popular Support who proceed from the petty bourgeoisie, who are not known as honest revolutionaries, have to be submitted to a methodic process of revolutionary education, free from prejudices, but geared to making each one of them into men and women conscious of their class vices and how to get rid of them to serve the people better. Anyway, in the Dominican Republic, which is the Latin American country for which this work is destined, we know in general terms all those who are willing and determined to carry out revolutionary changes, and the task of educating them to overcome their class vices will not be a difficult one; it may be more difficult in other countries with a larger population that is not going through a process of agitation as the Dominicans have gone through since 1961.

The working class will benefit as a whole from Dictatorship with Popular Support because it will become associated with private enterprises, which will give it security. It is likely that among the workers there will be several, and maybe many, who remain indifferent at the time of fighting to the implementation of Dictatorship with Popular Support, considering that in countries where unemployment is so high, those who receive a salary and have the advantage of social security are in certain ways privileged, but there probably will be few who will oppose it; among these one shall find without any doubt the leaders at the service of imperialism-pentagonism, such as salaried workers of the attachés, workers in the U.S. embassies, and agents of the American Federation of Labor-CIO.

Dictatorship with Popular Support will find ardent supporters among the semi-employed or underemployed of the lower sector, that is, those who come from the unemployed or street peddlers and are situated between these and the workers. Even though it may seem strange, in those two social sectors a petty bourgeoisie develops, which is understandable because the majority cannot even aspire to a factory job, since Latin American societies do not have the capacity to provide jobs for all those who need to work; and in this situation, members of those sectors seek their livelihood in personal activities, like street vending and cheap artisan work. The most logical thing is that among the lower petty bourgeoisie that comes out from the depths of the most oppressed groups in our countries, there are some who prosper and others who do not prosper; the former will feel naturally inclined toward the oligarchical fronts, and also naturally should become active enemies of the Dictatorship with Popular Support, so that it would be useless to find supporters among them; but the latter, who are the majority, will steadfastly support it.

All landless peasants, and those who have so little land that it is not enough to support their families at a decent level, as well as the rural workers who only find work during harvest time, and even then are poorly paid, will become supporters of the Dictatorship with Popular Support, since it will provide the former with lands to work in cooperatives, it will offer the next group the help of the cooperatives and good, fixed, and beneficial prices, and permanent jobs for the latter.

No social class or class sector will support the Dictatorship with Popular Support with as much enthusiasm as the unemployed, the ones without jobs or the urban street peddlers. In Latin American countries, these are truly the most exploited of the exploited. They are not even a cheap labor pool, since under the current economic, social, and political system, they do not have, nor will they ever have, any hope of improving their lot; they will never be able to live with decency or security. There will never be enough industries to provide them with jobs, nor sufficient land for them to produce, nor sufficient schools and hospitals for them and their children, unless the current system is totally transformed, just as the Dictatorship with Popular Support will do. To put these men and women, who are and represent more than one hundred million human beings in Latin America, to produce implies doubling in a short time the production of all or almost all basic consumer goods. This is absolutely impossible to achieve now, when five out of one hundred people take for themselves 30 pesos out of each 100 pesos that are produced, but this will not be so when the Dictatorship with Popular Support implements a system where out of each 100 pesos produced everybody will benefit equally.

Finally, Dictatorship with Popular Support will find ardent supporters among the youth sectors of the population that range from the unemployed or street peddlers up to the upper lower bourgeoisie, students in particular. In the portion of youths who come from the petty bourgeoisie, we will have to foresee that besides the class vices there will be deviations toward adventurism and opportunism, but we must also keep in mind that there is in it plenty of leadership material and decisiveness for the struggle.

The struggle that our peoples will have to carry out in order to radically, really and truly change Latin American structures will be long and hard, and for that reason it would be foolish to reject any force that contributes or might contribute to the great task. In fact, in the mammoth task that awaits us, anyone who adds an enemy to the cause of the Dictatorship with Popular Support will be acting as a traitor. But also acting as a traitor will be he who takes to the struggle for the Dictatorship with Popular Support the vices and deviations that are part of the habits of certain classes and social sectors, and those leaders who ignore the manifestations of those vices and those deviations without trying to amend them will act with results as harmful as treason.

General Principles and Organization

The implementation of Dictatorship with Popular Support must be the result of methodical work, which excludes all possibility of adventurous, reckless, and precipitous actions, and guarantees the participation of the people in all the policies implemented during the process of consciousness raising, of organization, and of the conquest of power.

Any activity that takes place without consultation of the people, behind their backs, and without taking them into consideration over all other things, is profoundly reactionary. When at the time of decision making the leaders act in the belief that the people desire what they desire, an act of supplanting the masses for the leaders takes place, and this means that this group of leaders considers itself superior to the people, more intelligent or more competent than the people. The substitution of the people for those who lead them or aspire to lead them always results in the desertion of the masses, since they know better than anyone else what it is they want and need, and they end up turning their backs on those who consider themselves as their representatives without respecting their freedom of speech, without having gained with a genuinely popular conduct the right to represent them. In order to represent the masses one must sincerely and honestly cohabit with them, one must know their problems, their concerns, and their ideas.

Dictatorship with Popular Support will only be able to achieve power when it counts on the support of the masses, and that will take place when the people have acquired trust and faith in the idea, in the organization and in the men entrusted with implementing the Dictatorship with Popular Support, to the extent that they will identify that idea, those men and their organization with their need of freedom and justice, of respect and well-being. Dictatorship with Popular Support must thus become eminently popular before, during, and after assuming power, and its sole source of power must be the people's will.

In order to become the depositories of the people's faith and their leaders, the supporters of Dictatorship with Popular Support must organize themselves into a front to work methodically, with discipline and, at the same time, with creative freedom. The tasks of developing the thesis of the Dictatorship with Popular Support, as well as of elaborating the strategy, the tactic and the programs that shall be applied on each occasion, shall be the product of the teamwork of all the forces assembled by that front.

The presence in the Dictatorship with Popular Support Front of all anti-oligarchic forces, that is, anti-imperial and anti-pentagon forces, each one enjoying its independence but all united for a common goal, will guarantee that through mutual ideological, strategic, and tactical vigilance the objective of radically transforming the social structures of our countries in order to build with them the home of liberty and the reign of justice will be kept perennially alive and alert.

Paris, May 6, 1969

The 1978 Elections

While Bosch and his party refrained from campaigning, the PRD sought to defeat Balaguer at the polls. Peña Gómez and the PRD leadership decided to form a broad-based opposition against Balaguer in 1974. Yet once again they had to abstain from participating due to government repression. By 1978, however, the situation had changed. Balaguer was hell-bent on seeking a fourth term, a move that by now most political forces, and even some within his party, opposed. Balaguer was no longer as popular as in the early 1970s. Years of repression and governmental corruption had tarnished his image, while his "economic miracle" had come to a screeching halt by the mid-1970s. The oil crisis, as well as falling sugar prices, had caused a recession in the Dominican economy, and the growing Dominican middle classes no longer viewed Balaguer as their best option. Even the international context had changed. The foreign policy of the newly elected U.S. president, Jimmy Carter, was based on respect for human rights. For Carter, the Dominican Republic, just as it had been a showcase for democracy in the 1960s, was now to be a showcase for clean elections in the late 1970s. Carter publicly urged and challenged Balaguer to organize clean, transparent elections, free from political intimidation.

On May 16, 1978, elections were held in which the PRD participated with S. Antonio Guzmán, a self-made, wealthy businessman, as its presidential candidate. Early results showed a strong lead for Guzmán. In the early hours of May 17th, the Dominican military burst into the offices of the Junta Central Electoral (Central Electoral Board, or JCE) and stopped the vote counting. For the next thirty-six hours there was no official response from Balaguer, who either did not approve of the move or was considering his options. Under intense pressure from the Carter administration and other friendly nations, Balaguer finally ordered the resumption of the process. The final results confirmed Guzmán's decisive victory. However, Balaguer exacted a heavy price for his concession: four provinces that had originally been won by the PRD were turned over to his party, thus giving him control over the Senate, the body that confirms judiciary nominees. The JCE argued technicalities in the counting of votes in the rendering of a questionable judgment known as the "historical decision." Balaguer thus managed to retain an important quota of power—even though he lost the presidency—and he now forced the PRD to negotiate with him on important issues such as the passing of new laws and the approval of the country's annual budget. The conclusion of the JCE's decision is reproduced below.

[THE JCE] DECIDES[11]

First: To declare as regular and valid in their form the appeals submitted by the Reformist Party and to reject those same appeals regarding the decisions of the Electoral Boards of Azua, Baní, Barahona, Bisonó, Castañuelas, Castillo, Comen-

---

11. Translated from Miguel Guerrero, *Al borde del caos: Historia oculta de la crisis electoral de 1978* (Santo Domingo: Editora Corripio, 1999), 363–365.

dador, Cotuí, Dajabón, Distrito Nacional, Duvergé, El Cercado, El Llano, Esperanza, Fantino, Gaspar Hernández, Guayubín, Imbert, Jarabacoa, La Romana, La Vega, Loma de Cabrera, Luperón, Moca, Monseñor Nouel, Pepillo Salcedo, Pimentel, Restauración, Sabana Grande de Boyá, Salcedo, Samaná, Santiago, San Cristóbal, San Francisco de Macorís, San José de las Matas, San José de los Llanos, San José de Ocoa, San Juan de la Maguana, San Pedro de Macorís, Tamboril, Villa Altagracia, and Villa Tapia, and the decisions made are confirmed in all of their parts.

Second: To declare, and in effect declares, regular and valid the appeals submitted by the Dominican Revolutionary Party against the decisions of the Municipal Electoral Boards of Bánica, Cabral, Enriquillo, Padre Las Casas, Pedernales, Pedro Santana, and Villa Vásquez, and as a consequence, revokes, in all their parts the decisions appealed by that Party and rejects the injunctions made by the Reformist Party of the elections that took place the past May 16th in those Municipalities.

Third: To reject and, in effect rejects, the appeals submitted by the Dominican Revolutionary Party against decisions of the Municipal Electoral Boards of Castillo, Higüey and San Cristóbal, for lack of evidence.

Fourth: To certify the desist action made by the Dominican Revolutionary Party regarding the appeal submitted by that Party against the decision of the Municipal Electoral Board of Duvergé.

Fifth: To reject, and in effect rejects, the appeals submitted by the National Civic Union Party against the decisions of the Electoral Boards of Altamira, Bayaguana, Bohechío, Cabrera, Distrito Nacional, Jánico, Jimaní, La Descubierta, Las Matas de Farfán, Miches, Monción, Monte Cristi, Monte Plata, Río San Juan, Tenares, Villa Riva, and Yamasá.

Sixth: To certify the desist action regarding the appeals made by the National Civic Union against the decisions of the Municipal Electoral Boards of Oviedo and Paraíso.

Seventh: Rejects the appeal submitted by the Municipal Movement Of The People against the decision taken by the Electoral Board of the National District, because it has no grounds.

Eighth: Rejects the appeal submitted by Dr. Rafael Duarte Pepín in the name of the Popular Democratic Party, against the decision of the Electoral Board of the National District, and as a consequence, the appealed decision is confirmed.

Ninth: To declare as regular in form the appeals submitted by the Reformist Party against the decisions of the Municipal Electoral Boards of Neiba, Tamayo, Villa Jaragua, El Seibo, Hato Mayor, Miches, Sabana de la Mar, Higüey, San Rafael del Yuma, Nagua and Río San Juan, and regarding their content, based on its own authority, declares the Reformist Party, as the winner in the provincial candidacies in La Altagracia, Bahoruco, María Trinidad Sánchez and El Seibo.

Tenth: To order that the present decision be notified to the different political parties and independent groups, and to the Electoral Boards, and [to order] its publication in the gazette, in accordance with the law.

Dr. Hugo E. Vargas Suberví, Substitute President; Dr. Luis A. González Vega, Member; Lic. Danilo E. Santana, Member; Dr. Rafael José A. Bergés Peral, Substitute Secretary

Democratization

The triumph of the PRD was a liberating experience for the Dominican people. After thirty-one years of dictatorship, five years of intermittent chaos, and twelve years of Balaguer's rule, finally a government that fully respected human rights and civil liberties was in power. President Guzmán was to make those freedoms the hallmark of his administration. Political prisoners were released, exiles returned, and there was a euphoric outpouring of political ideas, publications, and the creation of unions, and all sorts of organizations. Dominicans, who for so long had contained their urges to express themselves freely, now vented their repressed desires. Moreover, Guzmán managed to tame the pro-Balaguer military by dismissing and rotating officers, until eventually a new, more professional and apolitical generation of officers was promoted through the ranks. The country experienced a veritable "democratic opening." Unfortunately, the political successes of the Guzmán administration were not matched in the economic arena. The PRD inherited a shaky economy from Balaguer, and things got worse during the troublesome 1980s. Troubled by the nation's economic woes, corruption scandals involving close relatives, and the triumph of his archrival Salvador Jorge Blanco in the PRD's convention to nominate the party's presidential candidate, President Guzmán ended up taking his own life on the night of July 3, 1982.

Guzmán's inaugural speech is reproduced below. It was remarkable not only for his ambitious political and economic agenda, but also for the criticisms that he levied against Balaguer (who was in attendance at the ceremony), and the latter's autocratic and repressive style while in power.

SPEECH BY PRESIDENT
ANTONIO GUZMÁN FERNÁNDEZ OF AUGUST 16, 1978[12]

It has been exactly one hundred years since the last transmission of presidential power from a losing candidate to a winning one took place, when in 1878 President Cesáreo Guillermo transferred power to Ignacio María González. This fact demonstrates the tremendous significance this inauguration has for the strengthening of democracy in our people, since after one century of a troubled political history char-

---

12. Translated from Miguel Guerrero, *Al borde del caos: Historia oculta de la crisis electoral de 1978* (Santo Domingo: Editora Corripio, 1999), 367–381.

acterized by the weakness of our institutions, with this solemn act beautiful and promising perspectives for our institutional order are opened.

The event should serve to reinforce the faith of Dominicans in the benefits that derive from the democratic system, since these people had, with plenty of reasons, moments of great skepticism in the face of the performance of governments that essentially negated the principles that serve as the basis of our social organization. Today these people are spectators of a ceremony that signifies the sovereign popular will has been respected, at least in many of its fundamental aspects.

I hope that God will help me to contribute so that, in the future, periodic electoral consultations will constitute normal events in the life of the Nation, without altering in the least the activities of the national life. I cannot fail to point out what I hope will be a happy historical coincidence for the Americas. We were the first city of the New World in 1492; it was then when Santo Domingo irradiated culture and civilization toward all that was then known of the Continent. In 1978, with the elections and all that came afterward, we set an example for our sister nations that with determination, patriotism, optimism, and solidarity, we can save democracy. That is why, it has more significance for the Government and for the Dominican people the prestigious presence in this act of illustrious heads of state and special missions from friendly nations, distinguished ecclesiastical dignitaries and national and foreign personalities linked to political, social, economic, and cultural institutions and activities, which we value as an encouraging proof of faith.

It is worth remembering, letting history judge the deeds and the men who have intervened in this process, the events that culminate today. After twelve years of Reformist government, we began the electoral campaign, which, we must acknowledge it, developed in a climate of relative tranquility but that, however, was characterized by the polarization, increasingly stronger, of two options: the Reformist Party and the Dominican Revolutionary Party.

Dominicans had then the opportunity to witness how the Reformist Party utilized, in an unscrupulous way, all the resources of the State in its eagerness to remain in charge of the public administration. On the other hand, the efforts, the honesty, the spirit of sacrifice, and the mystique of the Dominican Revolutionary Party, aptly named the Party of national hope, shone forth. In spite of everything, I never doubted electoral victory. Victory achieved with the support of the vast majority of the Dominican people. However, there have been attempts to tarnish it by pointing out that we won thanks to an electoral fraud. To what reasonable person could it occur that a political party that has been in the opposition since 1963 had the means and the resources to commit fraud in an electoral process!

This argument served as a pretext for the unconstitutional decision of the supreme electoral tribunal, by which, thanks to some arbitrary mathematical calculations, and to a capricious allocation of votes that were not cast, the Dominican Revolutionary Party was deprived of the senate seats of the provinces of Bahoruco, La Altagracia, María Trinidad Sánchez, and el Seibo. The unfortunate procedure employed consisted thus, in the addition of a percentage of non-voters to the Reformist Party, which obtained in that manner a majority in those provinces, even though the votes that were cast in the ballots boxes had given the victory to the candidates of the Dominican Revolutionary Party.

The state of uncertainty created by the massive objections from the Party that today becomes the opposition, generated days of economic recession with negative repercussions for the immediate future of the country. We should feel satisfied because we knew how to overcome, with a great civic spirit, the obstacles which arose to hinder the consolidation of democracy in our country.

I have just been invested with the Highest Authority of the Republic when the functions of the Executive Power were deposited in my hands, and upon assuming, on this memorable occasion, under oath, the greatest responsibility that any citizen can assume before the nation: To obey and enforce obedience to the Constitution and the law.

Such a solemn pact, with God and with the Fatherland, synthesizes the high moral duty that I assume by accepting . . . the generous mandate the Dominican people have granted me to govern the destiny of the country during the next four years with unrestricted conformity to the law, and with the duty of safekeeping the independence and the sovereignty of the nation.

As I assume the functions of President of the Republic, I am fully conscious that this arduous and difficult task cannot be the exclusive work of the government, but that it requires, to be successful, the participation of all national sectors. For that reason, it is my the duty to examine, before the nation, the reality of the institutional and economic life we confront today upon assuming office.

As for the life of the fundamental organizations of the State, I am convinced that a nation is as solid and stable as its institutions are strong. Men move on, but institutions acquire increasingly strong permanency. Experience shows us that from the fragility of institutions to a state of frustration, of distrust toward everything established and of questioning, there is just one step. It is indisputable, and I say this without intent of accusing anyone, that during the past few years our country has gone through a grave moral and institutional crisis. This situation has generated as its foremost characteristic the huge administrative corruption that the former Government itself has had the courage to recognize.

The moment has arrived when men will be rewarded again for their dedication to work, for their devotion to serving the Fatherland and their fellow citizens, and not for the fruits of their lust for profit or their ability to increase their private capital with public funds or the peddling of influence power supplies.

Regarding our economy, it is fair to recognize that it has enjoyed years of plenty in the recent past, especially as a result of the high sugar prices as well as for coffee, cacao, and gold. The high revenues these exports generated for the treasury, and the hard currency obtained, were mainly used toward financing huge investments in urban and rural infrastructures and to beautify some cities, but the very own enterprises of the State were neglected, such as the State Sugar Council, the Dominican Electricity Corporation, and others from the Corporation of State Enterprises.

The country achieved, for several years, high economic growth rates and the private sector responded to the incentives, fiscal as well as financial, created to direct the investment toward pre-determined sectors. This process helped to expand a middle class that should greatly contribute to our future development.

However, this growth did not benefit the lower-income groups due to the freezing of the salaries in the public sector; to the neglect of public services such as health, social security, and education; to the almost complete absence of maintenance in the state's public works; to the abandonment of our people from the countryside; to the scarcity of food and the supply of agricultural inputs, as a consequence of a misguided agricultural policy, which did not promote production. On the other hand, our public administration has become disorganized, due to the excessive centralization of decisions, and at the same time, a lack of coordination of economic policies between the institutions and the organs that have influence over Dominican economic events. All this means that since 1975 the growth of our economy has slowed because of a lack of significant increase in the demand capacity of our domestic market, of a reduction in the prices of the main export products, with the exception of gold, and of the decreased efficiency of the state as an administrator.

The situation sketched above, should not be a reason for uncertainty nor pessimism, since I have faith in the honest men and women of our country who are willing to contribute to achieve a more promising future for our children.

In that sense I commit myself, at the helm of the government that starts today, to direct all of our efforts toward the achievement, first, of a true institutionalization. Just as I said on previous occasions, in order to reach this coveted goal, it is necessary to consecrate a change in power and, therefore, to incorporate into the constitutional precepts the principle of non-reelection. Also, it is necessary to fortify the powers of the state.

Regarding this particular, in my position as head of the executive power, I must emphasize that the work of the government should be carried out through joined efforts of the legislative, judiciary, and executive powers. I hope that the legislative power, in its lofty mission of making the normative laws of our social development, always place the supreme interests of the Dominican people above partisan interests and passions.

For my part, I can guarantee that the projects I will submit as President of the Republic for consideration by the National Congress will be inspired by the search for viable solutions to the major national problems, to the development of the country, and to the happiness of all my fellow citizens.

This attitude, which I consider necessary to maintain an environment of national concordance, I hope will be followed by the legislators from the government's party, as well as by the others who belong to the parties of the opposition.

Let us never forget that the people and history will be called to judge the attitudes each one of us assumes in the next four years!

Regarding the judiciary, the need to clean up the administration of justice is of great concern to the citizenry. Prestigious voices have been heard, demanding the creation of a judicial career path, the improvement of the living and working conditions of the judicial workers, the permance of judgeships, and the independence of our judiciary in its acts. I totally agree with that demand, which has to be complemented by reform of our penal system.

In conformity with our constitutional provisions, the appointment of the auxiliary judicial personnel corresponds to the Executive Power, but the grave responsibility of appointing the judges of our tribunals corresponds to the Senate of the Republic. This means, we can only count on a truly exemplary judiciary if its members are dedicated to integrity, competency, and honesty.

It is now necessary, gentlemen, to refer to the rules that will guide the Executive Power as supreme rector of the governmental administration. In the first place, just as I promised during the electoral campaign, we will fashion a government of national unity, because in the cabinet and in the state institutions the best minds of the country will be represented, without distinction based on political leanings. With this measure, we guarantee that, by leaving aside political sectarianism, the activities and decisions of the government will result from a fruitful diversity of knowledge, ideas and potentialities that will guarantee the primacy of the general interest and the achievement of the common good.

One must not confuse the unity of all the sectors of the national life around goals and purposes common to the fatherland's greatness with post-electoral partisan alliances. In other words, real national unity is above party politics.

As President of all Dominicans, it is now my duty to find new solutions to our old problems. Fundamentally, we have ahead of us two tasks from now on: to invigorate the economy, so that the welfare of our people will increase at the same time. To achieve this, we will expand our internal market and decisively foster our exports, in order to generate demand for national products, which will result in an increase in production and, therefore, in an increase in investment and employment in the national productive sector.

In the same manner, we will carry out a clean-up and capitalization work in the State enterprises; such as the State Sugar Council, the Dominican Electricity Corporation, and the Dominican Corporation of State Enterprises, so that in this manner the State may contribute to national production without competing either directly or negatively with the private sector.

To expand the internal market, we plan to improve public services, the functioning of the Government's programs, and the maintenance of public works, giving room this way to those Dominicans who want to serve the Fatherland. Equally, we believe that it is necessary for constructions, public works, and, if possible, private works to offer more employment than what has been achieved so far, utilizing more workers and less heavy machinery, as long as the nature of the works allows it. Also, and this is necessary for multiple reasons, we will do whatever is possible to improve the conditions of people in rural areas for their own benefit and that of other Dominicans, when we achieve an increment in agricultural production.

Our exports will grow as the result of various incentives and financing, so as to make our products more competitive overseas, since we are certain that the markets exist. To identify those markets, our diplomatic corps must be at the service of our exports. And to be able to maintain those markets, we must meet the commitments we incur and achieve acceptable quality levels.

At the same time that we grant incentives to national producers to increasingly raise their production, we will keep under observation prices and internal costs to avoid undue inflationary pressures, as well as our balance of payments, in order to avoid harmful effects on our currency.

I also believe that the state should pay more attention to the mining and oil sectors by increasing the well-supervised prospecting of our potential deposits, so as to obtain afterwards an exploitation that preserves our resources and results in net benefits for the country.

It is clear that the changes in the orientation of the economic policies require dedication and sacrifices from all participants, and that the State will require in the future new revenues to meet its new obligations.

I also firmly believe that the moment has arrived to pay more attention to our agriculture, necessary to the welfare of all Dominicans, especially when considering that we are a country that fundamentally lives off its land. I have repeatedly stated, in the course of the electoral campaign, that it is necessary to invigorate this important sector of national life. Our agricultural policies strive to initiate a truly scientific and just agrarian reform, that is, one that will not consist of simple distribution of land guided by essentially partisan criteria. The dominant criterion for the selection of the peasant beneficiaries will be, above all, their proven devotion to the cultivation of the land.

Agrarian reform must also be accompanied by a just credit policy, directed toward the sectors that influence production the most, that is, the mid-size and small producers, so that the necessary resources get into their hands at the right moment. Technical assistance and the market will play corresponding roles within this process and the peasants will be provided with certified seeds of highly productive varieties. Furthermore, we will carry out balanced studies for the zoning of crops in order to rationalize the types of products in each region as well as implement agricultural insurance, with the aim of providing our peasants with some compensation for losses due to climate and other conditions. This policy must start with the immediate improvement of the agrarian projects already in place.

With all of the above, we guarantee that the increase in production will immediately result in the lowering of the cost of living and the reduction of food imports, which presumes not only the improvement of the living standards of inhabitants of rural areas, but also of all the country's inhabitants.

In the health field, my government will spare no effort so that medical services, based primarily on continuous programs of preventive care and secondly on medical assistance, will reach even the most remote regions. The maternal-infant and nutrition programs will be strengthened with the aim of guaranteeing the health of Dominican mothers and their children, contributing thereby to attending to this neglected aspect in the health programs developed so far. Existing health centers need to be supplied with equipment, medical, paramedical, and administrative staff, and sufficient medicines in order to make them truly workable.

In this area, another one of our goals is the restructuring, revising, and updating of the social security system, administered by the Dominican Institute of Social Security, to guarantee an efficient service to its policyholders and pensioners. I have already pointed out in previous speeches that the future of our youths is being generated in the present. That is why we need to adjust education to the demands of economic, social, and cultural development.

The government, which begins today, will promote education as a function of development. But for that, it is necessary that existing programs are implemented with efficiency and schools are supplied with the equipments, materials, and human resources for optimal functioning. The expansion and progressive improvement of preschool education and the prolongation of general education will be our goal and concern; [also] the coordination between vocational education and general education;

the improvement of rural elementary schools with the aim of guaranteeing the same educational opportunities of the cities to the rural population; the restructuring of vocational learning, keeping in mind the characteristics of the labor force and the anticipated human resources needs for our development plans.

We will contemplate the possibility that the basic cycle of elementary learning will be within the reach and possibilities of everybody. I promise that we will start studies so that, in a gradual and regional manner, free school supplies will be distributed up to a certain grade level and to implement, in the same fashion, school breakfasts.

We will support, within available resources, the realization of systematic adult education campaigns, oriented toward the development of communities, the training of the labor force, cultural development, and the eradication of illiteracy.

The reunification and expansion of middle school programs is necessary for a greater proportion of youths to have the opportunity to continue their general education, at the same time as they receive some kind of high-quality vocational instruction.

The revision and the establishment of emergency programs for the training and accelerated formation of the teaching staff are pressing.

The country's universities can be assured that we will always be open to frank dialogue, with the purpose of making a significant contribution to the expansion and the improvement of post-secondary education.

As a complement to the government's educational activity and for the recreation of the whole population, it is fundamental to pay more attention to sports. In that sense, we strive to implement a policy of maintenance of the existing sports installations. The construction of new installations will be oriented to incorporate into the benefits that the practice of sports brings the inhabitants of the neighborhood communities, always paying special attention to the rural zone.

Professional sport events, which have a strong following and tradition in our society, will count with our sympathy, which does not mean that the government will neglect what is its primary obligation: amateur sports and the recreation of its citizens.

The housing policy of my Government will be oriented toward the construction of low-cost housing, since I believe that it is the only way to effectively contribute to reducing the huge housing deficit we have. It is inconceivable that the Government participates in the construction of luxurious and costly residences and apartments, which constitute a distortion of the goals the State should pursue in this type of social initiatives. When the cost and design exceed what we consider indispensable because it is necessary, hygienic and decent, this very important task must be left in the hands of affluent people and specialized credit institutions; both efforts should be accompanied by adequate urban planning.

All of this aimed at achieving the development of our social and economic potential, presupposes the existence of an honest, competent, expeditious, and dynamic public administration. As I have pointed out before, it has to be an instrument for development, not an obstacle to it.

For these reasons, I have called for a decentralization of the public administration [sector] which will allow us to simplify and expedite administrative procedures. I have also advocated for a revaluation of the condition of the public servant and, to that end, we will examine the possibilities and mechanisms for establishing the civil service and the administrative career.

Just as I pointed out at the beginning, officials and public employees must be characterized by strict performance of their duty and, above all, by the honesty with which they carry out their tasks. I will act with energy in those cases in which administrative corruption is established. Therefore, we demand from our most distinguished public servants a sworn affidavit of their assets when they assume their positions; and we will do whatever it takes to wipe out the noxious practice of soliciting gifts from our citizens in offices and departments of the public administration, as they attempt to solve different kinds of problems. At the same time, we will lay off those public officials who do not truly and effectively perform any labor that will justify the payment of a salary, which is money that ultimately comes from the funds contributors give to the Treasury.

On this anniversary of the restoration of the Republic, a patriotic act in which our invincible troops, dressed up in the glory of the battlefield, recovered our national sovereignty, I want to reaffirm my purpose of fostering, as their commander-in-chief, the institutionalization of our Armed Forces and National Police, of respecting their promotion ladder, of defending their integrity, of continuing and expanding their professionalization, and improving the living standards of the selfless men who serve the nation with dedication, generosity, and patriotism in their sacred mission of guaranteeing our independence, as pillars of the national sovereignty and preservers of the public order.

In accordance with our respectful submission to the law, in the national ambit as well as on the international level, I want go on record to show that the Dominican Government will faithfully fulfill its international compromises and will honor all treaties and subscribed conventions, including the Charter of the United Nations and the Charter of the Organization of American States.

Our country's foreign policy will be based on the principles of non-intervention in the internal affairs of other nations, of international cooperation, and of mutual respect among states.

We also seek to strengthen the ties of friendship and cooperation with the nations that are so honorably represented on this memorable occasion, as a show of solidarity with our country.

The issue of human rights has acquired a new dimension. The era in which they were considered in isolation, within the narrow limits of the territory of a particular state, is gone. Human rights constitute a truly common patrimony of humanity. By virtue of their indivisible and binding nature, their violation in a particular country reverberates in the others and represents an affront for all men.

I intend to rigorously apply the precepts and norms that consecrate those rights, as a principal obligation of the state, in compliance with the terms of our Fundamental Law, and I quote: "The effective protection of the rights of human beings and the maintenance of the means that will allow them to progressively better themselves within a milieu of individual freedom and social justice, compatible with public order, general welfare, and everybody's rights."

With the aim of assuring the strictest respect for those rights, I intend, in the course of my presidential mandate and in my condition as head of the Executive, to submit for consideration by the National Congress a project for the creation of a tribunal of constitutional guarantees. I regret being precluded from conceding the benefit of a pardon, today, as I am entitled by the Constitution, to the citizens who are incarcerated in our prisons. It has been literally impossible to utilize the normal mechanisms for such purposes, whose first phase consists in the preparation of a list of inmates with possibilities of being pardoned, that the General Prosecutor of the Republic submits to the Executive for its review and decision.

It is also up to the General Director of Migration to make an evaluation of the situation of the individuals banned from returning to the country, with the goal of submitting it to the consideration of the President of the Dominican Republic.

As you have seen, the fundamental change the Dominican Revolutionary Party has been advocating is a change in the moral attitude before the law. It is not only a change of men and public officials, but also a profound change in the conception of the rights of citizens regarding the nation and the state, as a just compensation to the full enjoyment of all their rights.

The labor of conciliation and of development, at the present moment and circumstances, demands, from each one of the children of this land: work, sacrifices, patience, patriotism and, above all, a great faith in God and in the capacity of the Dominican people to overcome difficult moments as they have done on so many occasions.

My government is fully conscious of its historical responsibility, which is shared in equal measure with the parties of the opposition, especially the Reformist Party. I make an appeal to all opponents, for them to scorn barren criticism and adjust their activities and their attitudes within a constructive spirit of devotion to the existing legal canons.

It is only fair to recognize that the victory we obtained in the booths and the way in which we have been able to advocate for the respect of our rights are due to the way in which freedom of the press, the fundamental backbone of a democracy, is exercised in our country.

I cannot let this opportunity go by without also recognizing the huge and valuable contribution of His Excellency, Doctor Joaquín Balaguer, to the crystallization of this historical peaceful transition of presidential power.

We also have to recognize that in the last years of his administration, infrastructure works of great value to the future development of our Nation were started. These works will be concluded and existing ones will be maintained as they deserve.

Before ending, I want to refer in a special way to the selfless men and women of the Dominican Revolutionary Party. A party and a membership with a clear record of sacrifices, of heroism, which have contributed so much to the establishment and strengthening of democracy in this country.

Thanks to the forcefulness and to the organization of this political institution, to the good sense and to the mystique of its members, we opened new horizons in Dominican political life.

Far from feeling satisfied with the arduous task carried out to this day, we must not dismay, we must continue working for the well-being of all Dominicans, with detachment, love, and self-abnegation.

Now allow me to pay tribute to the venerable memory of the Fathers of the

Nation, Duarte, Sánchez, and Mella, and with my thoughts placed on the sacrosanct Book of the Gospels, open in the center of the national shield, [I] elevate a prayer to the Almighty and to our spiritual mother, the Virgin of La Altagracia, so they may shower our people with blessings and enlighten our decisions, to enable me to fulfill the solemn oath I took, and contribute in this way to forging an increasingly prosperous, flourishing, and happy nation.

A "Gentlemen's Agreement"

As the PRD's popularity waned amidst the economic crisis of the 1980s, Balaguer was preparing for a political comeback. Dismissed by many in 1978, Balaguer looked increasingly appealing by 1986 and he once again promoted himself as the experienced, moderate candidate who will bring order to the country's governance. With the PRD bitterly divided into two contending factions, Balaguer waged an effective election campaign that won him the presidency by a narrow margin. Once in power, the "new" Balaguer used the state's resources to get himself reelected in 1990 against Juan Bosch of the PLD, and in 1994 against José F. Peña Gómez of the PRD. On both occasions, Balaguer was accused of rigging the elections, which he won by increasingly narrow margins. Particularly in the 1994 election, he won by less than twenty-two thousand votes in an election where over two hundred thousand Dominicans were unable to vote because their names had been removed from the voting lists.

Peña Gómez and the PRD, as well as foreign observers, documented these grave irregularities and the country was plunged into a prolonged post-electoral crisis. By early August 1994, an understanding was reached between the leadership of the three main parties with the mediation of the Catholic Church. In a "gentlemen's agreement" known as the "Pact for Democracy," they agreed to recognize Balaguer's victory in exchange for a shortened eighteen-month term (later extended to two years), after which new elections were to be held. In addition, Balaguer would not be allowed to run in the 1996 election, as consecutive presidential reelection would be banned. The majority runoff electoral format (or *ballottage*) was also introduced for the presidential election by which, if no candidate obtained more than 50 percent of the valid votes, a runoff election would be held between the two candidates with the most votes in the first election. Finally, presidential elections would be separated from elections for congressional and municipal authorities by a two-year interval. These changes were introduced into the Dominican constitution later that same month. The Pact for Democracy is reprinted below.

THE PACT FOR DEMOCRACY[13]

CONSIDERING: That elections are the foundation of the delegation of powers in democratic and representative regimes, like the one currently established in the Dominican Republic;

CONSIDERING: That the conflicts generated as a result of the elections of May 16, 1994, have affected the unity of the Dominican family;

CONSIDERING: That the legitimacy of the democratic system rests on credibility regarding transparency in the working of its institutions;

CONSIDERING: That it is essential to establish the foundations for a political reform, as a guarantee of the consolidation of our democratic system;

CONSIDERING: That peace is a nation's most precious asset, since it constitutes the foundation of order and development;

CONSIDERING: That dialogue represents in the modern world the most appropriate tool to solve in a harmonic and civilized way the conflicts that affect and divide nations;

CONSIDERING: That we Dominicans are capable of contributing to the solution of our national problems without pressures coming from foreign forces;

AS SUCH, for the previously mentioned reasons, the undersigned, representatives of the county's main political forces, and in the presence of national witnesses, from the social and economic sectors, and from the Church, as well as the Organization of American States, in its condition as regional hemispheric institution:

HAVE CONVENED AND AGREED

First: To participate in the National Assembly for the examination of the acts and the proclamation of the election of the President and Vice President of the Republic, declared by the Central Electoral Board as winners in the elections of May 16, 1994, according to article 36 of the Dominican Constitution;

Second: To participate on this coming sixteenth of August in the election of the leadership of the Senate and the House of Deputies of the Republic, as well as guaranteeing the presence of legislators from the different political forces of the country, in the swearing in ceremony of the President and the Vice President of the Republic;

Third: To reform the Constitution of the Dominican Republic to adopt the following measures:

1) To limit the constitutional period that begins on August 16, 1994, to February 27, 1996.[14]

13. Translated from Juan Bolívar Díaz, *Trauma electoral* (Santo Domingo: Editorial AA, 1996), 335–338.
14. Later extended until August 16, 1996.

274

PARAGRAPH I: The Legislators, Senators and Deputies, elected in the elections of 1994, and asked to carry out the constitutional reforms foreseen in this pact, will remain in their positions until August 16, 1998. Likewise, the Mayors and the City Council Members will remain in their positions until August 16, 1998.

PARAGRAPH II: The elections for Senators and Deputies, and Mayors and City Council Members, will take place every four years, starting on May 16, 1998.

2) To celebrate new presidential elections on November 16, 1995.[15]

3) To prohibit the reelection of the President of the Republic for two consecutive periods.

4) To establish the majority runoff electoral system, which consists of the fact that if in a first electoral round none of the candidates for the Presidency and Vice Presidency of the Republic obtain more than half of the cast ballots, there will be a second electoral round or runoff election forty-five (45) days after the first round had taken place, in which only the two candidates with the largest amount of votes in the first round would participate;

5) To establish the voting system of Electoral Assemblies in closed voting centers;

6) To reform the current judicial system;

Fourth: To introduce the following legal reforms:

1) To modify the current electoral law in order to harmonize it with the constitutional reforms and other legal issues agreed upon;

2) To create a new Central Electoral Board whose members are not representatives of the political parties;

3) To depurate the civil service offices (Civil Registry), as well as the identification and electoral card, and to reorganize the Electoral Registry and the electronic archives of voters of the Central Electoral Board, of the Electoral Board of the National District and other Municipal Boards of the country, with the goal of creating a new electoral registry;

Fifth: The Government that will rule from August 16, 1994, until February 27, 1996, will employ to a feasible extent, the collaboration of the fundamental political forces of the country, and there will be a major emphasis on programs aimed at diminishing poverty;

Sixth: The President of the Republic promises to submit to the National Assembly, at his swearing in ceremony, the forthcoming sixteenth of August, the law project convening the National Assembly to revise the Constitution of the Republic regarding the points that are raised in this document;

Seventh: The legal and constitutional reforms outlined in this agreement, must be approved within a limited time that should not exceed October 30, 1994.

Eighth: The undersigning in the current document promise to secure that the legislators of their respective organizations will be present and will vote favorably for the reforms considered here.

PARAGRAPH: To guarantee the fulfillment of the above stipulated, a notarial act that is annexed to the current document, which forms an integral part of it, and in which the signatures of the legislators elected for the period from August 16, 1994,

---

15. Later changed to May 16, 1996.

to August 16, 1998, are included.

Ninth: The compromise of all the undersigning forces regarding the preservation of social peace, public order, and respect for the constitutional regime is established.

Prepared and signed in the city of Santo Domingo, National District, Capital of the Dominican Republic, in as many originals as undersigning parties on the tenth (10) day of the month of August of the year nineteen hundred ninety-four (1994).

Signed August 10, 1994, at the National Palace by President Joaquín Balaguer, licentiate Jacinto Peynado, Monsignor Nicolás de Jesús López Rodríguez, licentiate Lidio Cadet, Doctor José Francisco Peña Gómez, John Graham, as well as by businessmen, newspaper directors, ecclesiastical authorities, university rectors, political leaders, union leaders, and representatives of social and popular institutions.

Race and Politics

With Balaguer barred from running for the presidency in 1996, the road now seemed clear for Peña Gómez, who felt cheated out of certain victory in 1994. Back then, Balaguer's supporters had carried on a vicious mudslinging campaign in which they accused Peña Gómez, who was black, of being of Haitian origin, of being emotionally unstable, and even of practicing witchcraft. As the 1996 presidential election approached, these charges were brought up again. This time Peña Gómez faced Leonel

The National Patriotic Front. From left: Juan Bosch, Leonel Fernández, and Joaquín Balaguer.

Fernández of the PLD, a young lawyer and substitute for Bosch as the party's presidential nominee. Balaguer, unable to run and bent on preventing a PRD victory, quietly backed Fernández, while showing little interest in supporting his own party's candidate, Vice President Jacinto Peynado. When Fernández obtained a second place in the presidential election, while Peña Gómez, who finished first, was unable to get the required 50 percent of the votes, Balaguer openly threw his support behind Fernández.

In an emotional public act on June 2, 1996, Balaguer, Bosch, and Fernández concerted an electoral alliance designed to stop Peña Gómez. The alliance, known as the Frente Patriótico Nacional (National Patriotic Front), grouped together former political foes in a symbiotic relationship. While the PLD needed Balaguer's votes to win the runoff election, Balaguer needed the PLD to defeat Peña Gómez and to guarantee legal immunity to his party faithful for acts of corruption committed in the past. Moreover, the PLD was a weak party with a small congressional representation. In his speech, Balaguer drummed up anti-Haitian Dominican nationalism by urging all "real" Dominicans to vote in a patriotic manner against foreign, un-Dominican forces—a clear reference to Peña Gómez's presumed Haitian ancestry. Balaguer's support tilted the scales; Fernández easily won the runoff election. In his concession speech, an embittered Peña Gómez lamented that "the Dominican Republic is still not ready for a black president." Balaguer's brief but incisive speech is reproduced below.

JOAQUÍN BALAGUER'S SPEECH OF JUNE 2, 1996[16]

It is a great honor for me to preside with my eminent friend, Professor Juan Bosch, over this event, which does not have a political character but rather an eminently patriotic one.

In his brief words, Professor Bosch has drawn the line of Pizarro for Dominicans. One side leads to chaos and disorder, and the other side leads to democracy, to progress, and to the stabilization of institutions.

If numbers do not lie and mathematics still retains its value, regardless of the fact that science has erased all absolute concepts in the world, we have already won the battle. The one million one hundred thousand votes the Dominican Liberation Party received in the last electoral contest plus the 435 thousand votes of the Social

16. Translated from Joaquín Balaguer, "Discurso del Dr. Joaquín Balaguer," June 2, 1996, photocopy.

Christian Reformist Party represent an overwhelming victory.

The bad road is closed, closed definitively to evil and to demagoguery, and open, wide open to Dominican patriotism.

This is the first time, gentlemen, in the history of the country that a treaty has been signed exclusively inspired by patriotic goals and not by the distribution of the nation's budget. In 1905 President Morales[17] signed an alliance with his adversaries, and in 1924 the alliance of General Horacio Vásquez with the National Progressive Force of licentiate Federico Velázquez. On both historical cases the budgetary end was taken into account. In this case, however, we are taking into account only reasons of a patriotic and historical nature. What we want is to prevent the country from falling into hands that are not truly Dominican.

Gentlemen, I therefore invite all Dominicans, not only the members of the PLD and the PRSC parties, but all my fellow citizens to vote for the Fernández-Fernández Mirabal[18] candidacy because that candidacy represents the sacred interest of the nation. All those who have the Dominican flag hoisted in their hearts should vote for that candidacy. I solemnly promise to work for it, to work for it night and day, without asking anything in return, and just for the satisfaction of being able to continue being Dominican on Dominican soil.

There were many abstentions in the past elections. I ask those Dominicans who did not vote out of apathy or indolence, or for whatever reason, to exercise their civic right on this occasion by voting for the Fernández-Fernández Mirabal candidacy.

Keep in mind that one vote is not just any figure, a vote represents a part of the Fatherland. As the Spanish adage says, one grain does not help the granary but it helps its companion.

All Dominicans, therefore, are being called on for this civic event of June 30th. All of us must attend this event and solely keep in mind the words on the national seal, of God, of the Country, and of Liberty.

17. Carlos F. Morales Languasco.
18. Referring to presidential candidate Leonel Fernández and vice-presidential candidate Jaime David Fernández Mirabal.